Bulletin Board Systems for Business

Lamont Wood

Dana Blankenhorn

John Wiley & Sons, Inc.

New York ■ Chichester ■ Brisbane ■ Toronto ■ Singapore

Publisher: Katherine Schowalter
Editor: Laura Lewin
Managing Editor: Ruth Greif
Production Services: Publication Services

In recognition of the importance of preserving what has been written, it is a policy of John Wiley & Sons, Inc. to have books of enduring value published in the United States printed on acid-free paper, and we exert our best efforts to that end.

This publication is designed to provide accurate and authoritative information in regard to the subject matter covered. It is sold with the understanding that the publisher is not engaged in rendering legal, accounting, or other professional service. If legal advice or other expert assistance is required, the services of a competent professional person should be sought. FROM A DECLARATION OF PRINCIPLES JOINTLY ADOPTED BY A COMMITTEE OF THE AMERICAN BAR ASSOCIATION AND A COMMITTEE OF PUBLISHERS.

Printed in the United States of America

10 9 8 7 6 5 4 3 2 1

Printed and bound by Malloy Lithographing, Inc.

To Mathilda O'Donnell Blankenhorn and Grace Bequette Wood,
who always believed their sons could be writers

Acknowledgments

We would like to thank our patient editor at John Wiley & Sons, Laura Lewin, as well as our agent, Jeff Herman, and our long-suffering wives and two children (each).

Especially helpful in preparing this book were Bob Mahoney of Exec PC, George Matyasak of Chicago Syslink, Rick Heming and Jim Harrer of Mustang Software, Phil Becker of eSoft, Jack Rickard of Boardwatch Magazine, Paul Waldinger of the Sound of Music BBS, attorney Lance Rose, and Andy Keeves of ILink. Dennis Hayes of Hayes Microcomputer Products was helpful in many ways. Kirill Tchashchin, Masyuki Miyazawa, Steve Gold, and Detlef Borchers helped with the international material. But most especially, we wish to thank Ward Christensen and Randy Suess, who started it all.

Trademarks

Apple and Macintosh are registered trademarks of Apple Computer.
AT&T is a registered trademark of American Telephone and Telegraph Co.
AutoCAD is a trademark of AutoDesk Inc.

BIX and Byte Information Exchange are trademarks of McGraw-Hill Information Services.

CompuServe is a registered trademark of CompuServe Inc./H&R Block Co.
Crosstalk is a registered trademark and CASL is a trademark of Digital Communications
     Associates Inc.

dBASE and Multimate are registered trademarks of Ashton-Tate.
DEC, VT52, and VT100 are trademarks of Digital Equipment Corp.

Galacticomm, the Major BBS, Galacticomm Software Breakthrough, and GalactiBox are
     trademarks of Galacticomm Inc.
Galaxy is a trademark of Galaxy Communications.
GEM and Digital Research are registered trademarks and CP/M is a trademark of Digital
     Research Inc.
GEnie is a trademark of General Electric Co.

Hayes and V-series are registered trademarks and Smartcom III, Scope, Smartmodem, ESP,
     and Smartcom Exec are trademarks of Hayes Microcomputer Products Inc.
Hercules is a registered trademark of Hercules Computer Technology Inc.
HyperAccess/5 and HyperPilot are trademarks and HyperAccess is a registered trademark
     of Hilgraeve Inc.

IBM, AT, XT, OS/2 and PS/2 are registered trademarks and VGA is a trademark of Inter-
     national Business Machines Corp.
Intel is a registered trademark of Intel Corp.

Kermit is a trademark of Henson Associates.

LaserJet is a registered trademark of Hewlett-Packard.
Lotus 1-2-3 is a registered trademark of Lotus Development Corp.

MCI and MCI Mail are registered trademarks of MCI Communications Corp.
Microcom Networking Protocol and MNP are trademarks of Microcom Inc.
Microsoft, MS-DOS, and Microsoft Word are registered trademarks and Windows is a trade-
     mark of Microsoft Corp.
Mirror III is a trademark of SoftKlone Distributing Corp.

Contents

Chapter 8

File Manipulation   103

Chapter 9

BBS Software   133

Chapter 12

Online Etiquette   209

Chapter 13

The Law of the BBS   219

Chapter 14

Viruses, Hackers, and Other Dangers   231

Chapter 15

The BBS Future   239

Chapter 16

Glossary of Jargon and Abbreviations   247

Appendix A

BBS Echo Networks   267

Appendix B

BBSs Around the World   285

1

The New World
of BBSs

ABOUT THIS CHAPTER

We'll define the term *BBS* and see:

- Benefits offered by BBSs
- Uses of BBSs
- How BBSs differ from electronic mail

We'll also examine the history of the BBS phenomenon.

BBSs, THE NEW MEDIA

Somewhere in your city there is probably a large corporate office or government agency that harbors, deep in its headquarters building, a mainframe computer tended by white-coated technicians. Employees or clients can use it from computer terminals located inside the building or, indeed, from anywhere on the planet served by a phone line, tapping the mainframe's data files and sending electronic mail to other users. It's an expensive, prestigious artifact, the mainframe.

It's also a dinosaur. Thanks to the emergence of BBS technology, now the smallest organization (even a hobbyist) can accomplish much the same thing for a comparative pittance, with the results differing mostly in terms of scale. Instead of 2,000 users at a time, there might be 2. But computers are computers, phone lines are phone lines, and modems (the computer–to–phone line connection devices) are modems. The 2 users of the BBS can be as well served as the 2,000 users of the mainframe.

WHAT ARE BBSs?

BBS stands for bulletin board system. An alternative term is CBBS (computer bulletin board system). Physically, a BBS is a microcomputer (usually some variety of PC) that is left running and is connected to a phone line through a modem that can answer the phone automatically. It runs software that will let a caller perform certain commands from a remote computer or data terminal. (See Chapter 3 for more details.)

A BBS is, in other words, a small-scale version of the mainframe. It can't do everything that a mainframe does, but it may very well do enough to adequately serve the needs of your business or organization. After all, not everybody needs to support 2,000 simultaneous users filtering multi-million-item databases. (But with the power of microcomputers doubling every 18 months, there may come a time when a BBS will be able to do so.)

ADVANTAGES OF BBSs

BBSs arose from the world of computer hobbyists, allowing them to socialize and use their technical skills at the same time. As explained in detail in Chapter 3, the hobbyist sets up a BBS and devotes it to online forums or conferences on topics of personal interest. Thanks to "echo networks," (detailed in Appendix A), users of such a BBS can exchange views and information with other computer hobbyists literally around the globe. Communication is the key word.

For the business use of a BBS, communication is again the key word. Business uses of a BBS include:

- *Publishing without paper.* Catalogs, inventory updates, policy statements, technical data, minutes of meetings—all these things and more can be posted online, where they can be updated instantly and where users can find what they need with a few keystrokes.

- *Automating mail-order sales.* Anything that can be sold over the phone can probably be sold through a BBS, using software that will validate credit card numbers. Combining this capability with the concept of publishing without paper, you can even sell products (generally, computer software) that exist only electronically. After validation of the credit card number, the user is given a validation number that can be used to trigger the transmission of the software from the BBS to his or her computer, where it can be used immediately. Alternatively, the user can get a demo version of the software free from the BBS and then send payment for the full version.

- *Computer-literate customer relations.* You can set up a forum or conference about your products to field comments and questions from computer-using customers. Feedback can be immediate and personal. Software companies can use BBSs to post updates, bug patches, useful macros, and user tips.

- *Non-real-time meetings.* An executive can post a comment or suggestion on a topic, and others can post their responses. Business can be moved forward without a meeting taking place.

- *Real-time remote meetings.* Through a BBS with multiple call-in lines, simultaneous users can chat with each other. The advantage over a conference call is that you can get a transcript automatically, since everything is in writing to begin with.

- *Electronic memos.* Similarly, BBS conferences can replace the circulation of "for comment" memos. Executives can view a memo electronically and type in comments.

- *Coordinating remote employees.* Salespeople on the road can call in to make reports and check inventory levels and price updates at any time of the day or night.

- *Offering services.* Of course, you can run the board for profit, offering BBS-based services to paying subscribers. Such services include online games (usually text-based adventure games), access to collections of programs and graphics files, and access to specialized databases. Business subject areas currently available on publicly accessible BBSs include:

Used car prices
Bird breeding
Computer book listings
Government jobs
Government economic statistics
Government energy statistics
Government educational statistics
The hay market
Pilot weather information
Stock market quotes

■ *Electronic mail.* If your division's planning is based on spreadsheets, why compose elaborate reports for headquarters when you can just transmit your quarterly spreadsheet to the headquarters' BBS? And if your internal correspondence is generated by computers, why ever print any of it on paper? Just transmit it to the BBS of the department it needs to go to.

BBSs VERSUS ELECTRONIC MAIL

Electronic mail is the sending of messages in the form of computer data either from one computer to another through some kind of data network or between users of the same, large computer. The system informs the recipient of the arrival of mail when that person next uses the computer, and the recipient can read it on the screen, print it out, incorporate it into a word-processing document, download (transfer from a remote to a local computer) it into a PC, forward it to someone else, or anything else the system allows.

Electronic mail services such as MCI Mail® and CompuServe® function as one large computer with multiple users. To use such services, you must have a microcomputer or data terminal; all traffic is in the form of computer data. Anyone with an account can call in, read any incoming messages, and send messages to any other subscriber. Some services can also print a message for standard postal delivery or provide gateways into other electronic mail systems or into the telex network.

Voice mail systems provide similar capabilities without requiring access from another computer or data terminal. Through an ordinary telephone, users record spoken messages for other users through what amounts to a large, computerized answering machine. You have to be a subscriber to receive mail, but generally anyone can call in and leave a message.

But electronic mail and voice mail services are just that—services, whose features are limited to the provider's conception of that service, filtered by the demands of the market. A feature will be added only if enough people seem willing to pay for it. Your stated needs may or may not have any impact. Most of the benefits of a BBS noted in the last section would be difficult to implement through one of these services.

A BBS, on the other hand, can be thought of as a tiny electronic mail service that you own. Its features are entirely under your control, and your users need not be subscribers to any third-party commercial service. They only need to know the BBS's phone number and be equipped with computers and modems.

The respective advantages of the three approaches break down this way:

- Voice mail is good for organizations that are not heavily dependent on computers and whose main logistical concern is the old one of overcoming "telephone tag."

- Electronic mail services are good for organizations that depend on computers but communicate in a uniform way with a fairly static community—salespeople or journalists, for example.

- BBSs are better for those who rely on computers, need flexibility, have an ad hoc user community, and benefit from having a wide range of material available online.

BACKGROUND: THE BBS NATION

Predictions of an explosion of commercial online consumer services have been circulating since cheap microcomputers and modems appeared in the late 1970s. Surely, pundits thought, home computer users would race to dial into huge commercial services with their plain-vanilla offerings. And although services such as CompuServe, Prodigy® and BIX™ do seem to have found a certain toehold in the market, others who invested with great fanfare have suffered badly.

Meanwhile, a quiet revolution was going on. Those millions of newly minted computer users were dialing into remote computers all right, but they preferred to dial into BBSs set up by their neighbors, leading to the growth of a (virtually underground) "BBS Nation." Many BBSs are still operated as hobbies, but others have become second or even primary careers for their owners. These digital tinkerers have gradually honed the technology, making it more reliable and easy to use—and they continue to do so as you read this. Any stigma of amateurism is evaporating as the BBS Nation's software and hardware suppliers become more and more professional and commercialized.

So it's no surprise that businesses have discovered this tool. Today, makers of BBS software report that 80 to 85 percent of their customers are businesses. These customers have discovered that you can set up a BBS with as many as 32 call-in lines for under $10,000, put nearly any employee in charge of it, and be reasonably certain that the system will work reliably within a very few weeks, possibly days. Once a case is made for the system, you can get clients, customers, and remote workers to invest in modems and software—on the off chance they don't have them already—and teach them quickly how to link with the board. Such systems can also be expanded easily, using standard tools from professional software authors, who offer excellent support.

As for users, today almost anyone can afford the equipment needed to call a bulletin board, just as almost any business can afford to set one up. You can buy a first-generation PC, perfectly suitable for the task, with a modem for under $500. Or you can get a good laptop computer with a modem for under $1,000. A faster modem by itself may cost well under $200. The software may cost another $100 or less. In addition, there are numerous services designed to cut a BBS user's phone bills (see Appendix C). This means you can now afford to go online from anywhere—even your car, using special modems designed for cellular phones.

The result? Estimates of the number of publicly accessible BBSs in the United States range around 30,000, with private or corporate BBSs running to several times that number.

This book is intended for those who want to participate in this quiet revolution. We'll present the necessary background information and lay out the available options.

THE BBS NATION'S HISTORY

It was a dark and stormy night. On January 26, 1978, a blizzard hit the city of Chicago. Two frustrated computer hobbyists, anxious to stay in touch despite this nuisance, wound up changing the world.

Ward Christensen was a young, bookish IBM engineer who belonged to the Chicago Area Computer Hobbyist's Exchange, or CACHE. Bright and extremely organized, Ward was taken with these new things called PCs and was having great fun tinkering with them.

He graduated from college in 1968 and went to work for IBM, but for years mainframes were too expensive for even an IBM engineer to get hold of. "In the early 70s I got interested in having my own machine to program. In January 1974 I went to a class in New York City on 'Large Scale Integration.' The teacher held up an 8008 chip. [This was one of the first Intel microprocessors—the "computer on a chip."] I asked, 'Can you make a real computer out of one?' They said, 'Yep.' 'What do I need to know to understand it?'"

He was told he'd need to understand transistor-to-transistor logic (TTL). So Christensen got some books and some old boards, and he started popping chips off the old boards with a blowtorch to make new boards. The following January, *Popular Electronics* put the Altair 8080 computer on its cover. Christensen bought one. He then began going to CACHE meetings, where he met Randy Suess. They worked together on projects such as saving data on tape cassettes using a speaker, a microphone, and an acoustic coupler.

In 1976 came CP/M™, the first true microcomputer operating system. A year later Christensen bought a license for CP/M and took his diskette to the home of a friend, Robert Swartz. "He showed me the CP/M editor and assembler, and I wrote a program to 'beep' the contents of my floppy to cassette via a modem." Every 128 bytes the modem would check the sum of the digits sent—that was the beginning of Xmodem, "although I didn't think of it as a protocol at the time."

"Sometime around there Randy also got CP/M, but he got the 'real thing'—IBM format 8 inch diskettes." Needing a way to swap data around, he wrote a program called MODEM.ASM in the summer of 1977 and offered it to the CACHE CP/M users group. "That program became the single most modified program in computing history—due to the many hardware environments in which it had to operate," Christensen remembered. MODEM.ASM was later modified into Xmodem.

Then Dave Jaffe, another CACHE member, wrote a routine called BYE that would let other people dial into his CP/M system and operate it. "I put up a 70,000-byte diskette-based CP/M system with BYE and my modem program. Fellow CACHE member Keith Peterson would call from Michigan and fill the diskette in one night or so." Christensen had unwittingly created the first remote CP/M system.

Which brings us to that snowstorm. "January 26, 1978, was a very snowy day. I couldn't get dug out, so I called Randy. I had the CACHE message recorder phone line in my house, and Dennis Hayes had 'invented' the hobbyist modem. Randy and I talked about putting up a second computer on the CACHE line as a way for people to call in with newsletter articles. Randy suggested we put the extra computer at his house, in the city, so more people could call it toll-free. He added, 'Forget the club, a committee project will never be done—make it just the two of us—you do the software, I'll do the hardware. When will the software be ready?'"

Out of such dares history is made. While the snow came down, Ward and Randy toiled and burned up the phone lines to Dennis Hayes in Atlanta. Hayes had started selling PC modems the previous summer, made on his kitchen table in "production runs" of five or so. He compiled his own manual and, under "applications," wrote that one of the things you could do with a modem is create a bulletin board. Like the corkboards in churches, schools, grocery stores, and clubhouses around the world, a computer bulletin board could feature notices of goods for sale or wanted, meetings scheduled or canceled, and anything else of interest. And the readers and writers of those notices wouldn't have to be physically close to the board—they could access it via a phone line. It was just one of several ideas put forward as a way to sell modems.

But these two customers in Chicago were taking him seriously. "I prototyped a bit of a dialogue in BASIC, patterned after (1) the corkboard bulletin board at CACHE meetings, and (2) the kind of bulletin board you see at the food market—you know, 'garage for rent,' 'dog grooming,' etc.," Christensen continued. Randy called Ward's program Computer Elite's Project C Communications.

Within two weeks, they began testing it at Randy's house in Chicago. "This was very early in February. No one believed it could be written in two weeks of spare time, so we called it 'one month.'"

As soon as he saw it, Dave Caulkins of the software distributor PCNET became convinced that the program, now called CBBS—Computer Bulletin Board System—had commercial potential. Ward agreed to a price of $50 "to keep people from bugging me (if it were free), yet making it cheap enough for anyone to buy." Since Christensen's work with IBM made him concerned about a possible conflict of interest, he insisted that Randy get all the money.

To this day Ward Christensen insists "anyone could have done it"— anyone could have written Xmodem and the CBBS. "Xmodem was born of the necessity of transferring files mostly between Randy and myself, at some means faster than mailing cassettes (if we'd lived less than the 30 miles apart we did, Xmodem might not have been born). CBBS was born of the conditions 'all the pieces are there, it is snowing like @#$%, let's hack.'"

Sometimes Ward Christensen shows up at meetings of bulletin board sysops, a short, owlish, quiet, and surprisingly young man wearing a suit and sneakers. When he makes a few comments at these meetings, everyone becomes quiet and respectful. His comments on the future of technology are always worth hearing. But he gets embarrassed by too much attention and the idea of his "place in history." He doesn't like being pigeonholed as a figure from the past. "I'm much more interested in the future than the past," he explained as we bid him goodnight.

Building an Industry

The story of Ward and Randy is, to an extent, the story of BBSs to this day. Altruism is transformed into a business and then into an industry.

Within months of the opening of CBBS, Dennis Hayes recalls, boards spread like wildfire, popping up everywhere. Since the boards helped sell his modems, Hayes kept on top of the movement, keeping a current list of boards and sending a copy of the list with each modem sold.

Not all the new boards ran CBBS. One board in Texas ran a program its operator called the Remote Bulletin Board System, or RBBS. No one claimed authorship of RBBS—"it was just sitting there," in the words of Richard Couture, who now runs a board for the San Francisco PC Users' Group. "Some people took it, played with it, and developed it."

Hayes kept track of boards for three years, until the list became overwhelming and the company noticed the appearance of some boards with "unclean" motives. Some were discussing sex, for gosh sakes—is that anything to send a kid buying a modem?

Until 1981 most boards ran on either the Apple® II or what was called the S-100 bus, a large box with plugs for add-in cards that ran the CP/M operating system from Digital Research, Inc. (DRI is now owned by Novell, which makes local area networks.) A few boards appeared for the Commodore Pet, which ran CP/M but had a different case, and the Tandy TRS-80, which ran an operating system called TRS-DOS, but these were a minority.

One of the early BBS programs for the S-100 bus was TBBS by Phil Becker (who has since become head of eSoft, a maker of commercial BBS software), written in 1980. "I first got involved in late 1979 or early 1980 through a friend named Dave Ebert," Becker said. "He was into the technology, and I was an inveterate mainframe chauvinist. I thought microcomputers were hopeless toys. He got me to call a bulletin board, and it was one of those moments where you stand still, the world spins a quarter-turn and it's never the same again. It was something called Connection 80 running on a TRS-80. The idea that microcomputers could do something useful got me. The idea they could store messages, and retrieve them, impressed me. I'd used microprocessors as embedded controllers, but the concept they could be real PCs hadn't caught on with me."

After Becker complained about the quality of bulletin board software, Ebert dared him over their Friday night poker game to write something better. The result was TBBS, the first commercial bulletin board software package. The first TBBS version was placed on the market and sold in 1981. Today there are over 10,000 TBBS installations in 34 countries worldwide.

Two events changed the computing world in 1981. The Osborne portable came out, offering a "real computer" in a box you could carry for under $2,000. More important, the IBM PC was released.

When the IBM PC emerged, Tom Mack took another look at RBBS. Mack, then president of the Capitol PC Users' Group in Washington, D.C., found it in his own shareware library, written in BASIC under CP/M. "Tom played with it and rewrote it in BASIC for the IBM PC," recalls Couture. "He played with it a while, and through the shareware libraries, it came to the attention of John Martin in Concord, California.

"John was looking for something like RBBS but thought the program wasn't well written. He contacted Tom, said he'd rewritten it, and sent a copy along. Tom was happy and told him he'd copyright it and give him half credit."

But neither wanted money for his efforts. Mack wanted to make RBBS available to the deaf. Martin saw RBBS as a way to show that BASIC was a viable language. Thus, the program became "user ware." Couture, whose board runs RBBS, explains the concept: "The code is copyrighted, but it's absolutely free, and it's distributed through BBSs." If you see it, you can download RBBS and use it. Your support will come from other bulletin board operators who use it, however, not from an organized company or club.

Tom Scott, then living in Virginia, also had his life changed by a bulletin board. In 1982 he dialed George Matyasak's Syslink board in Chicago, then running TBBS on a Radio Shack Model 1 with 4 floppy drives. Within a few years Scott was a computer dealer. Within a few more, he was selling services such as USA Today and the UPI News wire to bulletin board operators. Later he moved to Albuquerque and opened Starlink, reselling packet-switch services for bulletin board users. "My own telephone bill was the major motivator," he admits. Today Scott also runs Connect USA, the Galaxy™ BBS, and a magazine for BBS users called *Telecomputing*.

Bob Mahoney recognized the power of the IBM PC right away. He moved to a job at American Appraisal Associates in Milwaukee in part to work on PCs. Soon he started dialing boards on his own, including a board run by Gene Plantz, a BBS pioneer in Hoffman Estates, Illinois. "He set a good pace for being friendly with the good users, which is the vast majority, being strong, and keeping the annoying users from hurting everyone else," Mahoney said. "He had good policies and recognized the IBM PC as a defacto standard real early on."

Mahoney was hooked instantly and, after playing with others' boards for a few years, decided to open his own. "I wanted to get into computer consulting. I wanted my name out there as someone who knew what he was doing. I hoped to get online customers from local businesses, so I could do consulting." His Exec-PC board opened in November 1983 and was instantly one of the biggest in the country, "because by accident I'd gotten a 30-megabyte hard drive from Tecmar. Shell Oil, a consulting client, had ordered me a 10-meg drive they said I could keep after the project—Tecmar accidentally gave me a 30. So I collected business-oriented files from every board around for the IBM PC." At last count, Exec-PC had 250 lines, the largest board in the world.

Tim Stryker wrote bulletin board software before he ever dialed into one, starting in 1984. "Prior to that I'd been doing all kinds of things, primarily factory automation, process control, that sort of thing," he recalls.

After using a few boards, he created a multiplayer game called Fazuul that supported 46 simultaneous users on an IBM PC/XT® with a 10-megabyte hard disk. "It was quite an accomplishment in those days. It was pay-for-play, an online entertainment medium. We went online May 22, 1984, in Bay Harbor Islands, near Ft. Lauderdale, Florida."

Stryker, a 1977 Brown University physics graduate whose dad was a foreign service officer, had been playing with computers since 1968, when his high school gained access to Dartmouth's time-sharing system as part of an experiment. "They wanted to find out if lowly high school students would have a need to access a computer." At least one did.

Fazuul was a technical and artistic success but a financial flop. "There weren't enough people with modems to make a go of it." But the idea stayed in the back of his mind, and he formed a company called Galacticomm in July 1985 to operate a board using Fazuul. After reading a magazine column describing a new communications chip, Stryker built a 16-line modem card using it, called the Model 16. It came out in July 1986. "To facilitate sales I had to create a programmer's toolkit, which became the Galacticomm Software Breakthrough™. As a way to demonstrate how powerful that was, I needed a demonstration system. That became the Major BBS™."

Fred Clark opened Clark Development to write software that car dealers could use to check buyers' credit. David Terry contacted him about a similar project he was working on; the bank he worked for needed to link its branches. PCBoard® emerged as a support service for the other products, and it quickly became something more.

"We started in 1983 writing the finance and insurance software," says Clark. "The car dealer would enter your car deal into his computer, and the software produced documents. At the same time, our package linked to the credit bureau, via phone, and ran a check on the individual. They could decide whether to sell it to you right then.

"Part of our idea was we would program our dealers' documents for them. They had to send us their forms, or a copy, and we'd code their forms into the program and send back the files they needed to run their system. Sending disks back and forth was a hassle, so we wrote a program where they could call in and download their document forms."

After a few years of running the PCBoard as a service for software customers, local hobbyists found out about it and started dialing in. "Little by little the PCBoard program started to take shape. We did some work for RBBS and did some programming for them. Then it got to be that PCBoard was taking so much we sold the F&I software to a company in Texas." PCBoard is now at version 14.5, and Clark Development has seven employees.

Throughout the 1980s, every technical advance made in a factory quickly found its way to the hobbyist bulletin board market. Gary Young, author of the Oracomm™ BBS package, notes: "You can now run 32 lines for under $10,000. Ten years ago you couldn't get 32 lines on a mainframe." Oracomm, written in 1982, started as "a single-user board for me and a few friends to exchange files. It was written in Assembler and ran on an 8080 machine I had. It became popular, the line was busy, so I began developing it for the CompuPro™," a CP/M machine. "We ran multiple copies, and seven lines at once. Then people wanted to buy it, so I rewrote it in C for the PC. We've been improving it ever since, and the C version has been around 5 to 6 years." Oracomm is available in both shareware and commercial versions.

Wildcat® is the newest of the big BBS software companies, founded in 1987. Jim Harrer, a cofounder, had worked on a board program called Colossus, but the project fell through. Working from the concept of a database-based bulletin board, he came up with Wildcat. His partner, Rick Heming, is a former private investigator who started using boards in the early 1980s.

Says Harrer, "Mustang was started as a consulting firm, and Wildcat was a shareware product we thought would be nice. I decided to join the staff here, and we made it a partnership before it was incorporated in 1988." As with Exec-PC, Mustang was starting a consultancy, but within a few years software revenues overwhelmed consulting income, and it became a business.

The Rise of Netmail

Early bulletin boards had two basic functions. One was to exchange programs, either "userware" files, which are free—sometimes called "freeware"—or programs which can be distributed and used free of charge but whose authors request a payment from regular users in exchange for support—so-called shareware.

The other function was to exchange messages. Some messages are private, one-to-one, or mail messages. Others are organized into conferences on specific topics. Sharing such messages among boards, either "netmail" messages addressed to a specific user or "echo conferences," in which a number of users share messages, has become an industry in itself. Its origins are in a program called Fido.

Couture explains: "Tom Jennings, some time ago, was developing a software package called Fido. He was having trouble passing code among his beta testers," who were using the program before its release to find bugs, which Jennings could then stamp out. "So he set up a mail system to get the code back and forth." In the middle of the night the software would dial the beta testers, send along Jennings' own messages or bug fixes, and pick up the new input. Then the beta testers suggested that

Jennings put his software onto a BBS, to create an electronic mail system among hobbyists.

Thus, the FidoNet network was born in San Francisco. It has since spread around the world, with thousands of boards participating. It is organized hierarchically, with zone coordinators covering entire continents and passing (or "echoing") messages to regional coordinators, who pass them to hosts, who in turn pass them to nodes, and from nodes they are passed on to points.

It's all done by volunteers, and it's pretty anarchistic. Right away there were problems. "Some conference topics would wander off the topic, and sysops would complain about the cost of passing them around," Couture says. The result, within FidoNet, was a succession of attempts in the late 1980s to set up some rules. All were failures. People thought they could do better and set out to prove it.

This led to the proliferation of "echo networks"—SmartNet, RelayNet, NorthAmeriNet, ILink, and others. Each has its own sponsors, its own rules, its own specialties. Many boards belong to more than one network, but passing messages between networks is not permitted. "We couldn't figure out the legal liability there," explains Paul Waldinger of SmartNet.

Most of the echo networks, including FidoNet, use similar software for passing the messages around. Some of these programs are freeware, others are shareware, and still others, such as QMail™, are commercial ventures.

Tom Jennings, by the way, is still a member of FidoNet, in Net 125 covering San Francisco. Couture recently asked him if he had any idea what he might have been starting. "He laughed, and said, 'If I knew what was to come I probably wouldn't have done it.'" He was kidding.

An Unlimited Future

Phil Becker is convinced that the real history of bulletin boards has yet to be written. While he's collecting stories and papers on the past, he says that the future looks bright. "I really believe where we are now is just the beginning of BBS software as a market.

"1991 and 1992 will be big years of awareness and growth. It takes time for awareness to penetrate. We're just now reaching the point where there are mature software products available. That's only been true about a year. Our product was there a couple of years, but many people saw it as shareware."

Heming of Mustang agrees. "This market is huge, and it's a business market. We started looking at it that way, and the evolution reflects that."

So, it would seem that something that began as a hobby and grew through altruism has evolved into a serious business tool. Today, Stryker of

Galacticomm estimates, four out of five new boards are private, business-oriented systems. The hobbyist board market will continue to grow, and so will the number of boards run as profit-making businesses. Jack Rickard of Boardwatch estimates that in a few years some BBS operators will be millionaires. But it seems that the majority of boards in the future will be run by businesses, for solid business reasons.

It's time to put this tool to use for you.

2

Should You Run a Board?

ABOUT THIS CHAPTER

We'll look into:

- Examples of BBSs in business

- Pros and cons of setting up a BBS

- Alternatives to running a BBS yourself

BBSs FOR PROFIT

Computer companies have known it for years: Bulletin boards are big money-makers. They reduce costs for product support. They reduce costs for internal and external communications. They maintain customer loyalty. And they can help sell goods.

Any business that collects or distributes information can do it at a lower cost with a BBS. The next section lists just a few examples.

SUCCESSFUL BUSINESS BOARDS

Journal Graphics Inc. in New York uses a two-line Major BBS system as an integral part of its business. The company sells transcripts of interview shows such as "Oprah" and "The McNeil/Lehrer Report." President Jim Smith has transcribers working at their homes around the country. Those in the first market to broadcast a show enter every word spoken and then upload text files to the BBS. Once there, transcripts become part of a database that is resold in many ways.

TV Data uses its BBS in the opposite way, distributing its products using a TBBS system. As its name implies, TV Data sells TV listings to newspapers for publication. The data are very time-sensitive. The BBS lets newspapers pick up the listings when they want, and the eight-line board is busiest from 9:00 A.M. to 12:00 noon on weekdays. The board links via a local area network to a Digital Equipment PDP-11 minicomputer, which has the storage and speed to maintain separate databases for every market in the United States.

The state of Colorado runs a free BBS called Colorado TravelBank, which offers information about cultural activities, fishing, tours, travel, and in the winter season, data on snow, weather, road conditions, and more. The board is run by Jay Melnick and has been open seven years, with a growth rate of 15 percent per year.

Did you know that a BBS helped win the 1991 Gulf War? Chief Warrant Officer Rogerio Perez ran a TBBS system for the 25th Light Infantry on the battlefield. Field units using laptops sent standardized situation reports to the BBS, and these were compiled into reports for field commanders. The main board was loaded into a laptop computer on a Humvee, the modern version of a Jeep. In this case, all data traffic was encrypted and transmitted via microwave. In peacetime the same BBS is based in Hawaii and is used to retrieve messages from officers on the mainland.

Professional Office Systems, a subsidiary of Blue Cross–Blue Shield in Washington, D.C., runs a 16-line TBBS board to collect health insurance claims from doctors and hospitals. Claims are paid in 48 hours instead of two to four weeks, and doctors can use their existing billing systems to submit claims automatically. Todd Inman, manager of telecommunications operations for the company, says that the company saves $1.50 for every one of the thousands of claims it handles on the board, considering the cost of mailings, microfilming, data entry, and handling of paper claims.

Winthrop College in South Carolina once used a DEC VAX™ minicomputer for electronic mail but switched to an eight-line TBBS system on an IBM PC/AT®. Now students and teachers who never exchanged files on the VAX are using the BBS. The Winthrop board has a special section for the physically handicapped and a section for students at risk of dropping out of school, where "pen pals" on campus help each other through the tough times.

BBSs are best known, of course, for supporting computer hardware and software, although they could support any complex product. Quarterdeck Systems Inc. in Santa Monica, California, runs some excellent BBS support. Gary Faxer offers a three-line PC Board system to support his firm's DesqView™ operating environment. The board opened in 1984 with technical files and messaging. People get on and off quickly, he says. First-time users get limited access to mail and files, and Quarterdeck charges for access to its customer support people, who dial into it through a local area network to answer questions. Faxer has also joined SmartNet℠, maintaining the board as a hub on that network. This helps Quarterdeck link to overseas users, by passing echo mail to its offices in Ireland, France, Germany, and the United Kingdom through leased lines.

Mike Fitz-Enz, who runs bulletin boards for Borland International in Scotts Valley, California, explains the objective behind his board. "We're trying to get people off the phones. It's more cost effective. We can have one person talking to many people." Fitz-Enz runs internal boards for distributors and international subsidiaries, and external boards for customers, using TBBS. "The subsidiary board has questions and answers about products. We answer product questions from Argentina, for instance. The files are the same on both systems—utilities, sample code, technical information, tips and traps on the different products." His goal is to create an "echo network" among Borland boards around the world, so that users in Hong Kong can get support economically from California, and vice versa.

IBM's product support board in Atlanta, Georgia, runs under OS/2®. Wyn Easton is the sysop (404-835-6446). The 34-node board uses MultiNet software, from MultiNet Communications (in Oregon). It is divided into a 20-line public access system, a 10-node system for technical advisors, and a 4-line system for PC user groups; the last system runs on toll-free lines. "We're trying to promote messaging—users helping users with IBM hardware and software," says Easton. Experts dial in to answer questions from dealers, and files include corrective service diskettes for both OS/2 and PC-DOS™ 5.0. The board now gets 20,000 calls each month, or 300 hours of use each day. The number is listed in every manual for DOS 5.0. Does the board pay for itself? "Consider this," says Easton. "We have two full-time IBMers supporting 20,000 users. It's cheap."

Digital Communications Associates of Alpharetta, Georgia, uses a PC Board to support its IRMA™ and Crosstalk® products. The PC Board system contains technical tips, product information, and technical spec sheets for downloading. The three-line board helps win new customers for Crosstalk, Miller says. "Crosstalk's CASL™ language and its Windows™ files have scripts—some are extensive. A BBS user in France wrote a BBS in Crosstalk Mark 4, which is posted free. We can also exchange files between users and engineers privately." DCA has conferences on each product line, with questions answered by conference administrators who act as assistant sysops. When sales engineers go on calls, they can use the BBS to get current files from their laptops. "We do have users in other countries who call into the system. Most are dialing direct, and those links go by satellite.

Some are asking for contacts in their areas; more often they're support calls like others."

In some cases, of course, the BBS can become the business. Wayne Gregori runs a store inside a BBS. The Compact Disc Exchange's low subscription price is waived after the first year if members buy at least four discs through the exchange. Members can also list used discs on the system. Gregori uses TDBS to create a database of discs available and takes a 20 percent commission on all sales. Gregori sells membership packages through record stores, and says that any product that doesn't need to be seen can be sold through a BBS, including stamps, coins, and fine wines.

In Wisconsin, Buyer to Builder collects building permit listings and offers them to construction suppliers on a subscription basis. Builders pay (at press time) $895 per year and $49 per hour, and contractors pay $495 per year and $49 per hour, for access to the system. The board maintains qualified lists of potential buyers of construction supplies; those lists cost $495 per year and 50 cents per name. Homeowners can get limited system access for $189 per year plus $20 per hour. Behind Buyer to Builder is a database written with TDBS software. Its high price is justified because its information is specific. Information on new homes can be retrieved by homeowner name, and contractors can create detailed reports on the work of individual builders. The database can be searched for builders that build homes of a given size, total price, or price per square foot.

RULES FOR NEW SYSOPS

As you can see, the uses of a BBS system are as varied as the businesses and organizations using them. Here are 10 simple rules, culled from interviews with system operators, to get you started:

- *Define the information* you want to collect or distribute, and build your application around it.

- *Start small.* It's cheaper to add lines as they're needed than to pay for unneeded lines.

- *Keep your initial expectations modest.* A BBS costs very little to set up; you don't need to bet your business plan on it.

- *Move gradually.* Nontechnical customers may be upset if you close other support avenues all at once.

- *Support your users.* Using a BBS is easy once you get the hang of it, but getting the hang of it can be scary—especially for users calling long-distance. If you have toll-free phone lines, link your BBS experts to them so they can walk new users through the board.

- *Stay focused.* Don't try to do work online that you don't do offline.

- *Back up all data on your system to tape every day.* An uninterruptible power supply is another must.

- *Dial the BBS supporting your software regularly,* not only to solve your own problems but to learn of others' troubles that you can avoid in the future.

- *Price based on value.* If you're saving money by moving traffic to the BBS, price the service low or make it free. Price database access along the lines of paper reports. Don't charge more for transactions on the board than you would for the same transaction done in your store.

- *Be consistent.* Remember that your BBS is another storefront. Its policies, its look and feel, and its treatment of customers should be identical to or better than that offered to customers face to face.

MAKE OR BUY?

Regardless of the benefits, you don't have to go through all the trouble of buying, building, and running your own BBS. You can hire someone else to do it.

Jim Appleby runs his Business Board in Los Angeles as a BBS service bureau (see Chapter 11). "A customer support department head may not be aware he has a make-or-buy opportunity here. Once he learns he can purchase space on the Business BBS, he's overjoyed," he said.

That's not the only function of Appleby's BBS. It's also used to sell goods, through spot sales. "We have a full order entry system. Our database is the mirror image of one on a customer support person's desk." Appleby estimates that a customer who goes to the trouble of putting together a database of common support questions and answers can reduce the number of calls to his toll-free support lines by as much as 30 percent.

Appleby competes against mainframe systems such as GEnie™ and CompuServe. He wins customers because his costs are lower and he can deliver a comparable level of service. One feature of his board that even the big boys don't offer is its link to FaxtsNow, a fax service bureau that shares the Business BBS database. Users without PCs can dial FaxtsNow, receive a list of available files, and order files by their numbers.

Appleby provides in all contracts that customers can take their boards in-house if they want. He turns over all files, lists required software, and documents changes that he's made.

A Professional Setup Man

If hiring a service bureau sounds like too much of a loss of control, consider a firm such as Intercom of Anaheim, California. Paul Curtis started his company in 1989 to set up bulletin boards for corporate clients. All his business is coming in by word of mouth. "We're not even listed in the phonebook," he says. Clients are found all around the United States and in Canada. Curtis spends most of his time on the road.

A call to Intercom frequently results in an interview. Sometimes a BBS isn't the answer, Curtis admits. "I often suggest a faxback system, or voice mail, or an audiotex system instead of a BBS," he says. Good prospects for a BBS might be a group of hospitals that need to share information with each other, or distributors of technology-related products.

Customer support is Curtis's most popular application. File transfers are also important, especially for internal communications, as is electronic mail. "Order placement and information distribution are key. If someone calls in who's a prospect or potential customer and wants to find what products are available, we set the board up so they can go in and get specifications, and make their own decision. Then they can come back on line and make a purchase using a credit card or other arrangement." The only thing he can't do—yet—using TDBS and TBBS is get credit card authorizations, only because he's had a problem finding banks that will approve such charges.

Curtis prefers to write TBBS systems, but he's flexible. "I've used Galacticomm's Major BBS. On single-line systems I prefer Mustang's Wildcat, because it's easy to use and set up and easy for the client to change. Our whole goal is to make these folks self-sufficient with their systems."

Curtis writes formal proposals for each system, based on a labor rate of $125 per hour plus hardware, software, and the cost of phone hookups. "You have to see it as a potential profit center," he says, as an investment that will pay for itself both in new sales and in reduced phone expenses. "Once the initial cost is amortized, it's practically free," unless you're offering access on a toll-free line.

"Sometimes we go back, but as a rule we can handle maintenance remotely." Setting up and starting the system can take as few as 45 days or as many as 120. Most of the time is spent making sure the installation is bug-free. "We're not debugging the BBS so much as what we've done with it. Wildcat and TBBS and Galacticomm are pretty stable systems—it's rare to find something not functioning. But when you put in a complex menu that chains through a series of screens," there are a lot of things that can go wrong.

BBS Consultants

You can also hire a consultant to help you set up and run your board while you retain control.

In East Brunswick, New Jersey, Fabian Gordon has made BBSs a regular part of his consulting and service business since 1984. He calls his company Advanced Microcomputer Technologies. "I've been working on BBSs 13 years," he says, and his own hobbyist board is a node on FidoNet. Because of that experience, which he buttresses with work as a network controller for hobbyists in the area, he has no problem recommending shareware packages such as RemoteAccess or even freeware packages such as RBBS to his clients.

"Whenever I see a customer who has a remote sales staff, clients who are bogged down by the way they do their business, or clients whose customers have computers, I'll talk to them about a BBS," Gordon says. Sometimes they'll look at him like he's nuts, he admits. "But when you explain how it works, they catch on. They get creative quickly."

Many of Gordon's clients wind up with order entry systems and database systems based on TBBS. "I use Wildcat for single-line systems, but in a commercial environment they usually have more than one line. QuickBBS and RemoteAccess are both good messaging boards," he adds.

Pete White of GW Associates has also been recommending BBSs to clients in Holliston, Massachusetts, since 1984. White is committed to supporting a single system—TBBS.

Like Curtis, White sometimes finds that a BBS isn't necessary. For interoffice connectivity he'll sometimes put in a simple mail program such as SEAdog®. "They don't need a BBS, they only need to improve communications—they just need to leave the computer on," he explains.

White's clients include many companies outside the technology area, such as St. Louis Music, a music distributor. Another client, in Maine, distributes marmalades, mustards, and other condiments to smaller dealers. "I'm telling him to put a system in the corner which can act as a 24-hour-per-day salesman," he says.

Applications that White has handled include messaging, customer support, and product updates. "Normally my rate is fixed at $100/hour unless there's a contract, which runs about $2,000 for a basic system."

White asks his clients to give him an outline of what they want and to identify their goals. But customers seldom stick to those outlines. "They quickly want more." The outline is usually used to come up with a first estimate of costs.

White says his worst clients are so-called MIS executives, who run large mainframes. "They want things done their way, which is often an archaic way. I still hear people say that you need a dedicated line to run at 9,600 baud."

If you decide you need a BBS but don't have the capability to create and run one in-house, these three companies are just a few of your choices. "My main advice is to deal with someone who knows bulletin boards and what they can do," White says, and the advice is sound.

Every major U.S. city now has dozens of dedicated, experienced hobbyist system operators, anxious to find a way to profit from what they know. Among them are devotees of nearly every BBS system described in this book, and their ages range from 8 to 80. You can hire one by the hour, by the day, or full-time. And you can fully control the final result.

3

What Happens Online

ABOUT THIS CHAPTER

We'll cover the basics of what a BBS is and does. We'll look at:

- The physical description of a BBS
- The functional description of a BBS
- How a caller uses a BBS
- What the BBS user can do

WHAT IS A BBS?

A bulletin board system (BBS) is a microcomputer that is left on and hooked to a phone line through a modem so that it can answer incoming calls. It runs software that lets callers use the machine. As we'll explain in detail, callers can do things such as read and leave messages, participate in conferences or forums, run special programs, and retrieve computer files for later use.

This description includes two basic assumptions:

- *Everything is computer-based.* The callers are also using computers and modems. Their modems are calling the BBS's modem (usually via automated methods), and a computer-to-computer connection is created almost from the moment the BBS's modem answers the call. If a person answers, the caller's computer will treat the event as a malfunction.

- *Everything is digital.* All message traffic is in computer form and requires a computer (or at least a data terminal) to be read. Most of the traffic consists of computer "files"—stored computer data—that is either read on the screen by the caller or downloaded (sent to the caller's computer to be read at leisure later on that computer's screen). The caller may also upload material to the BBS.

In computer terms, the caller becomes a remote user of the BBS, and the caller's computer becomes a remote terminal.

What the caller can do depends on how the BBS's software is set up. It is possible for the caller to have full use of the BBS machine, just as if he or she were sitting directly in front of it. In this case the caller can do anything with the machine that is possible through keyboard commands. More likely, though, the software that the BBS is running will allow the user to perform only set functions, generally involving the reading, sending, and receiving of files. Only the system operator—the "sysop"—will have full control of the machine.

PHYSICAL DESCRIPTION

Most BBSs happen to run on PCs (microcomputers based on the architecture of the IBM PC and capable of running software intended for the IBM PC). It is possible to use any of a wide variety of computers, but the vast majority of BBSs do, in fact, run on PC compatibles. Even the slowest first-generation PC is capable of running a BBS of one to four lines, since the data-carrying rate of phone lines is usually too slow to challenge the capacity of even the crudest microcomputer. In terms of machine capacity, the main concern is the amount of file storage available to store the message traffic and whatever files are being offered. BBSs boasting hundreds of megabytes of disk storage are not uncommon.

As we'll explain in detail in the next three chapters, the computer must have a serial port and a modem (the two may be combined into one circuit card inside the computer), and the modem has to be connected to a working phone line. And the computer must be turned on, running special BBS software. If these conditions are met, nearly any PC or microcomputer can be used.

Since no one needs to sit in front of it for extended periods, the BBS machine can be left on a shelf instead of a desktop. Thanks to the simplicity of the hardware and software, minimal maintenance is required. Prudence suggests checking the machine once a day or so to correct any malfunction or counteract any mischief by the users. However, the authors have used BBSs that showed no signs of maintenance over the previous 18 months.

BBSs that support multiple call-in lines often use networked PCs, with each PC supporting one call-in line.

WHAT THE USERS CAN DO

When someone calls into a BBS, his or her computer becomes a terminal for that BBS. Material shown on the screen of the computer is actually coming from the BBS, and what the user types at his or her keyboard is sent to the BBS, which controls it. The details of how this is done is handled by the modem software, which must be running on the caller's computer. (See Chapter 7 for details on how modem software works.)

Having called into a BBS and established the connection, the user will be presented with "menus" of commands by the BBS's software. The user can respond by typing one of these commands. (Examples and details are shown in Chapter 9.) Commonly, the menus allow the user to do six things:

- *Read bulletins.* Bulletins are brief messages about the system itself or the organization that sponsors it, posted by the sysop. There is usually no provision for downloading them to the caller's computer, but the caller may wish to record them as they are read.

- *Participate in conferences.* Conferences are series of messages posted by users about a particular topic; they can be thought of as non-real-time conversations. A user "joins" a conference and can then read its "message base," starting with the first posting and continuing to the end. Some postings are classified as comments to earlier postings, and it may be possible to isolate and read such comments as "threads." The caller, of course, is generally free to type his or her own postings.

  The postings may represent traffic that has occurred only on that BBS, or they may be collected postings from other BBSs (perhaps hundreds of them) that share the same conference through an echo network. (See Appendix A for details on echo networks.)

  Conference topics can range from hard technical discussions of a particular brand of computer hardware or software, to sports and the weather. Echo networks may offer hundreds of conferences, of which several dozen may be carried by the average participating hobbyist or small-business BBS. The choice is entirely up to the sysop.

  Each conference generally has a moderator, an ordinary but presumably avid participant who has been asked to keep the conference clean and on-topic. For this purpose, the moderator is given the power to remove the postings of offenders.

  Hard technical conferences are often moderated by someone from the customer service department of the firm that makes the product under discussion. Or at least someone will be watching the conference to answer specific questions addressed to the vendor. (On the other hand, some technical conferences boast of being "untainted by commercialism" and have no vendor participation.)

- *Download files.* Many hobbyist-oriented BBSs offer long lists (tens of thousands, in some cases) of computer files. These may be free for the taking, available only to those who have paid a subscription fee, or free but limited by the number of usable files that the user has uploaded to that BBS. (The nature of PC computer files is explained in Chapter 8.)

    The files may be programs of general or niche interest, on topics varying from word processing to astrophysical calculations. Or they may be product catalogs, graphics, works of fiction—anything within reason, depending on the aims of the person running the BBS.

    The files are generally uploaded and downloaded using "data file-transfer protocols," as explained in Chapter 5. The files are often compressed to save transmission time, as explained in Chapter 8. Avid participants of multiple-BBS discussion conferences often use sophisticated combinations of data file-transfer protocols and file compression to help them cut their online time and phone bills, as explained in Appendix A.

- *Run doors.* A "door" is a specialized program that a user can run on a BBS after calling in. Common doors include games, BBS management tools, and retail sales systems that take credit card orders.

- *"Chat"*. If a BBS has more than one access line, any or all simultaneous callers may be able to chat—exchange messages in real time, as if they had data terminal connections with each other.

- *Send electronic mail.* Unlike conference postings, which are to be read by all participants, electronic mail involves messages intended to be read only by the addressees. For various reasons explained in Chapter 13, electronic mail is not a major thrust of hobbyist BBSs, but such "messaging" is a common use of private BBSs.

By combining these six features, the sysop can achieve the kinds of benefits listed in Chapter 1, all for a surprisingly small investment of time and money.

But to explore the BBS world further, we first have to get online—we have to be able to make a computer call to a remote BBS. We'll discuss how to do that in the next chapter.

4

Getting Online

ABOUT THIS CHAPTER

We'll cover the four requirements for getting online:

- A phone line
- A computer
- A modem
- Modem software

INTRODUCTION: THE SYSTEM

To get online you have to "configure" a "system," meaning that you have to get several discrete items to work together: a phone line, a computer, a modem, and modem software. None of these things will, by itself, get you online. Having them all together on one desktop is not good enough either; they have to be configured to work together. Also, many system parameters—the number of bits in a character, the speed of data transmission, and so forth—must match those of the computer you are calling into. (For more information, see Chapters 5 and 6.)

We can make an analogy to driving: you need a car, fuel, and a road, plus you and your fellow travelers must follow a complex set of driving rules. Lacking any of these ingredients, you won't arrive safely. Of course, the online world offers an extra benefit: training accidents are reasonably painless.

The Phone Line

Any phone line that reaches the PSTN (public switched telephone network) will suffice. If you can hear a dial tone, dial a number, and reach it without having to use the operator, you're in business. Both tone and rotary dial connections can be used.

However, not all phone lines can work with all modem speeds. The newest 9,600 bps modems must sometimes "back up," or slow down, on noisy lines. If your fast modem isn't connecting at its rated speed, even to another modem with the same speed, the phone line could be the cause.

Phone lines within a standard PBX (private branch exchange, or corporate switchboard) can be used by any modem. But to dial out of the system you have to remember to add digits in front of the number you're dialing when setting up your modem software. (This usually means adding a 9 prefix, to dial outside, followed perhaps by a comma to force the system to pause until the new dial tone is obtained. For more information, see the AT entry in the glossary.) If you have a digital PBX, you may also need a special connector, or a special data line, to reach the outside world.

The phone company service known as "Call Waiting" can also cause problems for modems. Call Waiting alerts you of another incoming call while you're talking; you can switch back and forth between two calls by rapidly pressing the "flash hook" (the receiver button). However, the tone signaling the second incoming call can cause a modem to hang up or can inject "garbage" into the data stream. In many areas you can add a dial code, such as *70, in front of the number you're dialing to disable Call Waiting. But this is no help with incoming calls. If you are setting up a BBS or a similar system that takes incoming data calls, don't order Call Waiting.

Using a cellular phone to dial out may also require special equipment, since the momentary outages that occur as the caller moves from cell to cell cannot be endured by standard modem systems. When making a cellular call, it's also important to always use error-checking protocols in data file transfers, since the lines are notoriously noisy. When making a cellular call with a modem, you can improve transmission by stopping your car so that the call remains within a single cell.

Besides the PSTN, you may also want to use a "packet-switching network" to cut the costs of your modem calls. Such networks consist of leased phone lines that have been specially conditioned for digital use. They run at very high speeds and carry multiple modem calls as "packets"; your data are tucked in with data from other calls and then sorted out at the end of the line so that it looks like a direct connection.

Packet-switching networks have "points of presence" in most metropolitan areas that can be reached through local phone calls. Once your call is logged into the network, it can be carried a long distance for much less than a long-distance call would cost, because you're sharing the line with other modems. Unfortunately, not all packet connections can run at the top speed of today's fastest modems—9,600 bits per second. The upgrade process of the network to this speed is ongoing. Until it's completed, however, you should recognize this speed limit and consider dialing direct on a long call.

It's important to remember that although the PSTN, public data networks, and cellular networks are ubiquitous, they can all impose speed limits on your data transmissions.

The Computer

Nearly any computer will suffice, so long as it has a "serial port" or plug for connecting your modem. Serial ports are usually called RS-232 ports. They are distinguished from printer ports, sometimes called parallel ports, by being "male"; the printer ports of a computer are normally "female." (See Chapter 6 for the difference between male and female plugs.) Older serial ports have 25 pins and are used by most desktop PCs. In an effort to create space for more ports on the back of PC adaptor cards, newer models use smaller plugs with 9 pins. (All 25 pins are usually required only in certain mainframe uses. Most PCs can get by with 7.) Plugs that translate between the two standards are inexpensive.

Early 300 bps modems made no major demands on serial ports. The new 9,600 bps modems actually run faster than most older serial ports can accept data, making them a real bottleneck. To correct the problem, Hayes Microcomputer Products offers an "enhanced serial port," or ESP™, that will let even a slow PC use a 9,600 bps modem efficiently. The ESP creates a buffer that holds incoming data until the computer can process it.

Computers do not send pictures to each other in the way that fax machines and TV sets do. They send data, which must be translated by software. Having matching configurations at both ends is imperative, and if you're sending pictures or compressed files, having matching translation software is also a necessity. (More on this is covered in Chapter 5.)

It is possible to use a data terminal by itself instead of a computer. (By data terminal, we mean a monitor and keyboard with just enough circuitry to interpret incoming data and display it on the screen.) Of course, since a terminal has no internal storage, any material that scrolls off the top of the screen is effectively gone and cannot be retrieved (except by repeating the actions that brought it onto your screen in the first place).

The Modem

A modem connects your computer to the phone line. With conventional phone lines, there is no way to get around using a modem.

You must use a modem that is compatible with the one at the other end. (There are many varieties. For more information, see Chapter 6.)

Fortunately, there are industry standards for PC modems, so getting modems to link up isn't difficult. But if your modem doesn't meet the standards of the modem it's linked to, no communication will take place.

Modem Software

To your computer, the fact that there is a modem connected to it means nothing. To communicate, the computer must be told to pay attention to the modem and do something with the data coming from it, and to use the modem when there is something to send.

Therefore, going online with a computer and modem requires modem software. There are many varieties. (For more information, see Chapter 7.) Most of what is required for matching your computer's configuration to that of the computer on the other end of the line can be done using the modem software.

WHAT HAPPENS

To go online, hook up your modem and computer, configure it with the modem software, and then order the modem to dial the phone through the software. You can do this either with a set of menus or a modem command that starts ATDT (for tone dialing) or ATDP (for pulse dialing). (For more information, see Chapter 7.)

Once you finish dialing, you should see activity on the screen produced by the online connection. With many modems you'll hear what sounds like static as the connection is begun—a process called "handshaking." With many modem software packages, you'll also hear a set of tones when the connection is established.

At this point, everything you type at the keyboard will be sent to the other system. Your typing affects your system only to the extent that it is echoed on your screen. You are now using the other system, not your own, and any commands you type in should be aimed at controlling the remote system.

To control your own computer again you must get your communications software to pay attention to your commands; you must reach "command mode." The command for doing this varies from package to package. (For more information, see Chapter 7.) Most early packages used the Escape key. Most of today's popular packages use some Alt-key combination, depending on the type of command you want to issue.

Note that we emphasize keyboard activity. At this point in the development of modem technology, the use of mouse point-and-click commands are limited. Those commands that do exist only translate between the AT command set and your modem software. (See the profile of Crosstalk for Windows in Chapter 7.)

Most of the time, your interaction with a remote computer will involve only the ASCII character set. (See the glossary for an explanation of ASCII.) Even the graphics seen in ANSI terminal emulation represent only high-end ASCII characters. The only way to deal with other types of data—spreadsheets, pictures, music—is as part of a data file transfer.

5

Basics of
Telecommunications

ABOUT THIS CHAPTER

We'll cover the fundamentals of data communications techniques, including what you need to understand for successful use of a BBS. We'll define such concepts as:

- Serial, full duplex, async communications
- Framing bits
- Transmission speeds
- Character codes and screen graphics
- File uploading
- Data file-transfer protocols
- File compression
- Terminal emulation
- ISDN
- Related topics

We've divided the material into fundamental, additional, and advanced topics.

INTRODUCTION

Whenever you go online, you are delving into the world of telecommunications. It's an arcane world; people get engineering degrees in telecommunications, and experts are well paid. But remember, people also get degrees in automotive engineering—but you can drive a car without one. The situation with BBSs is similar: you're going to drive (use) the car (modem), not reengineer it. Don't be afraid of the learning curve.

Still, there are some fundamental things you need to know in order to telecommunicate. This chapter covers these, as well as additional subjects that you may need to understand in a passing way, and advanced topics to prepare you for some of the jargon you might encounter in the field.

FUNDAMENTALS

On listings of BBSs you may see a phone number followed by a notation that looks something like this: 2400,8,N,1. This example refers to a board with a 2,400 bps modem, sending and receiving eight-bit data words, with no parity bit and one stop bit. The notation tells the caller how to set up software to use that BBS, and it sums up most of the basics of telecommunications as practiced in the BBS world.

Bits and Bytes

There are a few very important points that the notation doesn't address. They concern standard functions, shared by all BBSs.

The first and most obvious consideration is that we are sending digital data. The fact that nondigital phone lines are in use is immaterial; a modem modulates (translates) the digital data into analog tones on one end of a phone line, and then demodulates (retranslates) on the other end— hence the term *modem.* If you had two computers in the same room, you could get them to communicate quite easily by connecting them directly, with no modem at all (except perhaps for a "null modem," to make sure the "in" and "out" data lines match).

The basic unit of digital information is the bit (short for "binary digit"). In discussing the contents of computer memories, it's common to say a bit is either a 1 or a 0, the two numerals in the binary number system. Printed characters (our primary concern) are represented by units composed of up to eight bits, called bytes. Simple math (raising 2 to the eighth power) shows that a byte can have 256 combinations, easily enough to represent all the upper- and lower-case letters, common punctuation marks, numerals, and other standard characters.

The translation between a set of bits and a character is called a character code. In the BBS world, the code used is ASCII (American Standard Code for Information Interchange). (See the "Additional Subjects" section for more details.)

The actual, electrical nature of the bits need not concern us; that's handled by hardware. In modern systems, bits are represented by changes in voltage level. In older equipment (such as telex machines), they are represented by the presence and absence of current—"mark and space" on a "current loop."

Serial versus Parallel

Also not explicit in the notation is that you'll be using "serial" communications as opposed to "parallel." A microcomputer has two types of communication "ports" (specialized jacks to connect to outside devices; see Chapter 6): serial and parallel.

The parallel ports are almost invariably used for printer connections. They're called "parallel" because there are eight simultaneously transmitting data lines, one for each by bit of a byte, plus some control lines for "handshaking." You might say that a parallel port transmits bytes rather than bits. The connector cable has to be thick, and it can't be very long, or the devices at either end may get out of sync with each other.

With a serial connection, the bits of each byte are sent and received in serial fashion, one after another, over a single line. Since you have only one line in your phone connection, modem connections are always serial. (Some printers also use serial connections.)

Full Duplex versus Half Duplex

Having established that we are moving digital data in a serial stream, we should also mention that we are moving the data in both directions. This is called a "full-duplex" connection.

In a full-duplex connection, the computer does not display a letter when you press a key on the keyboard. Instead, it transmits the letter to the remote computer, which "echoes" it back to your computer, which then puts in on your screen. If nothing happens on the screen when you type, the connection may be lost, or the other computer may be momentarily too busy to echo the signal. Either way, there's a problem.

In half-duplex communications, a letter is shown on the screen and transmitted at the same time. If you notice that all the letters are rreeppeeaatteedd when you type something, that probably means that your software is set for half duplex but the other computer is still echoing all incoming text, so you should reset to full duplex. (Some mainframe systems, such as GEnie™, use half-duplex communications. If you use full duplex while online to GEnie, you won't see what you type.)

Duplex is sometimes referred to as "echo-plex," which is probably more accurate. "Duplex" technically refers to whether the communications channel can handle two-way communications or not. Half duplex, technically, is no duplex at all.

Sync versus Async

Also left unsaid by the notation is that you will be making an "asynchronous" (nonsynchronized) connection. Unless special equipment is added, PCs and other microcomputers can communicate only in asynchronous mode. So, obviously, the use of this mode is not a big distinction, but it determines the meaning of most of the "2400,8,N,1" notation.

"Synchronous" implies that two machines that are in constant, direct communication with each other, exchanging data in a constant stream, or in blocks whose contents amount to a constant stream. The position of a bit in the stream or block determines its meaning; every eight bits is a byte. Synchronous communication is used mostly in the mainframe world. (There's also a variant in IBM mainframes called "bisync.")

The best way to envision asynchronous communication is to think of an old electromechanical telex machine (which is where the technology began, incidentally). At some random moment a person sits down and starts typing. Each keystroke is transmitted immediately. But the typing is jerky; as far as the machine is concerned, the timing of the transmission of each byte is random...uneven...not synchronized with anything... asynchronous!

Therefore, each byte (or character) has to be sent down the line "packaged" as a separate data item, whose meaning is self-explanatory and independent of any other data that may be sent. This requires "framing bits"—start bits, parity bits, and stop bits—placed around the data bits that make up the byte. As we'll see, you also have to send them at the right speed.

Start Bits.   Each byte sent on an async connection begins with an extra bit called a start bit. With the original telex machines this bit had a special length that caused it to literally disengage the machine's clutch so that succeeding pulses would be treated as data. With modern equipment it's just another bit, but one that serves to warn the system of impending data.

Data Bits.   Following the start bit of a byte are the data bits. You would expect there to always be eight, but seven is equally common. If you examine the character code charts in the glossary you'll notice that the first 128 ASCII characters include all the letters and numerals. So if you are sending only text, then you need only seven bits. If you're sending something other than text (for example, graphics or a raw data file) and you send it with a setting of seven data bits, you'll get garbage at the other end. What's most crucial to remember is that if the board you're calling uses seven-bit words, you use seven bits. If the board uses eight-bit words, you use eight.

Parity. The parity bit follows the data bits and acts as a mechanism for the machine to check if the preceding data bits are all correct. The main thing you need to do is confirm that your setting and that of the board match.

If you are using "even parity," there must be an even number of 1s between the start and stop bits, and the parity bit is set to make the number even. For example, if there are three 1s, then the parity bit is set to 1 to make the total four.

"Odd parity" works in reverse: the result must be an odd number. So if there are two 1s in the data bits, the parity bit will be set to 1 to make a total of three.

With "no parity," the condition of the parity bit is not checked, and no parity bit is added to the frame.

Through the parity bit, the receiving machine should be able to tell if the bits in a byte have been garbled. If odd parity is used and a byte comes in with two 1s between the start and stop bits, then that byte must be bad.

Actually, parity checking works best when only one bit has gone bad; if two go bad, they may cancel each other out, in parity terms. In any event, the parity bit is rarely used or checked with PC communications systems. If a character is garbled, then you get a garbled character. (On the other hand, this lets you blame your typos on "line noise.") With text, a few ga*bles ar/ not a severe probl?*. But when you are sending numbers, program files, or other forms of pure data, things need to be perfect, and you might want to consider using a file transfer protocol, with its built-in error checking.

Stop Bits. The stop bit was originally included to make sure the telex had enough time to reset its mechanism before the next character arrived. With telex machines two stop bits are used (sometimes even 1.5), but with other equipment only one is needed.

8-N-1, 7-E-1. Most BBSs use a setting of eight data bits, no parity, and one stop bit (8-N-1), since it facilitates file transfers. Others, especially those that carry only text, use seven data bits, even parity, and one stop bit (7-E-1).

Baud Rate (Bits per Second)

Having lined up our bits and bytes, we then have to send them. Following are the standard speeds for microcomputer modems:

110 bits per second (telex machines)

300 bits per second (hobby units, with acoustic couplers)

1,200 bits per second

2,400 bits per second

9,600 bits per second

14,400 bits per second

Modems using 600 and 4,800 bits per second are also around, but you'll rarely encounter them.

The modems at the two ends of a connection have to be running at the same speed. Faster modems cost more but can normally handle all slower standard speeds. If a BBS runs at 2,400 bits per second and you call it at 1,200, that modem should connect—unless the sysop has made the board "2,400 only" to weed out slowpokes.

The term "baud rate" is often used in reference to the speed of a modem. This is generally used as a synonym for "bits per second," although technically it is not. The baud rate actually refers to the rate at which the modem is "changing the state" of the line, that is, introducing noise into it. At slower speeds, there is usually one chirping noise per bit, so the baud rate and the number of bits per second are the same. At higher speeds, modems use sophisticated schemes to cram multiple meanings into the waveforms they're transmitting, so the baud rate may be much lower than the number of bits per second.

You'll note that each byte (assuming the use of 7 data bits and parity, or 8 bits and no parity) often ends up being 10 bits long, thanks to the framing bits necessary in asynchronous connections. Therefore, you can expect a throughput of, at best, 240 characters per second on a 2,400 bps call.

Summary

The variables in an async connection are speed, parity, the number of data bits used, and the number of stop bits. Therefore, it should be fairly evident that "2400,8,N,1" means that a caller should set the system to 2,400 bits per second, eight data bits, no parity bit, and one stop bit. These are often the default settings in modem software packages. For some packages, you'll need to check your software manual to find out how to set these parameters. Once transmission begins, each character will arrive in its own little "data packet," so that any line noise should affect only one character.

Fortunately, you don't really have to worry about the internals of each character. All you have to realize is that certain parameters will need to be set in your software. A quick glance in your manual (try the index) should tell you how to set them.

ADDITIONAL SUBJECTS
Character Codes

ANSI ASCII. The universal code for BBSs is ASCII, as defined by the American National Standards Institute (ANSI). Familiarity with the ASCII code can pay off since, when you get right down to it, a lot of data processing and data communication amounts to manipulation of the ASCII code—since the data are in ASCII form. The full code appears in Chapter 16, the glossary.

Although ANSI ASCII offers far more characters than most people need for normal correspondence, specialists complain of its deficiencies. For instance, there is no printer's em dash, and there is only one kind of quotation mark; you can't emulate a printed page with opening and closing double quotes that curve in and out.

For BBS and electronic mail use, the problem with ASCII is that there is no end-of-paragraph character, as distinct from an end-of-line marker (the carriage return, code value 13). This is another holdover from the old telex days, when transmissions were printed out on the remote machine, one line at a time, and that was the end of the matter. The important thing was that the line did end, and the platen was advanced (by the line feed character); otherwise the next line of the message would overprint the previous line. Today, transmitted text is often reformatted by the receiver, but the paragraphing may be lost, with every original paragraph getting chopped into new, one-line paragraphs.

The most common solution to this problem is for the sender to put a blank line between paragraphs. In the process of reformatting the text, the receiver can have the word processor remove all single carriage returns and replace all double carriage returns with single carriage returns.

Most word-processing files, however, are not pure ASCII. They must be "exported" or translated into ASCII and then sent once it is made certain that there's a blank line between paragraphs. In order to achieve formatting that's not inherent in the ASCII code—such as boldfacing, line spacing changes, margin changes, and headers—word-processing software includes a large number of extra characters in the text (usually from the upper 128 code values of eight-bit ASCII) with values that differ from package to package. Sending a word-processing file from a program such as Microsoft Word® or WordPerfect® as is will usually result in a flow of text that is repeatedly disrupted by what looks like garbage on the screen.

On the other hand, if the recipient is using the same word processor as you, it might be appropriate to send the material as a data file with an error-checking protocol. You may then be able to load the file into the same word-processing program and use it immediately.

Eight-Bit ASCII.   The characters represented by ASCII codes 128 through 255 include a number of "dingbats" such as © and ®, characters specific to European languages such as German and French, and a collection of fill characters used to create "character graphics." The trouble is that the upper 128 characters of the ASCII set are not standardized; they are used differently by different systems and software packages. Microsoft Windows™, for instance, does not use the graphic fill characters. The IBM version of eight-bit ASCII is shown in the glossary.

EBCDIC.   Extended Binary-Coded Decimal Interchange Code (EBCDIC) is a character code used by IBM mainframes and their imitators. If your PC is connected through a modem to an IBM mainframe, there is probably an EBCDIC-to-ASCII converter on the mainframe side of the connection, and you can remain blissfully unaware of this code.

Baudot.   Baudot is a five-bit code used on old telex and Teletype machines. (For once, the name isn't an acronym.) Five bits gives you only 32 permutations, which would not be enough for alphanumeric communications; however, the code includes upshift and downshift characters (called *letters* and *figures*) to give each code value two meanings. (Heaven help you if a *letters* or *figures* character gets lost in transit, since everything after that will be garbled. When a Baudot message contains numbers, it is common to list those numbers again, as a sort of appendix, after the message.) However, even the resulting 64 characters are not enough to include all the lower-case letters. If you have the intuitive feeling that electronic messages ought to be all upper-case, then you've been exposed to Baudot telex messages.

(One peculiarity of Baudot is that R and Y are the inverse of each other in terms of the way the 1s and 0s are arranged, so typing RYRYRYRY as a line test message "exercises" the levers in a telex machine, melting any cold grease. If you come across material preceded by a paragraph of RYRYRYRY, it means that someone is warming up an electromechanical Baudot telex machine. With ASCII, the de rigueur test message is the beloved "The quick brown fox jumped over the lazy dog 1234567890 times." This message contains all the letters and numbers on the keyboard.)

Text File Uploading: "Autotyping"

As you have probably figured out, the way to send a long online message is not to simply dial up and start typing. You write and edit the message first on your computer, using whatever software you're comfortable with, and then convert it to an ASCII file. Then you go online and send your message, uploading it from the disk file you just created. This procedure is sometimes called autotyping, since, for all the remote system knows, you're just typing very fast.

Most communications software has upload settings along with an upload command. The settings to use will depend on the details of the bulletin board or electronic mail system you are dealing with, but your software will probably offer such options as:

- *Timing delays.* The system at the other end may not be able to accept the text as fast as you can send it, so to make sure you are not "overrunning the buffer" (which would result in random strings of text being lost from your transmission), you'll want to put in time delays. These can be slight pauses (measured in milliseconds) after each character, word, or line.

- *Echo prompting.* Using the full-duplex setting, your software can delay the sending of a character, word, or line until it has received the echo from the remote computer of the last character, word, or line sent. (However, if there is so much noise on the line that the echoed data item gets lost, the transmission may simply come to a halt. If this happens, try pressing Enter.)

- *Screen prompts.* Often you will be transmitting text into the "scratchpad" text editor of the remote computer. The scratchpad assumes that you're typing by hand, so it signals the beginning of a new line by sending you a "prompt," such as a colon or angle bracket. Therefore, your system needs to be told what prompt to look for before sending the next line.

- *Flow control.* In case the receiving system is getting more data at any moment than it can handle, it must be able to signal the sender to stop and restart the data flow. These two signals, called XON and XOFF, are handled automatically by the software, if they are handled at all.

- *Other settings.* The remote system may want every line to end with a carriage return/line feed, or a carriage return may be enough. Some systems cannot endure blank lines (to them it signals the end of the file), so your software may have a facility to replace blank lines with lines containing one space (thus fooling the system) or a period. Similarly, there may be a facility to replace a tab character with a certain number of spaces, although you're generally better off using spaces to begin with.

Log-On Scripts

Log-on scripts are similar in form to text upload settings but different in intent. They're more like tiny programs used to automate logging on to a system. Generally, the remote system will ask for your user name and password, using the exact same query each time. So the log-on script is a program that looks for that query and responds appropriately, preventing you from having to remember the arcane password you were assigned. Your modem software may have a "learn" capability that watches you log on manually once and then mimics your action on subsequent log-ons, in effect creating the log-on script or program for you.

However, line noise can alter what your computer sees when it logs on, throwing it off. And if other people get access to your computer or a disk containing your modem software, your log-on script may get into the hands of people you don't want to have it. Also, if you're on the road much, you may have to log on manually from someone else's computer. Log-on scripts are a little like the buttons on memory telephones that dial long strings of numbers automatically when you enter a simple code: you may forget the number and become dependent on your memory telephone. Therefore, even if you use log-on scripts, keep a list of the codes you need where you can get at it.

File Transfer Protocols

So far, we have talked about telecommunications as if personal computers were merely emulating telex machines. And that's a pretty fair analogy. In both cases, you type text from the keyboard that is immediately printed at the other end, or you type it in advance and then go online and send it—from a file with a computer or from a paper tape with a telex.

But computers have a feature missing from telexes: data files. Your executable program files, word-processing files, graphic files, database files, and others are often saved in a form that only accidentally resembles straight text. Try using the Type command to see a file on the screen of a PC and you'll see a stream of visual garbage, often truncated long before the end of the file, when the system encounters a byte that happens to have the same value as a text end-of-file marker. Trying to send such a file as text will produce similar, useless results.

But you can still transmit such files, using data file-transfer protocols. Such protocols send the files in native form, without trying to render them as text. The bytes are packaged in blocks, which are checked on the other end of the connection for accuracy. If there is an error, the block is resent.

Generally, you'll choose an error-checking command from a BBS menu and then tell your software to begin sending or receiving the file using the same protocol. Instead of watching the file scroll past, as you would with a text file, you'll get a screen message saying that the file operation is under way. There may also be an indicator reporting how much of the file has been sent.

Several protocols are in common use in the BBS world. The important thing is that your communications software include one of the protocols supported by the BBS. Some common protocols are described next.

Xmodem. Xmodem was the original personal computer file-transfer protocol. It was created by Ward Christensen, the man who wrote the first BBS program, CBBS, in 1978. (See Chapter 1.) Most other protocols are extensions of Christensen's ideas. (More accurately, Xmodem and the others are extensions of MODEM7, used first on CP/M microcomputers.) Xmodem is widely used, mainly because it is a sort of least common denominator, as it's the protocol most likely to be supported by a remote system. Also, since it's in the public domain, software developers can use it without worrying about copyright.

With Xmodem, data are sent as blocks of 128 bytes accompanied by a "checksum" computed from the code values of the data bytes. The receiving machine calculates the checksum for the block as it arrives and compares it to the checksum that was transmitted. If it matches, the block is assumed to have arrived intact, and the receiving machine sends an acknowledgment to the sending machine, triggering transmission of the next block. If the checksums don't match, the block is assumed to have been corrupted by line noise, and the receiving machine sends a negative acknowledgment, which triggers retransmission of the block.

Xmodem/CRC is an enhancement of Xmodem that uses a two-byte checksum, which makes undetected errors less likely. (Otherwise, two garbled characters can cancel each other out, for error detection purposes.) CRC stands for "cyclic redundancy checking."

The original Xmodem was fine when 300 bps modems were the rule on PCs. Even with the acknowledgments and checksums, it was fairly efficient. With a 2,400 bps modem, however, the waiting, checksums, and acknowledgments slow the transfer time considerably. A variant called 1K

Xmodem uses data blocks that are 1,024 bytes long, and this speeds things up, but not enough for most users. Another way around the problem is to use a "relaxed" Xmodem, with wider timing constraints. The relaxed version is recommended for use with CompuServe. Still another solution is WXmodem, which requires an acknowledgment only after four data blocks. It is intended for use on packet-switching networks and reduces the time lags caused by the acknowledgment messages.

Ymodem.   Ymodem was the first "batch" protocol, and it can be used to send many files at once. The first Ymodem, part of programmer Chuck Forsberg's "YAM" program under CP/M, transmits the file's pathname, length, and date in one Xmodem block and then sends it with Xmodem. Christensen tried to define and standardize the name Ymodem in 1985, and although an increasing number of programs meet his definition, others, such as Crosstalk, still don't.

Ymodem-G is a version of the protocol that does not offer error correction; it assumes that you are using an error-correcting modem.

Kermit.   Named for Jim Henson's Muppet frog, Kermit™ was written at Columbia University for computer environments that were hostile to Xmodem. It avoids network-sensitive control characters with a technique called "control character quoting." Ctrl-P, used in many word-processing files, may be sent as #P, for instance. When used with compression programs such as ARC and ZIP, however, this character translation adds about 25 percent to the data transfer time.

Worse, there are two dialects of Kermit. One transmits eight-bit characters when they appear in the data. The other uses "eighth-bit quoting" to transmit binary data over seven-bit connections. As a result, some Kermit programs may fail to operate with each other.

In addition, the original form of Kermit used packets even shorter than Xmodem's 128-byte blocks. It was designed to work with computers that choked on input that didn't look like regular text; thus, packet lengths were limited to one line of text. A variation called Kermit Sliding Windows, or SuperKermit, works faster but is more complex. Like Kermit, SuperKermit sends an acknowledgment packet for each 96 bytes transmitted. But SuperKermit doesn't wait for an acknowledgment; instead, it maintains a buffer of a few thousand bytes, retransmitting only after an error. This reduces transmission delays; however, SuperKermit has not been widely accepted.

Zmodem.   In 1986 Telenet, now SprintNet[SM], funded a project by Chuck Forsberg to eliminate the previously described problems. At first, Forsberg thought that just a few changes to Xmodem would be necessary, changes that would make it more like SuperKermit. The problem was how to add a block number so that errors could be corrected after they were found and the sending computer had gone on ahead a few blocks. Binary blocks couldn't be passed backward through some systems, Forsberg found. And some operating systems could not recognize the acknowledgments, or ACK packets, without stopping to wait for a response.

To solve these problems, Zmodem uses the actual file position instead of block numbers in its headers. The range of synchronization is the entire file; Zmodem returns to the point of error when retransmitting garbled data. Rather than being a simple protocol, Forsberg writes, Zmodem is "an extensible language for implementing protocols" that can be adapted to many different environments.

As a batch protocol, Zmodem also lets you upload, or download, a large number of files at once. In other words, you can search a file listing on a BBS, tag the files you want to download, turn on Zmodem, and go on to something else. All the files will be separated and waiting for you at the end of the transfer.

The basic Zmodem technology was introduced into the public domain in 1986. Unfortunately, not all implementations were perfect. Forsberg's Omen Technology now offers a shareware program called DSZ that solves most of the problems and can be made to work with most common modem programs. Even if your modem software doesn't support Zmodem, it should have a mechanism for escaping to your computer's command level, with the modem software in the background. From there, you can start DSZ separately, going back to your main program when the file transfer is done.

Note: Zmodem can usually be counted on to give the best results, but it is not always available at both ends.

Compression (Archiving)

Files on hobby bulletin boards are often posted in an "archived" format, meaning that they have been compressed using special software. Such compression means that files will take less time to transmit and allows sophisticated netmail activities that would require burdensome amounts of long-distance phone calling. (They are normally transmitted using one of the data file-transfer protocols described earlier.)

Compression also makes files easier to fit on diskettes for—you guessed it—archiving. However, compressed files may serve mostly to complicate your life, since you have to decompress them after receiving them, and you'll have two versions of the files taking up room on your hard disk.

The most popular compression utility is PKZIP® and its opposite, PKUNZIP. Files that have been compressed can be recognized by their

.ZIP extension. ARC is another common compression protocol. (See Chapter 8 for details.)

If a board offers compressed files, it will also commonly offer a copy of the compression utility it's using, which you can download. It's usually in the form of an executable file; if you type its name from the DOS prompt, it will decompress itself, including its documentation.

X.25

Packet-switching networks use a standard multiplexing scheme called X.25 that allows for multiple data connections over the same line. Data from slower lines are collected on a faster line, with each slower connection getting its own "time slice." The data are sorted into their constituent connections at the other end.

The use of X.25 is not restricted to the modems used within the packet-switching networks. An end user with a modem and software containing an X.25 packet assembler-dissassembler, or PAD, could call into a packet-switching network and set up multiple, simultaneous connections on a data service, perhaps downloading or carrying out a search on one line while doing an interactive job on the other line. The Hayes Ultra 9600 is an example of a modem with an X.25 PAD.

There is also a scheme called X.75, which is a way of combining data from multiple X.25 lines.

ADVANCED TOPICS
Videotext

Everything we have talked about until now involves the sending of data, which your machine will interpret and display according to its programming. What is displayed on your screen may or may not bear any resemblance to what was on the screen of the person who sent the material to you. (That scene in the movie *War Games* where the young hero calls up the school computer, displays his grades on the screen, moves the cursor over to a particularly bad one, and changes it, is Hollywood moonshine.)

Videotext involves the transmission of screen graphics so that the user interacts with a graphic display, rather than typing responses to the text that is rolling up the screen. To work, videotext requires special interface software to turn your computer into a "front end" for the "host." Examples of videotext codes include NAPLPS, used by Prodigy, and Teletel, used by the Minitel system in France.

Telex/TWX

Many of our basic data communications techniques are derived from those developed for the telex and TWX networks. Telex is short for "telegraph exchange," and TWX is short for "Teletype exchange." Telex goes back to the mid-1920s and involves electromechanical terminals exchanging Baudot code at about 50 bits per second. TWX arose later, using ASCII (although printing was still limited to upper-case letters). In North America telex is rapidly disappearing, being replaced by fax and electronic mail, but it is still used in parts of the world where crude phone connections and language barriers make other forms of communications problematic.

A high-speed modern replacement for telex that has found some support in Europe is called teletex. It should not be confused with teletext (although this seems unavoidable), which is a scheme for sending data to home televisions.

Answerbacks

If you delve deeply into one of the major modem software packages, you may find a parameter you can set called the "answerback." It's a short upper-case character string, and you probably will never need to use it— although if you need it, you will need it badly.

Telex machines commonly had a key labeled WRU, for "Who Are You." Pressing this key transmitted the enquiry character, which triggered the answerback of the telex at the other end. The answerback mechanism consisted of a little drum covered with studs. When it rotated, it activated switches that sent a character string that served to identify that telex terminal. The answerback string was typically just the terminal's telex number, but it could also be a word or short phrase.

In countries where the telephone and telex networks were owned by the government, answerbacks were assigned by a central authority, so that the identity of the calling party was always known. Such telex messages could serve as legal contracts. More prosaically, it's considered good practice to begin any telex connection with an exchange of answerbacks, and to exchange them again at the end of the message (especially with overseas connections). Since telexes are half-duplex, there is no other way to be sure you have remained connected during the entire transmission.

But unless you're rigging up some kind of overseas connection with someone who uses a half-duplex terminal, answerbacks will probably remain exotica.

Terminal Emulation

The way your system responds to incoming data is not written in stone. (You may have come to suspect that not much is written in stone in the field of data communications, and that the subject is being made up by the practitioners as they go along. You're right.) The manner in which your system responds is based on the "terminal emulation" it's using.

TTY.   TTY is an old abbreviation for Teletype or telex. Its electronic equivalent is referred to as a "glass TTY" or "dumb tube." A Teletype can be thought of as a remotely controlled typewriter. You type one line, and then you perform a "carriage return" to bring the printing position back to the left margin and a "line feed" to bring it down one line. Then you start typing another line. You can perform a backspace, do a carriage return without a line feed (for overprinting), or ring a bell. But that's about as fancy as you can get.

So with TTY; text is printed a line at a time, with previous lines scrolling upward to the top of the screen, as though they were printed on a piece of paper rolling on a typewriter's platen. The main difference with a telex is that the text, being on paper, will not disappear at the top of the screen. (And with a telex things were noisier and slower—10 characters per second.) Hence, you always want to make sure your communications software can perform "captures" to save all incoming material on a disk file.

PC ANSI.   PC ANSI, often called merely ANSI, is the emulation encountered most often on a BBS, although if the BBS is not doing anything fancy (if it's not using screen graphics or color), you might not notice any difference from TTY emulation.

As well as using the first 32 characters of ANSI ASCII as control codes, PC ANSI defines a number of "escape codes" (short strings of characters that begin with the Escape character, so that the device will know not to interpret them as text) to define certain screen and cursor control functions. Screen control functions include setting the color of the screen background and foreground; setting blinking, bold, or underscored characters; and clearing the screen. The cursor control functions include jumping the cursor to a given row and column.

3270.   In the IBM world, names are numbers and numbers are names, and 3270 is the generic name of a mainframe terminal. It's not quite a dumb tube, but what intelligence it does possess is devoted solely to arranging data on the screen. Normally, a 3270 connection is synchronous, and a PC connected to a mainframe doing 3270 emulation requires the addition of a special synchronous interface card. With special equipment and software on the mainframe, ordinary async connections are possible. But the mainframe could just as easily do TTY emulation, so you don't generally see 3270 emulation being done over modems.

VT100 or VT52. What 3270 is for the IBM mainframe world, VT100™ or VT52™ is for the Digital Equipment Corp. (DEC™) world. It lends itself more to async use. There is no particular reason to use it in the BBS world, where PC ANSI is well established, but you do see it in some corporate BBSs where the main corporate computer is based on DEC hardware or DEC emulation.

Break

The Break character is sent to a remote terminal to, basically, get it to shut up and listen to you. It will interrupt transmission, allowing you to take over. If you've begun downloading a long text file and immediately see that it's really not what you want, you can send the Break character to abort the transmission.

With most BBS-like systems, a break is accomplished by typing Control-C, Control-P, Control-S, or even Control-Z. Some PC keyboards have a Break key that normally sends a Control-C (although you may have to press Control-Break or some other combination).

On the old telex networks (especially private ones used by news services), a break signal was really a burst of line noise that lasted for about half a second. Some mainframe systems may require such a break. If so, your software should have some way of simulating it, although you'll have to find the parameter and set it.

Fax

Fax (an abbreviation for facsimile) is a digital data format that predates computing and has, with new technology, become increasingly popular because it's easy to use. Some BBSs are starting to share databases with faxes. (See the profile of the Business Board in Chapter 11 for an example.)

Since it uses digital data, a fax transmission can be captured, stored, and sent from a computer, using a special fax modem. But there the similarities end. Communicating with a BBS or electronic mail service is really nothing like fax, and the two communications protocols are completely incompatible.

With a fax machine, the contents of a page are scanned, digitized, and sent to another fax machine for printing; it's a remotely controlled photocopy machine. If the scanner sees a dot it sends a dot; if it sees no dot, it sends no dot. In this way, fax is a binary medium. The fax protocol also has a sophisticated handshaking procedure built into it so that, at the start of a call, the sending and receiving machines can "negotiate" what speed and mode they will use.

The modern international standard for faxing is called Group III, which transmits 200 dots per inch. Most fax machines feature 9,600 bps modems, which can send a double-spaced typewritten page in about 40 seconds. (Vendors often call such units four-page-per-minute machines, but only a blank page can be transmitted in 15 seconds.) Some lower-priced machines have 4,800 bps modems and send a page in 80 seconds. Coming soon are Group III faxes with 14,400 bps modems, which will transmit a page in less than 30 seconds when connected to another fax running at the same speed.

Fax machines are easier to use than data modems but have disadvantages. You can't load and edit a fax transmission as you would a page of text or a spreadsheet. To edit a faxed graphic, you need to convert it to a graphics standard used by your software. To edit faxed text, you need an optical character recognition (OCR) program to convert the text to ASCII. But there are many sources of possible error, not the least of which is the standard resolution of 200 dots per inch for fax images, which at common print sizes is too crude for highly reliable character recognition.

Limited data/information services are nevertheless possible with fax machines thanks to the "polling" function of the fax protocol; it is possible for one fax machine to dial into another fax machine that already has material loaded into it, and trigger the transmission of that material. It is even possible to call in and select the material you want from a list by responding to an automated attendant with your Touch-tone phone's keypad, before switching to fax mode.

T1 Lines

A T1 line is a common phone trunk line. It combines a lot of digital phone connections and packages them wholesale. A T1 line moves data at 1.544 million bits per second—the equivalent of 24 regular lines on one wire, leased to you by the phone company at a price lower than the cost of leasing 24 individual data lines. (The break-even point varies, but it's generally said that if you need more than 7 phone lines you might as well get a T1.) Local connections to the line are made by industrial-strength modems called CSUs—customer service units. If you have a branch bank whose computers need direct connection to the headquarters bank across town, T1 may be the way to go.

T3 Lines

Today's fiber-optic networks can transmit data at a rate much faster than 1.544 million bits per second. This has created a new standard, equivalent to about 30 T1 lines. Such a 45 million bps line is called a T3 trunk line. A T3 line can handle a full-motion TV show without compression.

ISDN

ISDN, which stands for "Integrated Services Digital Network," is a concept that will convert the phone system to digital technology. A single ISDN line, called "base-rate ISDN," consists of two 64,000 bps data channels, called the B channels, plus a 16,000 bps signaling channel, called the D channel. It's often called "2B + D" for that reason. You do not need a modem to use these lines, although you may need a packet assembler-disassembler, which is why Hayes includes PADs in some of its fast modems.

ISDN has been a subject of heavy discussion in the telephone industry for the last decade, but (compared to the pace people in the PC world are used to) progress has been slow, leading to interim conversions to T1 and such cracks as "ISDN: I Sure Don't Need (it)." However, the pace is accelerating, and as of this writing it is projected that basic-rate ISDN connections will be available to about half the business phone users in North America by 1994, at prices ranging from 1.3 to 1.7 times the base business rate.

Computers linked to ISDN will use PADs instead of modems as terminal adaptors. The adaptor will take care of speed differences between the computer and the ISDN line and will reformat the data from the RS232C async format to the ISDN sync format. For a call from one terminal adaptor to another, the connection would be almost instantaneous since the two devices could exchange call setup messages without having to ring the phone. Call Waiting would no longer be a problem, since the Call Waiting signal would be a data message like any other.

ISDN trunk lines move at T1 speeds and consist of twenty-three 64,000 bps lines and one 64,000 bps signaling channel. This is usually referred to by phone company executives as "primary-rate ISDN" or "23B + D." With the single D channel, you should be able to "dynamically reconfigure" the other 23, meaning that you can change what they do on the fly. (With analog T1, the lines are usually configured on installation.) For instance, you could combine six or so ISDN lines into a data-compressed stop-motion video channel to support a teleconferencing call. After the call, you could divide them into individual phone lines again.

ISDN's implications for the BBS world are vast. Files you can't send with today's fastest modems, such as multimedia presentations, could easily be sent under ISDN. Of course, the BBS community will require real hands-on experience with ISDN before it becomes clear what is practical and what isn't. (For more information, see Chapter 15.)

6

Basics of Modems

ABOUT THIS CHAPTER

Phone lines carry voices. Modems trick the phone lines into carrying data—with some difficulty, since data in no way resemble voices. In this chapter we'll cover:

- Why you need a modem
- Functional varieties of modems
- Modem speeds and standards
- Compression and correction methods
- Nonstandard modems
- Special modems
- Related devices
- Connectors

INTRODUCTION

You cannot participate in the BBS world without a modem. Telecommunications cannot take place without one.

The word "modem" has crept into common language as both a noun and a verb ("Turn on the modem," "We'll modem it to you"), but it is actually an abbreviation, for "modulator-demodulator." Put simply, a modem allows your computer to communicate with other computers over the phone lines. Your computer can act as if it were directly wired to the distant computer.

To reuse an analogy from the previous chapter, you don't need to know what's going on inside your modem to use a BBS, just as you don't need to understand what's going on under the hood of your car to drive. But you do need to understand the difference between varieties of modems, just as you need to understand the controls of different cars, and you need to know what's possible for a modem and what isn't, just as you need to know what your car is and is not capable of.

WHY DO I NEED A MODEM?

You can wire your computer directly to a terminal or a printer, but you can't wire it directly to a phone line. (You may find yourself plugging a phone jack directly into the back of your computer, but only if the modem is a card inside the computer.) Why not? First, a phone line carries about four times more current than you want to expose any computer circuit to. Second, the telephone system uses analog technology, whereas your computer uses digital technology. Both technologies involve wires and electricity, but there the similarity ends.

Digital signaling involves the transmission of on/off, yes/no, or 0/1 pulses. (See Chapter 5 for more information.) Meaning is derived from the pulses through some kind of "intelligence" on the part of the receiver— either electromechanically, as with old telex machines; through digital logic, as with computer systems; or by the listener's perceptual framework, as in the case of Morse code.

Analog signaling in the phone system involves "modulating" (inducing vibrations in) an electrical circuit to make it an "analog" (hence the name) of whatever sound was exciting the microphone. Sounds picked up by the mouthpiece at one end of the line will be reproduced by the earpiece at the other. There is no "intelligence" in the system; vibrations are simply translated between media.

Similarly, a modem takes the computer's digital signals and modulates them into a sound that can be transmitted by the phone line like any other sound. At the receiving end another modem demodulates the sound and converts it back into computer signals.

LIMITATIONS OF THE TELEPHONE SYSTEM

A modem connection will probably not be as fast as a direct connection between two computers. This is not the result of some scandalous global incompetence on the part of modem engineers, but stems from the "limitations" of the environment in which modems must work: the telephone network.

The word "limitations" is in quotes because the phone system itself isn't limited. After a century of tinkering and expansion, the phone network is a globe-spanning tool superbly adapted to its stated purpose: the transmission of the human voice. From that specialization arises the problem that modems are built to solve: translating between complex analog sound waves that can carry the subtleties of the human voice, and the rigid on/off bits of digital signaling.

Analog equipment must respond equally well to signals in a broad range of wavelengths. Every few miles the current must be "boosted" to keep it from fading out, but the signals must be faithfully preserved in the process. Nothing can be lost as the current passes through all the connections in the switching system. And the signals must survive intact even when hundreds of conversations are sharing the same "multiplexed" cable.

To simplify this, the phone system makes no attempt to transmit the whole sound spectrum. Whereas you might be able to hear sounds between about 60 and 16,000 vibrations per second, the phone transmits only sounds between about 300 and 3,300 vibrations per second. This 3,000-cycle "bandwidth" covers most of the capacity of the human voice, but it creates a severe limitation for data transmission; since you have to use sound waves to represent data bits, it's hard to move more bits per second than you have vibrations per second.

BITS AND BAUDS

The modem therefore is faced with a 3,000-cycles-per-second "pipe" through which to force data. For this purpose, fast modems have been engineered to do astonishingly complicated things: each sound wave is made to serve multiple purposes, and whether a wave is rising or falling in frequency and in amplitude can have meaning. The only reason modern technology seems simple and cheap is because the necessary computer logic can be compressed into a chip and mass-produced.

As mentioned in Chapter 5, the rate at which a modem induces sound waves into the line is its baud rate, sometimes called "symbols per second." The rate at which it is sending data is its number of bits per second. Only with slower modems does the baud rate and number of bits per second mean the same thing; faster modems run fast due to their sophisticated handling of the sound waves.

All modems do basically the same things: encode data as sound and send it over the phone system, and decode it at the other end. But beyond that they vary enormously. Modems that you would use on a PC vary by functional description, compatibility, and "transmission protocol." (Speed, the chief consideration we've discussed so far, is actually defined by the transmission protocol.) Functional descriptions include acoustic versus direct-connect, manual versus autodial, answer versus originate, internal versus external, dial-up versus leased-line, and synchronous versus asynchronous. Compatibility refers to the way the software controls the modem, the commands that the modem will accept to perform basic functions. For example, the "AT" of the Hayes command set refers to the command that tells the modem to be attentive to a command. The transmission protocol refers to the transmission method the modem is using.

There are hundreds of different types of modems on the market, and most of them can be defined using the preceding categories. Some cannot, however, and these will be discussed in the "Special Modems" section. When using BBSs, stick to the main varieties.

FUNCTIONAL DESCRIPTIONS
Acoustic versus Direct-Connect

Acoustic modems are the oldest, simplest, cheapest, and slowest kind. There is no physical connection between the computer and the phone line; the modem actually makes noises that are picked up by the earpiece of the phone. You can listen if you want—it sounds like a thousand crickets gone mad.

The body of the acoustic modem generally has two rubber cups that look like earmuffs, and the handset of the telephone is pushed down so that the mouthpiece and earpiece fit into those cups. (Old 1930s or new 1930s-revival phones, fancy "Mickey Mouse" phones, and newer phones with tiny microphones and square earpieces obviously won't work, except with some acoustic modems that have the cups hanging loosely on wires.) The rubber cups and the circuitry behind them are referred to as "acoustic couplers." Of course, turning digital signals to sound so that they can be turned into analog signals so that they can be turned back into sound so that they can be turned back into digital signals is a rather roundabout and potentially error-prone way of doing things, so acoustic couplers are generally not used for signals above 300 bits per second. The carbon granules inside the mouthpiece of a standard phone also cause problems. When you talk on the phone, the constant movement of your body keeps the granules from settling, but a modem, being inanimate, just lies there as the granules get packed together, causing distortions. Special microphone elements are available that avoid this problem.

If you have a standard North American residential telephone, you'll notice that the wire leading to the wall can be unplugged from the phone. At the end of the wire is a little rectangular four-wire plug called an RJ-11 phone jack. You plug one of those RJ-11 jacks into a direct-connect modem to connect it to the phone network—just like a regular telephone or an answering machine. There are no little rubber earmuffs, and the signal is never converted to sound waves.

Although fancier options are possible with direct-connect modems (such as autodialing, described later), they have not driven acoustic couplers off the market. Try using a direct-connect modem with a pay phone or some hotel phones, and the reason behind the acoustic coupler's survival will dawn on you. (There are little tool kits available that let you take apart a hotel phone and use a direct-connect modem, but try using one with a pay phone on a city street.) In addition, if your hotel has a digital phone system, you will not be able to use a direct-connect modem unless you find a phone jack in your room marked DATA. Finally, as you travel from country to country the electrical specifications of the local phone systems may change and render your direct-connect modem useless. But sound is sound, so your acoustic coupler will still work.

Manual versus Autodial

With an acoustic modem you're generally limited to manual operation: you dial the number, wait for the answering tone of the modem at the other end, and slam your phone's handset into the rubber cups. A direct-connect modem, however, ought to have an auto-answer, autodial feature. It should be able to dial the phone itself (either with tones or, in older phone networks, pulses) in response to commands sent to it by your computer's software. It should also be able to answer any incoming call with a modem tone. This is called auto-answer mode.

(Since there are people who don't understand this point, let's state it here clearly: No one can "hack" into your computer unless it is connected to a modem that is in turn connected to a functional phone line and, under the control of communications software, is in auto-answer mode. If your computer is turned off or the modem is not ready to take calls, no one can break into it without coming into your home or office.)

Answer versus Originate

When two modems begin a connection with each other, there is a moment of "handshaking" when one modem waits passively until it hears a special tone produced by the other. It then answers back with its own tone, and the connection is complete. The modem waiting passively is in "originate mode." The modem issuing the initial tone is in "answer mode." (It doesn't matter which made the call and which answered, as long as they are in opposite modes.)

Any new modem on the microcomputer market will handle both modes on command, so the inclusion of answer/originate as a functional description is not terribly meaningful—except that you will see older or special-purpose modems advertised as "answer only" or "originate only." These should be left on the shelf.

Internal versus External

An internal modem plugs into an expansion slot inside your computer. Such a modem must be of the direct-connect type; you plug a phone line into it through an RJ-11 jack in the back of your computer.

An external modem is a little flat box that generally sits atop or to one side of the computer. Unless it is "line-powered," it will have a separate power cord. It will have an RS-232C port, which you can connect to your computer via a "serial cable" to its "serial port."

External modems generally cost more because they need their own box and their own power circuitry. They can be an annoyance because you have to remember to turn them on and off. (Internal modems in laptops, incidentally, save battery power by remaining off until turned on from the keyboard—a discovery that has crushed more than one harried laptop user who could not get his modem to work.) However, an external modem can be used with any computer—desktop or laptop, PC or non-PC—with a serial port.

An external modem usually has a panel with a row of condition lights that you can use to troubleshoot or at least to easily see if the unit is turned on. (The signals conform to the logical pins on the RS-232C port; see a later section for details.) Although many internal modems can be used only on COM1 or COM2, an external modem will link to any port it's plugged into. It is also possible to have an external modem that can switch between async and sync (see Chapter 5), if that's what you need.

Internal modems require an expansion slot, and if you are interested in adding a scanner with a bus interface, scads of RAM, a CD-ROM controller, or a bus mouse to your system (all of which take up slots), you may want to go to an external modem.

Serial ports are also in limited supply; an IBM-compatible PC usually has only four. (If you have a serial mouse, a modem, a serial-interface scanner, and a serial printer, your expansion options are limited.) The IBM PS/2®is limited to eight serial ports. Whether it's internal or external, a modem will consume one of the available serial ports. An internal modem usually has some kind of "jumper" setting whereby you can set its port identification—1, 2, 3, or 4. Just make sure the setting doesn't conflict with an occupied port. With an external modem, you just need to note which port it is plugged into. Either way, the software will have to be given a "port setting" so it will know where to find the modem.

Dial-Up versus Leased-Line

Dial-up modems are intended for use on the public telephone network. To make a connection they have to dial a number.

Leased-line modems operate on special "conditioned" lines leased from the phone companies. (The repeaters and boosters, which normally make hash out of high-speed modem signals, have been tamed on leased lines.) They often use four wires rather than the two used for POTS (plain old telephone service) connections. Generally, there is no dialing; the two ends of the line remain "hard-wired" to each other.

The highest speed a modem can achieve on the public telephone network is debatable. It was once thought impossible to build 9,600 bps modems for the public network. Recent progress in modem technology and the quality of long-distance lines shows that 24,000 bps service can be sustained. Few dial-up modems operate faster than 9,600 bits per second, and that's generally the only speed you see leased-line modems running at.

Leased-line-only modems generally have no place in the BBS world. You need to know about them only to avoid buying one by mistake. However, if you are considering setting up your own private telecommunications network, for a corporation or a government agency, then you should probably look into them further.

Sync versus Async

As mentioned in Chapter 5, there are two main methods of computer data transmission: synchronous (sync) and asynchronous (async). Sync assumes that two computers are sending a constant stream of data to each other, and the meaning of a bit is determined by its place in the stream. Async assumes that someone is typing on the keyboard of a remote terminal, with each character (byte) sent in an independent manner.

In the BBS world, async is the only mode you'll encounter. If you want to connect your computer remotely to an IBM mainframe, you'll need to investigate sync modems.

AT Command Set

Compatibility refers to the software commands that the modem will respond to. Although the modem may have a few DIP (dual-inline plug) switches that you can set to perform certain options, control of the autodial and auto-answer features has to be done through commands from the computer. For autodialing, for instance, a typical command would amount to: "Go online, use tone dialing, and dial the following number."

The trouble is, the modem's only connection to the computer is the same serial port that the data are being passed through. The modem must have some way of distinguishing commands intended for it from the data it is supposed to be running through the phone line. There are a number of ways of doing this, but the standard method is the Hayes®AT command set, so named because all major commands begin with AT. A modem that uses this command set is called "Hayes-compatible." Details of the AT command set appear in the glossary (Chapter 16).

What you need to know is that the communications software you plan to use must be compatible with your modem. A communications package generally supports a variety of modems (just as a word processor typically supports a number of different printers), so you just have to make sure your modem is on the list. If it is not, you may still be able to use it as if it were, if it is Hayes-compatible.

Transmission Protocols

To ensure that modems from different makers communicate with each other, there are standards-setting bodies. In the days when the Bell System of AT&T ran the U.S. telephone network, whatever Bell said went, so we had the Bell standards. Since the breakup of the Bell System in 1984, standards have been set by the United Nation's Comité Consultatif International Télégraphique et Téléphonique (the Consultative Committee on International Telegraphy and Telephony), usually referred to as the CCITT. The CCITT standards for telephony are denoted by "V-dot-number," such as V.32, and are thus sometimes called the "Killer Vees." There is a swarm of them these days.

Modems using both Bell and CCITT modulation methods exist. Hayes, for instance, has the Smartmodem™ 2400, which optionally uses either CCITT V.22 or Bell 212 as its "fallback" speed. But the use of both standards does not mean that a modem can be plugged into any North American or European phone network—the line voltages are different.

(You want fallback speeds, incidentally, because line noises or equipment problems sometimes prevent you from operating at full speed. And some corporate systems set up in the 1970s still operate at 300 bits per second. The system doubtless seemed ultramodern when it was installed.)

Modem protocols you may encounter include the following:

■ *Bell 103*. This is the standard 300 bps American modem. Today, 300 bits per second is mainly a fallback speed for faster modems, and some won't even go that slow. Many BBSs, in fact, no longer support 300 baud; some don't even support 1,200. Bell 103's speed is often listed as 0–300, meaning that it will handle speeds slower than 300, including the 110 bps Teletype speed. Any old hobby modem you see for sale at a flea market with an acoustic coupler is probably a Bell 103 unit.

- *Bell 108*. This is the Bell standard for a 300-baud modem used on private, leased lines.

- *Bell 113*. This is the Bell standard for a 300-baud originate-only modem.

- *Bell 202*. This 1,200-baud modem was used on four-wire leased lines. Faster modems have passed it by.

- *Bell 212A*. This is the standard American 1,200-baud dial-up modem, with the Bell 103 protocol as the fallback speed.

- *Bell 212B*. This is the same as Bell 212A, except that it does not support the Bell 103 speed; it runs only at 1,200 baud.

- *V.21*. This CCITT standard is functionally equivalent to (but not compatible with) the Bell 103 standard. It is used only in Europe.

- *V.22*. This CCITT modem standard is functionally equivalent to (but not compatible with) the Bell 212 standard, at 1,200 (and also 600) bits per second.

- *V.22 bis*. Note the suffix "bis," which is French for "twice," or in this case, "mark 2." It represents the second iteration of, or an enhancement to, the V.22 standard. This label represents a CCITT standard for modems running at 2,400 baud.

- *V.23*. This CCITT standard was intended for a cheap videotext modem, running at 1,200 baud in one direction and a much slower speed in the other. It is used only in Europe.

- *V.26*. This is the original CCITT standard for a 2,400 bps modem. There is a version for the public phone network and another for four-wire leased lines.

- *V.27*. This is the CCITT standard for 4,800 bps modems. There are versions for the public phone network and for leased lines.

- *V.29*. This is the CCITT standard for 9,600 bps modems on leased lines, or modems running at half-duplex on the public phone network.

- *V.32*. This CCITT standard covers modulation at 9,600 bps, with a fallback to 4,800.

- *V.32 bis.* This is a modulation standard for 14,400 bps transmissions, with fallback speeds of 12,000, 9,600, 7,200 and 4,800. It's the newest of the CCITT V standards, and chip sets supporting it are just reaching modem makers at this writing.

Only Bell 212/103, V.22 bis, and V.32 modems have a long-term future. Serious users should not consider getting a modem slower than 2,400 bits per second (the V.22 bis variety). And such modems should feature Hayes compatibility—nearly every 2,400 bps model on the market does. For 9,600 bps modems those following the V.32 or V.32bis standard appear to have the most promising future.

CORRECTION/COMPRESSION PROTOCOLS

High speed modems achieve some of their throughput from data compression, which squeezes out duplications and patterns in the data not unlike the way the ZIP file compression utility works. (See Chapter 8.) A 4-to-1 compression ratio is possible, but 3 or 2 to 1 is more likely. By their very nature, compression protocols can also serve to detect errors.

Since they stretch the limits of what a phone line can do, high-speed modems need this internal compression and error correction capability more than slow modems. That's why you'll find error correction techniques built into most 9,600 bps modems and why it is addressed in V.42 and V.42 bis standards.

If a modem uses error correction techniques, it will "negotiate" that fact with the modem at the other end. Both must use the same technique, or no compression or correction will occur internally. If you are sending text, the use of an error correction scheme by your modem may negate the need for file transfer facilities such as Xmodem. For non-ASCII data you'll still want a file transfer facility, however. Try the Ymodem-G protocol, which uses the modem's error correction facilities.

MNP (MNP-5)

The Microcom Networking Protocol™covers both error correction and data compression through several "classes." Classes 1 through 4 involve error correction, and class 5 covers data compression. If a vendor just mentions MNP™, it usually means class 5, which is the most common data compression technique on the market now. It can double the effective data rate. Class 5 also embodies class 4 error correction. It's usually referred to as MNP-5. (There's also MNP-10, for use in cellular-phone modems.) Of course, the modem at the other end must be using MNP at the same class level.

V.42

V.42 is an error correction and data compression standard for fast modems, agreed upon in 1990. It covers 9,600 bps modems under V.32 and represents a variety of the Lempel-Ziv compression algorithm (see Chapter 8) from AT&T, with amendments from IBM and, finally, Hayes.

V.42 bis

V.42bis is the second iteration of the V.42 data compression standard and covers 14,400 baud modems with fallbacks to slower speeds.

SPECIAL MODEMS
Proprietary Modems

The premium cost of compatible high-speed modems such as V.32 has led to the appearance of nonstandard high-speed modems. Although adequate for connecting two computers point to point (sometimes at speeds up to 38,000 bits per second), they are not much use in the BBS world, where wide accessibility is desired.

A recent exception is the CompuCom SpeedModem (CompuCom, 1186-J Miraloma Way, Sunnyvale, CA, 94086; 408-732-4500, fax 408-732-4570), offering standard protocols to 2,400 bits per second and a proprietary 9,600 bps protocol, tied to a proprietary data compression protocol. However, its low cost (less than $200) has made up for its lack of industry standards in the eyes of many, especially sysops of echo network hubs, who send large volumes of data to each other. (See Appendix A.)

In addition, older, slower modems often turn out to be using proprietary standards. In the "old days" there was no pressing need for your computer to be accessed by the public.

Proprietary modems also include "asymmetrical" modems, which send data much faster in one direction than in the other. The theory is that most connections involve someone calling in to download data. The downloading computer therefore ought to have access to most of the line's "bandwidth," while the receiving computer needs only enough capacity to send commands. The download channel may be 9,600 bits per second, the control channel only 450 bits per second. If they notice that the flow of data has reversed, the two modems can renegotiate which gets the high-speed channel. Asymmetrical modems are often built around fax modem chips. That does not mean they can be used for fax, however; too much tinkering has taken place. An asymmetrical modem may use a Bell or CCITT standard for one of its fallback speeds, but that would be its only claim to membership in the BBS world.

Fax Modems

Facsimile machines use modems that transmit in half-duplex at 4,800 or 9,600 bits per second. Many vendors sell fax modems for computers that will transmit and receive images to and from fax machines, and to and from other computers with fax modems. A received fax image can be viewed on the screen or printed with a laser printer or high-quality dot matrix printer, like any other black-and-white graphics file. To send a fax, the modems generally come with software that will convert an ASCII file to a fax image, turning the remote fax machine into a dot matrix printer. With special software, you can also convert graphics files to fax format and send them, or convert desktop publishing documents to fax format and send them.

The thing you need to keep in mind is that fax modems and data modems generally occupy different worlds. They don't communicate with each other, because they don't use the same standards. Don't let the fact that they are both called "modems" confuse you; a cattle truck and a cattle barge both carry cattle, but you can't exactly interchange them.

However, many fax modems are sold with data modems built in. These are two devices on one plug-in board. The vendor will usually supply software to control the fax modem, and you'll be expected to control the on-board data modem with a standard data communications software package. Whether the unit is acting as a fax or data modem will depend on which software is controlling it at the moment. (There is a service-software combination called On the GoFax from Ibis Software [625 Second Street, Suite 308, San Francisco, CA 94107; 415-546-1917] that claims to offer both data and fax communications in one package. In fact, to get a fax transmission you send data to an AT&T service bureau, which translates it to the fax format and then sends it on to a fax machine. Two sets of modems and two sets of standards are still involved.)

With fax modems, there are still functional descriptions and CCITT standards to consider. The functional description centers around what kind of background operation the fax modem offers. Full background operation means it can receive and send a fax without interrupting what is happening on your screen, so you may continue other work while faxes are coming and going. To do this, the unit needs its own microprocessor. Partial background operation means that the unit can sit in the background and wait for incoming fax calls, but when one arrives it has to take over the foreground, interrupting other work.

The CCITT standard for modern digital fax machines is called Group III. A Group III machine should be able to connect with any other Group III machine, sending images at a resolution of (about) 100 × 200 dots per inch (or 200 × 200 in "fine" mode). Transmission is at 4,800 or 9,600 bits per second, with various fallback speeds in case of line noise. (Some new models can run at 14,400 bps.) Transmission times depend on the contents of the page; blank lines are essentially skipped over. At full speed using standard resolution, a fax machine will take about 40 seconds to send a double-spaced typewritten page. When vendors talk about four-page-per-minute units, they're referring to sending blank pages through a 9,600 bps fax modem.

There are other CCITT fax standards you may encounter. Group IV machines have a resolution of 400 × 400 dots per inch and transmit at 56,000 bits per second. They're found mostly in in-house, corporate networks. Group II machines are old analog machines that transmit a page in three minutes at a resolution of 96 × 96 dots per inch. There are also Group I machines, which send the same page in six minutes. (The CCITT is also working on a standard called Group III bis, which would add V.42 data compression to Group III transmissions, for an effective throughput of 38,400 baud. This could obviate the need for the incompatible Group IV standard.)

Group I machines have pretty much gone the way of the dinosaur, and Group IV machines are of interest only if you have your own network. Group II still has some presence in parts of the world, and if you do business with such places you might look for a Group III device with Group II compatibility.

Null Modems

A null modem is a device that lets two computers that are directly connected transmit to each other as if they are connected via modems over a phone line. As we'll explain in the "Getting Connected" section, simply running a serial cable from the COM line of one computer to that of another won't do the job; some of the lines must be shorted or crossed over. That's really all a null modem does.

Communications software usually has a "local" command that you should use when you're connected through a null modem. The handshaking signals from the modem that the software normally looks for will be ignored.

The speed at which you can operate using a null modem varies with the length of the line. Standard dogma is that you can't go farther than 50 feet at 9,600 bits per second, but your results may differ. If you're interested in going thousands of feet with a direct connection, you should look for a device called a "line driver," which boosts the line current.

There are also "short-haul modems" that can achieve high speeds at low costs, but they work only inside private telephone networks, between phones connected to a corporate PBX. Once the signals venture out of the switchboard and into the public phone network, with its rude boosting and filtering, they won't survive long.

Security Devices

Security is usually handled by the BBS software; the user has to give a valid name and password before being allowed to use the system.

The spread of laptops and the parallel demand that users on the road have full access to their corporate systems has led to increased attention to telecommunications security. (Hacker threats have helped this movement.) The result has been a search for hardware security solutions.

Modems with dial-back functions were embraced initially. Having received a call from a remote user who has given a valid name and password, the modem hangs up and then calls back. And it won't return the call of some teenage hacker holed up in his bedroom; the user has to be at his or her assigned phone number, a line that is on file with the host.

Unfortunately, this means that the valid user can't be out on the road. Worse, a user with Call Waiting on the phone line could be knocked offline the moment another call comes in. Moreover, hackers have found ways to defeat dial-back modems through clever manipulation of phone company call-routing features.

Therefore, favor has fallen lately on security "tokens," which usually are devices that resemble tiny (credit card size) calculators. They have a keypad and a built-in encryption key. The host knows the key and issues a random number to a caller, who is supposed to enter that number into the token and then enter the number the token generates into the host. The host knows what number the token should have generated, and the odds against guessing the number are astronomical. Just in case, however, the user may be required to respond to two such "challenges."

There are also time-based tokens, which require no input from the user. The token just has a readout with a number that changes every 30 or 60 seconds. The number is generated by encrypting the current time and date against a "seed number" unique to that token. The host has its own clock in sync with the tokens, and a list of the seed numbers and encryption algorithms. The user gives identification and inputs the number shown on the token's readout, and the host knows what that number ought to be.

A business-related BBS may require more attention to security than a hobby BBS. Primary attention should be paid to proper password selection and to what the users are doing once online. (Accidents can be as disastrous as sabotage.) But the use of a BBS implies that access to the corporate mainframe is not granted, so security is not as paramount as in other types of computer access. Just use good judgment about what data are copied to the BBS and left exposed there, and leave everything else in the mainframe—unconnected to the BBS.

Current Loop Modems

The old electromechanical Teletypes used a "current loop" interface, with voltages completely different from (much higher than) the electrical specifications of modern serial connections. Current loop equipment should be avoided unless you actually have a Teletype that you want to connect.

Local Area Networks

To be connected to a local area network, or LAN, your computer needs a special interface device called a LAN card or a network interface card. This device is not a modem per se. LANs are designed from the ground up to carry high-speed data and are thus not bound by the design limitations of the phone network. Speeds of millions of bits per second are routine. Sitting at your LAN-based PC, you can access a file in a file server down the hall as quickly as if it were in your own personal hard disk. Transmission, however, is usually limited to a few thousand feet.

A LAN may include a "communications server" with a modem that can be shared (in turn) by all other users of the network. But from the viewpoint of the end user, such a modem would function like any other.

GETTING CONNECTED

Your modem has to be connected to the outside world, and to your computer. Assuming you're not using an acoustic coupler, its connection to the outside world is through a phone jack, which in North America is the RJ-11 jack.

Whether your modem is internal or external, your computer sees it as a serial port. If you're using an external modem, the serial port takes the form of an RS-232C connector (in Europe this is called a V.24 connector), which your modem's connector cable plugs into. An internal modem fits into an expansion slot of your computer, and you connect it by following the vendor's installation instructions.

Phone Connections

That little rectangular plug with the spring-tab at the end of your phone line is an RJ-11 phone plug. It has contacts for the four wires of a standard phone line on one side, and the spring-tab on the other is designed to hold the plug firmly in the receptacle.

A direct-connect modem will generally have two RJ-11 receptacles, one marked LINE and the other marked PHONE, SET, or something similar. The LINE receptacle connects the modem to the outside world. The PHONE receptacle lets your telephone use the line when your modem isn't using it. The PHONE line ought to be dead when the modem is in use, but this is not always the case. Plugging anything into the PHONE receptacle is optional; the modem doesn't care.

Of the four wires in the plug, only two are actually used in a standard connection: the red and green wires (called, for reasons dating to the dawn of telephony, "tip" and "ring"). If you have to cut into a phone line to create your own connection, you normally just need to splice connections to the red and green wires.

(If you live outside North America, the preceding material may not apply to you. Socket jacks may be the standard. You must acquire equipment that conforms to local connection standards, or you must be willing and able to adapt it.)

Serial Ports

A computer's data connections to the outside world are called ports. In the PC world these are called COM ports, and there are four of them (eight on a PS/2): COM1, COM2, COM3, COM4, and so on. Although the computer need not have any serial ports, most PCs these days are shipped with at least one. If you install a serial port board, you have to set the port numbers on the board and make sure that two ports aren't trying to use the same number.

Besides connecting modems, serial ports are often used to connect the computer to a mouse or other pointing device, certain scanners, certain types of printers (especially certain PostScript®printers), special-purpose business devices, extra terminals, and laboratory equipment.

The opposite of a serial port is a parallel port, which is normally used to support printers. Each bit of a byte has its own data line. Data can be moved much faster, but not very far. Parallel ports are not normally used to handle two-way data communications, although there are software packages that trick them into doing so.

On a PC the parallel port may use a 25-pin connector, as may the serial port. If it is not otherwise labeled, the parallel port is usually female (containing holes awaiting wires), and the serial port is usually male (with plugs sticking out the end).

If an internal modem is installed in the computer, the system will see that modem as the serial port. Otherwise, a serial port is embodied in an RS-232C connector.

RS-232C

Having analyzed the phone signal it's getting through its connection to the phone line, the modem supplies the computer with a wide range of signals through a multiline connection called an RS-232C port. (The name means "Electronic Industry Association Recommended Standard 232, revision C." The C is often dropped.)

An RS-232C port has electrical, physical, and logical characteristics. The electrical characteristics (concerning voltage levels and such) are always the same, reducing the danger of your computer getting fried by unwanted voltage levels. However, the physical and logical characteristics differ, so let's discuss them.

Physical Characteristics.   RS-232C connectors differ by size and by gender. An RS-232C port has either 9 or 25 pins, each connected to an insulated wire in the connector cable. The original standard was for 25 pins, but in the microcomputer world it is rare for more than 9 to be used. (The pinout is discussed in the next section, but most of the other 16 were for "secondary data channels," test lines, and clock signals.) When the PC/AT came out, it was deemed desirable to put more than one serial port on an interface card, and to make room for this IBM adopted the 9-pin RS-232C port, eliminating the unused pins. Nine-pin connectors are now very common on 286 and 386 PCs and on laptops, as well as on the Apple Macintosh®. Adapters to go from a 9-pin cable or receptacle to a 25-pin cable or receptacle are widely available.

"Gender" refers to whether the wires of the RS-232C port are present as pins (male) or as holes (female). "Male" and "female" may also be called, respectively, "plug" and "socket." The receptacle on the computer is normally male (but not always), so you normally want the cable from the modem to be female. Extension cables usually have opposite sexes at the two ends. But if there is oddball equipment in use, things can get complicated fast, and you may find yourself trying to plug same-sex receptacles into each other—something contrary to computer nature, if not social norms. Fortunately, "gender mender" cables and plugs are available, with the same sex at either end.

Logical Characteristics.   The nine wires of the RS-232C connection used in the microcomputer world have set functions and their own names.

GND (Ground): In some situations there may be two ground wires, one for the computer and one for the signal line.

DTR (Data Terminal Ready): The modem uses this line to tell the computer that it is turned on, or that it exists at all.

DSR (Data Set Ready): The modem uses this line to signal to the computer that it is turned on, connected to a phone line, and ready to function.

DCD or CD (Data Carrier Detect): The modem uses this line to tell the computer that it has picked up the line and has detected a "carrier tone" from a modem at the other end.

RI (Ring Indicator): The modem uses this line to tell the computer that it has detected a ring signal on the phone line. (Your phone's bell is rung by an added voltage on the line that is easily detected by the modem.)

RTS or RS (Request To Send): The computer uses this line to tell the modem that it has data to send. Some modems with built-in error control require that this line be present.

CTS or CS (Clear to Send): The modem uses this line to tell the computer (in response to an RTS signal) that it can begin sending data. Some modems with built-in error control require that this line be present.

TXD or TD (Transmitted Data): The computer sends data out to the modem over this line.

RXD or RD (Received Data): The modem uses this line to send incoming data to the computer.

The pinouts for the two types of RS-232C connector are as follows:

25-pin unit	9-pin unit
1 GND	1 DCD
2 TXD	2 RXD
3 RXD	3 TXD
4 RTS	4 DTR
5 CTS	5 GND
6 DSR	6 DSR
7 GND	7 RTS
8 DCD	8 CTS
20 DTR	9 RI
22 RI	

You may be able to identify these pinouts by squinting into the end of an RS-232C connector. You should see tiny numbers, either just in the corners or by each pin/hole.

You'll notice that there are two data lines: incoming and outgoing. This can cause a problem since the computer's outgoing data has to be the modem's incoming data, and vice versa. So we have to add a further distinction, between data terminal equipment (DTE) and data communications equipment (DCE).

DTE refers to the computer side of the connection and has the received and transmitted data lines as shown in the preceding list. DCE refers to modems, serial printers, and terminals meant to be connected to a serial line from a computer. DCE data lines are the reverse of DTE lines, so that line 3 goes to line 2, and line 2 goes to line 3.

However, you may run across printers and terminals that are meant to be connected to a modem and thus will be DTE. Or if you want to connect two computers together via their serial ports, one of them will need to be DCE. Use of a null modem, described earlier, will correct the problem by reversing the received and transmitted data lines and doing some desirable jumpering on the other handshaking lines. Also, a few modems have a selector switch to reverse their data lines.

HISTORICAL NOTE

When confronted with the fact that scores of vendors now sell modems in the United States, some people get a little confused. They recall that there's something vaguely illegal about the whole industry.

True, it used to be a shade illegal in North America, and in some countries it still is. At one time only equipment provided by the phone company could be connected to the phone network. AT&T even went to court for nearly 10 years to keep someone from selling little rubber cups (noise mufflers) for phone mouthpieces.

But in 1969 the courts handed down the "Carterphone" decision, saying that the phone companies had a de facto but not a legislatively granted monopoly, so there was no legal problem with using "foreign" (non–phone company) equipment on the network. The phone companies then required that foreign devices be connected to the network through a Data Access Arrangement (DAA), which they rented for $2 to $10 per month. The DAAs were supposed to filter out any dangerous voltage levels coming from the foreign devices. (Acoustic couplers became popular because they involved no direct connection.)

The vendors complained that the dangers the DAAs guarded against were imaginary, and in 1975 the Federal Communications Commission agreed to change the rules, saying that if a sample modem passed safety tests, it could be manufactured and sold for direct connection to the network.

AT&T gave up and stopped leasing DAAs in July 1979. If you have an old modem that requires a DAA, you might find one for sale from an independent vendor, but you're probably better off getting a modern modem.

Some of the local Bell Operating Companies continued to, on paper, charge higher line fees for modem lines. These fees became a dead letter when it was pointed out that if the phone company tried to enforce the charge, it would be admitting to illegal eavesdropping on your line, listening for modem tones.

In many other countries the phone system is owned by the government, and rules against foreign devices are a point of law. In some of these countries you may have to rent your modem from the authorities. In places where the connection of foreign answering machines is allowed, some users connect their modems through their answering machines.

This situation is changing, however. Germany, once one of the strictest "licensors" of individual modem users, now requires only a formal license for the modem itself, to prove that it won't hurt the phone line. No license is needed if the modem is attached to a licensed private branch exchange (PBX). These regulatory changes have increased the cost of modems in Germany, but people are no longer prevented from using them. These trends of deregulation and privatization are expected to continue.

7

Basics of Modem Software

ABOUT THIS CHAPTER

Your computer cannot function online unless you have modem software (also called telecommunications software). Modem software varies widely. We'll look at:

- Common features
- Common functions
- Some packages popular with BBS users

INTRODUCTION

There are literally dozens of modem software packages, just as there are dozens of word processors. Like word processors, the modem package to use depends on your tastes and needs. In word processing, the choices range from simple line editors to full-blown desktop publishing systems. In modem software, choices range from utilities that do little more than connect the screen, keyboard, and serial port, to systems that come with their own programming languages.

To get you online, there are several things any package must do:

- It must toggle between an online mode and a local or command mode. In online mode your PC is simply a conduit for data going to and from the remote system; everything you type is sent to the remote system. In command mode, anything you type is a command for your computer.
- It must understand what's called the Hayes AT command set. The command to toggle between online and command modes is just a part of this command set. The Hayes command to dial a remote system with Touchtone tones, for instance, starts ATDT. The com-

mand set's "escape key sequence with guard time," which lets you move between the command and on-line modes, is patented by Hayes and licensed to other modem makers. The primary purpose of a good modem package is to serve as translator between the complexities of the Hayes command set and the average modem user.

- It must set system parameters for your online sessions, such as the speed of communication and the number of bits assumed to represent a complete character.
- It must be able to recognize the serial port and modem that you'll use to go online.
- It must let you upload and download files to and from the remote system.

To win your loyalty, there are some other things that a modem software package should do:

- It should perform data file transfers, preferably using several different transfer protocols.
- It should store all the settings, configuration data, and phone numbers for dialing specific online systems in a "phonebook" file.
- It should let you write "script files" for automating log-ons and other common procedures.
- It should provide a specialized programming language that will let your PC and modem perform tasks when you're not around.

Other beneficial features include a simple text editor, a "chat" mode for real-time online discussions that separates incoming and outgoing text, and support for PC ANSI graphics, which can add color to your online sessions and makes many boards easier (or at least more interesting) to use.

It's also nice to have modem software that supports a wide variety of modems, newer file transfer protocols such as Zmodem, and a "host mode," which can take incoming calls and act as a rudimentary BBS.

No software can be all things to everybody, but all the packages described here can get you online. Choose one that meets your budgets, your needs, and your tastes.

Price range codes rather than prices will be shown. The codes are:

!	Free
$	Up to $20
$$	$20 to $50
$$$	$50 to $75
$$$$	$75 to $150
$$$$+	Above $150

TELIX VERSION 3.15

Exis Inc.
P.O. Box 130
West Hill, Ontario, M1E 4R4 Canada
Phone: 416-289-4641
Price range: **$$**

Telix is a shareware package that you can acquire online from many bulletin boards. More accurately, you can acquire an evaluation copy. This is a full-featured copy of the program, but the documentation notes carefully that Telix is not a public-domain program. Should you elect to use it after 90 days, you are expected to send in the purchase price and get a registered copy.

Before using Telix, you configure it to the brand of modem you want to use via the MODEMCFG utility. However, the modem "initialization string" and other parameters can be reset with each call.

Once loaded, you toggle between the online mode, called "monitor mode" in the software, and the local mode, or "command mode." As with Procomm®, this is done with Alt-key commands. Typing Alt-Z brings up the list of available commands shown in Figure 7.1.

```
+------------------------------------------------------------------------------+
:                      Telix v3.15 Command Summary                             :
:                                                                              :
:          Main Functions                            Other Functions          :
:                                                                              :
: Dialing directory..Alt-D  Queue Redial #s....Alt-Q : Run editor........Alt-A :
: Send files........Alt-S   Receive files......Alt-R : Local echo........Alt-E :
: Exit Telix........Alt-X   Run script (Go)....Alt-G : Screen image......Alt-I :
: Comm parameters....Alt-P  Configure Telix....Alt-O : DOS command.......Alt-V :
: Key defs./macros...Alt-K  Terminal emulation.Alt-T : Translate table...Alt-W :
: Capture toggle.....Alt-L  Scroll back........Alt-B : Chat mode.........Alt-Y :
: DOS functions......Alt-F  Jump to DOS shell..Alt-J : Status toggle.....Alt-8 :
: Hang-up modem......Alt-H  Clear screen.......Alt-C : DOORWAY mode......Alt-= :
: Usage log toggle...Alt-U  Misc. functions....Alt-M : Printer on/off...Ctrl-@ :
:                                                    : Send BREAK.....Ctrl-End :
:      Select function or press Enter for none.      : Add LF toggle.....S-Tab :
:                                                                              :
: Copyright 1986-91 by Exis Inc., P.O. Box 130, West Hill, ON  CANADA  M1E 4R4 :
+------------------------------------------------------------------------------+
:   Time .. 01:18:25  Online .... No    :   Capture ... Off                    :
:   Date .. 07-08-91                    :   Printer ... Off                    :
:   Baud .. 2400      Terminal .. ANSI  :   Script ....                        :
:   Comm .. N,8,1     Port ...... COM2  :   Reg. Key .. TELIX.KEY              :
:   Echo .. Off       Add LF .... Off   :   Dial Dir .. TELIX.FON              :
+------------------------------------------------------------------------------+
```

Figure 7.1 Commands Available in Telix 3.15

You make a call from the dialing directory by first pressing Alt-D; this gives you the list of phonebook entries you've created. You make a call by scrolling the highlight bar over the entry you want and pressing Enter. To make a new phonebook entry, move to an empty line and edit the (mostly blank) field, using a screen like the one shown in Figure 7.2.

Most online settings are taken care of on this screen. Once you have set everything and exited, you can immediately make the call. The monitor-mode screen, again for the PC Pursuit℠ BBS, has the format shown in Figure 7.3.

The bottom line in Figure 7.3 is the status line, which in this case shows that you're using ANSI terminal emulation at 2,400 bits per second; no parity bit, eight data bits, and one stop bit; and full duplex. The timer indicates that this call has not been online for a full minute yet. Uploads, downloads, and data file transfers are also handled with Alt-key commands, and you can still use Alt-Z to refresh your memory. After the session is over, press Alt-H to hang up the phone.

Telix includes a script language called Salt to automate online procedures, and a script is provided with the software to create a mini-BBS. (In Procomm, which is in many ways similar to Telix, this is handled through a separate host mode.) There is no learn, or record, feature for easy log-ons, however. The editor command will invoke whatever DOS-based

```
+-: Dialing Directory :-------------------------------------------------+
:               Name                   Number    Line Format    Script  :
+-: 1  MCI Edit entry 2 :-------------------------------------+          :
:   2  PC Purss:                                              :          :
:   3  Ilink  : Name ............. PC Pursuit                 :          :
:             : Phone number ...... 2253444                   :          :
:             : Baud rate ......... 2400                       :          :
:             : Parity ........... None                        :          :
:             : Data bits ........ 8                           :          :
:             : Stop bits ........ 1                           :          :
:             : Linked script .....                            :          :
:             : Default terminal .. ANSI-BBS                   :          :
:             : Default protocol .. Xmodem                     :          :
:             : Local echo ........ Off                        :          :
:             : Add line feeds .... Off                        :          :
:             : Strip high bit..... Off                        :          :
:             : Rcvd BS is dest ... On                         :          :
+--------------: BS key sends ...... BS                        :---------------:
:     Mark/Unma: Dialing prefix # .. 1                         : and PgDn.     :
:             : Password ..........                            :               :
:             :                                               :               :
:             :                                               :               :
+--------------:                                               :---------------+
Dial  List  Tog+----------------------------------------------------+rk  Other  eXit
Edit an entry
```

Figure 7.2 Telix Dialing Directory

```
US Sprint's THE NET-EXCHANGE, home of PC Pursuit!
    Reston, Virginia

The following limits are in effect:
    Max Kbytes: 382 +/- bytes (daily)   Usage time: 60 minutes +/- dt
    Login time: 5 minutes               Response time: 5 minutes


*******************************************************
*                    WARNING!                         *
*                                                      *
*   You are being billed for this call if you used    *
*   ''C PURSUIT,id,pw'' to get here.  Please, only    *
*   use ''C PURSUIT'' to access this system!          *
*******************************************************

New users should use the name: Sprint Guest
            with a password of: outdial
REMEMBER:  passwords are case sensitive!

On at Mon Jul  8 14:20:09 1991


Enter your first name ( or first and last )   =>
  Alt-Z for Help ¦ ANSI-BBS ¦  2400.N81 FDX ¦      ¦  ¦       ¦ Online 00:00
```

Figure 7.3 Telix Monitor Mode

editor you specify, but there must be enough memory available for it to run in with Telix in the background. There is a chat function, which splits the screen into incoming and outgoing text windows, but it provides no pretransmission editing.

Appropriate to its lower price, Telix has a narrower scope than packages such as Procomm Plus, with which it shares many commands. However, it probably still has all the functionality the average user needs. As for simplicity, we know of a 13-year-old boy who installed it and put together his own BBS, using the mini-BBS function, in one sitting.

QMODEM VERSION 5

Mustang Software Inc.
P.O. Box 2264
Bakersfield, CA 93303
Price range: **$$$$**

Qmodem™ became popular with BBS users, in part because it was shareware: you could download a copy free from many BBSs, and if you found it useful, you could send a registration fee to its authors. Mustang Software bought Qmodem in late 1991 and turned it into a commercial product. But the old software version is still available on some BBSs.

Qmodem is unpretentious and easy to use. Commands are not really toggled. Instead, you press Alt and a letter to invoke a local command. Remembering all these Alt commands would be a nightmare for a new user, but pressing the Home key calls up a list, as shown in Figure 7.4.

Note that the commands are broken down into those you would invoke before, during, and after an online session. Setting up your modem—defining its speed, the number of bits in a character, and the serial port where it's installed—can be done from the command menu screen, by using the QINSTALL installation program, or by entering phone numbers and parameters in the program's phone book.

You enter numbers into the phone directory by pressing Alt-D. To dial a number, simply place the cursor on the number you want and press Enter. Qmodem emits a series of little bell tones once the connection is completed.

Once you are online, the screen (if you're logging into the ILink hub) will appear as shown in Figure 7.5. The bottom line on the screen is the Qmodem status line, showing your current emulation mode, online status, speed, and other settings, and the time you've spent online during this call.

```
+------------------------------- COMMAND MENU -------------------------------+
¦ ------------------- BEFORE -------------------     -------- TOGGLES --------- ¦
¦ Alt-D  Phone Book        Alt-G  Term Emulation     Alt-0  Session Log        ¦
¦ ------------------- DURING -------------------     Alt-1  Backspace DEL/^H   ¦
¦ Alt-C  Clear Screen      ^Home  Capture File       Alt-2  80x25 (EGA/VGA)    ¦
¦ Alt-F  Execute Script    ^End   Send BREAK         Alt-3  Debug Status Info  ¦
¦ Alt-Q  QuickLearn        PgUp   Upload Files       Alt-4  80x43/50 (EGA/VGA) ¦
¦ Alt-S  Split Screen      PgDn   Download Files     Alt-5  Host Mode          ¦
¦ Alt-T  Screen Dump                                 Alt-6  Batch Entry Window ¦
¦        Scroll Back                                 Alt-8  Hi-Bit Strip       ¦
¦ ------------------- AFTER --------------------     Alt-9  Printer Echo       ¦
¦ Alt-H  Hangup Modem      Alt-X  Exit Qmodem        Alt-B  Beeps & Bells      ¦
¦                                                    Alt-E  Half/Full Duplex   ¦
¦ ------------------- SETUP --------------------     Alt-I  Order Information  ¦
¦ Alt-A  Translate Table   Alt-N  Configuration      Alt-M  ANSI Music         ¦
¦ Alt-J  Function Keys     Alt-P  Change Baud Rate   Alt-U  Scrollback Record  ¦
¦ Alt-K  Change COM Port                             Alt-Z  XON/XOFF Flow Ctrl ¦
¦                                                    Alt-=  DoorWay Mode       ¦
¦ -------------------- DOS ---------------------     Alt--  Status Lines       ¦
¦ Alt-L  Change Drive      Alt-V  View/Edit File     ShTab  CR/CRLF Mode       ¦
¦ Alt-O  Change Directory  Alt-W  List Directory     Alt-+  Status Line Info   ¦
¦ Alt-R  DOS Shell         Alt-Y  Delete File                                  ¦
¦                                                                              ¦
+------------ Qmodem SST Version 4.2F Production  Compiled 01/21/91 -----------+
---------- Select a Command    F1-Help    ESC-Return to TERMINAL Mode ----------
```

Figure 7.4 Qmodem Command Menu

Figure 7.5 Qmodem Online Screen

Uploads, downloads, and data file transfers are triggered by pressing either the PageUp or PageDown key and selecting the data file transfer protocol you want from the list. Selecting ASCII is the same as selecting no error-checking protocol.

Qmodem has a script language for writing automated procedures. There is also a QuickLearn command you may use to have Qmodem write a script file as you perform an operation—think of it as a Record key. Qmodem also has its own editor, whose commands are based on the WordStar® model; you'll like it or hate it depending on your word-processing background. Additionally, you can program text into macro keys to quickly sign off on messages and perform common functions.

Qmodem also has a Host mode command that turns your PC into a mini-BBS. A caller can read messages; perform file uploads, downloads, and transfers; and chat with you, if you're in.

Full-featured software can be hard to use, but Qmodem manages to be simple yet powerful, allowing easy, direct access to all its features. Its popularity is understandable.

CROSSTALK COMMUNICATOR VERSION 2 REVISION A

Digital Communications Associates Inc.
1000 Alderman Drive

Alpharetta, GA 30202
Phone: 404-442-4000
Price range: **$$$$**

Crosstalk Communicator is DCA's low-end offering and includes only major, generic features of Crosstalk. DCA's Crosstalk Mark 4, by contrast, includes a professional-level programming language and just about any online function you can think of.

Selection of modem brand and serial port is made during the installation procedure, although you can change the settings later. As with Procomm Plus and Qmodem, you invoke commands using Alt-key commands, and you make a call by highlighting the entry you want on the dialing directory screen, which is shown in Figure 7.6.

Note that entries and phone numbers have already been supplied for major online services such as CompuServe. These phonebook entries include scripts, written in Crosstalk's CASL language, into which you need only place your user name and password to use them. (Procomm Plus and some other programs also include such scripts, but they must be called up separately.)

To create a new phonebook entry, you need to complete a screen of information concerning your desired framing bits, speed, terminal em-

```
Dialing Directory                  Offline              Alt-H  for help
+-----------------------------------------------------------------------+
:>Name      Description                        Calls    Last called  :
:---------------------------------------------------------------------:
: ANSWER    Answer a call                                            :
: CSERVE    CompuServe Information Service                           :
: DIRECT    Direct (hardwired) connection                           :
: DOWJONES  Dow Jones News/Retrieval                                 :
: EASYCALL  Create a new entry and make a call                      :
: MCIMAIL   MCI Mail                                                 :
: MODEM     Terminal mode, direct to modem                          :
: NORMAL    Default settings for new entries                        :
: OAG       Official Airlines Guide                                 :
: PCBOARD   Bulletin Board Systems (BBS)                            :
: XTALKBBS  The Crosstalk BBS                              never     :
:                                                                    :
:-------------------------------------------------- 11 entries -:
:                                                                    :
:      Enter            Ins             Alt-S            Del         :
:  call MCIMAIL   add entry manually  check entry setup  delete entry :
:                                                                    :
:     Alt-M           Alt-E            Alt-Y            Alt-Q        :
: utilities menu   edit text file   system & port setup  quit to DOS :
:                                                                    :
+------------------------------------------------ Esc  for offline options +
```

Figure 7.6 Crosstalk Communicator Dialing Directory

ulation, and other parameters, as shown in Figure 7.7. Use the Tab key to move from one option to another, and press Ctrl-Enter when you're through.

After you have made a call (in this case, using the system's MCI Mail script), the screen looks as shown in Figure 7.8. The bottom line reminds you to use Alt-A for a list of online commands, for file uploading and downloading, for file transfers, and for other functions. Alt-H, on the other hand, delivers a series of help screens. The status line notes that you are using the MCI Mail script, that the capture function and the printer function are off, and that you've been online for 27 seconds.

Crosstalk Communicator includes a text editor with its own idiosyncratic set of control keys, and a learn function to automate log-ons and other procedures. A subset of Crosstalk Mark 4's CASL programming language is also included. It consists of only 14 command words and seems barely powerful enough for log-on scripts. In answer mode, an incoming caller is greeted with a list of remote user commands, amounting to a mini-BBS. There is no chat mode.

Crosstalk Communicator is aimed at the user who wants to get online fast, and it can do that right out of the box. But sophisticated users might find its functionality limited. That's intentional. DCA would prefer that

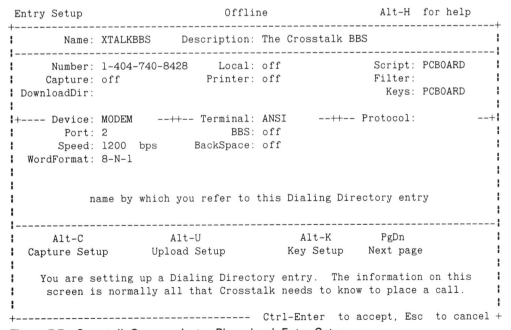

Figure 7.7 Crosstalk Communicator Phonebook Entry Setup

```
Connection initiated. . . Opened.

Welcome to MCI Mail!

Holiday letterhead is free.
Valentine's Day, Birthdays and more.

Type HELP HOLIDAY for dates.

Today's Headlines at 12:30 pm EDT:

--Borland To Acquire Ashton-Tate
   In $439 Million Stock Swap
--Motorola Net Fell 26% In Quarter
  * Corporate Earnings Report *
Type //NEWS on Dow Jones for details.


MCI Mail Version V9.0.B

   There are no messages waiting in your INBOX.
Command:
 Alt-A menu, Alt-H help ┆ MCIMAIL  ┆ Capture Off       ┆ Prn Off ┆ 0:00:27
```
Figure 7.8 Crosstalk Communicator Call

sophisticated users buy its Mark 4 program or, better yet, Crosstalk for Windows.

HYPERACCESS/5 VERSION 2.0

Hilgraeve Inc.
111 Conant Ave., Suite A
Monroe, MI 48161
Phone: 313-243-0576
Price range: $$$$

HyperACCESS/5™ uses Alt-key commands and pop-up screens to control events. Most system parameters are set within the phonebook facility. When you load the software, you can quickly configure the system to any of a long list of modems from a single menu screen, and then quickly change to a new modem later. Once you run the software, the initial screen is as shown in Figure 7.9.

You can use a numberless phonebook entry; the software just asks you for the number before proceeding. To set up a permanent entry, call up the Define System Settings screen, shown in Figure 7.10, with the D command. After you have set all the parameters needed to call a particular

```
+--- Main ------------------------------------------------- HyperACCESS/5 ---+
: +-----------------------------------------------------------------------+ :
: :   Press first letter of option                                        : :
: +-----------------------------------------------------------------------+ :
: :>>Call a system          ---Initiate a connection with a remote system : :
: : Define system settings---Add or change systems and settings           : :
: : Answer                  ---Answer calls or be a direct-cabled host     : :
: : Use DOS                 ---Use DOS commands or programs                : :
: : Editor                  ---Run text editor or word processing program : :
: : Keys                    ---Assign keys and manage automatic sequences  : :
: : Preferences             ---Set overall behavior of HyperACCESS/5       : :
: : Quit                    ---Exit from HyperACCESS/5                     : :
: +-----------------------------------------------------------------------+ :
:  System                                          Telephone number       :
:BIX............................................................<none>   :
: MCI Mail (2400 bps)...............................1-800-456-6245         :
: Another PC via cable............................................<none>   :
: Another PC with HA5.............................................<none>   :
: CompuServe (CS net).............................................<none>   :
: Dow Jones.......................................................<none>   :
: Easylink..........................................1-800-325-4112         :
: GEnie...........................................................<none>   :
+----------------------- PGDN, PGUP to page list -----------------------+
ALT-Comm ALT-Learn ALT-Run ALT-Files ALT-Help              N-lock   0:40
```
Figure 7.9 HyperACCESS/5 Setup Screen

```
+--- Main ------------------------------------------------- HyperACCESS/5 ---+
:+----- System settings ------------------------------------------------------+
:: +-----------------------------------------------------------------------+ :
:: : Enter a new setting                                                   : :
:: :   ESC to leave: <none>                                                : :
:: +-----------------------------------------------------------------------+ :
:: : Name of system           : PC Pursuit                                 : :
:: : Telephone number         :                                           : :
:: : Rate (50-115200 bps or baud)                     : 2400               : :
:: : Duplex (Full, Half)                              : Full               : :
:: : Bits per character (5-8)                         : 8                  : :
:: : Parity (None, Odd, Even, Mark, Space)            : None               : :
:: : Stop bits (1, 2)                                 : 1                  : :
:: : Emulation                                        : ANSI               : :
:: : Logon script                                     : <none>             : :
:: :                                                                       : :
:: : ASCII protocols        ---Set text sending and receiving details      : :
:: : File transfer protocols---Set file transfer protocol details          : :
:: : Hardware               ---Set port, modem and printing details        : :
:: : Colors                 ---Set display colors                          : :
:: : Miscellaneous          ---Set assorted other details                  : :
:: +-----------------------------------------------------------------------+ :
+: Communications errors: framing = 0    overrun = 0    parity = 0         :
 +-----------------------------------------------------------------------+
ALT-Help                                                   N-lock   0:30
```
Figure 7.10 HyperACCESS/5 System Settings Screen

service, including the name and phone number, you can go back to the main screen and call a system with the C command.

Once online, you can press Alt-M for a pop-up menu of commands. Figure 7.11 shows the screen for the Hilgraeve BBS. The HyperAccess Capture command captures all incoming material to a separate file. The Transfer command is used to upload and download files. Quote and Send-keys let you send Alt-key combinations to a remote system. The line along the bottom of the screen is the mini-help line, reminding you to use Alt-M for menus, Alt-H for help, and so on. This line also indicates that the Numlock key is on, which activates the numeric keypad, and that you've been online 25 seconds.

HyperACCESS/5 offers a script language called HyperPilot™ and a learn, or record, function. There's a built-in editor and also a mini-BBS function (although it's not called that) so that people can call you. In addition, you can assign macros to keystrokes for features such as online signatures.

One unique feature of HyperACCESS/5 is a virus filter which inspects the files you're downloading for the "signatures" of known viruses. It can also scan existing disk files for known viruses. Updated lists of viruses can be downloaded from Hilgraeve's own BBS.

HyperACCESS/5 offers a lot for the money. It makes more use of color than any other modem program. Additionally, its wide range of compatible modems helps to get it up and running quickly and easily.

```
+------------------------------------------------ Comm screen options --+
|   Press first letter of option                                        |
|   ESC to cancel                                                       |
|-----------------------------------------------------------------------|
|>>Capture  Print  Transfer  Review  Display  Sendkeys  Quote Hangup Menus |
+-----------------------------------------------------------------------+
            ---------                    ---------
            -------          Hilgraeve   -------
            -------                       -------
            -------          Product      -------
            -------                       -------
            -------          Support      -------
            -------                       -------
            ---------                    ---------

   Please enter your first and last name, and then your password.  If you
   are a new caller, you will be asked to verify your new password.


First name:


ALT-Comm ALT-Menus ALT-Learn ALT-Run ALT-Files ALT-Help        N-lock   0:25
```
Figure 7.11 HyperACCESS/5: Online Command Menu

PROCOMM PLUS VERSION 2.01

Datastorm Technologies Inc.
P.O. Box 1471
Columbia, MO 65205
Phone: 314-443-3282
Price range: **$$$$**

Procomm Plus enjoys a popularity in the BBS world similar to that of Qmodem. This is understandable, since the two packages are very similar. Procomm Plus, in fact, can be thought of as a fancy, expanded version of Qmodem. There are more options in the way of, for instance, the number of file transfer protocol supports, and more "bells and whistles."

Procomm began as a shareware program, but all the newer versions are commercial products with "shrink-wrap" license agreements. Version 2 of Procomm Plus was released early in 1991, but Datastorm quickly decided to do a "maintenance" update—Version 2.01—which corrects bugs that users had found. If you happen to buy Version 2.0, you can upgrade to 2.01 for free.

As with Qmodem, you toggle between the command mode and the online mode by pressing Alt and a command letter. The help screen, a list of commands, is invoked with Alt-Z and appears in Figure 7.12.

```
PROCOMM PLUS Ready!

+------------------------------------------------------------------------+
¦          P R O C O M M   P L U S   C O M M A N D   M E N U             ¦
¦------------------------------------------------------------------------¦
¦---------------- COMMUNICATIONS ----------------------- SET UP ---------¦
¦------- BEFORE -------------------- AFTER --------¦ Setup Facility .. Alt-S ¦
¦ Dialing Directory Alt-D  Hang Up ........ Alt-H ¦ Line/Port Setup . Alt-P ¦
¦                          Exit ........... Alt-X ¦ Translate Table . Alt-W ¦
¦------- DURING -----------------------------------¦ Key Mapping .... Alt-F8 ¦
¦ Script Files ... Alt-F5  Send Files ....... PgUp ¦--- OTHER FUNCTIONS -----¦
¦ Meta Keys ....... Alt-M  Receive Files .... PgDn ¦ File Directory .. Alt-F ¦
¦ Redisplay ...... Alt-F6  Log File On/Off  Alt-F1 ¦ Change Directory Alt-F7 ¦
¦ Clear Screen .... Alt-C  Log File Pause . Alt-F2 ¦ View a File ..... Alt-V ¦
¦ Break Key ....... Alt-B  Screen Snapshot . Alt-G ¦ Editor .......... Alt-A ¦
¦ Elapsed Time .... Alt-T  Printer On/Off .. Alt-L ¦ DOS Gateway .... Alt-F4 ¦
¦------- OTHER ------------------------------------¦ Program Info .... Alt-I ¦
¦ Chat Mode ....... Alt-O  Record Mode ..... Alt-R ¦ Clipboard ....... Alt-= ¦
¦ Host Mode ....... Alt-Q  Duplex Toggle ... Alt-E ¦ Monitor Mode ... Ctrl-\ ¦
¦ Auto Answer ..... Alt-Y  CR-CR/LF Toggle  Alt-F3 ¦ Toggle Status .. Ctrl-] ¦
¦ Init Modem ...... Alt-J  Kermit Server Cmd Alt-K ¦ Toggle Lines ... Ctrl-- ¦
¦ Reset Terminal .. Alt-U  Screen Pause .... Alt-N ¦ Pulldown Menu Key ... ' ¦
+------------------------------------------------------------------------+
              Press Alt-Z for On-Line Help
```

Figure 7.12 Procomm Plus Help Screen

Like Qmodem, Procomm Plus offers macro keys, a host mode to turn your computer into a mini-BBS, and PageUp and PageDown keys to perform file transfers, downloads, and uploads. You can press the ` (accent grave) key to place a list of menu commands along the top of the screen. Additionally, there's a chat mode that splits the screen, showing incoming text in one window and the text you're typing in another window. The text you type is not sent until you press Enter at the end of a line; this feature allows you to do some basic editing while chatting online.

A script language called Aspect lets you automate procedures, and a record mode, invoked with Alt-R, writes Aspect scripts while you enter commands.

Default speed, bit settings, and the modem serial port can be set from the setup menu, and individual settings—including a default file-transfer protocol and terminal emulation—can be entered for each service you dial in the program's dialing directory. This directory is saved by the software as a separate file, so you can copy it onto another disk when you take your laptop on the road.

Once online, the screen looks as shown in Figure 7.13 (in this case, for the PC Pursuit BBS). The bottom line is the Procomm Plus status line, showing current settings (FDX means full duplex). The rest of the screen consists of data from the BBS.

```
US Sprint's THE NET-EXCHANGE, home of PC Pursuit!
     Reston, Virginia

  The following limits are in effect:
       Max Kbytes: 382 +/- bytes (daily)   Usage time: 60 minutes +/- dt
       Login time: 5 minutes               Response time: 5 minutes


  ***************************************************
  *                    WARNING!                     *
  *                                                 *
  *   You are being billed for this call if you used  *
  *   ''C PURSUIT,id,pw'' to get here.  Please, only  *
  *   use ''C PURSUIT'' to access this system!        *
  ***************************************************


  New users should use the name: Sprint Guest
              with a password of: outdial
     REMEMBER:  passwords are case sensitive!

On at Wed Jun 26 16:33:08 1991


Enter your first name ( or first and last )   ==>
  Alt-Z FOR HELP ¦ ANSI   ¦ FDX ¦  2400 N81 ¦ LOG CLOSED ¦ PRINT OFF ¦ ON-LINE
```

Figure 7.13 Procomm Plus Online Screen

The major complaint about Procomm Plus concerns its support of the Zmodem protocol, which is based on an old, free version of the protocol, and not the DSZ program presently offered by Omen Technologies. This can, however, be fixed in a rudimentary way by specifying Zmodem as one of the program's "external" protocols.

Procomm Plus gives more value for more money yet is no harder to use than the old shareware version of Qmodem.

SMARTCOM EXEC VERSION 2.0A

Hayes Microcomputer Products Inc.
P.O. Box 105203
Atlanta, GA 30348
Phone: 404-840-9200
Price range: **$$$$**

Hayes started as strictly a modem maker. Its Smartcom Exec™ is marketed as a simple, straightforward package for use with the Hayes Smartmodem™ and V-series® modem lines. But if your modem is merely Hayes-compatible—and nearly every modem sold in the United States these days is—you should be able to use the software.

Instead of using Alt-key commands, Smartcom Exec uses function keys to toggle between offline menus, which is its command mode, and online menu screens. The offline menu is used to create phonebook entries and to set other parameters. The off-line menu is illustrated in Figure 7.14.

```
+------ Offline Menu -----+        Smartcom Exec          6/28/91 2:34 PM
:------------------------:
: Online           [O]:
: Online Status    [S]:
:------------------------:
: Editor           [E]:
:------------------------:
: Update Phone Book [U]:
: Program Settings  [P]:
:------------------------:
: Exit to DOS      [X]:
: Quit Smartcom Exec [Q]:
+------------------------+




     F1: Help : F2: Offline Menu : Esc: Back to Sign-on Screen
```

Figure 7.14 Smartcom Exec Offline Menu

To make a call, you first select the Update Phone Book item, resulting in a screen such as the one shown in Figure 7.15. The list of parameters on the right side of the screen is related to the major heading on the left side of the screen that you select. In this case, the major settings are shown—for phone number, framing bits, speed, and so on. Upload settings (called "autotyping"), terminal emulation, and technical modem settings can all be changed under the other headings.

To make a call after setting the parameters, go to the phonebook menu, highlight the entry you want to call, and press Enter. The software puts through the call, and an online screen such as the one in Figure 7.16 (calling Hayes' own BBS) appears.

You can call up the offline, or command, menu while online simply by pressing the Escape key. The command menu is shown in Figure 7.17. You can do uploads, downloads, and data file transfers from the command screen while online. The line at the bottom of the screen is a mini-help line, reminding you what the operational function keys do.

Smartcom Exec also features its own text editor, a script language called Scope, and a learn feature that can record your log-on sequences

```
                    Smartcom Exec          6/28/91 2:29 PM
+------------------------ Modify Phone Book Entry: mci ----------------------+
|                         |                                                  |
| Major Settings    [S]   |         Phone number:  18004566245               |
|                         |                                                  |
| Terminal Emulator [E]   | Connection Settings                              |
| Key Assignments   [K]   |                                                  |
|                         |    Connect through port:  COM2                   |
| File Transfer Settings [F] |   Type of connection:  Direct connection      |
|                         | Transmission speed (baud):  2400                 |
| Capture Settings  [C]   |        Character format:  7 - Even  - 1          |
|                         |                                                  |
| Autotype Settings [A]   |       Terminal emulator:  TTY                    |
|                         |                                                  |
| Modem Settings    [M]   |       Start connection:  Yes                     |
|                         |                                                  |
| V-series Settings [V]   | Protocol Settings                                |
|                         |                                                  |
| Network Settings  [N]   |   File transfer protocol:  XMODEM standard        |
|                         |   Flow-control protocol:  Start /Stop             |
|                         |       Autotype protocol:  Send lines              |
|                         |                                                  |
|                         |                                                  |
+-------------------------+--------------------------------------------------+
F1: Help | F2: Offline Menu | F5: Switch | F8: Save & Exit      ...Shift-Tab
```

Figure 7.15 Smartcom Exec Phonebook Update Screen

```
                    +---- * ONLINE WITH HAYES  * ---+
                    +-------------------------------+
                Hayes Microcomputer Products, Inc., Norcross GA, USA
: O :-----------------------------------------------------------------: O :
:   :  1-800-US-HAYES is for information and support of Hayes products :   :
: O :  and other Hayes support programs. All callers are welcome to use : O :
:   :  this system, but technical support is limited to Hayes customers :   :
: O :  only. If you are calling for public domain/shareware files or    : O :
:   :  user-to-user e-mail and message bases please call 404-HI-MODEM.  :   :
: O :                                                                    : O :
:   :  Selecting your CONFIGURATION:                                     :   :
: O :  If this is your first call you'll be asked some questions to set  : O :
:   :  up your initial system configuration. You will need to know what  :   :
: O :  type of terminal emulation your software is set for.  VT-100/102  : O :
:   :  or ANSI is recommended.                                           :   :
: O :                                                                    : O :
:   :  PLEASE use your REAL name and address. NO HANDLES ALLOWED!!!      :   :
: O :  DO NOT USE YOUR COMPANY NAME! **_Passwords_are_Case-Sensitive_**  : O :
:   :-----------------------------------------------------------------:   :
```

First Name?
 Fl: Help : F2: Offline Menu : F3: Online Menu : F4: Rotate   ...Shift-Tab

Figure 7.16 Smartcom Exec Online Screen

```
+-------- Online Menu --------+------------------------------------------: O :
:----------------------------:formation and support of Hayes products    :   :
: Choose Phone Book Entry  [C]:programs. All callers are welcome to use   : O :
: Stop Connection          [S]:al support is limited to Hayes customers   :   :
:----------------------------: for public domain/shareware files or       : O :
: XMODEM Transfers         [T]:message bases please call 404-HI-MODEM.    :   :
: Show Keys (TTY)          [K]:                                           : O :
: Turn Disk Capture On     [D]:TION:                                      :   :
: Turn Printer Capture On  [P]:ll you'll be asked some questions to set   : O :
: Turn Autotype Text On    [A]:onfiguration. You will need to know what   :   :
:----------------------------:on your software is set for.  VT-100/102    : O :
: Use a Script             [U]:                                           :   :
: Learn a Script           [L]:                                           : O :
:----------------------------:e and address. NO HANDLES ALLOWED!!!        :   :
: Offline                  [O]:NAME! **_Passwords_are_Case-Sensitive _**  : O :
+----------------------------+------------------------------------------:   :
```

First Name?

 Fl: Help : F2: Offline Menu : F3: Terminal Screen : F4: Rotate   ...Shift-Tab
Figure 7.17 Smartcom Exec Command Menu

or other procedures and turn them into scripts automatically. You can also assign text to keys to create macro signatures that let you sign letters with a single key combination. There is no mini-BBS function, although there is an "answer mode" that would let another computer call yours for simple file transmissions and perhaps chatting.

Smartcom Exec's weak point is that it is dedicated to Hayes modems and includes no configuration list of other modem brands and models. Although some customization features are included (for initialization and dial prefixes, for example), they are likely to mystify the novice. None of this will matter if your modem is fully Hayes-compatible or made by Hayes.

MIRROR III VERSION 2.0

Softklone
327 Office Plaza Drive, Suite 100
Tallahassee, FL 32301
Phone: 904-878-8564
Price range: **$$$$**

Mirror was originally a software "clone" of Crosstalk XVI. Its Version 1.0 was released as Version 3.6 to conform to Crosstalk's version number. A lawsuit resulted, but even before it was settled, Mirror was evolving in its own direction. Mirror III™ now has two interfaces: a "status screen" interface reminiscent of the original Crosstalk clone version, and a "dialing directory" interface, which is more like Procomm Plus. The status screen requires that you input command words, such as RQ for Request. The dialing directory lets you pick commands from menus. Obviously, the latter is easier to use.

As with HyperACCESS/5, Mirror lets you pick your brand of modem from a menu during the installation procedure and select a default interface—dialing directory or command interface. (You can switch to the other one at any time.) Assuming that you pick the dialing directory interface (which is recommended), the screen you get upon loading Mirror looks like the one in Figure 7.18.

As with Procomm Plus, you make a call with Mirror III by placing the highlight bar on the phonebook entry you want and pressing Enter. To create a new entry in the phonebook, press Esc to activate the menu along the top of the screen, and choose the Entries item. You then get a pop-up screen asking if you want to add, copy, delete, or edit an entry. Next another pop-up screen lets you enter the necessary information. If you choose Add, the screen (with the pop-up menus overlaying the original dialing directory screen) looks like the example in Figure 7.19.

```
                        Dialing Directory

    Connect   Entries   Tagging   Locate   File   Utility   Help Quit
+------------------------------------------- DIALDIR2 has 3 entries (Pvt)---+
¦    System Name                    Phone Number   Speed Port    Emulation ¦
¦  1.Default Entry (SoftKlone BBS)  1-904-878-9884 A2400 2         ANSI     ¦
¦  2.ILink                          19146674567    A2400 2         ANSI     ¦
¦  3.MCI                            18004566245    A2400 2         ANSI     ¦
¦                                                                          ¦
¦                                                                          ¦
¦                                                                          ¦
¦                                                                          ¦
¦                                                                          ¦
¦                                                                          ¦
¦                                                                          ¦
¦                                                                          ¦
¦                                                                          ¦
¦                                                                          ¦
¦                                                                          ¦
¦                                                                          ¦
¦----------------------- Tagged Entries (0 entries tagged) -------------------¦
+- Return to Dial Highlighted Entry ---- ESC to Activate Menu --F1 for Help --+
```
Figure 7.18 Mirror III Dialing Directory

```
                        Dialing Directory
+---------------------------------------------------------------------+
¦ Connect   Entries   Tagging   Locate   File   Utility   Help Quit  ¦
+-----------+-------------------------------+--------------------+ (Pvt)-+
¦    System ¦ Add new entry...        Alt-A ¦mber   Speed Port    Emulation ¦
¦  1.Default¦ Copy highlighted entry... Alt-C ¦8-9884 A2400 2        ANSI     ¦
¦  2.ILink  ¦ Delete entry...         Alt-D ¦567    A2400 2        ANSI     ¦
¦  3.MCI    ¦ Edit highlighted entry... Alt-E ¦245    A2400 2        ANSI     ¦
¦ +- Entry Editor --------------------------- DIALDIR2,  4 of   3 (Pvt) -+ ¦
¦ ¦ Name:                                      Phone:               ¦ ¦
¦ ¦                                                                  ¦ ¦
¦ ¦ Speed:     A2400      Script:              Last Call:            ¦ ¦
¦ ¦ Data Bits: 8          Emulation:                at:              ¦ ¦
¦ ¦ Parity:    None       Protocol:    None        for:             ¦ ¦
¦ ¦ Stop Bits: 1          On-line Menu: Pulldown                     ¦ ¦
¦ ¦ Duplex:    Full                            Total Calls: 0        ¦ ¦
¦ ¦ Port:                                      Total Time:           ¦ ¦
¦ ¦                                                                  ¦ ¦
¦ ¦ Comments:                                                        ¦ ¦
¦ ¦                                                                  ¦ ¦
¦-¦                                                                  ¦-¦
¦ ¦                                                                  ¦ ¦
¦ +-- Alt-S to Save Changes ----- ESC to Abandon Changes ---- F1 for Help --+ ¦
+---------------------------------------------------------------------+
    Type new value.
```
Figure 7.19 Mirror III Pop-up Screen for Adding an Entry

The modem speed, number of framing bits, serial port, and other basic information are defined using this screen. If you are unsure of what to enter, you can either press F1 to call up a list of possible entries, or press the space bar to cycle through a list of possible answers.

Once you select a phonebook entry, the software dials the modem and optionally emits tones when it gets online. If you are running a log-on script, it will look as if invisible hands are responding to the screen prompts, inputting your name and password, and so on.

At this point you can press Esc to get a menu of commands for file uploads, downloads, and other functions. The menu invoked while calling Softklone's own BBS is shown in Figure 7.20. The bottom line is the status line, as with Smartcom Exec or Procomm Plus. In this case, you're being reminded that you can press Esc to get the online menu or press Home (on the numeric keypad) to reach the status screen, that the capture facility is off, and that you're using ANSI emulation.

Mirror includes a script programming language called Prism and a learn (record) feature for easy automation of log-ons and other functions.

```
+-------------------------------------------------------+
: File  Chat  Transfer  Capture  Printer  Status  Quit :
+-------------------------------------------------------+erating 24 hours daily
-----------------------------------------------------------------------
2400/1200/300 Baud                              8 databits, no parity

Use ''ANSI'' Emulation for highlighting and graphics.

Please use your Full Name on this system (no 'Handles').

This system is running dBBS, a fast and flexible bulletin board program
written in C and Assembler, by Daniel Doman 212 427-1805 (BBS).
MNP is a registered trademark of Microcom Incorporated.


dBBS Version Ver 5.7E  08-23-90  - Copr. 1985 - 1990 Daniel B.  Doman


Welcome To SoftKlone Information Exchange
Please Log In



Please Enter Your FIRST Name:
 Esc for Command?, Home for Status   :    Capture Off   :    ANSI
```

Figure 7.20   Mirror III Command Menu Invocation

(Log-on scripts written for Crosstalk's CASL programming language re-main compatible with Mirror.) A chat mode not only splits the screen into incoming and outgoing text windows and lets you edit a line before send-ing it, but also lets you compose and edit as many lines as will fit into the window before sending them. You can use the cursor control keys for editing. In addition to the chat windows, there is a separate text editor using many WordStar commands.

Mirror offers a backscroll feature so that material that has scrolled off the top of the screen can be recalled and examined. There is no built-in mini-BBS, although there is an answer mode, with special password and screen message commands.

Although Mirror includes Zmodem as one of the data file-transfer options, Zmodem's DSZ program is not built in. Instead, the package includes DSZ separately. If you elect to use Zmodem, you're expected to send (as of press time) $20 to Omen Technology in Portland, Oregon.

Mirror is richly featured and includes more functionality than the average user will ever need, yet the program remains easy to use.

CROSSTALK FOR WINDOWS VERSION 1.2

Digital Communications Associates Inc.
1000 Alderman Drive
Alpharetta, GA 30202
Phone: 404-442-4000
Price range: **$$$$+**

Crosstalk for Windows Version 1.2 requires Microsoft Windows 3.0, the increasingly popular graphical user interface for the PC. Figure 7.21 shows the program in use to log on to a BBS. If the BBS's screen graph-ics look slightly odd, it's because Microsoft Windows has its own way of representing eight-bit ASCII characters.

As with all Windows applications, commands are input through menu items listed along the top of the screen. You toggle to command mode by moving the mouse cursor (not shown in the figure but always present on the screen) from the data window to the command line, where it turns from an arrow into a pointing hand. You put the hand over the menu item you want and then click, getting in return a list of commands associated with that item. You then click on the one you want from the list and continue.

Begin using Crosstalk for Windows by choosing Setup and its 10 com-mand items (Figure 7.22). To enter the phone number, click on the Ses-sion command. To set the serial port, framing bits, and speed, click on the

Figure 7.21　Crosstalk for Windows Welcome Screen

Device command, and then select the settings you want by clicking on the appropriate "radio buttons" (Figure 7.23).

Click on Terminal to select your terminal emulation; you'll want the IBM PC selection. Select your file transfer protocol under the Protocol command. (You can change it online if you need another.) Upload settings are selected under the ASCII Upload Settings command. The Function Keys command lets you assign your own definitions to function keys, which are then shown as screen buttons along the bottom of the screen. They can be activated by clicking the screen buttons with the mouse cursor, so that you need not actually press any keys. (In the screen shown in Figure 7.21, the user has set them to give log-on information.)

The Display command lets you select various options concerning the screen's appearance. The Fonts command lets you choose what the screen text will look like. The Modem command lets you pick the brand of modem you're using from a long list. Finally, the System command lets you choose where files will be stored.

Having made your selections, save them by clicking on the File menu item in the upper left and selecting Save As. Your selections then become a "phonebook file."

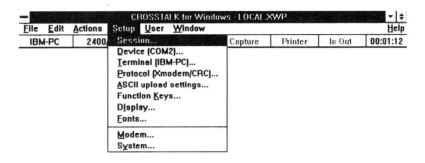

Figure 7.22 Crosstalk for Windows Setup Menu

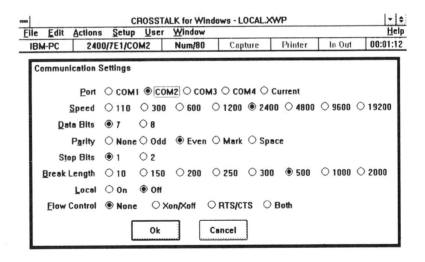

Figure 7.23 Crosstalk for Windows Communications Settings Menu

To dial a number, click on the Actions menu item, and select the Dial command. You will be presented with a list of phonebook files. Double-click on the one you want, and the software commences dialing.

Text uploads, downloads, and data file transfers are performed by selecting the appropriate commands from the list you get after clicking on the File menu item.

Log-on scripts can be written from the Scripts command under the Actions menu item. The scripts are actually compiled in Crosstalk's CASL programming language. However, there is no learn or record facility.

This being a Windows program, you can save incoming text to the Windows Clipboard or transmit Clipboard text directly to a remote system. Before you do this, however, make sure the line lengths are appropriate. You're expected to toggle to the Windows Notepad utility and use it as a text editor.

Using the Scroll command under the Edit menu item, you can freeze the screen and scroll up through the material that's already come in.

Crosstalk for Windows incorporates the Windows DDE (dynamic data exchange) protocol, so that an experienced Windows programmer should be able to control it in the background from another application.

Crosstalk for Windows is feature-rich, lacking only a learn facility. Its major weakness is that it runs under Windows. Although Windows allows multitasking and graphical ease of use, it also means that ANSI screen graphics may not look as intended. And not only is the software comparatively expensive, as with all Windows applications you need at least a high-speed 286, and preferably a 386-based machine, to get acceptable performance.

SMARTCOM III VERSION 2.0A

Hayes Microcomputer Products Inc.
P.O. Box 105203
Atlanta, GA 30348
Phone: 404-840-9200
Price range: **$$$$+**

Like Smartcom Exec, Smartcom III™ is modem software offered by Hayes Microcomputer Products, the modem maker. But it's more than just a fancier version; Smartcom III offers features that are genuinely unique.

For instance, the main menu, following an online session using TTY emulation, takes the form shown in Figure 7.24. Note that the top part of the screen resembles the Smartcom Exec screen, whereas the bottom is devoted to "sessions." With the Smartcom III user interface, "session" has two meanings.

The first is a rather grandiloquent term for the combination of "activity" (software) and "connection" (modem and serial port) settings needed to get online to a particular host. All the settings combine to form a particular session, which is basically the case with every other modem software package.

The second meaning is unique to Smartcom III. The package lets you have multiple online sessions going at the same time with up to four different hosts. The session display will show the status of each (whether it's transmitting, receiving, or standing idle), and you can toggle between sessions by pressing the F4 "Rotate" key. Hayes spokespeople say it's common for conference moderators to set up two sessions, one for uploads or downloads and the other for the interactive functions required in maintaining the message base.

However, to run multiple sessions with Smartcom III, you need a Hayes modem with X.25 circuitry. You call into an X.25 packet-switching network and set up multiple calls to hosts reached through that network. The network's X.25 circuitry combines the data from the connections and

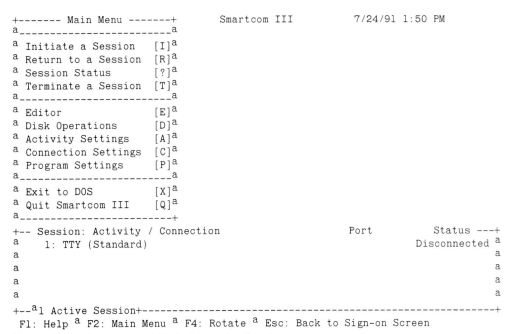

```
+------- Main Menu -------+        Smartcom III          7/24/91 1:50 PM
a_____a
a Initiate a Session   [I]a
a Return to a Session   [R]a
a Session Status        [?]a
a Terminate a Session   [T]a
a_____a
a Editor                [E]a
a Disk Operations       [D]a
a Activity Settings     [A]a
a Connection Settings   [C]a
a Program Settings      [P]a
a_____a
a Exit to DOS           [X]a
a Quit Smartcom III     [Q]a
a_____+
+-- Session: Activity / Connection              Port         Status ---+
a    1: TTY (Standard)                                   Disconnected a
a                                                                     a
a                                                                     a
a                                                                     a
a                                                                     a
+--a1 Active Session+--------------------------------------------------+
  F1: Help a F2: Main Menu a F4: Rotate a Esc: Back to Sign-on Screen
```

Figure 7.24 Smartcom III Main Menu for Session

sends them down your phone line to your X.25 modem, which parcels the data out to the correct Smartcom III sessions. Placing X.25 calls also requires consulting the documentation of whatever packet-switching network you are using.

But whether placing single calls with a conventional modem or placing multiple calls with a Hayes modem, you still have to do the usual thing: set all the parameters. You invoke the Activity menu to set software parameters (such as terminal emulation, data file-transfer protocols, capture settings, and upload parameters) and the Connection menu for modem and serial port settings.

You probably won't need to change much in the Activity menu, but you will in the Connection menu. After pressing C and selecting Modify from the next menu, select the type of connection you want from the list presented, using the cursor key. (You will almost always want Originate. Except for Answer, the other options are for special purposes, most involving local area networks.) Following selection of Originate, you'll get a menu of the form shown in Figure 7.25.

As with Smartcom Exec, selecting a major topic on the left brings up a list of options and settings on the right. After you're through with the settings, press F2 to return to the main menu and I to initiate the session.

Smartcom III includes a text editor, extensive online help features, a learn feature, macro keys, and a script language called Scope. There

```
                                    Smartcom III        7/24/91          1:59 PM
+------------------------ Modify Connection: Originate ----------------------+
|                                                                            |
|  Major Settings        [S]          Connect through port:  COM2            |
|                                                                            |
|  Modem Settings        [M]           Type of connection:  Modem originate  |
|                                                                            |
|  V-series Settings     [V]               Phone number:                     |
|                                                                            |
|  X.25 Parameter List   [X]      Transmission speed (baud):  2400           |
|                                      Split-Speed (baud):  None             |
|  Flow-control Settings [F]                                                 |
|                                         Character format:  7 - Even  - 1   |
|  Network Settings      [N]                                                 |
|                                 Protocol Settings                          |
|                                                                            |
|                                    Flow-control protocol:  Start/ Stop     |
|                                                                            |
+---------------------------+------------------------------------------------+
 F1: Help   F2: Main Menu   F4: Rotate   F5: Switch              ...Shift-Tab
```

Figure 7.25 Smartcom III Connection Modification: Originate Menu

is no chat facility and no mini-BBS, although there is an answer mode
to handle incoming modem calls. You can scroll backward through text,
although each session will claim its own screen memory block, so that
multiple sessions require all the RAM you can get. As with Smartcom
Exec, there is no configuration list of modem brands.

To make full use of Smartcom III, you really need a Hayes modem
with X.25 circuitry (all Hayes modems have it) and probably V.42 as well.
Smartcom III will be wasted on anything else.

CROSSTALK MARK 4 VERSION 2.0

Digital Communications Associates Inc.
1000 Alderman Drive
Alpharetta, GA 30202
Phone: 404-442-4000
Price range: **$$$$+**

You can get online fairly easily with Crosstalk Mark 4, but getting
online is about the least you can do with it; it comes with a very powerful script language called CASL (Crosstalk Applications Script Language)
that's actually a full-scale programming language.

Assuming you want to use it rather than program with it, you start
with the dialing directory screen, which is illustrated in Figure 7.26. You're

```
Dialing Directory              Session #1 offline          Alt-H  for help
+--------------------------------------------------------------------------+
┆>Name      Description                          Calls      Last called   ┆
┆--------------------------------------------------------------------------┆
┆ ANSWER    Answer a call (unconfigured)           0          never       ┆
┆ DIRECT    Direct connection (unconfigured)       0          never       ┆
┆ EASYCALL  Use this to make a call                0          never       ┆
┆ NORMAL    Crosstalk Mk.4 Normal Setup                                   ┆
┆                                                                          ┆
┆                                                                          ┆
┆                                                                          ┆
┆                                                                          ┆
┆                                                                          ┆
┆                                                                          ┆
┆--------------------------------------------------------------------------┆
┆                                                                          ┆
┆       Enter             Ins            Alt-S             Del            ┆
┆    call ANSWER    create new entry   setup ANSWER   delete ANSWER       ┆
┆                                                                          ┆
┆       Alt-M            Alt-E            Alt-Y            Alt-Q           ┆
┆  utility scripts   edit text file  your preferences  quit to DOS        ┆
┆                                                                          ┆
+-------------------------------------------------------- Esc  to exit +
```

Figure 7.26 Crosstalk Mark 4 Dialing Directory

given a list of preconfigured calls. On the lower half of the screen are listed the keystrokes needed to invoke or edit an entry, or call a utility. You can change the parameters for a particular call by pressing Alt-S to get the session setup screen, which is shown in Figure 7.27.

Alternatively, you can invoke the Easycall option and get a list of preconfigured calls, shown in Figure 7.28. To use one of the services listed, you must be a subscriber, of course, and the system will ask for your user name and password and then log you on automatically. If you select the BBS option, it will ask for the phone number.

Once online, you can perform file uploads, data file transfers, and other functions by pressing various Alt keys. To get the list of Alt functions on the bottom of the screen, you press Alt-A. Figure 7.29 shows what the screen looks like if you are logging onto the PC Pursuit BBS and have pressed Alt-A.

The package offers a learn facility, macro keys, and a text editor, but no chat function or mini-BBS. But to say that Crosstalk Mark 4 has or doesn't have something is fairly meaningless, since presumably you can program it to do about anything you want—the CASL reference manual is about 500 pages long, which is more than the documentation of most other

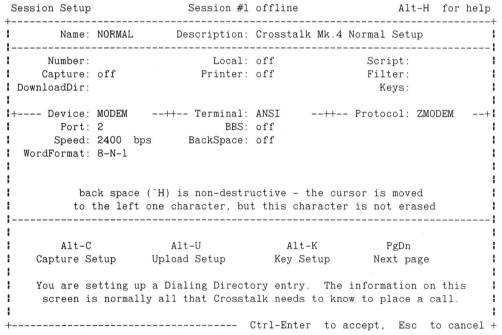

```
Session Setup              Session #1 offline            Alt-H  for help
+-----------------------------------------------------------------------+
|        Name: NORMAL       Description: Crosstalk Mk.4 Normal Setup     |
|-----------------------------------------------------------------------|
|     Number:               Local: off            Script:               |
|     Capture: off         Printer: off           Filter:               |
| DownloadDir:                                      Keys:               |
|                                                                       |
|+---- Device: MODEM    --++-- Terminal: ANSI   --++-- Protocol: ZMODEM  --+|
|        Port: 2                BBS: off                                 |
|       Speed: 2400  bps    BackSpace: off                              |
|  WordFormat: 8-N-1                                                     |
|                                                                       |
|                                                                       |
|         back space (^H) is non-destructive - the cursor is moved       |
|           to the left one character, but this character is not erased  |
|-----------------------------------------------------------------------|
|                                                                       |
|      Alt-C            Alt-U            Alt-K            PgDn            |
|   Capture Setup    Upload Setup     Key Setup        Next page         |
|                                                                       |
|   You are setting up a Dialing Directory entry.  The information on this|
|      screen is normally all that Crosstalk needs to know to place a call.|
|                                                                       |
+-------------------------------- Ctrl-Enter  to accept,  Esc  to cancel +
```

Figure 7.27 Crosstalk Mark 4 Session Setup Screen

```
+ Please choose a service to set up ----+
:                                        :
:              AT&T Mail                 :
:             CompuServe                 :
:              Delphi                    :
:       Dow Jones News/Retrieval         :
:             Lexis/Nexis                :
:               MCI Mail                 :
:               Newsnet                  :
:        Official Airline Guide          :
:               VU/TEXT                   :
:                                        :
:        Bulletin Board System (BBS)     :
:                                        :
:        Remote\2 Host or R\2LAN Host    :
:                                        :
:         System not listed above        :
:                                        :
:      Return to the Dialing Directory   :
:                                        :
+ Select with        and press  Enter    +
```
Figure 7.28 Easycall Services Listing


```
US Sprint's THE NET-EXCHANGE, home of PC Pursuit!
    Reston, Virginia


The following limits are in effect:
    Max Kbytes: 382 +/- bytes (daily)   Usage time: 60 minutes +/- dt
    Login time: 5 minutes               Response time: 5 minutes


*******************************************************
*                    WARNING!                         *
*                                                      *
*   You are being billed for this call if you used    *
*   ''C PURSUIT,id,pw'' to get here.  Please, only    *
*   use ''C PURSUIT'' to access this system!          *
*******************************************************
+ Online Menu--- Enter  to return online,  Alt-A  to hide or show ------------+
:                                                                             :
: Alt-C  capture incoming data        Alt-B  send 'break' signal             :
: Alt-R  review scrolled data         Alt-O  disconnect from host            :
: Alt-E  edit text file                                                      :
: Alt-U  upload text file                                                    :
: Alt-P  protocol file transfer       Alt-Q  quit Crosstalk Mk.4             :
:                                                                             :
+-------------------------------------------------------- PgDn  for others +
[#1] Command:
```
Figure 7.29 Use of Alt-A when Logging on to PC Pursuit BBS

packages listed here combined. You could write your own BBS package with it from scratch (and a DCA spokesmen says that this has, in fact, been done).

Considering that Crosstalk Mark 4 costs several times more than other packages that will get you online just as well, buying Crosstalk Mark 4 seems justifiable only if you do have an urge to write your own BBS software. If you have such an urge, don't let us stop you from trying to fulfill it. However, considering the complexity and scale of such a task, and the availability of perfectly good canned software, such a project should not be embarked on lightly.

SMARTCOM EZ

Hayes Microcomputer Products Inc.
P.O. Box 105203
Atlanta, GA 30348
Phone: 404-840-9200
Price range: **$$**

Smartcom EZ is the simplest modem control program in the Hayes line, but also the least powerful. There are only four files used in Smartcom EZ: the main program file, a phonebook, a help file, and a resource file used by the main program.

Installation is through an Install program that asks some basic questions about your modem and your PC communications setup.

To make a call with Smartcom EZ, toggle through the menu to Call or Answer, and then select a number from the phonebook and press Enter. New phonebook entries are created quickly, in much the same way as with Procomm Plus and HyperAccess 5. Once you're online, pressing the F2 key allows you to reach other features of the program, as when you upload or download files.

Smartcom EZ is limited. There are no script-writing capabilities, no online word processor, and only two terminal emulators: VT102 and TTY. But the features that are available should let you use nearly every MS-DOS–based BBS in the United States, and many of those in the rest of the world.

8

File Manipulation

ABOUT THIS CHAPTER

Doing anything online ultimately means manipulating computer files, either moving them or creating them. We'll examine:

- File compression techniques
- Identification and nature of PC files

FILE COMPRESSION

To save space on a board's hard disk and time in uploading or downloading files—and to employ many specialized netmail utilities used in echo networks—file compression is a must.

There are many file compression programs, but they have a lot in common. They look for redundant or repeated characters, create a table showing where they are, and consequently reduce the size of the file. The most popular compression scheme is the Lempel-Ziv Huffman, or LZH, format. It's used by all the popular PC compression programs and is also at the heart of the modem compression standard known as V.42.

Another thing the popular compression programs share is the ability to self-archive or self-compress. This means that they can compress themselves, or other programs, into an executable file with the extension .EXE. Once such a file is downloaded, you enter the name (without the extension) from a DOS prompt, and decompression will begin automatically.

Before using any compressed file, or any self-extracting file, be certain you have lots of extra space on your disk to hold the results. Many popular commercial programs come in compressed form, and they usually include a batch program—a sequence of commands—that will not only decompress them but will move them automatically onto your hard drive, in the correct subdirectories. The purpose behind this is as much to ensure that they fit on the disk as to offer you, the user, any convenience.

There's another reason to keep extra disk space on hand when using compression programs. Many compression programs, such as PKZIP™, temporarily create additional copies of the files they're working on during the compression and decompression processes. They also retain the original compressed file while creating the new, decompressed version of the file (or files—lists of files can be compressed into one file). Keeping at least 10 times the space you need on your disk for the final file is a safe rule of thumb.

The more redundancy in a file, the more it can be compressed. Generally, text or program files can be cut in size by half or more. Picture files can be compressed even further. Video files can be compressed the most, by adding to the file only those elements in the picture that change.

For PC text and programs, the major compression programs share more than a scheme. They share many commands, and they're started in the same way. From your computer's DOS prompt, enter the name of the program and then a specific command. Then use a "/" or "-" to separate any extra switches or options from this command, and follow it up with the drive and complete pathname of the file you want to compress or decompress. Here's the general format, taken from the documents for LHarc Version 1.13 from Japan:

```
LHarc [<command>] [{{\|-}{<switch> [-| + |2| <option>]}} . . .]
<archive_name> [{{<drive_name>:}|{<home_directory_name> \}]
[<path_name> . . .]
```

All this sounds horribly complex, but it need not be. The switches and options can be learned in a reasonable amount of time, as can the use of paths and subdirectories. If you need to start by simply moving programs to be compressed or decompressed into the same directory as the compression program, don't be embarrassed. The authors do this all the time!

For most major programs, you'll really need to learn only two basic commands:

a   Adds a file to a compressed file

x   Extracts a file from the compressed file

The PKZIP™ system makes this even easier, using separate programs for compressing and decompressing files. (The decompression program is called PKUNZIP™.)

In the following pages, we'll discuss most of the common formats and programs currently used on U.S. bulletin boards. But we won't discuss every program that handles compression—there are quite a few. Some, such as Expanz!™ from InfoChip Systems and Stacker™ from Stac Electronics, include an add-in board to make the job go faster. Others, such as SQZ!Plus™ from Symantec, are specialist programs for jobs such as spreadsheets. No doubt more compression programs, both commercial and public-domain, will appear in the coming years.

ARC™

System Enhancement Associates Inc.
925 Clifton Avenue
Clifton, NJ 07013
201-473-5153 (voice)
201-614-9605 (fax)

ARC™ is the oldest of the major compression utilities. In fact, "ARCing"—short for "archiving"—was for a long time a synonym for file compression.

ARC™ was first released in March 1985 as a shareware program. Today the only version of the program to be found on bulletin boards is XARC™, which decompresses ARC files. The current version of the product, ARC+Plus™, is a commercial product.

SEA founder Thom Henderson worked on mainframes and multi-user time-sharing systems before buying an IBM PC XT in the mid-1980s. He noticed two things about the PC right off. "It didn't get faster after 5:00 P.M., and it was lonely. Bulletin boards brought back some of the feeling of not being the only one at the keyboard."

But Henderson feels burned by the hobbyist bulletin board movement. When a competitor, Phil Katz of PKWare, came out with a PKARC™ program, Henderson sued to protect his trademark and code. Henderson won in court, but thousands of BBS operators switched to Katz' new product, PKZIP™, fearing Henderson might enforce his copyright on them, and resenting the idea that he wanted to be paid for his intellectual property.

"We have a more realistic feeling of the attitude of BBS operators," Henderson now says. Some think he's gone out of business because of the wide use of ZIP™ rather than ARC™. In fact, Henderson has been busy improving the program and porting it to other platforms, such as the IBM AS/400 minicomputer. He's doing fine, and he's turning ARC™ into a real business utility. The ARC+Plus™ disk also includes a version of the program for OS/2.

ARC+Plus™.   Unlike its competitors, ARC+Plus™ has a full menu interface, so using it is very simple. ARC+Plus™ features two types of menus. The ABC menu is designed for simple functions such as archiving, backing up files, and copying. The advanced menu delivers all the program's commands and options. Both menus are on the same screen.

Installing ARC™ is as simple as putting a disk in a drive and typing the word *INSTALL* from the DOS prompt referring to that drive. The Install program lets you put the program anywhere, even in a new sub-directory.

The ARC™ manual recommends that you put the program in your computer's main CONFIG.SYS file, and that you add it to your DOS path—specified in your AUTOEXEC.BAT file, which starts your computer—so it can be called up from anywhere within DOS.

The ARC™ program menus can all be accessed using a mouse or through the keyboard. All of the main features on the Menu Bar can be accessed through an Alt-key command; Alt-A brings up the Archive menu, for example. This makes using even the advanced commands within ARC™ painless.

The commands on the left side of the screen make up the ABC menu and represent the main features of the program. Besides being used to compress files, ARC+Plus™ can also be used as a backup utility, compressing files and copying them to floppy disks. You can use ARC+Plus™ to back up everything on a hard disk, or just files that have changed since your last backup. The same menu is used to restore the files.

The ABC menu also lets you do such things as change the current directory you're working with, or view, delete, or even run programs; ARC+Plus™ can in fact be used as a shell program, your main interface with the computer.

The advanced menu is on the same screen as the ABC menu, separated from it only by a vertical line on the screen. It features three sets of commands:

- *Sort*   You can sort files in the current directory by their name, extension, size, date, or even a comment tag. There's also a command on this menu called Filter that lets you use DOS wildcards, sorting and viewing only those files beginning with the letter C, for instance.

- *Mode*   The Mode commands let you quickly compress files to the maximum extent possible or to be compatible with older versions of ARC™—5.0 and 6.0. The Mode command also lets you add files to your compressed file without actually compressing them, or display comments about files.

- *Options*   The Options menu can be used to check off additional commands for compressing a file that would require extensive use of DOS command languages if used with other compression utilities such as PKZIP™, LHA™, or ALZ™. You can save paths and file attributes, add comments, compress hidden or system files, and even add or change passwords needed to decompress files. Just hit the Enter key, or click the mouse, next to the option you want, and a checkmark will appear.

For the corporate market, the ARC+Plus™ menu structure sets a new, higher standard. All the program's capabilities can be accessed directly from a DOS prompt, using many of the same commands offered by other compression programs described in this section. But with all that power on a menu, why would you want to leave it?

Because of the history of ARC™, however, and its suit with PKWare™, you will not likely see many ARC™ programs on hobbyist bulletin boards, or even major online systems. The only version of the program available on BBSs is the XARC™ program, which decompresses ARCed files.

PKZIP™, Version 1.05

PKWare Inc.
9025 N. Deerwood Drive
Brown Deer, WI 53223
414-354-8699

PKZIP™ and its companion program, PKUNZIP™, are currently the most popular compression schemes found on U.S. bulletin boards. They were written by Phil Katz of Glendale, Wisconsin. Katz got into the compression utility business with a program called PKARC™, but he was sued by Thom Henderson of SEA™ for using the term "ARC" to describe the program, for using SEA code, and for stealing the "look and feel" of ARC™.

The suit was settled on terms favorable to SEA™, but Katz had his revenge. Despite repeated attempts by Henderson to explain his position to BBS operators—he didn't mind sharing his code with the world, but he didn't want someone else making money from it—operators jumped on Katz' PKZIP™ as soon as it came out, and it's remained out front ever since.

PKZIP™ programs can be easily identified on a board by the file extension .ZIP. Most boards that support the .ZIP format keep a public-domain version of the self-archiving program, PKZIP101.EXE, online for downloading.

As with ARC™, you can pile many different files into a ZIP™ file. You can include a program's manual, a batch file directing the decompression of the file, or other files. Commercial users may want to include notes on performance with their ZIPped financial results, or combine all their daily uploads or downloads into a single ZIP, for easier handling by workers.

Following are some of the major features of PKZIP™ and PKUNZIP™:

- PKZIP™ and PKUNZIP™ are separate programs, which makes them easier for novices to use.

- Both PKZIP™ and PKUNZIP™ offer screen messages such as Storing, Shrinking, and Imploding, to describe to users how they're working. PKZIP™ also reports on technical information from within the compressed file.

- PKUNZIP™ features a short-cut command, PKUNZIP* or *.ZIP, that decompresses all ZIP files within the given subdirectory.

- PKZIP™ and PKUNZIP™ can be used on files compressed with ARC™, but the reverse will not work.

Following are some of the important commands that can help you in using ZIP™ and UNZIP™:

a   Add a file to a specific compressed file collection.

c   Create or edit file comments along with your compressed file.

d   Delete a file from the compressed file collection.

f   Freshen files. This replaces an old version of the same file in the compressed collection. If none exists, nothing happens.

h   Call up the program's help screen.

i   Add changed files to the ZIP collection.

j   Mask/unmask file attributes. Use it with the hidden, read-only, or system file attributes, setting them off like this: <h,r,s>.

k   Retain the original date of the ZIP file.

o   Set the time and date of the ZIP file to that of the oldest file in the collection.

p   Store recursed pathnames, so that when files are decompressed they'll move into their old paths.

q   Enable the addition of comments, including graphic comments, under the ANSI™ graphic scheme.

r   Recurse subdirectories. This lets you compress all files with a specified filename at once. The program will search your entire drive for them and add them to the ZIP collection automatically.

s<password>   Scramble files and add a password for security. The password goes inside the brackets.

u   Update files, adding them if they're not in the file or replacing them if they're dated after a file already in the collection. It differs from the **a** command in having this date-stamp protection.

m[u,f] Move files into a ZIP file, and automatically delete the original. The options in brackets are Update, which will add the new file to the ZIP file only if it doesn't already exist or has an earlier date, and Freshen, which puts into the Zip file only the latest version of the file.

v[b,r,t,c,d,e,n,o,p,s] View technical information on each file in the ZIP collection, including its original length, compressed size, compression ratio, date and time of its creation, and attributes. The options can give you more, or less, information than this.

e[x,s,a,b] This function lets you specify how the file is to be compressed. The **ex** command specifies the implosion method, which provides more compression than **es**, the shrinking method. The **ea** command will use imploding on text files and shrinking on binary files; the **eb** function does the reverse. The shrinking method takes 120,000 bytes of available memory to run, and imploding takes about 90,000.

w <h,s> Include hidden (**h**) or system (**s**) files in the files to be compressed.

W Do not include hidden or system files.

x Exclude specific files from the compression.

z Create or edit a comment, or descriptive label, which will be displayed as the compressed file is processed.

The following important options are unique to the PKUNZIP™ program:

d Create subdirectories that may not have existed upon extracting the ZIP file.

j<h,r,s> Mask or unmask file attributes, as in hidden, read-only, and system files.

o Overwrite existing copies of extracted files, if the filenames match.

s<password> Unscramble files, adding the password.

t Test the integrity of the ZIP file.

Self-Extractions. Like other major compression programs, ZIP and UN-ZIP let you create self-extracting files, that is, command files with the .EXE extension that will unzip themselves when you enter their names at the command prompt.

The command for creating such files is PKSFX, and it is used as follows:

PKSFX [options] [d:path\] [file...]

Most of the ZIP and UNZIP options, such as **d** for creating directories, **o** for overwriting old files, and **t** for testing file integrity, also work with PKSFX.

PKSFX also lets you create list files with any word processor. These are lists of the files, with their subdirectories, that should be included in your self-extracting ZIP. Precede the list filename with the @ symbol in the PKSFX command line to activate it. The list files can be mixed with other options.

PKWARE™ also makes a program called PKZIPFIX™. If your ZIP file won't open and decompress, try to reconstruct it using PKZIPFIX™. Such files will get the name PKFIXED.ZIP, and you can then try again to decompress them.

Like SEA™, PKWare™ also offers extensive technical support, including a 24-hour bulletin board at 414-352-7176, a voice line open from 9:00 to 5:00 Central time at 414-352-3670, and a fax line at 414-352-3815.

LHA Version 2.12

Haruyasu Yoshizaki
Nifty Serve: PFF00253
ASCII PCS: pcs02846
GEnie: K. Obuko
PC-VAN: FEM12376
Compuserve: 74100,2565
INTERNET: c00236@sinet.ad.jp.

The story of LHA™ proves that the ideas behind hobbyist bulletin boards have become universal.

Haruyasu Yoshizaki, known to his friends as Yoshi, got the idea for creating his own archiving utility from a book called *A Hard Disk Cookbook* by A. P. Labo, from Shouei Press. He explored existing utilities on the Nifty-Serve network, which is owned by Fujitsu and Nissho-Iwai Trading but affiliated with CompuServe of the United States. There he found a utility called Larc by Kazuhiko Miki, with better compression ratios than PKWare's Zip, and LZari by Haruhiko Okumura, which he said was even better.

The program uses static Huffman coding, and Yoshi admits it's not as fast as he had expected. An older version of the program, LHarc 1.13, is not completely compatible, but files made with the new program can be decompressed with the older version, if they're created with the **lo** option.

Yoshi admits that LHA™ is not for everyone—but it will be of interest to anyone for whom disk space is a bigger consideration than time. It may be slower, but it achieves the tightest compression ratios of any shareware archiving software, he says.

Although LHA™ is available free from GEnie, CompuServe, and some major bulletin boards, the copyright is reserved. The program includes its own decompression routine, so when you invoke the executable file for the first time after downloading, it will decompress both the main program and its manual.

Once it's loaded and decompressed, typing "LHA" will give you a help screen showing its command structure. Like other programs of its type, it includes a number of switches—invoked following a "/" or "-" delimiter. Typing Ctrl-break or Ctrl-C at any time will abort LHA operations and return you to the DOS prompt.

The command line synopsis is:

```
LHA <command> [/<option> ARC [[DIR\] [FILE]...]...
[-+012| WDIR]...]
```

Despite this synopsis, which appears in the program's documentation, LHA™ is relatively simple to use. Invoke the program, invoke a command for it, and then name the file you want the command to work on, being careful to include its subdirectory. You may also add optional commands and specify where the "working directory" is—where files created with LHA are to be placed.

Following are some common LHA commands, many of which are shared by other compression programs:

a Adds a file to a compressed file. For example, the correct form for adding file1.ext to the ARCHIVE.LZH package is:

```
LHA a ARCHIVE.LZH file1.ext
```

Note that if a file called file1.ext already exists, LHA will use the **a** command to replace it with the new file.

One more thing: Although the .LZH extension is the default for LHA, you can use another if you prefer. If you specify no extension, .LZH is used. But if you plan to pass any such files on a BBS or elsewhere, it's best to use .LZH so your recipient will know what program to use to decompress it.

u Updates a file to the compressed package. The difference between this and the **a** command is that **u** will check the date-time stamp on the file and delete the older copy.

m Move a file to the compressed file. This will erase a second copy of the file if it's found in the archive, so Yoshi wants you to be careful.

f Freshen a file in the compressed file. This replaces an old version only if one exists. If no second copy is found in the compressed file, nothing happens.

e or **x** Extract a file from the compressed file, or "archive package." Either command can be used. The **x** command adds the path of the original file and creates a new subdirectory if none exists. **e** extracts only the latest version of a file. You can also extract just one file from an archived package by specifying it. Here's the proper command to extract file1.ext from that package we made earlier:

LHA e ARCHIVE.LZH file1.ext

p Display files in the compressed file. You can print such a file or, using the /v switch, view it on your screen. That command would look like this:

LHA p /v ARCHIVE.LZH file1.ext

d Delete files in the compressed file. This lets you selectively eliminate files from an archived package, without extracting and recompressing it.

l List files in the compressed file. In addition to the name of all the files, you'll get their original size, stored size, the compression ratio, the date and time they were first created, the type of compression used, and a CRC check. You can use common DOS conventions to list only certain files. The following command would list only files in the archive with the extension .c or .h, or with the name readme.doc:

LHA l ARCHIVE.LZH *.c *.h readme.doc

v View a list of files in the compressed file. This provides a fuller description of each file than the **l** command, adding the files' complete paths.

s Self-extract a compressed file. This is how the original .EXE version of the LHA file on the GEnie service was compressed. A self-extracting file is the perfect way to pass along an extraction utility.

t Test a compressed file. This runs a CRC check on each file in the compressed file and compares it with the value stored for it originally. If you have any problem extracting a file with .LZH, using the **t** command is a great help.

Switches. Switches are a common DOS device for adding details to commands. Long-time DOS users who use shells for copying and moving files may have forgotten about them. You add switches to an LHA command by separating them from the main command with a "/" or "-". You can use more than one switch at a time—just don't add a second "/" or "-" when using them with LHA. One other caveat: Use only lower-case letters for switches. Yoshi writes that he may use the capital letters in future updates of the program.

Following are just a few of the common switches recognized by LHA. The latest version of the program adds numbers to these commands, which can be used to make them more specific. You can find out all about them in LHA's excellent English-language documentation file.

/x Allow extended file names. This lets you compress a number of files together that are in different subdirectories, and then extract them with the subdirectory tree intact.

/o (For "old") Make a compressed file compatible with the format of a predecessor program, LH113C.

/r Recursively search and compress. This lets you compress all files with a specified filename at once. The program will search your entire drive for them and add them to the compressed file automatically with this switch.

/p Use the full pathname when extracting the file. This lets you pull out only files in a certain subdirectory from the compressed file.

/m Skip messages. This turns off the program's attempts to query you about possibly nasty actions, such as the overwriting of existing files. This switch is not recommended unless you really know what you're doing.

/a (Attributes) Generally, the program won't compress read-only, system, or hidden files. This switch lets the program compress them.

/w (Working directory) This puts all newly compressed files into a separate, working directory, which must be specified with the command. It's used when you are running out of room in the current directory or if you want to handle compression in a faster RAM drive. Here's how you'd move compressed files into a new subdirectory called temp:

LHA a /w[d:\temp] ARCHIVE.LZH [file1.ext file2.ext ...]

Compressed Filenames and Paths.   Again, LHA uses DOS conventions in filenames and paths. You can compress or decompress files with certain extensions or in certain subdirectories, or move files to other directories. Set off these directory commands with square brackets, and if you're going to specify a home directory name—separate from the one where the utility is located—set it off with a "\" or ":" character.

The same applies to pathnames, which are set off in round brackets. If you don't specify names or paths, the program will work on files in your current subdirectory, compressing or extracting them to the same subdirectory.

Setting Switches.   You can permanently reset all the defaults of the program using the Set command. For example, the command

SET LHA = /we:

will set drive E: as the working directory and compress all files in directory mode.

You may also specify LHA's working directory with the environment variable TMP:

SET TMP = E:

However, the /**w** switch will override this setting.

Result Codes.   LHA returns the following result codes. Such codes tell you how the program has run and are shared by many other compression programs.

0   Normally finished

1   Process finished, with nonexistent file names ignored during archiving, or occurrence of a CRC error during decompression

2   Compression or extraction failed; no compressed file created or files moved

3   Unable to write temporary files into the compressed file. This result indicates that you may have a damaged file. This function changes the name of your work file to LHA.2(and deletes the original compressed file. When you see this, Yoshi suggests you try renaming LHA.)2(as your compressed file, although it might be damaged. Other temporary filenames created by LHA include LHA.)1 (the original compressed file, renamed) and LHA.TMP(a work file created for viewing by another utility).

Final Points. LHA can create "small" self-extracting compressed files, limited in size to the recipient computer's working memory, or larger files that can fit within the limits of the recipient's hard disk.

To protect against viruses, LHA thoughtfully includes two commands for use with these self-extracting files: telop and keyword. You invoke the telop command by putting a "!" in the name of the main file; the program will ask you if you want to proceed, and you can add your own message to the cryptic "[Y/N]" included with the program. "Thus, the telop will politely reassure the recipient of your SFX as to sender, contents and intentions," the manual states. All you need to do to create a telop is write it with a word processor and call it "!" before archiving it.

You invoke the keyword command inside a large self-extracting file by creating a batch file with your keyword in it, and adding that file to your set of compressed files. The batch file will be run only if the recipient types the required keyword.

You can also protect yourself from viruses by using the l command to list the contents of an .LZH file before extracting it.

Yoshi's distribution policy, stated at the end of his manual, allows for free copying and distribution as long as his copyright and the manual are included. He'll also let you modify the program, but you must distribute all source code free and make the fact that you've modified it clear. He also asks that you distribute the latest available version, and he disclaims all warranties.

For commercial use of the software, Yoshi asks that you not copy-protect the result so that the DOS Diskcopy command can create a perfect copy; that your package print the name of the program, "LHA," and the copyright banner; and that the distribution policy also be printed on the package or disk label.

Although LHA admits to being slower than its competitors, it creates more compressed files. Best of all, it's free. Next time a friend tells you the Japanese haven't given us anything lately, tell them about Haruyasu Yoshizaki. Better yet, give them a copy of LHA.

One more point: Starting with Version 2.00, Yoshi opened up his source code to the public domain. This has resulted in a number of enhanced versions of the program, with their own file extensions. ARJ, now at Version 2.00, is becoming especially popular with some sysops because it makes files 6 percent smaller than those of ZIP.

So many people have used LHA to create their own compression programs that Yoshi now includes a protection switch, /t. Once you get a self-decompressing copy of the program, simply type:

LHA t LHA.exe

to see "The original distribution from Yoshi" message, proving your copy is authentic.

PAK Version 2.51

NoGate Consulting
P.O. Box 88115
Grand Rapids, MI 49518-0115
616-455-6270
BBS: 616-455-5179
Fax: 616-455-8491

PAK is one of the newer compression programs making its way onto bulletin boards. It can compress and decompress ZIP and ARC files, as well as files created with its own .PAK extension. The program authors also note that each file PAK creates has a calculated CRC number, which ensures the detection of damage after the file is transmitted via a modem.

PAK uses the same conventions as the other programs, including use of the **a** command to add files to a compressed file, the **m** command to move files into a compressed file and delete old versions, and the **f** and **u** commands familiar to PKZIP users. The commands **l**, for list, and **v**, for view, are also supported.

The general command for creating a new compressed file collection with PAK is:

PAK a <*archive name*> <*filename or names*>

DOS wildcard characters such as "?" and "*" can also be used to add a number of files to the compression at once, and you can also specify subdirectories. These two attributes can be combined, so that c:\book\ch2?.* will compress all files from the book subdirectory on drive c that begin with ch2, regardless of extension. Many of the ZIP options, such as /path and /move, are also supported by PAK.

Other important commands for use with PAK include:

e Unlike ZIP, PAK does not have a separate extraction command. Just as you use **a** to add a file to compressed list, you must use **e** to extract it. Following is the correct format:

PAK e <*archive name*> <*filename or names*>

Wildcards and subdirectory specifications can all be used with the **e** command, just as they can with **a**. This can get complicated, as with this example from the PAK documentation:

PAK e project \c\objects*.obj \c\source*.c

This monster would extract all of the files with the extension .OBJ to the \C\OBJECTS directory, and all the files with the extension .C to the \C\SOURCE directory. If you can use such commands routinely, don't buy yourself a DOS shell.

x   This command decompresses files like **e**, but it also deletes the compressed version from the compressed file.

p   This command decompresses files but sends them to your screen for viewing. Use /MORE if you want to look at only one screen at a time, and add >prn to print them, like this:

PAK p docs >prn:

This would extract all of the files from the compressed file DOCS and send them to the printer.

/path   By adding this option to your decompression command, you can restore your files to their original subdirectories. The program will create the needed subdirectories on your hard disk if they don't exist.

PAK's documentation notes that it can decompress files made with any of its competitors, and compress new files of the following types. The list is useful for keeping track of the many synonyms for compression that are now used.

Packed: Repeated byte values replaced by codes, used by ARC

Squeezed: Huffman encoding, used by ARC 5.20 and earlier versions

crunched: Lempel-Zev compression, used by ARC 4.5 and earlier versions

Crunched: Lempel-Zev compression, used by ARC 5.0 and later versions

Squashed: Lempel-Zev compression, used by PKARC

Crushed: Lempel-Zev compression, used by PAK

Distill: Huffman/Sliding Window, used by PAK 2.51

Shrunk: Lempel-Zev compression, used by PKZIP™

Reduced: Sliding Window, used by PKZip 0.9

imploded: Huffman/Sliding Window, used by PKZIP™ 1.0 and later versions

Imploded: Huffman/Sliding Window, used by PKZip 1.1 and later versions

Following are additional commands used by PAK:

r Revise remarks. After you have created a compressed file, you may wish to change remarks that were originally put onto user screens. For example

PAK r saved *.doc

will first display the compressed file remark, and then it will display the files with the extension .DOC, one at a time, and ask for the new remark for each. If you wish to keep the existing remark, simply press <enter>.

h The "header" command is much like "revise," except it only changes a single remark: the one displayed as decompression begins.

c Convert files from another compression format to that of PAK 2.0. For example, to change all ARC files on your hard drive to PAK files, simply enter:

PAK c *.ARC /ren

In this example, the /ren option will rename the new files, from .ARC to .PAK.

Earlier versions of PAK were compatible with ARC compression. Those from Version 2.0 on are not. The **c** command can be used to revise new PAK files to the old format. There are a number of options available with this command:

/c Converts files to the type used by ARC, PKARC, and PAK Version 1.X

/s Converts files to compression types compatible with PKARC or PAK 1.X only

/cr Converts files to compression compatible with PAK 1.X

/z Converts PAK or ARC files to the ZIP file format and renames them with the .ZIP extension. For files to be used with Version 1.01 of PKUNZIP, you need the /bugs option, as in this example:

PAK c bonzo /bugs

BUGS implies the ZIP option.

/zs Converts a compressed file for reading by ZIP Version 0.9

Self-Extracting Files. Like its competitors, PAK can create .EXE files that decompress themselves. PAK requires no royalty for the distribution of self-extracting compressed files. The command is a simple option from the **a** command, as follows:

PAK a demo /exe

The /exe option directs the program to create the PAK compressed file with the .EXE extension. Entering its name at a DOS prompt will cause it to decompress by itself. You can also use pathnames to move self-decompressing files to a specific subdirectory. This is especially useful for commercial programs that will want their own subdirectories.

PAK can also convert files to self-decompressed format, with the **c** command and the /exe option:

PAK c sales /exe

The reverse would be:

PAK c sales.exe

Other Options. As noted before, PAK can compress files in a number of ways. These are options to the main command:

/C Use the crunch method.

/S Use the squash method.

/CR Use the crush method.

The following options are of primary interest when you are using the Convert command.

/g This will encrypt your PAK files and let you add a password. It stands for "garble." The complete notation for encrypting the file secret.exe in the compressed file dark.pac with the password "deep" would be:

PAK a /g = DEEP dark secret.exe

(Don't blame us for the joke. It comes from the PAK manual.) Extracting that file requires the following command:

PAK e /g = DEEP dark secret.exe

/r This is the equivalent of ZIP commands such as **c** (for a comment) or **q** (for an ANSI graphic command).

/h   This is similar to /r but puts the remark only at the top of the PAK file.

/ren   Use this with the Convert command to change extensions on converted compressed files to the .PAK extension.

/s   You can sort the files in a .PAK extension with this option, adding **n**, for "filename"; **e**, for "extension"; **t**, for "time"; and **s** for "size."

/t   This lets you specify a path for temporary files, the files created during the process of decompressing files.

/w   This command is used to replace an existing file, either within a .PAK or elsewhere. Options are **a**, for "always;" **p**, for "prompt;" **o**, for "replace older files;" and **n**, for "never replace."

PAK   Typing the name of the program by itself will bring up a short list of commands.

PAK tries to be a peacemaker between ZIP and ARC. Large groups on both sides of the ZIP and ARC dividing line are passionately committed to their side of the debate, and the dispute is really more about ethics than technology. If you want to stay out of that debate, but you also want a product with U.S. support, PAK may be a good alternative.

Zoo 2.01

Rahul Dhesi
GEnie: r.dhesi

Zoo is the newest of the major compression utilities. It uses the standard Lempel-Ziv compression algorithm of other programs, as well as the same commands as its competitors, which are often given in the same way.

Dhesi wrote the program using Microsoft® C 3.0 on a PC clone machine, with portability testing done on a PC clone running Microport™ System V/AT. The executable Version 2.0 for MS-DOS® is compiled with Borland's™ Turbo C 1.0.

The command **zoo h** gives a summary of commands.

Like ARC, Zoo has two modes: expert and novice. Unlike ARC, both modes are accessed from the DOS command, which means that you have to understand DOS to get the most from the program. All compressed files created with the program have the extension .ZOO, unless the user specifies a different extension.

Novice commands consist of a hyphen followed by a command word, which may be abbreviated. Expert commands consist of a command letter followed by modifiers and are case-sensitive.

When adding a file to an existing collection of compressed files, Zoo marks old versions of files as deleted. But these deleted versions can be undeleted.

Zoo Novice. The novice commands used by Zoo are common to most compression programs, except that Zoo allows the entire command name to be used. Each command starts with the "-" character. Here for review are the novice commands:

-add Adds the specified files to the compressed file

-freshen Adds a file to the compressed file if an older file by the same name already exists there

-delete Deletes a file from the compressed file

-update Adds a file to the compressed file, deleting old versions if they exist

-extract Decompresses specified files

-move Deletes source files after adding new files to an archive

-print Extracts files and prints them to the computer screen (and can, of course, be used to send extracted files to the printer)

-list Lists information about a specific file, including attached comments

-test Works like -extract, but also tests the file for errors

-comment Allows for the addition of comments to compressed files, to 64K of comments (end of comment indicated by typing /end on a line by itself)

-delete Deletes the specified files

Zoo Advanced. All the novice commands, shortened to a single letter, work in the advanced mode. However, **-extract**, for example, is shortened to **X** instead of **e**. All the switches and general commands used by other compression programs work with Zoo, and they can be piled one on top of another.

Zoo was one of many programs that emerged following the ARC-ZIP legal battle. How well it does from here on out depends on its creator and its users.

ARJ Version 2.10

Robert K. Jung
2606 Village Road West
Norwood, MA 02062
617-255-0061
Fidonet: 1:16/390.7
Internet: robjung@world.std.com
CompuServe: 72077,445

ARJ has been attracting considerable attention from BBS operators lately because it offers slightly better compression ratios than its competitors. Since it's also a free shareware program (for noncommercial users) it's won some BBS loyalty.

The program is not designed for commercial use. Companies must purchase site licenses to obtain registered copies; however, they can evaluate the program for 30 days without liability. ARJ 2.10 was thoroughly tested for use with DOS 2.11, 3.3, and 4.01, and it was lightly tested under DOS 5.0.

ARJ was written by Robert K. Jung, who wrote it in ANSI C with the idea of maintaining a single version of the source code for use with many different machines. Jung has announced plans to port ARJ to Atari, Amiga, and Unix™-based machines, as well as DOS systems. Using it is similar to using LHA™ or PKZIP™, with which it shares commands, but ARJ has its own format.

Jung admits in his manual that he's indebted to Haruyasu Yoshizaki for developing LHARC and distributing its source code. "LHARC gave me the impetus to start studying data compression," he writes. Jung also appreciated the work of Haruhiko Okumura and his AR001 and AR002 programs, which provided the basic design for early versions of ARJ. However, he writes, the LZ77 compression routine is new and original.

ARJ lets you write comments for files or input them from another file. It supports DOS volume labels and tests newly compressed files before overwriting originals. The program can compress multiple volumes with a single command, making it a competent backup utility, but it can also recover individual files. The program also lets you search for strings of characters within compressed files, offers a facility to recover files from broken compressed files, and offers a security envelope feature, which disallows changes to a secured compressed file and makes distribution of such files safer.

With ARJ, commands and switches may be entered in upper or lower case, and switches may be placed anywhere after the command ARJ. Switches can be set off with either "-" or "/," but the two may not be mixed in the same command. Jung suggests that switch options not be combined, so that **-k** and **-i** should be used instead of **-ki**, for instance. The switch option "--" tells the program there are no more switches to process in the current command.

The main commands, switches, and options of its competitors all work with ARJ, but there are some additional commands to keep in mind:

ARJ -?   This command will show you all of the program's extensive help screens.

jm, jm1   These options give you more compression and smaller files.

m2   This option compresses more quickly, with some loss of file size.

-   This tells the program there are no more switches to process in the current command. It's especially useful if filenames have the "-" symbol in them.

v   Verbosely list contents of a compressed file. To assist in building lists, there are two switches with this command: **-jv** and **-jv1**. The former displays only pathnames, and the latter displays all information about a file except the comment line.

a   Allow any file attribute. This switch lets you compress system or hidden files, which are not usually recognized by the DOS wildcard commands such as ***.doc** and **c??**.

j   Join compressed files together. This command attaches two compressed files, even if both contain multiple files. Not all switches are supported by this command. The same command can be used to convert a self-extracting module into a regular ARJ compressed file, as in this example:

ARJ j new_name arjsfx.exe

n   Rename files in a compressed file. The program will prompt you for the new name of each selected file. To skip renaming a file, enter a blank line. Specify the general names of the files you want to rename or you'll have to go through your entire compressed file (or "archive") with this command. This command, for instance, will give you prompts to rename all files with an extension of .c:

ARJ n archive *.c

c   Add a comment of up to 25 lines to the header of a compressed file, or to individual files. ARJ prompts for each line in the comment. [RETURN] will end the comment. To get rid of comments, use the **c** command again, then a space, and [RETURN] on the first available comment line. In all cases, new comments replace old.

! With ARJ, this command lets you input comments up to 2,048 bytes long directly from a text file. The full command to input the file archive.txt as a comment to the current archive would be:

!archive.txt

starting in column 1 of the first comment line.

z This switch adds archive comments, but not file comments.

i This command checks the integrity of the ARJ program. It's useful if you've just downloaded the program from a bulletin board.

k Keep archive in backup file. This enables you to avoid overwriting your most recent copy of a file. The archive is given the new extension .BAK, but other files with the same name and the .BAK extension will be overwritten.

q Query on each file. This switch leads you to prompts asking you to approve actions on each file in your archive or list in turn. This allows you to selectively delete, or add, files to a compression list with full control.

-v Spread a large archive across multiple diskettes. This command makes ARJ the only file compression utility that can also be used for making file backups.

y Yes on all queries. This overrides the overwrite queries for the **x** or **e** extraction commands, the pause during an **s** command, and the next volume pause using the **v** option. Use it only with batch files, and with caution. It can be combined with the **j** command to answer only certain types of queries.

REARJ This activates a program that accompanies ARJ used to convert files compressed with ARC™, PKZIP™, or LZH™ to the ARJ format. The conversion can be done all at once, from the DOS prompt, like this:

REARJ *.ZIP *.ARC *.LZH

ARJSFX This is the command to create a self-extracting file with the extension .exe from a set of compressed files. It works with most common ARJ commands, switches, and pathnames. If you're a licensed user of the program, this feature automatically supports the ARJ security option. This option disallows any type of modification to a secured ARJ compressed file and performs internal checks to make sure no modification has taken place.

ARJ's LZ77 compression algorithm, and its liberal licensing policy, have given it a good start among BBS operators. Whether it can hold this position depends on Jung's ability to make the program easier to use, and the efforts of other compression schemes to top it.

.GIF Version 89a

CompuServe Inc.
5000 Arlington Center Boulevard
Columbus, OH 43220
614-457-8600

CompuServe's Graphics Interchange Format, pronounced "Jif," was first announced in 1987 and extended in 1989. It's designed as a mechanism for storing high-quality color images that can be exchanged among users of different hardware.

.GIF stores raster images rather than bit maps or vector graphics. Although the images are somewhat resolution-dependent, the size and shape of the dots making up the image can be defined, as can colors. The clarity of the .GIF images you get is determined by the least effective equipment used in creating, transmitting, or translating them.

.GIF files can have very good resolution, up to 16,000 × 16,000 individual dots per image. This compares with 2,000 × 3,000 available with most laser printers. .GIF images can also use up to 256 simultaneous colors, specified from a possible set of 16 million colors.

Not all .GIF images, however, can be processed by all .GIF software. .GIF drivers are designed for specific hardware and are limited by hardware. Generally, detail is lost in translating a .GIF to the screen or a printer, but the quality is usually acceptable.

In business, .GIF has many potential applications. Business charts, merchandise catalogs, documentation illustrations, schematic diagrams, medical illustrations, and color radar maps can all be stored using the .GIF format. Unfortunately, .GIF is best known among many BBS users as a way to pass sexually explicit pictures around. Some .GIF boards of this type have proven highly profitable, while operators of other systems have been arrested on pornography charges based on .GIF files.

.GIF images are usually transmitted using a variation of the Lempel-Ziv Welch compression scheme, a variation of the scheme used in programs such as ARC and in the V.42 error-correction and compression standard for modems. LZW compression reduces file size by 50 to 87 percent. This means that an image of 320 × 200 pixels in 16 colors, normally requiring 32,000 bytes of storage, may need only 8,000 in the .GIF format.

CompuServe itself offers software for the display or creation of .GIF files. The company offers a limited, nonexclusive, royalty-free license for the use of .GIF in computer software, so long as authors acknowledge CompuServe's ownership and use its service mark. Usually, this acknowledgement appears as a banner on the opening screen of a .GIF file creation program, called an encoder, or a .GIF drawing program, called a decoder.

.GIF itself is defined in terms of blocks and sub-blocks containing both parameters for display of pictures and the data used to make them. Support for color comes from so-called color tables, a sequence of bytes representing red-green-blue color triplets. .GIF files can also define their own aspect ratios, the quotient of each pixel's width and height. Anything from 4:1 to 1:6, in increments of 1/64, will work. The scheme also includes room for comments, text, headers, and image descriptions, inside each .GIF file.

The conversion of an image into a data stream involves several steps. First, the number of bits needed to represent the picture is established. Second, the data are compressed. Next, the set of compression codes, each of which may run from 3 to 12 bits, are converted to a string of 8-bit bytes, providing a little more compression. Finally, those bytes are packaged into blocks, preceded by character counts and output.

A picture is worth 1,000 words. Using .GIF files, the power of bulletin boards is greatly enhanced.

PC FILE FORMATS

Once you get a file downloaded, or transferred to your computer, and decompressed, you are faced with this fact: The PC world is a jungle of file formats. Although the vendors (or sponsors) of other environments (notably the Apple Macintosh) have been able to maintain some minimal discipline among their software developers, the PC software world has been notable mostly for its chaos. Virtually every major package has its own way of formatting data.

This is true even in the relatively straightforward world of word processors, spreadsheets, and databases—where the data are ultimately alphanumeric and can often be examined with the DOS TYPE command. And it is even truer in the graphics field. If you've downloaded a graphics file, you need special graphics software just to see what the file looks like—graphics software that will work with that format.

But how do you even know what the format is? Look at the DOS file extension. If you see a file called STUFF.TXT, for example, .TXT is the file extension. DOS software packages normally use the file extension to tell them how to handle a file, and they can be counted on to produce files with appropriate file extensions. (Admittedly, any joker can use the DOS RENAME command to change the extension, leaving you in the dark, but this is generally not a factor.)

So, we can approach the file format jungle armed with file extensions as a classification tool. And, like naturalists facing a real jungle, we can be assured that the fauna all fall into higher classifications—in this case, into text, raster, vector, and metafile types.

Text Formats

There is a generic format for alphanumeric data, plus a wide variety of specialized formats, each belonging to a brand of word processor.

.TXT. The generic extension .TXT is widely used to denote a plain-vanilla text file in ANSI ASCII with a carriage return at the end of each line. (Alternatively, there may be a carriage return and a line feed, but this makes no difference to most word processors. Or there may only be a carriage return at the end of each paragraph.) Special cases include comma-delimited ASCII files, which are data files rendered as ASCII text files, with each record as one line and individual fields in each record separated by commas. Tabs and other characters can also be used as delimiters.

Beware: There is nothing to stop a word processor from using the .TXT extension to denote a file in its own specialized format.

Other Word-Processing Formats. Each word-processing package uses its own format to encode information not embodied in the ASCII code—such as margins and boldfacing—and its own methods. For proper results, you'll have to use the proper word processor with the proper file. However, many word processors can import files produced by other leading brands. Common formats are denoted by the following extensions:

.ASC   Another extension used to denote ASCII

.BAS   BASIC program code, either in the form of ASCII or BASIC "program tokens"

.BAT   Batch files: lists of DOS commands that run by invoking the name of the batch file. They are written in plain ASCII and can be edited with nearly any word processor.

.DAT   Generic data file, denoting no particular format

.DBF   dBASE® database files

.DOC   Document files for several different word processors, including Microsoft Word, Multimate™, and SmartWare™. The fact that they use the same extension does not mean that they use the same format.

.QWK   Semistandard format used by mail doors to package a user's conference mail. (See Appendix A.) As sent, a .QWK file is actually several text and index files compressed into one; the mail-reading software will decompress the file into the text format it uses.

.REP   Reply file—the opposite of a .QWK file

.SYS   A system configuration file, used internally by the operating system. Like .BAT files, these are written in plain ASCII.

.WK   A Lotus 1-2-3® spreadsheet

.WP   A WordPerfect™ word-processing document

.WRI   A Windows Write™ word-processing document

.WS   A WordStar® word-processing document

Raster Formats

A raster image codes each dot (or pixel) of a picture. A dot is there or it is not, and if it is there it may be some color or shade of gray. Simply bit-mapping an image from the screen to a file is not generally done, since most formats additionally employ some form of file compression. Group III fax produces crude raster images. Types of software that create raster graphics are called paint packages, since they paint dots on the screen.

Raster formats are used for scanned images and photo-realistic images. The drawback of raster formats is that the images are resolution-dependent and device-dependent; something that looks good on the screen may come out startlingly small on a laser printer, since the dots the printer uses are much smaller and closer together than the dots used by the screen. And magnifying raster images can produce disappointing results, since the magnified curves can end up looking like jagged stairways.

.TIF.   The Tagged Image File (.TIF) format was developed by Aldus for importing scanned images (which generally end up being bulkier than files produced by paint programs) into desktop publishing documents. .TIF is versatile and widely used, but it is also complex, with widely differing variants. It is doubtful that any one graphics program can handle every possible .TIF variant.

There are five major .TIF classes: monochrome, gray scale, color using a palette specified by the package that produced it, color using red/blue/green values for each pixel, and fax images with a .TIF header. A .TIF file may also embody several compression schemes, or none at all.

Most .TIF software can handle most .TIF images, but it may pay to have more than one .TIF-compatible package handy just in case.

.PCX. As the format used by Zsoft's PC Paintbrush, .PCX is about the oldest PC graphics file format, and most PC paint packages support it. It uses RLE (run-length encoding, where you indicate the equivalent of "three 1s and two 0s" instead of 11100) to achieve some compression. Formats include monocolor, 4-color CGA, 16-color (or levels of gray) EGA and VGA, and 256-color (or shades of gray) VGA. A .PCC file extension generally denotes material that has been cut from a .PCX file, for pasting into another .PCX file.

.GIF. .GIF is the color-graphics file format used by CompuServe for its rich Picture Forum. It is a fairly sophisticated format, supporting LZW file compression and multiple images per file. (See the "File Compression" section for details.)

.BMP. The .BMP extension denotes bit-mapped images created either by Microsoft Windows or OS/2 Presentation Manager. It is a very simple format without compression.

.PCL. A .PCL file is a Hewlett-Packard LaserJet® "print file"; in other words, data that would normally have been sent to a LaserJet printer were instead stored in a disk file. Such files can be quite large, and there is generally no way to edit them. They are commonly created for the purpose of being converted into the .EPS or fax format.

.CUT. A paint package called Dr. Halo creates files using the .CUT extension. Color .CUT images require a palette file using the .PAL extension.

Fax. Fax is not really a discrete format. Fax modems generally come with software that will store incoming fax images as data and convert graphics or PCL files into a fax format for transmission. However, each fax modem uses its own idiosyncratic approach and file extension. Although files created by one may be usable by another, you should not assume this.

Vector Formats

You can think of the difference between vector and raster formats as the difference between painting and drawing. Instead of each dot being coded, a vector format establishes two points and a connecting line of a certain width. Curves are based on arc fragments. Rather than merely describing the dots on a page, in other words, a vector format describes how the picture is created. This geometric approach can make the use of vector graphics device-independent for display or printing purposes, since each graphics display or printer can decide how best to draw and fill the lines. Vector shapes can also be rescaled and bent on command, which is useful for designers.

However, you won't see vector graphics used much in the BBS world. A complex drawing embodies all the shapes and forms the artist had to combine to achieve the final work. When a drawing is displayed on the screen, the software will lay down all the shapes and forms the artist used on top of each other, as if re-creating the history of the drawing. Although this underlying material is necessary if you want to edit the drawing (say, if one architect has sent a floor plan to another), it's deadwood for a read-only visual aid. If a drawing is posted on a BBS, it was probably first converted to raster form, a sort of screen printing of the drawing.

(Although converting from vector to raster is routine, converting from raster to vector is very difficult. It's easy for software to derive dots from the directions, but harder to derive directions from the dots.)

Some of the common vector formats are described in the following list.

.PIC. This is the (fairly simple) format that Lotus 1-2-3 uses when it generates a chart using spreadsheet data.

.DXF. The Document Interchange Format is used by Autodesk's Auto-CAD™ software to import and export drawings. Files can be encoded as ASCII or as pure unTYPEable data. Obviously, .DXF is used mostly for CAD drawings, and such drawings can be quite large.

.HPGL. The Hewlett-Packard Graphics Language produces printout data intended to be used by pen plotters.

.GEM. Digital Research's GEM® (Graphical Environment Manager) graphical user interface uses the .GEM format as its native vector file format. Although the GEM® interface has not received the market acceptance of its later rival, Microsoft Windows, the .GEM format remains in wide use because it is supported by Xerox Ventura Publisher®, a leading PC desktop publishing package.

Metafiles

Metafiles can contain both vector and graphics information. Common formats include:

.EPS. Encapsulated PostScript is a way of capturing PostScript printout data into desktop publishing documents. An .EPS file can contain bit-mapped images as well as vector information. There is generally no way to edit such pictures, or even show them on the screen; you can only print them out.

.CGM. The Computer Graphics Metafile format was created by the American National Standards Institute to facilitate the exchange of graphical data between software packages. However, it is mostly used for vector graphics.

.WMF. Windows Metafile is the format used internally by Microsoft Windows. In most cases, the size of a WMF file is limited by the capacity of the Windows Clipboard to 64K.

9

![chapter divider]

BBS Software

ABOUT THIS CHAPTER

After using your modem software to dial into a BBS, you then have to use the BBS and its software. We'll take a caller's view of the four leading commercial BBS software packages and list other packages available.

INTRODUCTION

BBS software packages, like modem packages, present you with interfaces that vary from package to package. But they all involve the same ideas; uploading, downloading, posting and reading messages, and invoking doors. (Doors are programs external to the BBS, that are run to perform a specific purpose, such as play a game, download conference mail, or even make automated sales. The door software is usually swapped into memory, replacing the BBS software, and it interfaces through the serial port using the call set up by the BBS software. When the door is finished running, the BBS software is reinvoked.) We'll examine some of the BBS software packages that you are most likely to encounter as a BBS user.

PCBoard

Clark Development Co. Inc.
P.O. Box 571365
Salt Lake City, UT 84157-1365
801-261-1686

PCBoard is the most popular bulletin board package among systems accessible by the public. It doesn't require a powerful computer, it works

```
        MAIL COMMANDS            SYSTEM COMMANDS
{E}nter a message
{R}ead messages             {O}perator page
{REPLY} to messages         {C}omment to SYSOP
{TS} Txt srch messages      {H}elp with commands
{Y}our personal mail        {X}pert On/Off
{Q}uick message scan        {M}ode [GRAPHICS]
{NEWS} file [DISPLAY]       {V}iew settings
{CHAT} between nodes        {P}age length set
                            {I}nitial Welcome
        FILE COMMANDS       {W}rite User info
{U}pload a file             {B}ulletin listings
{UB} Upload batch           {G}oodbye [HANG UP]
{D}ownload a file           {T}rans. protocol
{DB} Download batch         {J}oin a conference
{F}ile directories          {A}bandon a conference
{FL}ag for download         {OPEN} a door
{L}ocate files [NAME]       {SELECT} Conferences for scanning
{N}ew files [DATE]
{Z}ippy scan [DIRS]      Conference selected is: Main Board

(58 min. left) Main Board Command?
```

Figure 9.1   PCBoard Command Menu

with networks and multitasking DOS extenders such as DesqView, and there is a wealth of third-party software available for it, so each board that uses PCBoard can look unique.

Still, there are some basic PCBoard commands that are shared by most other packages, and learning them can help speed your use of any system and lower your phone bills. The main command menus is shown in Figure 9.1.

Getting Around

The simplest and most often used PCBoard commands date from the earliest shareware and userware packages such as RBBS. They include:

R   Read messages.

E   Enter a message.

G   Goodbye, or log off the board.

Under the Read command are a number of subcommands to help you get to specific messages faster. With PCBoard, these can be combined with the Read command on the same line or used in response to prompts as the board queries you about what you want to read. Some of the more common Read subcommands are:

Y   Read messages addressed to you.

F   Read messages addressed from you.

user   Read messages from a specific user. This can be combined with the user's name, or the board can prompt you for it.

The Scan command offers even more power than Read, especially if you're active on a particular board. Scan delivers a short summary of a number of messages. You can choose to read, reply, or download by a number off the list. It too can be combined with other commands. In addition to the Read subcommands, some of the more common Scan subcommands are:

Since   Scan all unread messages.

TS   Search all messages for a specific test string, such as your name, and scan them. Of course, this command should be followed by the name or phrase you want searched for.

All messages in PCBoard are given sequential numbers. This command lets you set a number to scan messages from.

Getting around the message base is only one way to use PCBoard. Most public boards feature large file libraries, accessed from the main menu with the File command. A file can be text, a program, a picture, or a set of other files, compressed using a utility such as .ZIP or .ARC. More important to a board user, a file can usually found be in a numbered file directory, with the order created by the system operator. Some of the more common File subcommands are:

Choose a directory number. If no directory number is specified, a prompt will request one.

D   Download. The system will immediately prompt you for the name of the file to be downloaded. Then, if you haven't established a default protocol, the system will prompt you for the protocol you want to use.

L   Locate by name. You'll be prompted for a text string, and filenames containing the string will be offered.

N   Locate by date. You'll be prompted for a date, often the last date you were online with this board, and the system will offer every file obtained since that date.

FL   Flag a file for later downloading with the **DB** command on the main menu.

Z Zip through the files in a directory for specified text (not to be confused with the ZIP compression utility). Whereas the **L** and **N** commands search filenames, **Z** searches entire files.

The Join command represents one of the more powerful features of PCBoard software. By organizing files and message collections under separate conferences, a single board can hold hundreds of files and thousands of messages, but won't slow down when a user asks to search those lists. There are three primary subcommands from Join.

Join a conference by its number. The main conference on any board is designated as conference 0.

[Name] Join a conference by its name. The conference designated by the number 0 on any board can be joined with the command **j main**.

Q Quick join. After joining a conference, use this command to bypass news files and introductions, going directly to the message base and file directories.

The Open command represents another powerful feature of PCBoard software. Doors are programs outside PCBoard, that are attached to it and available for use. Sometimes these are ordinary programs such as word processors or spreadsheets, but there is also a wealth of games programs, shopping programs, and others. This is where PCBoard add-ons such as PC Verify, a program that calls new users back to verify that they've left a real or valid modem number, are accessed. Subcommands here include the **#** and **[Name]** commands used for Join, as well as a **[parameter]** command similar to those used in DOS.

Other Commands

There are a number of other basic commands on the PCBoard main menu. Most are simple, but a few represent entrances to other powerful applications:

Chat between nodes Real-time chat, in that users accessing the same system can type conversations and save them, is not a specialty of PCBoard software, but it is supported. You need to enter a node number, and you can't just invoke a chat with a user name. But for business-related boards that want to use Chat for meetings between specific people at specific times, the capability is available.

{O}perator page The **O** command will, with most boards, ring an alarm, to which the board operator may respond by initiating a chat with the user invoking the command.

{**C**}**omment to sysop**   The **C** command is a specific variation of **W,** with all messages going to the board operator.

{**H**}**elp with commands**   PCBoard has extensive help facilities covering all the commands not listed here. General help can be invoked with **H,** and found by entering the command you need help with in response to the prompt.

{**X**}**pert on/off**   Once you learn all the PCBoard commands, you can get rid of the menus with this command.

{**M**}**ode [graphics]**   Using ANSI terminal emulation, that is a subset of the Digital Equipment VT100 standard, users can add color and graphics to their PCBoard sessions. This is one reason using PCBoard can be a more pleasant experience than using a larger system such as CompuServe, that doesn't offer graphics.

{**V**}**iew settings**   The **V** command lets you see what you originally told PCBoard about your computer, so you can make changes. If you first called on an Apple II and are now using an IBM PC, for example, this is especially useful.

{**P**}**age length set**   This is a crucial setting usually established when you first sign on to a PCBoard system. Because it is so important, the ability to change it is offered on the main menu.

{**T**}**ransfer protocol**   This is another crucial setting. The default file-transfer protocol established upon first signing up to a PCBoard system can be changed with the **T** command.

{**I**}**nitial welcome**   Every board operator will offer a welcoming message to new users, and it can be seen again with the **I** command.

{**W**}**rite user info**   In PCBoard, the **W** command refers only to information about individual users.

{**B**}**ulletin listings**   Bulletins may cover board policies or changes on the board and can be reread quickly with the **B** command.

TBBS VERSION 2.2

eSoft
15200 East Girard Avenue, Suite 2550
Aurora, CO 80014
303-699-6565

TBBS is excellent for applications that involve databases. It can be extensively customized, so no two TBBS boards look alike. It's a favorite for customer support and is used by such companies as US Robotics and Hayes. TBBS won't run the biggest boards with its 64-line limit. Using all this power can also be difficult for first-time sysops.

TBBS stands for The Bread Board System. It offers 40 separate menu commands and works on anything from the slowest PC XTs to the fastest 80386 machines.

Figure 9.2 shows certain lettered commands that are common to most TBBS systems and are offered as standard equipment. The command list includes:

<R>ead   The main command to read messages

<Q>uick scan   The main command to scan messages by number and subject

<M>ail   The main command for reading notes sent directly to you

<D>ownload   The main command for taking files from the BBS

<U>pload   The main command for submitting files to the BBS

<H>ello   The main command for paging the sysop.

<G>oodbye   The main command for leaving the board

```
LMMMMMMMMMMMMMMMMMMMMMMMMMMMMMMMMMMMMMMMMMMMMMMMMMMMMMMMMMMMMMMMMMMMMMMMMMMM9
:   Utilities    Messages & Mail    Msg & SIG Boards    Meetings    Offerings  :
HMMMMMKMMMMMMMMMMMMMMMMMMKMMMMMMMMMMMMMMMMMMMMKMMMMMMMMMMMMMMMMMMMKMMMMMMMMMMMMMK<
          .                    :                 :                    :
ZDDDDDPDDDDDDDDDDDDDD?        :     ZDDDDDDDDDDDDDDPDDDDDDDDDDDD?   ZDDDDDDDPDDDDDDDD?
3 <G>oodbye        3          :     3 <R>ead Msgs - General Bd 3   : 3 <C>ourses TNC 3
3 <T>ime Left      3          :     3 <Q>uick Scan Msgs - Gen  3   : 3 <B>CEN        3
3 <X>pert Mode     3          :     3 <L>eave Msg - General Bd 3   : 3 <J>obs Lists  3
3 <F>ormat Term.   3          :     3 <S>pecial Interest Group 3   : 3 <W> Services  3
3 <H>ello Sys Ops 3           :     3 <E>NA Position Statement 3   : 3 <O>rder Items 3
@DDDDDDDDDDDDDDDDDDDY      :         @DDDDDDDDDDDDDDDDDDDDDDDDDDDY : @DDDDDDDDDDDDDDDY
Select Menu Item     ZDDPDDDDDDDDDDDDDDDDDDDDDDDD?   ZDDDDDDDPDDDDDDDDDDDDDDDDDDD?
    of               3 <M>ail .. Ele#tronic Msgs 3   3 <1> General Assembly    3
Interest Using the   3 <N>ews Items .. Bulletins 3   3 <2> Scientific Assembly 3
1st Letter or Number 3 <D>ownload .. Get Files   3   3 <3> ENA Membership      3
 Shown in Brackets   3 <U>pload .. Submit Files   3   3 <4> Management Seminars 3
    s                3 <A>nd Other Medical BBS's 3   3 <5> National Calendar   3
.                    @DDDDDDDDDDDDDDDDDDDDDDDDDDDY   @DDDDDDDDDDDDDDDDDDDDDDDDDY
```

Figure 9.2   TBBS Main Command Menu

Not every TBBS board, however, uses even this scheme. Some boards, such as Hayes Online, put the major functions of the board behind numbers on a menu. For users, what's important is that the main menu be meaningful and its functions be accessed quickly by typing one key. Since TBBS is so easy to customize, your experience with every board will be different.

Some TBBS support boards, including eSoft's own, can disconnect a caller who inputs an invalid user name—even before the password prompt is reached. Others can be programmed to prevent users from leaving messages—even short notes to the sysop—until they are authorized as users. And a wide range of access privileges are possible, which are specific to the user name and password. This makes the "look and feel" of the same TBBS system different for different users.

Version 2.2 also includes internal support for Zmodem-90, the latest version of the DSZ Zmodem program from Omen Technologies. And, in keeping with the trend by sysops to add CD-ROM drives to their boards, Version 2.2 also includes improved CD-ROM support.

WILDCAT 3.0

Mustang Software Inc.
P.O. Box 2264
Bakersfield, CA 93303
800-999-9619
805-395-0223

Wildcat, from Mustang Software, has become especially popular for single-line corporate BBSs because it's easy to set up and run, as well as simple to use.

The main menu (Figure 9.3) shows all the major board options and is self-evident. Message and file collections are separated on the main menu but can be related at the option of the sysop.

The Entertainment option on this particular board refers to game doors, that can be added fairly quickly. The Order door refers to add-ins that can be used for on-line ordering.

Behind the main menu are more menus. Each menu is fairly simple, with no more than a dozen or so choices each identified by a single letter or character. The simplicity of Wildcat remains its strength, both for users and for sysops.

```
\\\\\\\\\\\\\\\\\\\\\\\\\\\\\\\\\\\\\\\\\\\\\\\\\\\\\\\\\\\\\\\\\\\\\\\\\\\\\\
\\\\\\\\\\\\\\\ZDDDDDDDDDDDDDDDDDDDDDDDDDDDDDDDDDDDDDDDDDDDDDDDDDDDD?\\\\\\\\\\\\\
\\\\\\\\\\\\\\\3  VD7VD7                      VD7VD7              3\\\\\\\\\\\\\
\\\\\\\\\\\\\\\3  : :: :                      : :: :              3\\\\\\\\\\\\\
\\\\\\\\\\\\\\\3  : S= :  VD7  R  RD7         : S= :  RD7  RD7  7 V 3\\\\\\\\\\\\\
\\\\\\\\\\\\\\\3  :    : GD6 :  : :           :    : GD  : :  : : 3\\\\\\\\\\\\\
\\\\\\\\\\\\\\\3  P    P = S P  P P           P    P PD= P P  SD= 3\\\\\\\\\\\\\
\\\\\\\\\\\\\\\CDDDDDDDDDDDDDDDDDDDDDDDDDDDDDDDDDDDDDDDDDDDDDDDDDDDD4\\\\\\\\\\\\\
\\\\\\\\\\\\\\\3          W I L D C A T !  ver 2.55 Multi-Node     3\\\\\\\\\\\\\
\\\\\\\\\\\\\\\@DDDDDDDDDDDDDDDDDDDDDDDDDDDDDDDDDDDDDDDDDDDDDDDDDDDDDY\\\\\\\\\\\\\
\\\\\\\\\\\\\\\\\\\\\\\\\\\\\\\\\\\\\\\\\\\\\\\\\\\\\\\\\\\\\\\\\\\\\\\\\\
\\\ZDDDDDDDDDDDDDDDDDDDD?\\\\\\\\\ZDDDDDDDDDDDDDDDDDDDD?\\\\\\\\ZDDDDDDDDDDDDDDDDDDD?\\\
\\\3 B ulletin Menu  3\\\\\\\\\3 C omment / Sysop 3\\\\\\\\\3 H elp Level      3\\\
\\\3 F ile Menu      3\\\\\\\\\3 G oodBye        3\\\\\\\\\3 S tatistics      3\\\
\\\3 M essage Menu   3\\\\\\\\\3 I nitial Welcome 3\\\\\\\\\3 V erify a User   3\\\
\\\3 W ho is Online  3\\\\\\\\\3 E NTERTAINMENT   3\\\\\\\\\3 ? Command Help   3\\\
\\\3 * WILDCAT! Info 3\\\\\\\\\3 U serlog Listing 3\\\\\\\\\3 Y our Settings   3\\\
\\\3   press the star3\\\\\\\\\3 O RDERS & INFO   3\\\\\\\\\3 P age Sysop       3\\\
\\\@DDDDDDDDDDDDDDDDDDDDY\\\\\\\\@DDDDDDDDDDDDDDDDDDDDY\\\\\\\\@DDDDDDDDDDDDDDDDDDDDY\\\
\\\\\\\\\\\\\\\\\\\\\\\\\\\\\\\\\\\\\\\\\\\\\\\\\\\\\\\\\\\\\\\\\\\\\\\\\\
```

Figure 9.3 Wildcat Main Menu

MAJOR BBS

Galacticomm Inc.
4101 S.W. 47 Avenue, Suite 101
Fort Lauderdale, FL 33314
305-583-5990

Galacticomm's Major BBS software has recently become widely used with large, public boards because it's simple to offer popular features such as shopping and chatting with it. Since the software is written in C, it can be customized or extended. Also, it's designed from the ground up as a multi-user system; Galacticomm sells expansion units that can let you run up to 16 lines from a single PC.

The command menu is divided into sections or modules, which are listed in Figure 9.4. However, many of the Major BBS commands aren't found in other BBS software packages, such as TBBS or PCBoard. Some are preceded by a slash (/). Others can be combined, or concatenated, into a single abbreviated command; for example, **SRQS** means quickly scan the board's special interest groups for new public messages. This can slow the learning process for experienced BBS users.

Even the command to exit the board is different—**x,** as in "exit," instead of **g**, as in "goodbye." But the **x** command is also used to go to

```
A) Your Account Information    B) Billing
C) Chat Lounge                 D) Dial Out Services
E) Electronic Mail             F) File Library
G) Multi-Player Games          H) HELP!
I) Information                 N) News
O) Online Shopping Mall        R) Registry of Users
S) Special Interest Groups
W) What's New                  Y) Speed Search Database
$) Classified Ads              ?) Additional Commands
Z) Purchase Credits
X) Exit the System
```

Figure 9.4 Major BBS Main Menu

a higher menu as well as to exit the board; the Goodbye command can usually get you off a board from anywhere.

Major BBS is designed around special interest groups, or SIGs. SIGs can be private or public, which makes this software useful for businesses that need to divide workers into many different work groups. Workers in multiple locations can be assigned to one or more private SIGs and exchange messages on their work, without seeing the work of other groups.

Within different modules, the same letter may be used to refer to different commands. **T,** for instance, means "check for messages To me" within the mail section and "enter the Teleconference (chat feature)" within the SIGs section.

Following are some of the commands commonly used to help you get around a Major BBS system.

X Exit. Either leave the board from the top menu, or exit to a higher menu from any other menu.

R Read messages.

T Read all messages to you.

ERT A combination command, this will list all messages addressed to you—private mail, replies to your public messages within SIGs, or public messages to you in a SIG.

SS? List all special interest groups. Adding a group's name and the command **RLBO** will give you a one-line summary of each message in the SIG you specify.

/p Page another user. Follow it with another user's ID and a message. This is an example of how the Major BBS is built from the ground up as a multi-user system.

/# Show who else is online.

W Write a message.

M Modify a message.

E Erase a message.

EW Write a message to another user. Follow it with a user ID. **EWSysop** is used to write a note to the system operator.

After entering the command to write a message, the user reaches the Major BBS editor menu. All of the commands here are self-evident and are delivered with one-letter codes but a few deserve mention for their uniqueness.

A Append. This lets you upload a file to accompany your typed message. It can be sent either as an ASCII text file or using the Xmodem or Ymodem protocols.

C Change. This lets you change the text of a message before uploading it with the **S** (Send) command.

L List. This lets you look at the message you just typed before sending it with the **S** (Send) command.

SIG Commands

The main-menu command for entering a special interest group is **S.** In a public system, SIGs may be organized around common interests. In a private system, they may be organized around work groups. Or they can be organized in any other way you wish. The Read and Write commands are used here also, but they refer to SIG bulletins, not messages. You can also use the **U** command to upload a message to a specific SIG, or **D** to download a message.

The Major BBS has some powerful commands for getting users around large SIGs quickly.

K Keyword search. You can enter one keyword or two. If you enter two, the system will search for messages with both keywords in them.

S Scan messages. Here's another example of a one-letter command with two meanings. In the main menu, it is used to enter a SIG.

Q Quick-scan the SIG. You can use this command to search bulletins in all SIGs you are a member of, or just the SIG you're presently in.

RQ Set up a quick-scan. This will let you create a list of SIGs to scan for messages with the **Q** command. It's combined with the + or − and / commands, as follows:

RQ–/BBS: Drop the BBS SIG from the list of scanned SIGs.

RQ+/BBS: Add the BBS SIG to the same list.

RQC Change the current quick-scan SIG list. You use the same commands as with **RQ** to add or delete SIGs from the list.

SIG messages are organized into threads. A thread is a set of messages that refer to one another. Threads are created by users, so some threads may seem to change topics as they go. Users can move through a thread after reading one message in it with the following commands:

TB Thread backward to the most recent message with the same topic.

TF Thread forward to the next message with the same topic.

TP Read the first message, or parent, of the current thread.

Using the thread commands won't interrupt a quick-scan, so you can follow them at your leisure. They only work when you're scanning or searching through the message base.

Teleconferencing (Chatting)

You can reach the teleconferencing system with the **T** command. Each SIG can have its own teleconference, or there may be a number of public teleconferences accessible from the main menu.

Teleconferencing in the Major BBS is referred to as chatting on other systems. As with CB radio, messages are typed at various keyboards and listed by the system in the order in which they're received. Many modem software packages, such as Procomm Plus, have a special chat mode to make using such systems easier.

In a public system, teleconferencing may be a lot like CB radio, complete with the use of "handles" and other in-words that may seem absurd to the novice. In a private system, teleconferencing can be used to hold meetings among workers thousands of miles apart; the log of the teleconference thus becomes a record of the meeting.

As you can see, teleconferences can be wide open or very narrow. They can relate to specific subjects, be tightly controlled, or consist of random discussions around the electronic campfire.

Following are some of the commands used for teleconferencing on the Major BBS:

PAGE <**Userid**> Page or invite another user of the system to your teleconference.

<Userid>   Send a private message to another teleconference member.

CHANNEL <#>   Switch to another teleconference.

CHAT <Userid>   In the Major BBS, chatting is a function between two users only; teleconferencing is a group chat. The same command is used to offer a private discussion, or to start the discussion. The request will appear only on the computer of the user you specify.

MODERATE <topic>   This command sets up a conference topic and makes the person giving the command its moderator.

APPOINT <Userid>   This command makes someone else the moderator.

SQUELCH <Userid>   This command is available only to moderators and is used to shut up an obnoxious or loud user. To avoid problems later on, it's best to offer a Chat command either before or right after using this command.

UNSQUELCH <Userid>   This command is the opposite of Squelch.

Classified Ads

You can reach the classified ads section of a Major BBS board with the **C** command. Classifieds are really a special type of public message. In a private board, there may be no need for them. Many businesses, however, run public boards to support their products, and for those boards this feature can be used to run specials or advertise add-ins. On public boards, of course, the classifieds work much like those in a newspaper, except they can be searched more quickly.

Users can scan for ads alphabetically under topics, and ads can be deleted after a certain length of time; that's up to the system operator. Here are the commands in the classified ads menu:

G   General information. This is used to explain the policies of the section, what types of ads are in or out, and how to search the section.

S   Scan or read ads.

P   Place an ad.

M   Modify or change an ad.

D   Delete an ad.

C   Check for responses. This is used, of course, only by the person who places an ad, or the system operator.

Other Features

Every Major BBS you dial into will be different. The main menu in Figure 9.4 may look nothing like the menu on your favorite board. It is the ability of the Major BBS to be extended or customized that is its main strength. The program itself is written in the C language, and add-in programs using the same language are available from Galacticomm.

Galacticomm offers special editions of its software with some additional features:

- *The File Library Edition.* This is a special edition of the Major BBS, released in July 1990, for use in systems where uploading and downloading files is a priority. Instead of being organized around special interest groups, the library edition is organized around libraries.

- *The Entertainment Edition.* This is a special edition of the Major BBS, released in June 1990, for use in systems where games and chatting, or teleconferencing, are the top priorities. It comes with two role-playing games, Androids and Magic, as well as a dating registry and a protocol called Flash, which makes it simple to put other multiplayer games online. Additionally, about 75 games that will run under the Major BBS are available from third parties.

- *The Shopping Mall Edition.* This is a special version of the Major BBS, released in November 1990, for use as an electronic mall. Merchants can use this BBS to offer their catalogs online, or entrepreneurs can use it to create their own "online shopping centers."

- *The MenuMan Edition.* This is a special version of the Major BBS, released in June 1990, that lets you organize every service on your board as part of a menu tree. This is especially important for systems run on behalf of many businesses, or for those with a wide variety of topics and closed user groups not supported in the main program.

OTHER DOS-BASED BBS PROGRAMS

Bulletin boards started as a movement by users to help one another. The first bulletin board program, CBBS, was distributed as shareware.

Today there are many bulletin board programs available. Some are distributed as shareware, and others are freeware, sometimes called userware. Still others have one-man companies behind them, hoping to break into the big time occupied by Galacticomm, Clark Development, eSoft, and Mustang Software. Using one of these offerings may cost less up front, and it may make your board unique. But there are also disadvantages, mainly in terms of the limited support you'll find for your software.

With all that in mind, this section describes some of the more popular shareware, freeware, and small commercial BBS programs. They are listed alphabetically and divided between single-line BBS systems and multiline systems. Price ranges are coded as follows:

!	Free
$	To $20
$$	$20 to $50
$$$	$50 to $75
$$$$	$75 to $125
$$$$+	Above $125

Single-Line Systems

DCI, $$$$, by Nordevald Software, P.O. Box 280138, Tampa, FL 33682, BBS: 813-961-0788

DCI provides facilities for multiple message bases, base formats, user identities, and file transfer options. It also features an internal callback verification system. It was written in Turbo Pascal Version 5.5 and Turbo Assembler Version 1.01 from Borland International. It requires an IBM XT with a minimum of 384K of memory and a hard disk in its single-line configuration, and it can take advantage of expanded memory and the DesqView multitasking environment. In addition to his own BBS, the author supports the software through messages in the BBS conference on BIX.

Feathernet BBS, Version 3.32, $$$, by Ronnie L. Pierce, Feathernet Software, 810-F Vernon Circle, Mountain View, CA 94043, BBS: 415-967-3484

Feathernet is a shareware program featuring enhanced message-conferencing features. It is designed for MS-DOS 3.0 or higher, and the author recommends it be used only with an 80286- or 80386-based machine, with 210K of memory used while the program is operating.

File transfers, manipulations of compressed files, and sysop utilities can be done outside Feathernet using batch files or a DOS shell, if there's memory available. All these options can be chosen in the process of setting the program up. External programs, or doors, are run through batch files after Feathernet terminates.

Users can "flag" files for later downloading while searching or viewing directories, and they can resume aborted uploads using Zmodem. Users can also view compressed files online or download just parts of a compressed file using the .ZIP, .LZH, or .ARC compression schemes. Text searches are enhanced by the highlighting of text when it's found, and an offline reader called FNREADER.EXE comes with the program. Users are notified of mail waiting in any conference at log-on, and they can customize their own scanning to bypass undesired conferences. Users can also be "forced" into an external program, or door, as they log on if the sysop desires this. This option is especially useful if you want to force new users to go through a registration process before they're given access to the whole board.

QuickBBS Version 2.65, **$$,** *by The QuickBBS Group Inc., P.O. Box 621735, Orlando, FL 32862, 407-228-9096; BBS: 407-856-0356*

QuickBBS was originally written by Adam Hudson but is now copyrighted by Darrell J. Cadwallader and the QuickBBS Group. One of the most popular shareware programs, it can be used for 30 days free. The minimum memory requirement is 512K, along with a hard-disk PC. Doors, or add-in programs, require additional memory.

QuickBBS is designed as a messaging and file system and is ready for use with netmail or echomail with only the addition of a mailer program and tosser/scanner utility. The message base is put into a database format, so messages can be retrieved quickly and require less storage space. The software supports message linking, meaning that threads of messages can be established and followed easily. The program also uses "hot keys," which can interrupt menus. The program also has built-in ANSI routines so that sysops don't need a separate ANSI.SYS file, and there are 32,000 different security levels available; you can password-protect individual menus and file languages. There's also a questionnaire command language.

RBBS Version 17.3A, **!,** *by D. Thomas Mack, Ken Goosens, and Doug Azzarito, 5480 Eagle Lake Drive, Palm Beach Gardens, FL 33418, 407-627-9767, BBS: 407-627-6969*

RBBS is the oldest and one of the most popular free BBS programs in existence. It has dozens of authors besides those listed, and its history goes back over a decade. The latest version has extensive capabilities, including the ability to link to dBase programs like TBBS, to work with doors like PCBoard, and to handle sophisticated message bases. The program also has over 700 kilobytes (350 pages) of documentation detailing all of this power and how to use it. The authors recommend use of an IBM/AT or compatible, with a color monitor, and 640 kilobytes of random access memory (RAM), plus a modem, for use of the software.

The authors recommend use of a text editor capable of producing simple ASCII text and a "test" computer, that a sysop can also use to access the system as a user. It's distributed freely, with source code. First copies of new versions are sent to the Capital City PC User Group in the Washington, D.C., area. The authors ask that improvements to the code be distributed free as .MRG files in the public domain, and that companies that like the software feel free to donate equipment, software, supplies or services to its developers. They also recommend that you join CPCUG, 51 Monroe Street, Plaza East Two, Rockville, MD 20850, 301-670-1737.

As with other systems, the main functions of RBBS are the passing of news or bulletins, electronic mail, the exchange of programs, the conducting of surveys or placing of online purchase orders, and the playing of games. The software not only supports all these functions, but works with networks and multitask operating systems, or as a "local" application on a LAN.

Unlike other shareware or public-domain BBS programs, however, RBBS support is pretty extensive. It has its own echo network, RBBS-Net, headed by Rod Bowman (714-381-6013), and conferences on RBBS are also found on RelayNet.

*Sapphire, Release 3.10A, **$$,** by Pinnacle Software, P.O. Box 714, Airport Road, Swanton, VT 05488, 514-345-9578, BBS: 514-345-8654*

Sapphire is a single-line shareware BBS package. It has the same messaging, filing, and doors capabilities as other BBSs, but it likes to rename functions. It calls users "members," for instance. It's aimed at store managers, consultants, and new sysops. Its operating credo is an "install-and-forget" design, but it lacks power.

To run Sapphire, all you need is a PC with 512K of memory and MS-DOS 2.0 or higher. It will run with only floppy disks, although that's not recommended. It requires only one change in the PC CONFIG.SYS file, with everything else done in a menu-based program called SCONFIG. Most of Sapphire works off the 10 function keys, or the same keys and the Alt key. You can banish a caller from the valid-caller list by simply hitting Alt-F8, for instance.

Sapphire's designers are proud that their system doesn't require maintenance but has some power. It can handle 225 message files, for instance. When the last file is used up, however, the first one is replaced. Sapphire maintains a list of 500 uploads. Again, when the list is full, programs are deleted, but in this case the program to be replaced is based on the popularity of the download. External programs, or doors, are supported; Pinnacle itself wrote a game door called Pyroto Mountain. The support is handled through batch files. Zmodem file transfers are also fully supported.

*Simplex BBS, !, by Christopher Laforet, BBS: 919-226-6984;
CompuServe, 76120,110; Genie, XTX74591; BIX, laforet*

Simplex is a single-line board based on the user interface of QuickBBS.
Currently available for DOS or OS/2, the author writes that he plans to
port it to Unix and make it multi-user.

Simplex can be distributed free. You can buy the source code from
the author and modify it, but you cannot redistribute it. It is designed
for use with FidoNet and other echo networks, and for file uploading or
downloading. As its name implies, the goal of the software is to be simple
to start and simple to run.

*Socrates, Version 1.10, $$, by Michael A. Jacobs, Mikronetics, 2114
Weatherton Drive, Wilmington, DE 19810; FidoNet 1:150/199*

Socrates is called a "bulletin board construction set" since all the
menus, user responses, and system activities are defined by the sysop, and
Socrates merely executes a "programmed" configuration. In that sense, it's
very much like TBBS.

Socrates is distributed as shareware. Those who register are promised
updates and support, as well as utilities not found in the evaluation pack-
age. The name is derived from Plato, a Control Data learning system the
author used while at the University of Delaware.

In addition to the usual choices—messaging, files, and so forth—
Socrates lets the sysop choose the format of the message bases. These
can be sequential or in Socrates' own format, that groups messages by
subject. The board is fully FidoNet-compatible and can be used with ex-
isting message utilities and mailer programs. The program will run with
only 200K of free memory on any PC.

*TriTel BBS, Version 1.1, $$$, by Mark D. Goodwin, P.O. Box 187,
Orland, ME 04472, BBS: 207-469-6556*

TriTel is one of the newer BBSs around, but it contains such features
as an internal version of the Zmodem protocol, netmail support, the ability
to run doors, written for BBS programs such as PCBoard, a method for
testing archives in the .ZIP format, and even a quick and easy way to lock
out obnoxious callers—a file called JOKER.DAT.

TriTel is shareware. It requires an IBM PC/XT with 256k of free memory and a hard disk drive. In addition to running doors from PCBoard
by internally generating door data files, it can also handle external programs written for other software. This relieves the sysop from setting up
a collection of door data-file conversion utilities. The archive tester checks
to make sure ZIP files were uploaded without errors and tests them for
viruses.

TriTel also has a number of add-in programs, available from the support BBS. TBANK12 lets callers save unused time for a later day, TriMail is an offline mail reader, TriMST13 is a file list maker that can update your file list every night as part of a maintenance routine, TTQ&A is a special help file for new TriTel sysops, and TTUT110 is a text interface for using programs such as PCRelay and MegaMail with TriTel. Further third-party development is encouraged; the program is written in C++.

Multiline Systems

ADTBBS, Version 1.4D, **$$$$,** *by Aaron David Thompson, Abstract Data Technologies, 2805 North Highland Avenue, Tucson, AZ 85719, BBS: 602-881-8570*

ADTBBS, named for its author, is a multinode BBS that requires use of ANSI graphics. It allows for remote updating by the sysop, and although it's based on MS-DOS, it uses some commands from Unix. It requires an IBM PC with a hard disk and DOS 2.0 or higher.

Installation is handled through a batch program, called Install, that creates necessary directories and places files in them. It divides echo mail addresses by registered node numbers and accepts things such as doors under an executable file. The program supports expanded memory under Version 3.2 or later of the Lotus/Intel/Microsoft specification.

Auntie, Version 5.11, **$$$$,** *by Wes Meier, W & W Associates, 1988 Via Appia, Walnut Creek, CA 94598, BBS: 415-937-0156*

Auntie is going through its fourth author. Originally compiled by Mark Fletcher in 1987, and then updated by Fran Guidry and Paul Thorpe in 1988, it's now being supported by Wes and Wilma Meier of Walnut Creek, California. It can support multiple nodes.

The program features threaded messages and offers four "expertise" levels, so that both beginners and experts can use it easily. Users can also extract individual files compressed with ARC, ZIP, or LZH, and 10 download protocols—including Zmodem—are supported.

New with Version 5.11 are QuickMail upload and download commands, so that new mail can be packetized and downloaded at once for use with offline message readers. The program also supports doors, or external programs. In addition, the support board supports an offline reader called QWiKer and a version called QWiKer Advanced.

Oracomm, Version 5.0, **$$$,** *by Surf Computer Services, 71-540 Gardess Road, Rancho Mirage, CA, 92270, 619-346-9430, BBS: 619-346-1608*

A two- or three-line shareware version of Oracomm is available for downloading from many bulletin boards and online services. An enhanced version called OracommPlus is a commercial product that can handle more modems and has many added features, including database functions. A 33-user version is available.

Oracomm is written in Microsoft C but incorporates many other libraries and functions, including QEMM from Quarterdeck, that allows it to perform multitasking. A Copy command moves the program onto your hard drive, from that the STARTUP.EXE file self-extracts with initial files, utilities, and a manual. Another self-extracting program, ORAnnnn.EXE (the *ns* refer to the number of nodes or modem connections ordered), contains the actual program. The file and buffer commands in your CONFIG.SYS program may also have to be changed. From there you use the BBS NOMODEM command to tell the program about your modems and where they're connected.

Most Oracomm commands are conventional, such as **R** for Read messages, **E** for Enter messages, **C** for Chat, **D** for Download, and **G** for Goodbye. But most can be modified with subcommands, enabling you to move through the message base more quickly or order an upload or download quickly using a specific protocol.

One feature that sets the regular version of Oracomm apart is what you can do with its user lists. You can go to the beginning of a thread and see who started it with the **W** command; its subcommands can give you profiles of users or lists of who logged on recently. Match commands turn user profiles into a rudimentary database. Within the chat feature, all commands begin with a backslash (\).

The top-of-the-line commercial version lets you create up to 99 subboards with 35 directories each, offers a general-purpose database and support for outside programs or doors, and features a number of doors that cost extra with other programs, such as a callback and verification program, a mass-mailing facility, and an order-entry system.

PowerBBS, Version 1.35, $$, by Russell E. Frey, 35 Fox Court, Hicksville, NY 11801, BBS: 516-873-8032

PowerBBS is a low-priced multinode BBS system that has links to PCBoard. It was written in Borland's Turbo Pascal and is designed to be fast as well as easy to install and use, according to the author. To run PowerBBS, you'll need DOS 3.0 or higher, 230K of memory, and a hard drive with at least 10 megabytes of available memory.

PowerBBS calls its message areas "forums", and each can have its own file area. The program supports up to 100 forums, and subsysops can be appointed within the software to handle the forums. Security features are supported, and each forum can have its messages put in a separate subdirectory and have its own news commands, or bulletins. Menu files and file listings can be edited simply. The program also supports questionnaires. PowerBBS fully supports Zmodem and can log Zmodem file transfers. Additional nodes on the system are run from their own .DAT files and must be started from their own batch files. PowerBBS will also run under multitasking environments such as DesqView and with local area networks. It is 100 percent NetBIOS-compatible.

PowerBBS also lets sysops create their own menus, although a number of standard menus are preloaded. Menus are written with a program called PowerLang, that is similar to BASIC. The program also supports doors, that requires the PCBoard .SYS file, and offers a conversion routine to handle such programs.

RemoteAccess, $$$$+ (commercial version, $$$ hobby version), by Andrew Milner and Richard Brannon, Continental Software, 625 Greencove Terrace #128, Altamonte Springs, FL 32714, 407-788-3736

RemoteAccess was written in Australia and was born when a sysop there who had been running QuickBBS decided to add an additional phone line. The software is designed to run by itself or with a front-end mailer for networks such as FidoNet. It offers its own menu structure, as well as a template to help you make your board look unique. Low maintenance requirements were also a design goal. The program offers greatest screen control when the Avatar terminal program is used.

RemoteAccess offers up to 200 message areas and up to 64,000 security levels with user-definable flags. A user can be assigned to one of 255 separate groups, with specific download limits, time limits, and upload/download ratios. As written, the software supports up to 99 phone lines, and it works with all kinds of multitasking systems, including DESQview, TopView, MultiLink, DoubleDOS, and PC-MOS/386. Six file transfer programs are supported, including Zmodem, and there are 15 slots into that you can put more. Support for CD-ROM drives is also featured, and there's extensive online help available to sysops. Finally, the program offers QuickBBS-style user and message database formats, so utilities written for that system can be used with RemoteAccess.

ROS Version 4.0, $$$, by Steve Fox, Associated Information Services, P.O. Box 13711, Albuquerque, NM 87192, BBS: 505-299-5974

ROS was updated to a multi-user version in the summer of 1991. The program was written in Turbo Pascal, and the new version is almost three times the size of Version 3.8, the single-line version it replaces.

A setup program is included that can lets the BBS program "get out of the way," taking up just 5,000 bytes while running large external transfer protocol drivers, doors, and compression programs. This is especially effective if expanded memory is available. The new version of the program also works with any mailers or doors that use Fossil drivers, and it's DesqView-aware. It can also be used on a local area network. The program supports most common file transfer protocols internally, including Zmodem.

Spitfire, Version 3.1, **$$$$,** *by Mike Woltz, Buffalo Creek Software, 913 39th Street, West Des Moines, IA 50265, 515-225-9552*

Spitfire is one of the most extensive shareware BBSs on the market, offering nearly all the features found on its commercial competitors. It's also one of the more expensive programs, but you can run it with multiple nodes. It was written with Borland's Turbo Pascal.

Spitfire requires only 256k of memory to run, and a hard disk is recommended. It requests a few changes in your computer's CONFIG.SYS file, but nothing major. Spitfire supports up to 255 message conferences, and each gets its own menu. You can configure each separately, so some may require more security while others may support netmail, for example. File areas can also be configured separately. Questionnaires can be created using any ASCII text editor that doesn't add special print control codes to the file.

Spitfire supports the use of ANSI graphics, like its big-time competitors. The program also supports 10 levels of security. Spitfire's documents recommend the use of batch files, not only to handle external programs or doors, but for routine maintenance. A program called SF.BAT is offered for just this purpose. Spitfire can handle up to 24 separate doors, that can be listed on their own menu. Spitfire supports a number of error-checking protocols, such as Xmodem, internally, and can be easily setup to support up to 14 external protocols, like Zmodem. Spitfire supports netmail both through doors and through front-end programs such as BikleyTerm or FrontDoor.

Setting up Spitfire to run with multiple phone lines, or nodes, is not much more difficult than having it work with one. Multinode systems can run in one computer, using a multitasking program such as DesqView or Windows 3.0, or in a local area network such as Novell Netware or Lantastic.

SuperBBS, Version 1.11, **$$$,** *by Risto Virkkala and Aki Antman, Porslahdentie 23 G 40, SF-00980 Helsinki, Finland, Europe, BBS: +358-(9)0-341-1398*

SuperBBS was written in Finland, and the author of the documents, who is Dutch, admits up front that English isn't his first language. The program is distributed as shareware, with site licenses available. Support is offered via a FidoNet echo mail conference called SUPERBBS. The multiline version came out in mid-1991. A single-line version, 1.10, is somewhat older and therefore more stable. As the support implies, SuperBBS is mostly built around messaging and file access.

Like QuickBBS and RemoteAccess, SuperBBS uses a menu system that must be built from scratch. If you don't want to do that, you can use a program such as MenuMaster Version 1.20 or any other menu program compatible with QuickBBS, as long as it supports 'unlisted' menu types, since SuperBBS has more menu options. The easiest menu setup would divide the board into message areas, file menus, and other menus—such as doors, games, or merchandise-ordering questionnaires.

Like TBBS, SuperBBS has a menu editor that relies on command "types," designated by number. You can also set up "hot keys" so that users can reach menus quickly, before they're painted on the screen. ANSI graphics as well as ASCII text are supported.

SuperBBS runs with DesqView and Digital Research's DoubleDOS, and it supports multitasking.

10

■────────■────────■────────■────────■

Operating BBS Software

ABOUT THIS CHAPTER

We looked at BBS software from the caller's or user's viewpoint in the last chapter. But BBS software packages have another face: the one they show to the sysop. We'll look at what options the four leading packages give the sysop, and the availability of third-party software for them.

INTRODUCTION

The remaining chapters do not represent a manual of BBS operations. Instead, think of them as a buyer's guide and a source of advice in making important business decisions regarding a BBS.

Over the last few years, four companies have come to stand out among developers of BBS software for the IBM PC, and we will profile their packages extensively. This is not to say that other packages are inferior, but if your business is to depend on any software in the 1990s, it's best to concentrate on those packages that are backed by companies of some size. All of the top four—Clark Development's PCBoard, eSoft's TBBS, Mustang's Wildcat, and Galacticomm's Major BBS—have at least a half-dozen employees and support their products both by voice lines and on their own BBSs. Each has a large installed base and hundreds of existing sysops who are happy to answer questions or, in some cases, go to work running your corporate board.

That brings up another important point: You don't have to put a top executive to work running your BBS. There are plenty of qualified sysop candidates running public boards on all four major packages. Other chapters of this book profile people who can set up your board, or run a board for you.

What you as an executive should be involved with is deciding what corporate functions your board will fulfill, what its general policies will be, and what its relationship will be to the rest of your corporate computing environment. You'll want to decide whether your board is open to the public, open only to customers, or open only to employees, for instance. Succeeding chapters will help both you and your sysop to define these policies. Pay careful attention to Chapter 13, on the laws involving BBSs, and Chapter 14, describing the true nature of the hacker risk.

Mainly, don't be afraid. BBSs are now a stable, effective technology. Increasing numbers of workers, retailers, and ordinary customers are becoming comfortable with modems and communications software. BBSs are a low-cost way to connect you to your customers, and your people to each other. At a time when budgets are under enormous pressure, BBSs can save your company money and expand its reach, with minimal risk.

PCBOARD VERSION 14.5

PCBoard has excellent documentation and many powerful features. It is a good first consideration among major BBS programs for the IBM PC.

PCBoard is among the BBS programs that behave best on a Novell or Lantastic network, although it can also be used in a multi-user configuration, with "slave cards" controlling individual nodes.

Installing PCBoard

Like many other programs, PCBoard provides a batch file called IN-STALL.BAT to help in installation. It runs from a hard disk's root directory. The main program requires 1.5 megabytes of space on a hard disk and 320 kilobytes of free memory, but it will run on any PC running DOS 3.1 or higher, even an old IBM PC XT.

To upgrade the program or run it on a network, first copy the program onto a new subdirectory, and then run the Install program, again from the root directory. In upgrading, this avoids the problem of accidentally erasing files used by the newest version, 14.5. For network users, this minimizes the impact on the overall network.

Setup for PCBoard

All the main files for PCBoard are in one directory, and all files relating to the board are in subdirectories below it. Thus, help files are in \PCB\HELP, and files used by the system operator are in \PCB\SYSOP.

Each available line, or node, on a PCBoard system will generate its own Call Waiting screen. To reach the system functions, simply disable one node through this screen, using an Alt command to enter the main system operator functions. You can reach this screen from the main PCBoard prompt with the batch file BOARD.BAT.

The sysop utilities of PCBoard require extensive use of DOS commands but allow wide customization of the user's environment. The utilities can be run using as little as 10 kilobytes of system memory. They can automatically credit users for uploading files and debit them for downloads, or let remote users quickly access door programs.

PCBSetup is the first program you'll access before putting a board online. The same program is used to change the way the board is set up. Clark Development recommends that you plan your system on paper before using PCBSetup; that's good advice. The problem isn't that PCBSetup is hard to use, but there are many different ways to configure a board, and some features can conflict with each other. Following are some helpful hints for using PCBSetup.

Security. Multiple security levels are featured. New users and novices will get little security, in order to keep them from harming the board accidentally or on purpose. But even expert users may not have the highest security clearance of the system operator. That would let them change the board's setup without permission.

File Locations. A board that has been running for a time may quickly run out of disk space. Be careful to specify other logical hard drives for files that are not essential to the actual operation of the board. Even files on users may be moved to another disk drive. And functions ancillary to the board—download directories, message bases, and chat logs—can be moved easily as well.

Modems. There are differences among modems. Fortunately, PC Board features a program called PCBMODEM that displays these different features so that you can set them up on the modem configuration screen.

Events. If you're planning to offer a public board with a lot of late-night usage, and you plan on late-night maintenance as well, check out the event menu carefully. You can use it to stop users from uploading or using other time-consuming board functions for some minutes before maintenance routines run. You may even be able to move these routines back in time, if you want, so that users can finish what they're doing.

Closing the Board.   Closing the board to people outside your company can be simple with PCBoard. It's done with a command on your options #1 PCBSetup screen. Be careful, however, to preload the names and phone numbers of registered users before closing the board.

Viewing Compressed Files.   If you like, you can let users view files that were compressed before being uploaded. This is very useful on both corporate boards and public boards, but it could keep users online longer. If you're trying to cut down on the time spent on individual online sessions, don't offer this feature.

Conferences.   Variables for setting up conferencing are in the options menu #3. Conferences take space, but they can be very useful. In a corporate board, you want to control the number of conferences to save hard disk space. A public board user will expect either a wide variety of conferences or none at all.

With PCBoard, each conference will have its own setup utility. You can make some conferences public and others private; the latter strategy is recommended for work groups. Since PCBoard lets you create up to 65,000 conferences, it's important to note where those files are being stored. If you have only a few conferences, keep them together. If you have a few hundred, spread them around among the hard disks on your network.

Main Board Configurations.   The location of crucial subdirectories, and the default privacy of messages, are saved from this screen to a file called CNAMES, which is copied to every active modem, or node, on your board. Letting users make their messages and uploads private is important—but remember that they're all public to the system operator.

There are many other parameters involved in setting up PCBoard, but the quality of the company's manual makes following them easy.

Running PCBoard

Mistakes in setting up PCBoard aren't fatal, even if the board is in operation. Most options can be changed easily by editing file locations, changing parameters, or adding and deleting sections from the board's menu. All changes are handled with the PCBSetup program.

Parameter files that can be changed include the password files; the FSEC file, which adds security to download directories, the SEC file, which does the same thing for uploads; the TCAN or trashcan file of forbidden user names, and the protocol files, a list of the download and upload protocols available with the board.

Text/graphics files that are common to most PCBoard systems include the welcome screen; the new-user bulletins, a file that appears when an unregistered user reaches a closed board; and a "warning and expired" file for boards with paying subscribers. Other common text/graphics files include a CNFN file, listing available conferences; a NEWASK file, which queries new users of the board; a NEWREG file, which handles answers to those questions; a new-user script; a log-off script; and a topic file for group chats.

Menus and configurations can also be changed easily. These files, which have the extension .LST, include the user menu, the system operator's menu, the news menu, the list of available doors leading to programs outside the BBS, the lists of available scripts and directories, and the configurations of bulletins, scripts, directories, download paths, and doors.

Doors make the purpose of your board obvious to even the casual user. Which outside programs you support tells a lot about what you want happening on your BBS. One advantage of PCBoard is that you can add security to your doors. This might be used to let only top executives work with specific spreadsheets, while allowing any caller to use the word processor or an accounting package.

Running a group of doors requires the system operator to create batch files, which are sets of commands directing the PCBoard software to the locations of specific programs. A program in a door may even be outside the main computer, linked only by a communication port.

Bulletins are a sysop's way of communicating to all users. You'll use the bulletin listing file often, but some listings, such as the board's warnings and policies, will remain constant. If you're going to be taking the board down for a time or make major changes in its operation, it's a good idea to leave a bulletin at least a few days in advance.

Scripts are important to any bulletin board. You can use any word processor or graphics editor to create them or to jazz them up. You also need to enter them into the SCRIPT.LST menu as part of your PCBSetup routine. Do this each time you create a new script or take an old one down.

Directories are especially handy if you're using your business-related board as an external mailing system. The main board and every conference will be listed separately here, and security can be added—if you're willing to do extra work to create that security. PCBoard doesn't recommend this.

Maintaining PCBoard

Unless you're changing scripts, directories, or some other major parameter of your board, much of your maintenance of a PCBoard BBS will take place from the main sysop menu. As with PCBoard users, sysops can quickly change any parameters once they learn the proper set of commands. One of the best aspects of the software, however, is that even the sysop can forget the commands and use menus. This lets you appoint subsysops for routine functions.

Among the major functions of the main sysop menu are the manipulation of the caller's log and user's list, the compression of sets of messages so that they'll take less space on the hard disk, the recovery of killed messages and list message headers, the viewing of files on the screen, and user maintenance functions.

User maintenance is very important in a business environment, because people are always being hired or fired. It's pretty simple with PCBoard. Simply choose this function from the main sysop menu, then use the **A** command to add a name, **C** to change a name, or **D** to delete a name. **F** will help you find a name, **L** will list all the names, **P** will print the list, **S** will scan the list, **U** will undelete, and **Q** is used to quit this menu. You can also find a specific user record by its number with the # command.

PCBSSYSMGR is a separate program with its own main screen. This is where you perform routine maintenance on the list of users. You can change their security levels, clear them to enter conferences, or force them out. You can use as much detail as you want in your conference permissions, giving users with the same security clearance different levels of access to different conferences. You can have long or short forms on individual users, and you can compress and sort the files in many ways. Essentially, the user list works like a database.

A separate user info file maintenance screen is used to change specific user records. You can use it to change the conferences that a user is permitted to access.

The same screen lets you edit your door list, allowing you to add and remove third-party software programs written to work with PCBoard. The same screen lets you quickly analyze problems by looking at CONFIG files; with so many functions going on at once, these can get complex and plentiful. If you like, you can also change the colors users see on your board, to give it some personality.

Public boards can take advantage of the ability to create file or byte ratio tables from the PCBSSYSMGR program. These tables make sure that users send along at least as much software as they take out of your system. Once the ratios are established, these functions run themselves.

PCBFILER works in conjunction with the setup and system manager programs. It uses files called DIR files, which are text files containing lists of other files. The power an individual user has to download specific files depends on how his or her security clearance interacts with the DIR files.

The DIR files point to other files, which may not even be on the main PCBoard hard disk. Each door and conference, as well as the main board, has its own DIR file.

The DIR file editor makes all this complexity easier to master. Once a DIR file is selected, its settings will appear on a separate screen for modification. This lets you do such things as move conferences to different disk drives, move software files to different drives, and even move files offline.

PCBMONI is used to monitor callers to the systems. It starts with a list of which users are on which nodes of the board. It also tells you which function each user is using. By invoking this program and then hitting the Enter key when a node is displayed, the system operator can, for example, lead a new user through the menus, challenge a caller who has caused problems in the past, or just hold an informal chat with a regular caller. As with most utilities in PCBoard, PCBMONI can be accessed directly from the DOS prompt or through a menu.

Conclusions

To the untrained eye, PCBoard does not look much different from other bulletin board programs. Its power, especially for the business user, lies in its ease of use, the support given it by Clark Development, and the fine manual that comes with it. The extensive use of menus for sysop functions and the ease with which it works with local area networks have made it the market leader.

There are, however, weaknesses to PCBoard. Its database functions are not the best. It's not the top choice for use in a single multi-user system; it performs best in multi-user mode as part of a network. And its chat function is a bit cumbersome. The company's support of its third-party door program authors is weak; they couldn't even supply the authors of this book with a complete list of such programs. But it's hard to go wrong with PCBoard, and you won't get fired for recommending it. (Wasn't that once said about IBM?)

Third-Party Software. Scores of doors are available to run under PCBoard. Among the more popular business-oriented ones are:

Sales Door, a system for selling products online, from Streamline Design, 1 Herron Place, Bramalea, Ontario L6S 1P3 Canada.

PC Verify, for user identification, from Curtiss Kowaliski, 2312 Vincinda Circle, Knoxville, TN 37924, BBS: 615-522-2498.

The Verify Door, for online user identication verification, from Jim Lockhart, 317 San Miguel Streets, Winter Springs, FL 32708.

THE MAJOR BBS, VERSION 5.30

One big advantage of the Major BBS is that it's easy to set up and run. With its preconfigured answers to technical questions, and setup routines on easy-to-follow menus, even someone who hasn't used a computer before can become a Major BBS sysop.

Before setting up a Major BBS system, however, think about what you want it to be. This process is more important with the Major BBS than with any other system profiled here, because the Major BBS is easier to extend and customize than other systems. You don't want to have to junk your system's organization in the middle of its growth path.

Installing the Major BBS

The Major BBS doesn't use an Install program. Instead, you create a subdirectory for the board from DOS, move into it, and copy files from the three program diskettes. These functions can also be handled with a shell program such as XTree.

Unlike such programs as PCBoard, which run best in networks, the Major BBS runs as a multi-user system, with all users generally sharing the same central chip, or CPU. So before starting your board, think about how many simultaneous users you want to support. Major BBS documents provide a chart showing how many users different types of PCs can support, depending on how fast the users' modems are. The slowest PC, for instance, will handle one fast 9,600 bps modem or four 2,400 bps modems. A computer using the fast Intel® 80386 chip at 25 MHz, on the other hand, can handle up to 32 users of 9,600 bps modems or 64 users of 2,400 bps modems. The basic software has a limit of 64 channels. To increase the usage of a Major BBS system, Galacticomm sells what it calls Breakthrough boards, which support up to 16 modems each; the Gallacti-Box, supporting 16 internal modems; and the GallactiBoard, supporting external modems.

Before proceeding to set up the Major BBS, you need to change the CONFIG.SYS file of the computer running it. This file is found in the computer's root directory. It should include the following specification to handle the largest number of files possible:

    FILES = 127

One more important point: Change the password in the software for the sysop. The password provided is simply Sysop. If you leave it at that, any hacker can enter with that password and tear up your board. Directions for changing it are in the documentation.

Setup for the Major BBS

The Major BBS is configured from a menu screen, so it's not necessary to understand DOS to set up a fairly complex system.

There is also a quick setup utility, invoked from the main configuration menu. To use it, simply enter the system's name, the company's name, its address, and the city and state in which the board is located. There's also a question 1, which asks for the arrangement of the host computer's function keys. If they're arranged along the top of the keyboard, you won't need to change the factory-installed setting. If they're along the side, change it to 2×5. If the host computer has a color screen, change the answer to question 2 to "color." However, "auto," the factory-supplied answer, will also work here.

A more complex configuration will involve accounting for users, handling the charging of fees, creating automatic routines to handle housekeeping, creating a main menu and audit trail, and setting up such functions as teleconferencing or chats, electronic mail, special interest groups (SIGs), classified ads, a registry of users, and polls and questionnaires.

Setting up each of these options is as simple as answering a set of questions. Up to 200 can be used. And in each menu there is online help available, along with "factory defaults" preset to the most common, workable answers. Following are some helpful hints.

Charging Users.   Most private boards won't charge users, but you can still use this function to track which users or departments are making the most use of the system and which aren't using it at all. Then your sysop can work on the low-usage departments with tutorials and other aids to help users reap the benefits of the system.

Configuring Hardware.   Some standard hardware configurations are shipped with the system, making this task easier than it sounds. Function keys can be used to quickly configure more complex systems, with each modem being given its own hardware channel.

Non-Hardware Channels.   Galacticomm recommends that you always keep a few channels open and available for internal use. If you buy a 64-user version of the software, for instance, activate no more than 60 or 61 channels with modems and outside lines.

Restricted Phone Lines.   If you're not charging users, don't worry about separating lines between demonstration and for-pay channels. If you are charging users, keep some lines open strictly for paying customers, and let only new users on a few lines offered as a demonstration and sign-up system.

Questionnaires.   The Major BBS comes with seven questionnaires demonstrating how this function can be used on both public and private systems. Each can have up to 20 questions, and reports are easy to generate.

In a publicly accessible system, questionnaires might refer to the system and preferences for it, or to current events of interest to the sysop. In a business system open to the public, questionnaires can help customers fill out warranty cards online, get their input for future products, or assist in product purchase by credit card. In a private system, questionnaires can quiz workers on company policy, get their opinions on recent changes in the business, and teach them about products or corporate history with a trivia quiz.

Customized reports on questionnaire results are available as new questionnaires are created. This is one of the more clever, distinctive functions of the Major BBS, and it is well worth taking advantage of.

Running the Major BBS

Operations on the Major BBS are handled through a screen called the operator console. This provides statistics on board usage, an audit trail, and a list describing current usage on the board. In addition, this screen presents a set of defined function keys you can use to access other functions:

F1   Through this function you can monitor the activity on each channel. You can follow chats or just keep track of what users are inputting on each node, or channel, of the board.

F2   This lets you send real-time messages to users. Follow this key with F1 to send the message to everyone, or follow it with a channel number to address just one user. Type the message, and tap F1 to send it.

F3   This gives you detailed statistics on the usage of the board—how many users there are and what functions they've used. If you're charging users, use the functions off this key to credit their bills and uploads.

F4   This function is for posting usage credits. If you have a private board with unlimited credits, you won't use it.

F5   Closed corporate boards aren't likely to need this function, either, but it can deliver a detailed accounting on each user of the board. If regular usage of the board is required—for salesmen or executives, for instance—this display can be used to identify the computerphobes at the firm.

F6 This function is used for log-on messages, which are like mandatory bulletins; they appear on everyone's screen as they sign onto the board. You can use it on a business-related public board to advertise specials, on a private board to let people know about special corporate events, or on a public board to give customers changing greetings or alerts on changing policies.

F7 This lets you enter the board and see it from the user's perspective. This comes in handy when you get complaints or, worse, when you're not getting the usage you expect. You can also use this function to chat with individual users.

F8 This displays real-time information about online users. This feature allows you to monitor what the board is doing at the present moment.

F9 This lets you analyze usage of the system by special interest group, by the types of callers you get, or by the type of function on the board.

F10 This is the most dangerous screen on the system. It lets you delete users, disconnect channels, and even bring the system completely down for maintenance.

Maintaining the Major BBS

The Major BBS provides a daily cleanup function. As it comes from the factory, the package activates this function at 3 A.M. each morning. As part of this routine cleanup, data on the previous day's usage are saved and the files reset to zero, and credit accounts are changed to reflect the previous day's use (or the previous month's or year's).

At the same time, it's a good idea to handle the backing up of all system files and user files as part of the daily maintenance routine. The Major BBS uses a program called Btrieve for all databases, so the last inputs are always saved to disk as you power down. You'll eventually need a powerful tape backup system to backup your mail and message databases.

There are also special considerations to maintaining the three specialized versions of the software.

The File Library Edition. The File Library Edition is designed mainly for the uploading and downloading of files: program files, text files, picture files. A large hard-disk capacity is crucial for such systems, as are regular backups of user files. You'll also need to move files around more than with other versions of the program.

It's best to keep all new uploads separate in order to check new programs for viruses, text files for relevance, and picture files. It wouldn't do to let users of a Southern Baptist board accidentally upload pictures from *Penthouse* magazine. So check all files before you move them to download libraries.

The Entertainment Edition.   Many sysops of the Entertainment Edition are hoping to make money from users' online time or from payment for messages collected in the dating registry. Account maintenance is most important here.

The Shopping Mall Edition.   Order fulfillment is the key word with the Shopping Mall Edition. You'll find yourself doing maintenance regularly, taking down changes, changing prices, adding new merchandise, and closing out lines. Handling invoices for merchants and collecting debts are also important considerations with this version of the program.

The MenuMan Edition.   With MenuMan, the maintenance schedule will be dictated by the menus added. These may be add-in programs written for the Major BBS or customized functions created by your company. The problems listed for shopping, entertainment, and libraries all apply here.

Conclusions

Of all the BBS vendors covered in this book, Galacticomm is the most dedicated to turning BBSs into successful businesses. That doesn't mean, however, that all businesses will find the Major BBS to their liking. The emphasis on tracking credits, for instance, is overdone if you're letting all verified users in free.

Although the Major BBS is great for chat, it's weak in file collections. Its basic multi-user structure makes it less appealing to those companies that put their online activities on a LAN.

If you are trying to make a profit off a BBS system, especially from chat, choose the Major BBS. If not, find something to fit the specific needs of your business. Even then, this might be the right package.

Third-Party Software

Galacticomm publishes a catalog of third-party software that runs with the Major BBS. Vendors offering business-related software include:

Prostar Software, 1821 South Central, Suite N, Kent, WA 98032, 206-949-0579, BBS: 206-941-0317. Offers a variety of netmail and system management utilities, plus "system enhancers" and games—enough to fill a 16-page catalog.

Logicom Inc., 1371 NW 80th Terrace, Plantation, FL 33322, 305-474-4850, BBS: 305-473-8203. Offerings include bulletin board forums offering anonymous postings and ANSI graphics, and Ad Master for online advertising using text of ANSI.

M.B. Murdock and Associates, P.O. Box 2194, Pinellas Park, FL 34665, 813-545-8050. Offers various system utilities plus the Adventure Writers Toolkit.

Parallax Development Co., #21 Lower Concourse, 2016 Sherwood Drive, Sherwood Park, Alberta T8A 3X3 Canada, 403-452-3626, BBS: 403-449-9199. Offers an executive billing system with credit card support, payment options, gift coupons, and electronic mail verification; and Data-View for account and usage analysis, with charting.

Infinetwork, P.O. Box 1241, Laurel, MD 20725, 301-498-6352, BBS: 301-498-6183. Offers the Electronic Classifieds, an online advertising and sales system.

MicroCom Communications Services, P.O. Box 17854, Irvine, CA 92713-7854, 714-552-5971, BBS: 714-639-7725. Offers its advertising package, featuring both "hook" and full-screen ads.

Onlinestore, Stadtle 2 Fl-9490, Vaduz, Liechtenstein, +41-75-20366, BBS: +41-75-82084, fax: +41-75-20367. Offers a German-language version of the Major BBS.

TBBS 2.2

TBBS's flexibility has a price: It takes longer to set up and customize than other programs. You'll also want to do some hard thinking before starting the process—deciding on policies and how the board will "feel" to its users.

It is possible to get a TBBS system started within minutes. The system's Install program can do everything but set up your modems, including changing your computer's AUTOEXEC.BAT file, which controls the start-up of the computer, and its CONFIG.SYS file, which sets up the computer's hardware and peripherals.

Even with the simplest system, however, you'll have to work with a TBBS package called CEDIT. This is the package's configuration editor and lets you tell TBBS about the modems connected to it. If you only have one or two modems, it should prove no problem. Switch settings for the most popular modems are included in the manual.

When you want more from the program, TBBS will deliver—but at a price. TBBS is not as difficult to use as a computer language, but it is far more difficult than most menued applications. Think of it as the dBase of BBSs.

TBBS Hardware

You can run a one- or two-line board under TBBS using an IBM PC AT compatible with 640K of memory and a hard disk. To increase the number of ports, you'll need more powerful hardware.

TBBS works with multiport serial cards such as the Digiboard. The manual features extensive documentation for getting these products to work with the software. The manual warns, for instance, that old IBM PC XTs and ATs won't let you address more than two serial ports, so if one computer will be running your entire BBS, you'll probably need a Digiboard (or something like it) to get going. eSoft sells an "Interrupt Daisy Chain" cable enabling you to install two Digiboards on a single PC AT. Adding more is technically possible but could leave you with very slow system. TBBS supports and sells the Digiboard but will not offer trade-ins on Digiboards that it doesn't sell. Other multiport boards are not supported but can often be used.

TBBS includes 40 separate menu commands, which you can mix and match as you prefer. Version 2.2 can support an unlimited number of message areas. These sections can be offered in the same treelike form that Unix systems use, with subdirectories separated by dots, as in TBBS.menu commands. To customize the program, you'll need to work with three editor programs: CEDIT, MEDIT, and QAL.

CEDIT

The program CEDIT.COM creates or edits a configuration file called CONFIG.CTL, which in turn controls the MTLBBS.EXE and ML-HOST.COM programs, which do the work of running a TBBS system. It is controlled from a series of menus.

Message boards come preloaded in a sample file called CONFIG.CTL, but you can define up to 63. Two board names are reserved: msg to sysop and netmail. You can limit the availability of other boards to users with specific access privileges and decide what can be done on each. You can limit some to e-mail or allow private messages, the enclosing of files with messages, and the combining of messages with those from other boards. There's a separate line, with options, for every conference you set up on the board. On a large board you may want to have assistants set their own policies on their own message boards. They'll either have to learn CEDIT or take change requests to the sysop.

TBBS comes preloaded to run with 25 different types of terminals. It will use one of these files in response to user prompts. Be careful in making changes: you may lose track of standard configurations and be unable to retrieve them. If you have a private board and know what type of terminal every user will have, you can define it here and avoid giving users terminal options each time they sign on.

Events that you can define within TBBS include both those internal to the software and those outside it. Internal events might include limitations on the use of chat or changes in your log-on and log-off greetings. External events include the use of housekeeping programs that will take TBBS down for a time. You'll want to set them to run late at night. Often such events as compressing mail messages and sending them to other boards can be handled from a batch file; an example is included in the manual.

CEDIT also offers an options menu, **o** off the main menu. This lets the sysop list the board's current configuration or change any of the elements within it.

System options include many policy questions, including the ability to disconnect an unregistered user before log-on, and a choice of time after which the system will hang up on inactive users of the board.

Ports, lines, and modem options let the sysop define precisely what types of modems are on what lines of the board. Whenever you move modems around, add modems, or change modems because of a failure, you'll need to use this screen to notify TBBS of the change. You can also set certain modems to work only at certain hours or change menus based on the modem speed used by a caller.

Message board options include more questions of policy. Will you let users delete their old messages? Can they forward messages? How will you handle chains of messages—should they be automatically followed? At what minimum privacy level can messages be forwarded? Should passwords be required on public messages? How many messages can be online at once? The answers will differ for every board, and they need to be considered before this screen is accessed.

Menu format options include the handling of ANSI graphic screens. TBBS lets you create the equivalent of "pull-down" menus for users who can handle ANSI terminal graphics. (Most modem software programs support ANSI.) This screen will also let you control the use of chatting between nodes and handle time limits for board use by various classes of users. In a paid system, these are true "billing classes," as indicated on the screen. For a private system, the classes might represent different types of users—employees, customers, and resellers, for instance.

Dayfile options control the logging of information on system usage. The answers to these reporting questions will be complied in a file called DAYFILE.LST, sent either to a printer or to a disk drive. You can also get more or less detail on the activities of callers by changing the options on this screen.

Log-on options control how the system acts when people attempt to call it. Here is where you have the most control over the security of a TBBS system. You can close the board off to new users, require only a password, or set the system to call back and verify new users. You will also use this screen to set your own sysop log-on here, as well as to file greetings, new files, and new user files.

New-user defaults specify exactly what new, unverified users will be able to do on a TBBS board, and for how long. You can set time limits, call limits, limits on the number of minutes spent downloading files, or restrictions on the use of other functions. If you're not allowing new users, this screen will be meaningless.

MEDIT

The ability to fully customize menus is one of the strengths of TBBS. One way to do it is with a program called MEDIT, which creates files of the form MENU????.CTL. These files, when displayed, form the command interface between users and the BBS.

A TBBS system can have as many menus as the sysop wants, and each can "call" another menu; the main menu can respond to a message base command to bring up a messaging menu, for instance. TBBS will support up to 132 columns in a single line, but not all user terminals can support this many; most IBM PC screens support just 24 lines of 80 columns. Whom you expect to log in, and with what equipment, will determine how you design menus.

To make life a little easier, TBBS comes preloaded with three sample menus, and some systems make do with them alone. If users are experienced with TBBS, it may be a good idea to use some of these commands in your menus, but it is not necessary.

Each menu line consists of three elements, and MEDIT will display each entry on three lines for the sysop during editing. The first line identifies the command's name, an explanation, and a one-character shortcut to invoking it. The second line features the various privilege codes relating to the menu item—who can use it, in other words. The third line shows the key to be used in activating the function, its command type from the TBBS control summary —there are 54 in all—and the location of data vital to the execution of the command (subdirectories for the TBBS program or mail, for instance).

Using MEDIT starts with two menus, one allowing for the creation or editing of menus and a second relating to the basic MEDIT functions. You can list entries, add an entry at the end of a menu, insert an entry in the middle, change an entry, delete an entry, move an entry, change an entry's title, change an entry's billing class, or save the changes and quit editing.

Each menu control file you create must provide some exit for users—either a log-off or transfer to another menu. Because TBBS menu construction is so flexible, omiitting this step is a mistake that is easy to make.

SDL

There's a second way to create menus: a compiler called SDL (for system definition language). SDL comes with extensive documentation and is a regular feature of TBBS. Programs written using SDL can be compiled into .CTL files used on either a single- or multiline TBBS system.

The compiling function is invoked with a simple DOS command:

SDL source[,{listing}][/T][/M:nnnn]

The source is the name of the file you've created in SDL, including a path or drive name, if needed. The listing switch indicates whether or not you want a listing file produced with the extension .LST. This will include the fully expanded SDL file along with source line numbers; it can become quite large. The **/T** option indicates you want a "test compile"; if you use it, no .CTL files will be written. The **/M** option with its **nnnn** qualifier indicates that you want to compile a specific, named menu.

Example: The following command would compile Menu0000.CTL from the source file Sample.lst and generate the listing file D:\listing\sample.lst:

SDL sample,d:\listing\sample /m:0000

SDL consists of a series of directives, keywords, and arguments, and it features a macro capability that can make the results more readable, controlling the source file during system creation and maintenance. It has two major operations: macro definition and menu creation.

Directives are followed immediately by a colon and may be indented for clarity. Directives that end blocks, however, cannot be indented. A directive may contain an argument, such as the name of a macro, but it cannot consist of fewer than two characters. The two most common directives are Macro: and Menu:.

Keywords are used to specify an argument. They end with an = sign and are followed immediately by an argument. Keywords and arguments can share lines or be put on separate lines.

Arguments are names of commands, either modified keywords, directives, or macros. Arguments must leave one or more spaces at the end of a line, except for the text parameter on the Opt Data= keyword, which must appear at the end of a line.

Macros are called into an SDL program with the @ character. For example, a macro called Benefit would be called into the program with

@Benefit. Each macro may pass up to nine arguments, placed in parentheses and separated by commas. They can be nested up to 25 levels deep and used as parameters in defining other macros.

Any line in an SDL program can refer to any of the powers, menu entry types, or other options used elsewhere in TBBS. That's what makes it so powerful. Think of SDL as a script-writing program under TBBS.

Messaging

A number of TBBS files have to work together closely to create a working message base, including MEDIT, CEDIT, and USERLOG.BBS.

MEDIT includes all the commands that are offered on TBBS menus. This file works with the CEDIT message board definitions to create message databases in files called MSGHDR.BBS and MSG.BBS. The first file consists of menu headers and index pointers, the second of the messages themselves. They all work together with the USERLOG.BBS file to tell users, when they log on, about the status of messages waiting for them.

A sysop can predefine nearly any type of message search procedure in MEDIT—searching backward or forward through the message base, looking for new or marked messages, those from a specific individual, or those on a specific subject.

You can also define what users can do with messages—whether they can forward them to other users, delete them, or download files enclosed with them. Sysops can even allow for the creation of chains, called "threads" in some systems. These are related messages that may not follow one another directly but relate to the same subject.

QAL

QAL lets you write question-and-answer scripts. But don't think of this as a mere election function. Surveys can be used for online merchandise ordering, for surveying customers, or for other purposes.

Three types of files are accepted by QAL. Survey files can be constructed to accept answers as long as 250 characters. Voting files accept only a single keystroke and are limited by the number of entries offered. You can build questionnaires using ANSI graphics, covering entire screens.

Surveys.   Surveys are created by typing in questions and appending a single-digit control code, that tells TBBS how to handle answers. The following types of questions are allowed, and you can mix or match types on a single survey.

Questions that save answers in a file, as in a consumer survey

Questions that save answers for verification, as in an order entry system

Yes/no questions that are aborted to the menu upon an **N,** so that users can "bail out" of the survey

Yes/no questions that verify orders with a "yes" answer and save them to a "verified" buffer

Yes/no questions that do not move "yes" answers to a "verified" buffer

Questions that display text with no expectation of an answer

Voting.   Voting files are simpler than survey files. They accept only single-keystroke answers, which are further limited by the number of options in the question. If you're giving users seven possible answers, for example, the number 8 becomes an invalid answer.

Answers to voting files can be displayed in a file called VOTESUM, which can be made a menu item in its own right.

You can also make sure on vote or survey files that users enter answers only once, by automatically resetting the flags on their authorizations after they vote. This makes such authorizations useful even on private systems.

Conclusions

If you want a bulletin board system you can set up and run quickly, TBBS may not be for you. It is not the best of the lot in terms of working on local area networks, either. But TBBS can be customized in many ways its competitors cannot be. And its database capabilities put it head-and-shoulders above the crowd for companies that need databases.

Third-Party Software

Most of the third-party software for TBBS systems is produced or published by Pete White and his firm, GW Associates, P.O. Box 6606, One Regency Drive, Holliston, MA 01746, 508-429-6227, BBS: 508-429-1784. A catalog of the latest offerings can be downloaded from his BBS.

Of the three dozen programs available at this writing, the main business-related ones include:

On-Line Sales Manager, which is touted as handling all aspects of selling, except inventory management, and lets you attach text files to items in the catalog.

User Manager, which handles user billing and access status and alerts selected users to software upgrades they are entitled to. It will accept credit card payment with algorithms to check for invalid numbers.

Message Manager, which replaces the message-base functions of TBBS with a new system that has no limitations on the number of messages and allows anonymous postings (popular on conferences devoted to nonmainstream practices).

Connection Exchange, software for online matchmaking and dating services. Users can attach .GIF files of themselves.

TDBS

TDBS is one of the most important BBS programs, and if you need the capability, it is a good reason to buy TBBS instead of a competitor. TDBS is, simply put, a dBase III+—compatible compiler program. It allows you to write programs in the dBase language, which can then be run on a TBBS system.

There are some differences between TDBS and dBase; some dBase commands make no sense in TDBS and are omitted, and TDBS has commands of its own to take advantage of the shared environment. But TDBS and dBase III+ files are generally compatible, and TDBS will directly compile both .PRG and .FMT format files, written to be used by dBase. One important difference is that TDBS data memory is limited to 48 kilobytes per user, whereas dBase lets you use up to the PC's 640 kilobyte limit.

Another important point: TDBS is by nature a multi-user program. It automatically arbitrates when two users access the same data, automatically updates screens of users when new data are input, and integrates mail with the database program.

TDBS Commands

The following list should not be considered a TDBS manual, but merely a sampling of the important TDBS commands:

@   Used in combination with directions to clear, display, and draw on sections of the user's screen

APPEND   Adds records from an ASCII text file or other database file to the database

CLEAR   Releases variables and other commands, or clears the screen

COPY   Copies files and databases, or creates an empty database file while saving field definitions

ON   Used for handling errors and unusual inputs, ranging from accidental disconnects from the board to the use of the Escape key

SET   Used to create defaults for users, ranging from whether exact matches are required for character comparisons to whether the Return key is needed to start a function

USE   Can open an existing database or mailbox, along with the associated commands

ZAP   Removes all records from the active database file

All of the TDBS commands are given a full page of explanation in the TDBS manual, which is actually better than the main TBBS manual in terms of clarity.

TDBS Functions

Functions are just as important to TDBS, or dBase, as commands. These are internal operations used in conjunction with commands either to confirm the status of items or to operate on specific pieces of data. TDBS provides all the standard dBase language functions, plus some extended functions. Use of the extended functions, of course, will make your TDBS program incompatible with other dBase dialects.

Functions can be nested up to 20 levels deep, making the programs easier to read, and they can be used to modify one another. They're more difficult to learn than commands because few are complete words. We've tried to define them in terms of complete words for clarity. Here are just a few:

ABS   Returns the absolute value of an expression

CAPFIRST   Returns a copy of an expression, with the first letter of it capitalized

DATE()   Returns today's date as a value in date type (for example, 010191 is January 1, 1991)

DESCEND()   Allows for creation and seeking of descending-order indexes

FCOUNT()   (Field count) Returns the number of fields in the current work area

FKLABEL   (Function key label) Returns the text name assigned to a specific function key by the program

ISSHARE   (Is shared) Can determine if a database or mailbox is currently being shared

LJUST   Left-justifies an expression as it's displayed

NUSERS()   Returns the number of users currently linked to the TDBS program

REPLICATE   Replicates a character string a specific number of times

UAUTH   (You authorized) Returns a list of your authorization files

UIBM()   (You have IBM graphics?) Asks whether or not you are using IBM graphics

USING   Determines which lines are using a shared work area

WAIT4RLOCK   (Wait for record lock) Waits for a record to be locked or for a specific amount of time to elapse before locking the record

Again, all of the TDBS functions are given a full page of explanation in the TDBS manual.

Conclusions

TDBS can be used to perform many important functions on a corporate board. It can let a distributor maintain a product catalog for use by retailers, for instance. It can let a retailer offer answers to customer support questions in a very user-friendly fashion. It can be used, in other words, for any kind of shared database function. Its possibilities are limited only by your imagination.

If you decide to use TBBS, find a use for TDBS as well. You'll be glad you did.

WILDCAT 3.0

In August 1991, Mustang Software delivered a complete rewrite of its Mustang BBS software. Version 3.0 is far easier for a sysop to use, and much more powerful, than the program it replaces.

Version 3.0 of Wildcat makes extensive use of menus. There are menus to set up each section of the board, menus to keep track of board activity, and menus everywhere for the users.

Version 3.0 is also a multi-user Wildcat. There are sections in the new manual covering the use of Wildcat with multi-user systems and slave cards, with networks from Novell and Lantastic, and with DesqView 386, a DOS operating environment that allows for multitasking.

Version 3.0 also has greatly improved support for external programs, or doors, through a DOORS.SYS file, which the company hopes to make a standard in the industry.

Finally, the new version of the program not only supports echo networks such as FidoNet, but it also can be linked with doors to outside services such as CompuServe and MCI Mail. This makes it a much more powerful tool in the corporate environment, where it can become a complete communications door on a local network.

Installing Wildcat

Installation of the program now starts from a program called Winstall, whose first screen controls the subdirectories to be used for needed files on your hard disk. The main program uses a directory called \WC30, and other sections of the board, including configuration files for modems and utilities, are put in subdirectories underneath it. Directory \WC30 must be part of your DOS path for the program to work correctly.

Upgrading from an earlier version of Wildcat is made easier by a program called WUPGRAD.EXE, which works off a menu listing all previous versions of the program. Behind these selections are configuration menus and pop-up windows, with defaults to convert all databases for use with the new version. When you're finished, selecting Start Upgrade makes everything else automatic.

There is one caveat: Due to the massive structural changes in this upgrade, no utility programs for earlier versions of the program that interacted with CONFIG files or databases will operate with Wildcat Version 3.0. However, updated versions of all popular utilities were tested along with Version 3.0, so upgrades on those should be available.

Configuring Wildcat

Configuration of a Wildcat BBS is handled through a program called MAKEWILD.EXE, which, like the program's other features, runs off a menu. Most screens behind this menu require you to simply fill in the blanks from your keyboard; the program also works with a mouse. A few of the screen fields use pop-up windows to simplify things further. Some have pick-lists, windows that allow for the selection of multiple items from the menu.

The General Information Definition screen in Makewild is filled in with simple information such as the sysop's or company's name, the board's name, the registration number of the software, and the number of conferences, file areas, doors, screen programs, and nodes on the board. Also listed here are the location of various Wildcat subdirectories, where the program can access data on users, files, nodes, and messages.

A second page of questions is even simpler to fill out. These ask about the use of ANSI color menus, the setting of a default file compression extension, and the setting a time for maintenance events. A third screen sets security defaults and even lets the sysop limit writing to the screen. Multiple choices are toggled using the space bar.

The Security Definition screen is used to close the board to outside callers, to allow or disallow a transfer to DOS for users, to verify callers' locations as they log in, to set a limit on the number of password attempts allowed, and even to lock out callers if they fail to pass the security test. You can require the use of birth dates and home phone numbers for added security and require passwords for downloading files.

There are two screens for defining modems. The first Modem Definition screen lists such things as the communications port, its IRQ and base address, the baud rate of the modem, and a number of other technical choices. Fortunately, there are three standard setups; one should be right for your modem. The modems that will fit each standard setup are listed in the manual. A modem with nonvolatile memory (NRAM) must also be set up with the program WCMODEM.EXE, and the same program is used to test and troubleshoot the modem interface.

The second Modem Definition screen features the messages used when modems of different speeds dial into your system. There are also standard error correction codes, on-hook and off-hook strings, and reset and answer strings, all taken from the Hayes AT command set. You should not have to set these codes differently than indicated in the manual.

The External Protocol Definition screen lets you add additional file transfer protocols to your system. This means you can use batch protocols based on the DSZ version of Zmodem from Omen Technologies, which offers a standard system of support for batch file transfers (see Chapter 5).

The Main Menu Definition screen lets you customize the appearance of your BBS main menu, allowing you to delete some commands or change the characters used to access them. You can also change the order in which commands are presented and the level of security needed to access them. The Message Menu Definition screen lets you customize message conferences in the same way you can customize the main menu, and the File Menu Definition screen allows you to customize your file collections. You can change the names of commands, the letters used to access them, and the security levels needed to use them.

The Sysop Menu Definition screen lets you define the security levels needed to perform the various duties of a sysop. Only the actual sysop should have absolute control over the system. The highest security level is 1,000.

Wildcat permits you to create up to 1,000 different security levels, each with different permissions and powers. The Security Profile Definition screen lets you create and maintain these security profiles. You can enable or disable the use of file transfer protocols, enable or disable access to specific conferences or doors, and even change the types of menus and displays accessed by different callers. Other standard security features supported here are daily time limits, upload/download ratios, and the maximum number or size of downloads available to users. The security profiles will be most extensive on public for-pay systems, but you may also define separate but related security levels for different work groups on a corporate system.

Wildcat supports up to 1,000 different file areas, defined on the File Area Definition screen using pop-up windows. Once you name a file area, the pop-up window will let you create a path where files from that area will reside. A second pop-up window will let you choose the level of security needed to reach it and the message conferences that can list it.

Wildcat 3.0 supports up to 1,000 different conferences, defined through a Conference Definition screen, which works much like the File Area Definition screen. You can list paths for the conference menus, display files and messages, appoint conference sysops, limit the length of messages and the number of questionnaires, and toggle such things as file attachments, return receipts, and private messages, as well as the use of aliases. This screen also lets you link individual conferences to netmail systems such as FidoNet or Novell's Message Handling System (MHS), which can store and forward messages among different applications. This is a crucial new feature, but a complete understanding of it requires use of Novell's MHS Gateway documentation. Once you create a conference, you can copy all the definitions quickly from the Conference Definition menu using the F3 key.

The Door Definition screen will reflect the number of doors listed on the first General Information Definition screen. Here you define them by name and specify whether a door can be used by more than once person at once.

The Idle Screen Definition screen also reflects back to the first General Information Definition settings. This lets you run programs from the program's Call Waiting screen via a menu. This is especially important for regular maintenance.

After running Makewild you'll still need to configure each modem to be attached to the board. This is done with a program called WCMO-DEM.EXE.

Running Wildcat

While Wildcat 3.0 is running you may still access many functions if no users are online, using function keys. You can turn the keyboard and printer on and off, turn on a bell that will page you if a user wants to chat, or run any of the Idle Screen applications defined in Makewild. You can also use Alt-key combinations to display space available on all drives used by Wildcat, show the status of various modems or nodes, reset the board's use statistics, or log on locally to see how the board looks from the outside.

Another set of Alt keys and function keys are used when callers are online. You can type F6 and chat with a caller, add or remove user time, and even upgrade or downgrade user security levels. You can also create up to nine text files alerting callers that they're being logged off immediately or in 15 minutes, activating them with an Alt-number combination. This is important if you're planning unscheduled maintenance.

Wildcat lets you create dozens of text files that can be sent to callers for specific purposes. They can be created using any word processor that delivers pure ASCII text, without print control codes. Some, activated by the Alt-number combinations as just mentioned, can be used to log callers off, immediately or later.

You'll also find such files as the BADFILES.LST, which prevents people from uploading files whose names duplicate existing Wildcat filenames, or related files such as ZUP.BAT, the Zmodem batch upload file. You can specify other disallowed filenames through a file called BADKEYS.LST. If your board won't accept handles or aliases, it's easy to prevent users from logging on with them by listing them in the BADNAMES.LST file, and then telling callers using aliases about their banishment with the BAD-NAMES.BBS message.

Some of the message files are pure public relations, such as BIRTH-DAY.BBS, displayed if a user calls in on his or her listed birthday. Others are more important, such as the bulletins you can write and list in the BULLETIN.BBS submenu file, saved under BULL#.BBS filenames. The DOORS.BBS submenu file will list available doors, and the CON-FLIST.BBS file will list the conferences available. By creating and updating these text files, you can easily give your Wildcat board its own look and feel.

One unique aspect of Wildcat is that it has two ways to deliver color menus to callers. The first uses ANSI terminal emulation. The second method involves embedded codes, set off by the @ key, which can be entered using a text editor. You can use these color codes to add colors to words within messages or to headings. You can also use color to set off important information about the BBS or about the user. A list of labels that can be customized in this way appears in the program's documentation.

Wildcat 3.0 Add-Ins

Mustang made a number of major announcements at the 1991 Fall Comdex computer convention in Las Vegas. As a result, companies that want to link a local area network to a BBS can now find excellent support for that effort. Says president Jim Harrer, "We are now a LAN-based

BBS. Our whole focus is linking people on a local area network to people dialing in remotely."

- *BBServer.* This was the lead announcement, according to president Jim Harrer. "It's a dedicated server for connectivity to manage the BBS. A lot of our corporate accounts load Wildcat on their server, and they get alarmed. This is a completely separate solution, where you have a server dedicated to the BBS, handling all incoming lines. When people locally want to log on they just attach to it. It's one-directional, so even if someone logs in with your name and password they can't get onto other servers in the network."

- *MCI Gateway.* This is an add-in to Wildcat 3.0, that lets you link to MCI Mail, from a local area network, through the BBS. Users on a LAN could share an MCI Mail mailbox.

- *MHS Gateway.* This program not only lets you link the BBS directly to a Novell NetWare LAN through its MHS standard, but it can also be used to link two Wildcat BBSs together. It works much like an echo-mail program, combining messages, sending them in bulk, and receiving messages in bulk from the other system. Through Wildcat, this could allow companies with operations in many different countries to link their LANs at the lowest possible cost.

- *CIS Gateway.* Like the other gateways, this is an add-in program that links to another type of system. In this case, the other system is CompuServe. With this feature, a company can answer user questions on CompuServe, which has over 850,000 members around the world, simply by purchasing a regular membership and mailbox, and then uploading and downloading mail messages each night. The alternative is to spend thousands of dollars creating a CompuServe "forum", which offers many BBS services but is maintained on CompuServe's own mainframes in Columbus, Ohio.

- *FAX Gateway.* In this case, it's not a system that's being linked, but fax machines. With this add-in, users of your board can create and send messages to remote fax machines directly from the board, once a separate fax card is installed in the computer housing your board. The current version of the gateway, however, does not support incoming faxes.

Wildcat Doors

Wildcat sells a number of add-in programs that run as doors with it. Some can be very important.

Wildcat has a provision for scanning file uploads for viruses immediately, while a caller is online. It's done through a batch file called SCAN-FILE.BAT in the program's home directory. The batch file can call up a standard virus-checking program as a door, run it even on compressed files, and report back immediately if a virus signature is detected.

Wildcat also offers support for CD-ROM optical drives. It can load directories of the CD-ROM drive onto a magnetic hard drive, speeding searches of them. Wildcat can also quickly find the location of a file on the CD-ROM, speeding downloads.

Wildcat is capable of integrating with several mainframe systems, including MCI Mail and CompuServe, as well as systems using Novell's MHS format. These gateways make use of the Wildcat event manager, which sets a time and date for the gateway to operate using a batch file. This means that messages on your BBS can be shared with CompuServe or MCI Mail users. This new feature can greatly reduce the cost of product support. Simply set up a CompuServe or MCI Mail mailbox, and then use this mail door to download those messages rapidly and at the lowest possible cost. Have your support staff answer the messages at leisure through the BBS, and then return them to your customers through the same door.

The MHS Gateway is also supported by a large number of corporate e-mail packages, including cc:Mail. This can help make your BBS a part of your regular corporate computer system.

Conclusions

Version 3.0 of Wildcat is a fine program, and it shows the direction that competitors will likely follow in their upgrades. Its menued operation structure will let even casual PC users become corporate BBS sysops. Its gateways to other mail systems point the way to greater integration of electronic mail worldwide. And the manual for Version 3.0 of the program is truly excellent. It sets a high standard, which we're certain the competition will in time meet.

Third-Party Software

Mail utilities for Wildcat systems are sold by Online Computer Resources, 4330-J Clayton Road, Concord, CA 94521, 415-687-0236, BBS: 415-687-0236. The chief product is Wildmail, a shareware package that distributes mail packets in the Fido protocol to the Wildcat message base.

Wildcat products are also available from Technique Computer Systems of Victoria, British Columbia, Canada.

11

Ten Top BBSs

ABOUT THIS CHAPTER

We'll look at 10 leading BBSs in North America.

INTRODUCTION

Hard work. Offering customers what they want. These sound like old-fashioned values, but in the new-fashioned BBS world, they amount to a prescription for success.

The boards profiled in this chapter are not the 10 largest BBSs in the United States, nor are they the most profitable. They were chosen because they represent the diverse threads along which BBSs are turning into profitable businesses, or because they offer services of particular interest to businesses.

Given the lead times and shelf lives of most books, and given the extremely high turnover rate for most boards—the average public board stays online less than a year—we also based this list on longevity and potential staying power. In this respect, a board's reputation among other sysops was considered crucial.

In the BBS world, it is possible for a hobby to turn into an avocation, and then into a career. Many of the sysops who got into the business for something other than money are earning the greatest rewards now. Within the decade, some of the sysops you'll read about here will likely become millionaires. And they'll have gotten there the old-fashioned way—by earning it, and by putting customers' needs first.

EXEC-PC

Sysop: Bob Mahoney
414-789-4210
Milwaukee, Wisconsin

There are many big public bulletin board systems in the United States. But everyone agrees that there's none bigger than Bob Mahoney's Exec-PC (main menu shown in Figure 11.1), with 250 nodes and growing. But Mahoney insists he didn't start out to become the CompuServe of the bulletin board business. Exec-PC just grew beyond his wildest dreams.

It started as a small, public board in 1983, dedicated like its fellows to the distribution of "shareware," software that the authors allow to be copied for free in the hope that active users will pay for documentation and updates. Mahoney's goal was to make his name public and, perhaps, to find some computer consulting work.

Mahoney was heavily influenced by Gene Plantz, who still runs the IBBS board in Hoffman Estates, Illinois. Plantz's was the second board Mahoney ever called, back in 1982. Plantz's user interface was "quick and efficient," Mahoney recalls, and while he was friendly with regular, well-behaved users, he kept the annoying eight balls from hurting others. Also, "Gene recognized the IBM PC as a de facto standard real early on. He was one of the first few boards for the IBM PC."

Bob's interest in telecommunications, however, reaches further back in time. He worked with very early online systems at the University of Wisconsin, getting a BS in computer science at the Madison campus, and

```
Exec-PC  T O P   M E N U
<?>help ....... HELP with this menu
<S>ubscribe ... Subscribe or Renew for Exec-PC full access
<B>ulletins ... Info about this BBS
<H>elp ........ HELP on the most often asked questions
<R>ead mail ... Read all pending messages addressed to me
<F>ile ........ File Collections
<M>essage ..... Message system
<E>nvironment . Change my password, address, prompts, etc.
<A>nsi/color .. Turn on/off color and graphics from BBS
<L>ist users .. Info on other users
<W>ho ......... Who is on the system right now?
<X>pert ....... Toggle expert mode (short or long menus)
<G>oodbye ..... Log off system (hang up)


(61 minutes left) < TOP (SBHFMREALWXG, ?=HELP) -> G
```
Figure 11.1 Exec-PC Main Menu

then an MBA with a business data systems orientation from the Milwaukee campus in 1978. He went to work right away with ADP Network Services, which was selling computer time from giant mainframes but, uniquely, allowing users to own their data.

In 1981 Mahoney switched jobs and began managing the information center for American Appraisal Inc., in Milwaukee. "They assigned me the task of helping users, taking care of telecommunication links. We gave users their first chance to access corporate databases directly, with their own user-friendly tools. When the IBM PC came out, I insisted on being the PC coordinator and introduced hundreds of PCs (to the company)."

By sheer accident, Exec-PC became one of the largest PC bulletin boards in the country when it opened in November 1983. "I'd gotten a 30 megabyte hard drive" on a consulting project from Shell Oil after ordering a smaller drive. So, "I collected business-oriented files from every board around for the IBM PC."

Within two months Exec-PC added a second phone line, or node. By the following November that line too was in steady use. By March 1985 Exec-PC had six lines and was charging $10 for a three-month membership, or $35 for a year. A month after that, Mahoney quit his job with American Appraisal, going into PC sales to fortify his income from the board. Among his clients were the NASA Ames Research Center and General Mills' corporate headquarters.

"A lot of people today still think they can collect $100,000 in venture capital, put up a system and retire," Mahoney notes. "People go bankrupt that way. I didn't push the system to be self-supporting. That helped me keep rates down and excitement up. We kept fun a priority above the desire to make money."

Mahoney finally hired his first full-time employee in 1991. Tim Semo runs the Exec-PC 64-line chat service under the nom de keyboard Data. That service, which runs the Major BBS software package from Galacticomm, opened in April 1991. Exec-PC is also installing five CD-ROM drives with 15 gigabytes of storage and is testing modems that run at 14,400 bits per second, from US Robotics.

To access Exec-PC, use eight-bit words, no parity, one stop bit, and the ANSI terminal emulation available in most communications packages. If you have a color screen on your PC, you'll be delighted with the color-coding Exec-PC offers. Even in monochrome, however, the menus are simple to understand.

Like most bulletin board systems, Exec-PC uses a set of single-letter commands, most of which are self-evident to regular BBS users. **F** leads to the file collections, **R** reads the mail, and **G** means goodbye, or log-off. Unlike the case with most boards, however, the actual software used by Exec-PC is proprietary. It makes extensive use of "hot keys," which you can use before a menu is painted to go on immediately to the next menu. The result is incredibly fast response for such a large system. This means you can get the benefit of the board's expert mode as soon as you learn a few commands.

In addition to letting callers move between collections quickly or search for files by keyword using an exclusive search feature called Hyper-Scan, Mahoney lets his callers learn about people who have uploaded software, and he lets them set a default transfer protocol from within the file menu. Most boards don't give out information on uploaders and allow protocols to be changed only on sign-up or from a special parameters menu. Exec-PC supports most of the popular upload and download protocols, which are also accessible with a single-letter command.

As with most of today's large boards, however, there's no real secret to Exec-PC's speed and power. Like its competitors, the board runs on a local area network, with its software running as an application under Novell Netware software. Each of the board's four file servers has its own PC network, but to users all this power is transparent. It really does feel like you're talking to one computer.

Besides going to a network, Mahoney's other major change came in 1989, when he moved the board out of his house and into a nearby office building. Wisconsin Bell dug a trench a quarter-mile from that office to its local switch. "We can easily have 500 PCs in this one room we've put together," he says. The chat system runs on a separate phone number with an X.25 packet link to the main board, which means that users can access it off Exec-PC's main number.

To protect against viruses, Mahoney tests every piece of software that comes in. He downloads it by wire to a floppy disk–based PC, and he unplugs that PC from the network before running the program. The custom software provides further protection. "And we warn people that if you are virus-nervous, don't download files until they've aged for two weeks."

Although Mahoney takes precautions, he downplays the threat. "When viruses first got popularized we were afraid it would be the end of our business. It slowed our growth, but not everyone believed the sensational news stories. We have yet to have an instance, with 600 kilobytes of downloads per month, of someone getting a virus infection from our BBS."

What makes Bob Mahoney special among bulletin board operators isn't just his board, but the way he approaches every question from a user's perspective. He knows that, in addition to his own charges, all his users must find a way to reach his board via phone.

That's why, when a small firm called CompuCom released an inexpensive, nonstandard 9,600-baud modem this year, Mahoney ignored the technical objections in his own mind (for example, it doesn't meet standards like the V.32 modulation scheme) and bought some for his users. "If the CompuCom isn't popular in two years, but it's paying for itself in four months, who cares?" he asks. That's also why he became a node on the Connect-USA network, offering inexpensive phone access to most users day and night.

By thinking like a user, Mahoney has expanded his business enough to take a niche away from huge mainframe-based services such as CompuServe and GEnie. The author of an uploaded program called PONYEZ.ZIP recently told Mahoney of his own experience. One week after loading the program on a variety of services, there were 15 downloads from McGraw-Hill's BIX service, 48 each on CompuServe and GEnie, and 122 on Exec-PC.

CANADA REMOTE

Sysop: Jud Newell
416-629-7000
Demo: 416-798-4713
Mississauga, Ontario, Canada

Despite having filed for bankruptcy in 1990, Canada Remote (main menu shown in Figure 11.2) remains the second most successful bulletin board system in North America. New president Neil Fleming says the board had 140 lines in mid-1991, 19 gigabytes of storage, and 9,000 registered users. Canada Remote solidified its position in October 1991 by buying CityLink, a Toronto board specializing in chat services and running TBBS software. Canada Remote itself runs PCBoard.

Like Exec-PC, it runs Novell Netware 386. Canada Remote has an Ethernet backbone, with four file servers and PC ATs chained off it using Arcnet. What the user sees is PCBoard software, says Fleming.

Aside from the annual subscription, there are no membership requirements, such as the upload/download ratios used by hobby boards to ensure fresh supplies of software, or the hourly charges of such services as CompuServe.

How could such a large system go under? Founder Jud Newell tried to use his profits to go into other businesses and became overextended, says Fleming. The board is now carrying only its own bills and is doing well financially.

Newell, who remains the board's system operator and driving force, was an accountant in Toronto when he opened a one-line Remote C/PM system in May 1981. "This became an obsession right away, a job in 1985," he says. "We got into dealing with other boards, calling over the world, running high phone bills. It just got too big to run as a hobby."

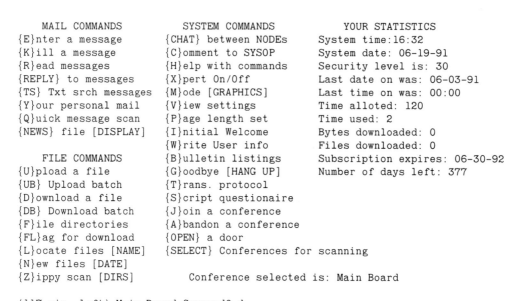

```
      MAIL COMMANDS           SYSTEM COMMANDS           YOUR STATISTICS
{E}nter a message        {CHAT} between NODEs       System time:16:32
{K}ill a message         {C}omment to SYSOP         System date: 06-19-91
{R}ead messages          {H}elp with commands       Security level is: 30
{REPLY} to messages      {X}pert On/Off             Last date on was: 06-03-91
{TS} Txt srch messages   {M}ode [GRAPHICS]          Last time on was: 00:00
{Y}our personal mail     {V}iew settings            Time alloted: 120
{Q}uick message scan     {P}age length set          Time used: 2
{NEWS} file [DISPLAY]     {I}nitial Welcome          Bytes downloaded: 0
                         {W}rite User info          Files downloaded: 0
      FILE COMMANDS      {B}ulletin listings        Subscription expires: 06-30-92
{U}pload a file          {G}oodbye [HANG UP]         Number of days left: 377
{UB} Upload batch        {T}rans. protocol
{D}ownload a file        {S}cript questionaire
{DB} Download batch      {J}oin a conference
{F}ile directories       {A}bandon a conference
{FL}ag for download      {OPEN} a door
{L}ocate files [NAME]    {SELECT} Conferences for scanning
{N}ew files [DATE]
{Z}ippy scan [DIRS]           Conference selected is: Main Board


(117 min. left) Main Board Command? d
```

Figure 11.2 Canada Remote Main Menu

Newell switched to PCBoard software in 1986 so he could network his many computers together. He's still not a technician; all he's learned about computers he learned running Canada Remote. "I like dealing with the members most," he says, emphasizing the social aspects of his job. "I spend my day talking to other members, on the system or the phone, and picking up new and wonderful things to put online. We tend to use outside consultants to do our programming.

"This is certainly a fun career for people who enjoy this kind of stuff. You've got to enjoy change."

To stay ahead of the online pack, Canada Remote is always changing and adding new things. At the time of the interview, Newell was adding 700 conferences from the Usenet network, a conferencing system running large computer systems under Unix, and putting through a gateway to Buffalo with eight phone lines so that U.S. callers can dial in with inexpensive packet services like PC Pursuit.

Before that, Fleming opened a fax service. "We have free local sending of faxes. If you have a PC and modem, leave a message in our Conference 106 and every half-hour they get faxed to Toronto and Mississauga. We're adding reciprocal agreements with other systems so faxes can be sent further." The fax service got a real workout during the 1991 Canadian postal strike and came through with flying colors.

What really sets Canada Remote apart, however, is the personal service it gives users in the Toronto area. It's really more of a user group and computer club than an online bulletin board. The board has its own office, in Toronto's West End, and each Saturday people can drop in to learn more about the system.

The board also offers technical support by telephone, from 1:00 to 7:00 P.M. each weekday, and runs seminars every two weeks. At one seminar, Microsoft representatives gave each attending member a free copy of their Excel program, remembers Fleming.

As with Exec-PC, Canada Remote's most popular service is the wealth of shareware programs available for downloading. "We collect 15 to 17 megabytes every day," scanning them with the latest antivirus software from McAfee Associates and Peter Norton Computing, says Newell.

Next in terms of activity is messaging. Canada Remote is linked to 10 major e-mail networks, including Hyperlink, Relaynet, EchoNet, and ILink. It even sponsors its own network, NorthAmeriNet. "That last is unusual in that we completely sponsor it. Two hundred participating BBSs get to call in on our toll-free 800 numbers. So our corporate clients can get point-to-point communications at no cost," says Fleming.

The Usenet access is unique among PC-based bulletin boards. Usenet is an international network of 50,000 Unix computers with 12 million users, who churn out 10–12 megabytes of notes each day. The board developed its own interface between Canada Remote's PCBoard software and Unix, which it can resell to other boards.

Canada Remote also offers stock quotes from Canadian and American exchanges, including the Vancouver, Montreal, and Toronto exchanges in Canada, as well as the NYSE and NASDAQ. Finally, there are the Canadian Press, UPI, and Newsbytes news wires.

Fleming has shown a great talent for marketing. His newest innovation is a dealer network to resell Canada Remote memberships. "It gives a dealer another new reason to sell hardware, boosts the value of his sale, and if he does directed mailings to his customers he can make money," says Fleming. The board also advertises in *PC* magazine.

RUSTY & EDIE'S

Sysop: Rusty Hardenburgh
216-726-0737
Boardman, Ohio

Rusty Hardenburgh was tired of rules. That's why he decided to open his own board, one without rules, on May 11, 1987.

Since then he's learned some hard lessons, among them the need for some rules. But he has built a great little family business. Rusty & Edie's (main menu shown in Figure 11.3) now has 89 phone lines and computers

```
PCBoard (R) v14.5a/X199 (beta 06/04/91 18:03) - Node 26

==================[   Main Menu   ]=================

A)bandon Conference  G)oodbye (Hang up)   O)perator Page     TS)Txt Srch Msgs
B)ulletin Listings   H)elp Functions      OPEN a DOOR        U)pload a File
CHAT between NODEs    I)nitial Welcome     P)age Length Set   UB Upload Batch
C)omment to SYSOP    J)oin a Conference   Q)uick Msg Scan    USERS List Users
D)ownload a File     K)ill a Message      R)ead Messages     V)iew Settings
DB)Download Batch    L)ocate Files(name)  REPLY to Msg(s)    W)rite User Info
E)nter a Message     M)ode (Graphics)     RM)Re-Read Mem #   X)pert On/Off
F)ile Directories    N)ew Files(date)     S)cript Question   Y)our Per. Mail
FLAG for download    NEWS file display    T)rans. Protocol   Z)ippy DIR Scan

          SELECT Conferences for Scanning or Reading

(57 min. left) Main Board Command? g
```

Figure 11.3   Rusty & Edie's Main Menu

filling the basement of the family home in Boardman, Ohio. In addition to Mrs. Edie Hardenburgh, Rusty, now 53, has a son and daughter working on his board. A stepson has also joined.

The board, which charges an annual subscription fee, has almost a pirate reputation among other system operators because of its wealth of adult-oriented conferences and pictures and its large number of program files. The reputation comes mainly from Hardenburgh's own anarchic attitude, which he developed as a hobbyist. "I was in the insurance business and got a computer in 1985. Someone mentioned bulletin boards, and I gave one a call. But they were run by people who wanted to be dictators . . . one had you fill out two long questionnaires in one session—if you didn't make it you were thrown off." Others demanded that forms be mailed in. "One day I said to myself, this is ridiculous. I got through to one guy and asked him why he did it. He said, 'people would crash his system' otherwise."

Disbelieving the threat, "I opened my board with no rules. No time limit, no byte limit, you didn't have to pay. Our banner said 'If you've been thrown off any other system, come to ours.' We ran that way until July 4, 1988. By that time I'd expanded to two nodes, adding a second phone line. But we'd become so popular that it might take a week to get on. We started getting hate mail. I talked to my wife, and we decided to close down."

That might have been the end of it, but before going out of business Hardenburgh decided to write a bulletin to his users, stating his case and asking for donations. "The money just poured in. As it did, we started adding equipment." Eventually, Hardenburgh retired from his insurance job in order to get the time he needed to keep expanding.

"It's kind of ironic, but as time goes on you get absorbed into the system. We started adopting the rules we hated so badly—we couldn't do everything the way we did before. But we managed to keep the remnants of the old system. We don't have download/upload ratios, we don't hassle anyone. You have to pay, but we still call it a donation. We still let kids on."

Hardenburgh's main worry is his adult files. He's a grandfather and understands the danger. His first move was a separate conference for adult conversations and files, which now has 3 gigabytes of material, including 2,000 text files. "We have 25 authors of erotic text who find an outlet here. We're a haven for those authors.

"We have a lot of more legitimate stuff too," he adds, and when the board adds its 101st line, which he anticipates would happen in late 1991, he says he plans to split the adult areas off into a separate system.

When Hardenburgh started Rusty & Edie's, he had a two-bedroom apartment, and he put his computer in the second bedroom. "We put so many in, you had to walk in sideways. It got to the point where despite air conditioning and new electricity we couldn't cool the place." So he moved to a house and put the computers in the basement, stacked in groups of 16. The Hardenburghs build their own IBM PC XTs from parts and link them with a Novell Netware 386 network and five file servers with 10 gigabytes of hard-disk storage. "It's hard to conceive," he marvels.

The board keeps Rusty and Edie warm in more ways than one. "We have a huge electrical bill. We can't keep the house cool no matter what we do." When the temperature outside rises above 50°, he runs the air conditioner. When the temperature is below freezing, he cools the house simply by leaving the windows open. However, "We have to turn off the A/C when the temperature goes below 50 outside, because the unit will freeze up. That causes real problems. We open the windows, but that doesn't cool the place enough, so we have to run huge fans." In some Ohio families, sad to say, the computer in the basement is never turned on and exists as an heirloom. At the Hardenburghs', it's the furnace that's the heirloom.

Hardenburgh says most of his users dial directly, some from far, far away. "We're very popular in Europe—I don't know why. We have more callers from London, England, than Youngstown."

The board is very busy from 8:00 A.M. to noon, again from 1:00 P.M. until 4:00. The evening traffic starts to build around 6:00 P.M. and peaks at midnight, but the board stays busy until 3:00 A.M.

Hardenburgh explains the traffic pattern this way: "From 8:00 until noon we're busy because these guys are calling from work. They can call from work for hours at a time. Obviously, they're vice presidents or presidents, important people. From noon to 1:00 they go to lunch. At 4:00 they go home, except on Friday, when it slows down at 1:00. Then at 6:00 the phone prices start getting cheaper. They drop again at 11:00." By midnight on the West Coast, however, even modem users head for bed.

Hardenburgh's biggest headaches are legal ones. He worries that moral crusaders may go after him for the adult files, although the same materials are available at local convenience stores. He's already faced down critics for his files on witchcraft; Wiccans (the followers of Wicca, the cult of witchcraft) find his board a haven. The lawyers' biggest worry, however, involves the privacy of electronic mail.

"You could be liable if a private message gets opened up. Privacy laws are explicit. We've put a disclaimer up that's proven effective in court," describing all messages as public.

One big problem for Hardenburgh arose when someone left a message with his former girlfriend's phone number. "We have 10,000 members, 2,800 calls per day, and we had to burn that phone number. That scared me to the point where I don't allow any open message to have a telephone number in it.

"There's also a disclaimer against commercial files. No one has ever been convicted of having a commercial file online, but I don't want to be a test case." Some software companies send demonstration versions of their programs to Rusty & Edie's. Hackers send the full versions, calling them "demos." "Every week I get a call that some obscure file is commercial."

One worry Hardenburgh doesn't have is viruses. He decompresses and checks every file he gets. "You could no more put a virus in my system than fly," he says. "We have 60,000–70,000 files, and never saw one."

Hardenburgh concludes that his personal philosophy remains intact. "We like to believe in the basic goodness of people. My wife and I are burnouts from the 60s, and we didn't like rules then. We don't like them now."

GALAXY

Sysop: Tom Scott
505-881-6964
Albuquerque, New Mexico

Tom Scott calls his Galaxy™ bulletin board, in Albuquerque, New Mexico, the most important in the United States, and he may be right.

Galaxy (main menu shown in Figure 11.4) serves as the nexus for Connect USA, which combines the CompuServe packet net with Galaxy's own equipment and trunk-line deals. The Galaxy board's own contents are

```
Top Menu

GALAXY INFORMATION NETWORK

A) Your GALAXY Account Info      B) CONNECT-USA & Starlink Billing
C) Chat Lounge & Fast Eddie's    D) Dial Out Services
E) Electronic Mail               F) File Library-OVER 19,000 FILES
G) Multi-Player GAMES            H) HELP!!
I) STARLINK Information          N) News
O) Online Shopping Mall          R) Registry of Users
S) Special Interest Groups       T) Telecomputing Magazine Online
U) CONNECT-USA Information        V) Dasnet E-Mail Information
W) What's NEW on GALAXY          Y) Speed Search Database
$) Classified Ads                ?) Additional Commands


Z) Purchase Credits For Local Use

X) Exit the System (Logoff)

TOP MENU
Select an Option (? or H for HELP):
```

Figure 11.4 Galaxy Main Menu

not remarkable—a collection of shareware, some interesting text games, and messaging. Scott admits it's intended mainly for local Albuquerque callers.

But Galaxy is also the home office of *Telecomputing*, still the only monthly, color, slick-papered magazine serving the bulletin board community. And it's the home office of Scott, a garrulous, opinionated man who may be the most controversial driving force in the bulletin board industry.

His enemies accuse Scott of favoring one software vendor over another, of arrogance, and of making inflated claims. Operators of large BBS systems, for instance, say that they get few calls from his packet nets, and that he claims credit for a revolution they created. None of this fazes Scott, who moved to Albuquerque from Virginia in 1989—for his health, he says.

Despite the controversy surrounding Scott, *Telecomputing* continues publishing every month, and his networks are among the data communication business's best bargains. And only Tom Scott could have brought most of the industry's leaders together in November 1990, during the Fall Comdex trade show, for a loud, raucous party in the Dunes Hotel in Las Vegas.

Scott is in a unique position to know where the BBS business is hottest. "From our statistics the most popular states are California, Texas, Illinois, and Florida," he says. "The heaviest concentration of inquiries from people about whether we serve an area is in the Upper Midwest." The Northeast is also an active calling area.

Scott refuses to release figures on his usage, saying only that he has several thousand users. And many are businesses. One customer in southern Maryland, he says, is setting up a master bulletin board in its home office, with other boards around the country maintained from the main location.

Galaxy uses the Major BBS software package from Galacticomm.

THE ECONOMIC BULLETIN BOARD

Sysop: Paul Christy
202-377-0433
Washington, D.C.

If you're an economist or an exporter, the best value in the U.S. government is the modest cost of joining the Economic Bulletin Board (main menu shown in Figure 11.5), run by the U.S. Department of Commerce.

The five-year-old board has 32 lines running TBBS software, says system operator Paul Christy. Its membership fee gives users two hours

```
ZDDDDDDDDDDDDDDDDDDDDDDDDDDDDDDDDDD?
3   THE ECONOMIC BULLETIN BOARD   3
3            Main Menu            3
@DDDDDDDDDDDDDDDDDDDDDDDDDDDDDDDDDDDY


<B> Go to bulletin system
<C> Leave a comment
<F> Go to file system
<G> Sign off system
<H> Help
<I> View welcome message
<M> Leave a message
<O> Call the operator
<P> Read personal mail
<R> Read messages
<U> Go to utility system


Command: c
```

Figure 11.5 Economic Bulletin Board Main Menu

of access to some of the most important business files in the United States. Above that limit, it costs 20 cents a minute in the morning, 15 cents a minute in the afternoon, and 5 cents a minute at other times. Daily files are updated each morning.

"The Federal Reserve in New York gives us daily quotes on Treasury notes, and we're the only source for the Treasury's Daily Statement, the government's balance sheet. We're also the only electronic source for Trade Opportunities collected by the U.S. Foreign and Commercial Service. That's a popular file—they're all qualified export leads, with full information on how to contact companies."

Christy came to the EBB in July 1990 from Capitol Hill, where he worked at the Congressional Budget Office. Besides running the board, he sells the National Trade Databank, a compact disc database with 600 megabytes of trade data each month. His actual title is Acting Division Director of the Business Statistics and Information Systems in the Office of Business Analysis, part of the Economics and Statistics Administration of the department.

Credit for starting the board goes to former department employees Jack Cremens and Ken Rogers. "They got it up and rolling and went through the initial throes of convincing other agencies to use us." They started with a single line running RBBS, a shareware program, and now have 32 lines running on an AST 386–based computer, whose 3,000 subscribers log on a total of 500 times a day.

Christy's goal for the next year is to move to 64 phone lines. But if you're worrying about your tax dollars, don't. The board is required to be self-sustaining, including that part of Christy's salary devoted to maintaining it. Prices were increased in July 1990 and may rise again as the system is expanded. "Fortunately, the technology of bulletin boards has come along to the point where you don't have to be a technician anymore. That's a small portion of the job," he says.

Who uses the board? "Our intended audience is anyone who needs access to federal economic data. Economists, businessmen, traders, exporters, students, librarians are all users," he says. "We have anecdotal evidence that our users are who we want. Our privacy restrictions prevent us from finding out exactly who our users are."

Christy says 85 percent of the board's callers come from outside Washington, and although it can be accessed using PC Pursuit, as well as Accu-Link and Connect USA services, Christy says he would still like to get the board its own X.25 PAD so that users of packet nets such as BT Tymnet and SprintNet can access it directly. "That would be easier for our users, who are not really computer-literate. They would like to dial a local number and not know anything else," handling all log-on details through a script file.

THE BUSINESS BOARD

Sysop: Jim Appleby
213-477-0408
Los Angeles, California

Many businesses that find they need a bulletin board, to support either their own salespeople or their customers, don't know that they are facing a make-or-buy decision in the matter.

But you don't have to become a sysop. You can hire Jim Appleby instead. Appleby's Business Board (main menu shown in Figure 11.6) is one of the newest of the large boards, having opened only in 1988, but it is one of the fastest-growing.

"BBS systems can be used to augment marketing, customer support, and sales. We sell slots in our database. That augments traditional customer support calls for those with a modem."

Appleby is aggressive in signing up corporate clients, for whom he provides customer support. Callers get a four-digit PIN that sends them directly to the section of the board they need from the board's main menu. These sections can also be accessed using a "go" command, as on CompuServe.

Appleby doesn't like to discuss specifics about his board for trade reasons, but he admits he's running a customized version of the Major BBS from Galacticomm. (In November 1991, the board became an authorized reseller of Major BBS software.) "In the classic sense, I run a service bureau," he says. "We are, as far as we know, the only company running a service bureau based on the Major BBS. We have most of the modules, exclusive of games."

Besides customer support, the Business Board also provides spot sales for customers such as the Bidtel Exchange, for which he offers an auction service. Businesses post specials for callers who dial in for support, and the board provides a full order entry system. Appleby urges his clients

```
Main Menu

    [I] . Information About     [R] . Read your Mail     [F] . The Support Forums
    [C] . Your Credit Balance   [W] . Write E-Mail        [L] . The Library
    [H] . Query On-Line Help    [N] . NewUser ToolKit     [O] . On-Line Shopping
    [A] . Ansi & 9600 access    [*] . Pagename List       [S] . Contract Services
    [U] . Registry of Users     [#] . BBS Credit Info     [T] . Tele-Conference
    [+] . What's New?           [P] . Purchase BBS        [X] . Exit and Logoff

-> Select a Letter or type GO *: #
```

Figure 11.6 Business Board Main Menu

to put up long lists of common questions and answers on their sections of the board, claiming that 30 percent of questions can be answered that way, without additional work on their part.

Instead of selling his services directly to users, Appleby is unique in aiming at corporations and government agencies that should be board operators. One recent contract is with the California Environment Business Resources Assistance Center, or CEBRAC, which is funded by state agencies in charge of environmental laws and enforcement. Laws are overlapping, and small businessmen are getting caught. CEBRAC previously answered questions about the law over the phone.

Now CEBRAC can answer those questions through the board or send copies of documents through the Business Board's affiliate service, FaxtsNow. FaxtsNow is a fax service; users dial a number, respond to menus using Touch-tone keypads, enter a code corresponding to the pages they need, and have those pages delivered on the same call. The fax service and the board share hard disks, so only one copy of the regulations is needed. "A future enhancement will allow us to make the call back to the fax while on the BBS; users will be prompted to send the fax number."

Late in November 1991, The Business BBS and FaxtsNow completely integrated their two services. That means users can dial the board through their PC and have documents downloaded to a fax machine, or vice versa. Applyby calls this capability vital for many businesses, which may offer customers schematics or other drawings and can't be certain that callers will have the necessary software to decompress and decode picture files.

Each Business Board client has its own page number off the board's main menu. These numbers are given out only to registered users and act as a first level of security. They're accessed with the "go" commands, and each client gets his own system of passwords and user IDs. There are eight levels of security in all.

Appleby provides in his contracts that all customers can take their boards in-house when they want. "We turn over all files they've built and make a list available of all the software they will need. There are a dozen minor modifications we've made, and we turn over that documentation. The only things we don't turn over are our Business BBS menus."

The biggest headache for Appleby is his early schedule. "A professional sysop has to go to work at 5:00 A.M. so maintenance functions can be done while use is low." And, like any good businessman, Appleby knows what he does well and avoids other aspects of bulletin board operation— like chat and games. "You do a few things and you do them very well. If you try to do all things you'll bump into giant competitors."

Appleby says he gets three kinds of phone calls. "We get programmers calling who've been told to bring up a BBS, referred to us by Galacticomm.

We answer their questions and make a few suggestions. The second caller is a businessman, and when we start explaining the role of a system operator he says he doesn't have time. The third kind of call is almost an immediate sale. This caller recognizes he needs a BBS, didn't know he had a make or buy option, and he learns from us he has an option."

CHANNEL 1

Sysop: Brian Miller
617-864-0741
Boston, Massachusetts

Brian Miller, system operator for the five-year-old Channel 1 bulletin board (main menu shown in Figure 11.7) in Boston, has high goals. "We aim to compete with CompuServe," he says of his 65-line PCBoard system.

"We planned this as a business from the beginning," he adds. But so far Miller, a psychologist, and his wife, Tess, an architect, are keeping their day jobs and have only one employee, who's 13 years old. The board had 13,000 validated callers in the past year, but actual paid membership may be only about 4,000 to 5,000, Miller says. He adds that over 100,000 files are downloaded from the board each month, and Channel 1 contains about 250,000 messages at any one time.

```
----------------------->  Channel 1 Commands Menu  <----------------------

E-Mail                   Menus                    Files/Transfers

E nter new message       J conference menu        F ile directories
R ead messages           J [#] join conference    F V view archives
Y our personal mail      A bandon conferences     D ownload [to you]
R Y read all your msgs   B ulletin menu           DB atch download
R Y A all conferences    S ign-up questionnaires  U[B] pload [to us]
RM reread msg. #         DOOR  gateways to other   N ew files [date]
TS text search msgs.     OPEN  system functions    Z ip scan [keyword]
Q uick mail scan                                  T ransfer protocols
SELECT conferences       Other Basic Commands     TEST an archive

WHO  see who's online    H use at all prompts      P age length [# lines]
CHAT talk online         V iew caller stats        W rite info [password]
NEWS reread news         C omment to sysop         I nitial screen
X pert [menus on/off]    M color on/off            G oodbye [logoff]

(xx min. left) [Node 39] Channel 1 Command?
```

Figure 11.7   Channel 1 Main Menu

Like other large boards, Channel 1 runs on a local area network. Like Exec-PC, its chief attraction is shareware available for downloading. Conferencing, using echo networks, is the second feature of Channel 1, and entertainment in the form of online games is the third.

Miller is proudest of how his board works. All nodes are either fast Intel 80286 machines or 386-SX machines on an Ethernet LAN with Novell Netware 386 software. That means more "MIPS per caller," or more processing power devoted to running each call, compared with competitors, he says.

The board is still located in Miller's home, with PCs lining the walls on racks. "We heat the house with the LAN," he says, much like the Hardenburghs in Ohio. "But we're looking at office space."

Adds Miller, "We're in a transition. We see ourselves in the Super BBS category and we're trying to move against CompuServe and GEnie," both of which are based on 20-year-old mainframe technologies. "We think we surpass them in a number of areas. All we need are some of the online database and gateway paraphernalia, then there'd be little separating us except price and interfaces," areas where he says Channel 1 is lower and better.

One improvement Miller is planning is giving users direct access to his LAN so that they can run programs. "CompuServe would never do that," he says.

But, after five years of work, Miller hesitates to recommend his lifestyle to others. "I don't recommend this to anybody. We think there's a pot of gold at the end of this rainbow, but it's a long rainbow and a lot of work. Unless you're prepared to risk your health or if you have a venture capitalist behind you, don't even think about it."

Much of Channel 1's conferencing is based on echo networks, which pass messages among boards at set times each night, using compression and fast modems to keep costs down. Among the larger networks through which Miller's board gets messages are the Relaynet Information and Message Exchange (known as RIME), ILink, and SmartNet.

Because Channel 1 passes along nearly everything it can echo, topic coverage is incredibly broad, Miller says, and users can get into arguments on anything. "It ranges from soap operas and pets to support for commercial applications, with everything in between," including politics and religion.

One problem for all the echo networks is a lack of technical standards, Miller adds. He's working on that problem with all three nets he belongs to. "But in any evolving technology—all these nets are only a few years old—both the technology as well as the sociological technology is in the process of evolution."

SOUND OF MUSIC

Sysop: Paul Waldinger
516-536-8723
Oceanside, New York

Portly, gentlemanly Paul Waldinger set up the Sound of Music (he's a music lover) BBS in 1985 to deal with the pressures of raising two children. "I wanted a way of reaching adults while staying at home," he explains.

Today, the SOM Premium Information Network (as he now calls his business, whose main menu is shown in Figure 11.8) has 20 call-in lines, including a "tie line" from the BBS's home office on the south shore of Long Island's Nassau County to New York City. This means New Yorkers can reach SOM with a local call. Each incoming line can run at 9,600 bits per second, and users have access to about 40,000 files (amounting to 4 gigabytes of online storage) for an annual subscription that varies depending on whether you are using the board's tie line into New York City.

Waldinger also has a number of corporate subscribers and a printed newsletter with a mailing list covering 5,000 people. Also, SOM is the hub of SmartNet, a nationwide echo network with about 150 member boards.

Each of the 20 modem lines is supported by a separate PC, and they are all linked by a 10Net LAN. Waldinger chose this configuration because 10Net did not demand expensive dedicated file servers. Five of the nodes

```
IMMMMMMMMMMMMMMMMMMMMMMMMMM[   Main Menu   ]MMMMMMMMMMMMMMMMMMMMMMMMMMMMMM;
GDDDDDDDDDDDDDDDDDDDDDDDDDDDDDDDDDDDDDDDDDDDDDDDDDDDDDDDDDDDDDDDDDDDDDDDDD6
:                                                                       :
: Abandon Conference  Goodbye (Hang up)   Operator Page     TS Txt Srch Msgs :
: Bulletin Listings   Help Functions      OPEN a DOOR       Upload a File   :
: CHAT between NODEs   Initial Welcome     Page Length Set   UB Upload Batch :
: Comment to SYSOP     Join a Conference   Quick Msg Scan    USERS List Users :
: Download a File      Kill a Message       Read Messages     View Settings   :
: DB Download Batch    Locate Files(name)  REPLY to Msg(s)   Write User Info  :
: Enter a Message      Mode (Graphics)     RM Re-Read Mem #  Xpert On/Off     :
: File Directories     New Files(date)     Script Question   Your Per. Mail   :
: FLAG for download    NEWS file display   Trans. Protocol   Zippy DIR Scan   :
:                                                                       :
:             SELECT Conferences for Scanning or Reading                :
:                                                                       :
HMMMMMMMMMMMMMMMMMMMMMMMMMMMMMMMMMMMMMMMMMMMMMMMMMMMMMMMMMMMMMMMMMMMMMMMMMM<

(45 min. left) Main Board Command? d
```

Figure 11.8 Sound of Music Main Menu

are, in fact, file servers, but they also support a modem line each—and have no problem doing it, since they are 25 MHz 386 PCs. Most of the other nodes are 286 machines, which Waldinger finds on the used computer market for about $300 each.

Waldinger notes that with 9,600 bps modems you have to have a 286 machine to keep up; a PC XT won't do unless it's "souped up." However, anything faster than a 286 machine is overkill. "People don't impress me when they say they have a board running on a 486 machine—the user can't tell any difference," he says.

The key to SOM's success, Waldinger says, lies in offering the customer something of value. "Files and technical support are what the users want. They have heard about Sound of Music and that we offer unique files. But files can't be your only reason you dial a BBS. With just files you will only have a run-of-the-mill BBS; you will not have a national system. Our online support and V.32 connectivity makes us unique."

For technical support, SmartNet is the hub for conferences run by Hewlett-Packard, Quarterdeck, Hayes, US Robotics, PKware, and Word-Perfect. Most of these companies have their employees call directly into the Sound of Music to participate, but some reach the BBS through the SmartNet echo network. Quarterdeck uses Sound of Music as a hub to connect its corporate electronic mail system between the headquarters in Santa Monica, California, and a branch office in Dublin, Ireland.

"It's not easy to say why any of these companies chose us [to host their technical support conference]," Waldinger says. "I worked at it and was able to demonstrate that BBSs have a unique calling, that not everyone calls CompuServe or can afford to. That means Sound of Music is an excellent alternative."

In addition, "We lease out areas of the Sound of Music for electronic mail; companies can pay $100,000 on salaries to do their own system, or they can pay us. General users can't get into the lease areas, unless the leasing group has opened it, as Hewlett-Packard has," he explains. The cost depends on the number of users, but for $50 per month you'll get a conference area serving 10 users, and for $500 per month you can get a full BBS with up to 40 conferences. Just to have a technician call in to moderate a technical support conference costs only $50 a year.

The Sound of Music sounds like a business, and Waldinger agrees that it is. "It's not to the point where it has any full-time employees, but I would call it a money-making enterprise. It is making money, but not to the point where I could leave my full-time job," he notes.

Meanwhile, there is the board to run. Waldinger has nine co-sysops, each with full power to run the board. As the hub of SmartNet, with more than 125 active conferences, Sound of Music gets about 800 to 2,000 messages a day. The message traffic is scanned four times a day.

Slanderous messages are marked so that only the recipient or the sysop can read them. If a message is out of context for its conference, it may be moved and the sender advised, or a message might be sent to the sender advising a better place to post the message.

"We don't see many credit card numbers and that kind of thing since users know we scan through everything," Waldinger says. As for files, about 100 arrive every day, and the sysops carefully extract each one from its compression scheme and make sure it contains no viruses or copyrighted software. It's no longer common for Waldinger to see copyrighted programs uploaded, but the sysops do run across such things as example files from various software packages. Since these, too are copyrighted they are deleted.

Waldinger says most virus scares are really the result of someone trying to run software in an incompatible setting. Waldinger's experience is that real viruses are rarely seen outside academic networks.

As for flamers (see the glossary), "That usually involves one person claiming to know more than another; the pen is mightier than the mouth. We always try to let them work it out themselves." But when they can't, the sysops will intervene—for the sake of professionalism.

BOARDWATCH MAGAZINE

Sysop: Jack Rickard
303-973-4222
Denver, Colorado

Perhaps no one has dialed into more bulletin boards than Jack Rickard. "I've probably dialed into 20,000 BBSs in the past four years," he says. Rickard, 35, is married to a woman from the Philippines and has three children. His family also includes her aunt and uncle. They live in the foothills of the Rocky Mountains southwest of Denver.

This very conventional man runs a very unconventional business. No BBS in America is more devoted to text files than Rickard's six-line Boardwatch board (main menu shown in Figure 11.9). It includes "USA Today," a 64,000-byte daily file from Gannett that costs downloaders a monthly subscription fee. Most of the board's callers are themselves board operators looking for unique things to offer their own callers.

And Rickard delivers them. Perhaps no file is more unique, however, than Rickard's own newsletter. *Boardwatch Magazine* is a sprightly monthly, usually 24 pages and printed in one color on heavy stock, that is avidly read by Fortune 500 executives who want to know the latest bulletin board trends. It is the best-known, least biased window into public bulletin

```
ZDDDDDDDDDDDDDDDDDDDDDDDDDDDDDDDDDDDDDD?
ZE?                                        ZE?
  3@Y        Boardwatch Magazine           @
  3              Main Menu                  3
  3     DDDDDDDDDDDDDDDDDDDDDDDDDDD          3
  3       1. Boardwatch Magazine            3
  3       2. USA TODAY Download Area         3
  3       3. News/Periodicals               3
  3       4. File Libraries                 3
  3       5. Message Areas                  3
  3       6. Games/Entertainment            3
  3       7. Closing NYSE/Financial         3
  3       8. Bulletins                      3
  3     DDDDDDDDDDDDDDDDDDDDDDDDDDD          3
  3     I System Info    U Utilities        3
  3     G Goodbye        H Help             3
  3Z?                                      Z?3
@EY $ Order Boardwatch Subscription @EY
@DDDDDDDDDDDDDDDDDDDDDDDDDDDDDDDDDDDDDDDY
Command:
```

Figure 11.9 Boardwatch Magazine Main Menu

boards. The letter is crammed with news, reviews, and wry observations belying the fact that its editor has no formal training as a journalist.

"My background is in the defense industry as a technical writer, documenting advanced weapon systems, radar, and communications systems, with a bit of automated test bed work. I was employed by McDonnell Aircraft, Emerson Electric Company's Electronics and Space Division, and Martin Marietta Denver Aerospace, and of course I did freelance projects for perhaps 30 other firms over the years," he says.

"I first took a fancy to personal computers during the mid-1970s. I wrote software for the Sinclair ZX-81/Timex™ computer in the early 1980s which sold well, including a word processor titled ZWryter™. I also wrote a tutorial program and book on BASIC for the Commodore C-64."

Rickard first dialed into a bulletin board while living in St. Louis in 1981. He was just an ordinary modem user until 1986. "I was using modems to transfer technical documentation around to various clients in the Denver area." Then he found a list of Denver BBSs and learned that all had closed. "I ran into a number of people who had telephone numbers that once belonged to a bulletin board but had been reassigned after the board closed. They told of receiving 12 or 15 mystery calls each day for months. They seemed to be really in distress.

"I thought I would put together a verified list of active BBSs in Denver to kill off these aging electronic lists. I printed it on paper, with a date, so it would show some 'age.' I started adding a few notes on how to turn off Call Waiting, how XMODEM worked, where the good deals on the then-pricey 1,200 bps modems were, etc. The list caught on, and in March 1987 we started regular monthly publication of *Denver PC Boardwatch*.

Quickly, his local letter began getting notice in other cities. "It didn't appear that other cities had such publications. We began picking up subscribers from across the country." In just 18 months, 80 percent of the subscribers were from outside Colorado, so he changed the title to *Boardwatch Magazine*, started a select national list of boards, and began adding lists from different cities, topical listings, and so forth.

The BBS came online a year after the magazine came into print. "People wanted to look up back issues," he says. "So we put in a database of article titles with a keyword search." Rickard's board has also become a haven for other authors looking to make a living from publishing their work online. There's a publication called *BekBits*, Alan Bechtel's *InfoMat* magazine, an online digital music review, and LONEWOLF.ZIP by Judy Heim, "a soap opera for technoids." He describes all of them as "experiments in distribution."

The Boardwatch Magazine file library started out with shareware the newsletter had reviewed. Users sent along a good collection of archive utilities and communication files. "By accident we wound up with a large Windows files area," he says, along with files of the board lists put out in the magazine.

Most messages on the board are from other system operators and consist mainly of questions and answers about various boards. There are also some echo conferences on such things as U.S. Robotics' HST Courier™ modems, and the TBBS software run by the board.

The games section, however, is not what it seems. It started as a sample of applications written for TDBS, the dBase-like language that is an extension to TBBS. "To encourage applications we sold those applications done by basement entrepreneurs," he says. Today, the most popular application is a program called Exactus, which lets users manipulate the NYSE data on the board.

"We get it (the data) from Max Ewell's Discount Brokerage in New York. The point of the experiment is to develop BBS applications that let callers maintain portfolios. The ticker application has historical data, you can get bar charts on a screen. The important thing is that you can keep a portfolio, enter it once, and after that it works like a spreadsheet." Rickard charges extra for the stock quotes.

Rickard's not modest about his accomplishments. "With a solid background in military computer, communications, and other electronic hardware, and assembly language programming for very small PCs, I've been able to fill in some of the blanks new callers and users have, and cut through some of the incredible pap coming out of PR firms on high-technology issues.

"I think Boardwatch has been successful largely because of the mostly accurate perception that most of the computer journalism field is a bit slimy," with magazines serving advertisers and PR firms rather than the readers. Rickard doesn't have that problem; most of his money comes from readers. "I can print pretty much what I like in the way I like it, and that translates into a reader perception that they are getting the straight story—at least as one eccentric in the Rocky Mountains perceives it— without a sales job.

"We've also enjoyed a surprising relationship with the companies we bash regularly. It is not at all unusual to do a story on a telephone company and receive a very official letter protesting the inaccurate rumor mongering we do. In the same mail, we routinely receive six to eight other letters from subscribers within the same organization assuring us that it was right on the mark."

The perception is that Boardwatch is a newsletter for hobby BBS operators. Actually, it is about hobby BBS operators. "The overwhelming majority of our paid subscriptions are from within Fortune 500 corporations, large consulting firms, telephone companies, modem manufacturers, and the rest of the computer press.

"There is a very high level of interest within corporate America in the technological developments of BBS communications, and a dearth of formal information on the subject."

ONLINE WITH HAYES

Sysop: Randy Cooper
404-446-6336
Norcross, GA

There are many companies today that do some or all of their customer support online, using bulletin boards. But according to Jack Rickard of Boardwatch Magazine, few do it as well as the company that helped start it all, Hayes Microcomputer Products Inc.

Actually, Rickard says, Dennis Hayes was for a time no big fan of bulletin boards. Sure, he helped Ward and Randy write CBBS in 1978, and sure, he kept track of the nation's bulletin boards for a few years after that. But once modems went mainstream and a few unsavory types got into running boards, he backed off as many others did.

Then, in the late 1980s, Hayes' company hit a hard stretch. Modem buyers began looking to price first and features later. Hayes' prices were among the highest in the business, and the company suffered. Dozens of people were laid off, including many people working the phones in customer support. The company moved out of its swank office building into a cheaper office-warehouse nearby. The "Fortune 500" salesmen in suits left, while engineers in Hayes' old mold remained.

Somehow, most Hayes users never noticed the changes—mainly because they had a friend in the Hayes BBS, which could answer their questions, tell them what was new, and maintain their interest in Hayes products.

Today Randy Cooper runs the Online with Hayes board (main menu shown in Figure 11.10). He upgraded it with TBBS in 1990 so that the 16-line board would be easier for novices to use. Many modem buyers make the Hayes board their first call, he points out, so ease of use is crucial. It's all done with TBBS hot keys—single-character commands. When this interview was made, for instance, the Hayes board was touting a cash rebate offer. Cooper created that menu and, to make it easier for users to remember it, used the $ key as the command to access it.

Besides running the Hayes BBS, Cooper also handles messages to the company written on the GEnie and CompuServe systems and on the SmartNet echo network. In addition, he coordinates the company's sysop program and works on testing unreleased products. Most of the time the board runs itself, he says, and all he needs to do is answer the mail, a job that can be handled remotely—even when he's at a sysop conference across the country.

```
---------------------- O N L I N E   W I T H   H A Y E S ---------------------
<P>revious Menu  <M>ain Menu   <H>elp   <S>ettings   <I>ntro News   <G>oodbye
------------------------------------------------------------------------------


    [1] About Online With Hayes - What's available here and about this system
    [2] What's **NEW** at Hayes - Find out about new products and announcements
    [3] Hayes File Library     - Read or download files in the file library
    [4] Hayes Technical Support - Search Knowledge Base or ask Tech Support
    [5] Hayes Connection        - Reseller info for Hayes Registered Dealers
    [6] Product Descriptions    - Learn more about the Hayes product line
    [7] Hayes Customer Service  - Info on upgrades - 3rd Party Products - BBS #s
    [8] Hayes Online Store      - Order manuals - power supplies - small parts
    [9] Special Support Areas   - Info for Resellers - Developers - BBS SysOps
    [A] The Hayes Advantage     - What sets Hayes apart from the competitors
    [B] Bulletin Board Lists    - Search for BBSs in your city or area code
    [$] ** CASH REBATE OFFER ** - Get $CASH$ Rebates on selected Hayes products!
    [L] LANstep                 - The *NEW* expandable network operating system
    [W] Warranty Registration   - Register your *NEW* Hayes product electronically
    [Z] Special Interest Groups - SIGs - Public message bases and shareware files

Command: g
```

Figure 11.10 Main Menu of Online with Hayes

Instead of using the MEDIT function of TBBS to create his menus, Cooper used SDL, a compiler that generates menu files from a program file. It's done in a block format so that each menu is a blocked section of code, Cooper explains. The menu command doesn't have to be in that section; it just has to be compiled somewhere. Entries can be taken out or written quickly.

Before taking on the board, Cooper had no previous programming experience, except for using the SCOPE scripting language, which is part of the company's Smartcom program. Learning SDL took three full days, he says, and although he's now conversant with the system, he's still learning it.

For hardware, the Hayes board runs an Intel 80386-based PC running at 25 MHz and two eight-port Digiboards linked, of course, to Hayes modems. A second computer is used for development of new software routines, which are ported to the main machine after they're tested. The whole system is economical in terms of space and hardware. The board is taken offline only for daily maintenance routines—usually at around 3:00 in the morning.

What does the board do? Its main functions are customer support and customer loyalty. Support for users—a list of common questions and answers, and a mail function linked to the company's tech support staff—is found behind menu option 4. Resellers, software developers, and BBS operators can get their own specialized questions answered behind option 9.

Many support boards offer nothing beyond messaging and file downloading. The Hayes board is an exception. Behind option Z— available only to callers dialing directly—are a number of special interest groups (SIGs) with their own files and message bases. There's one for IBM PC users, one for Macintosh users, and even one for Tandy users. All the SIGs are run by volunteers in the Atlanta area, not paid Hayes employees.

Perhaps the most interesting of the SIGs are those for BBS sysops. They're run by sysops using Hayes 9,600-baud modems around the country, and they're divided along the lines of major BBS software programs. There are SIGs for TBBS and PCBoard, for instance. There are even separate SIGs for some public-domain BBS programs such as Telegard and Spitfire. Users decide which SIGs they want to see, Cooper says, and programs without much traffic can be discussed in the "sysop's lounge" SIG.

Option 5 is a dealer registration section written with TDBS, and Cooper plans more use of the program once he learns more dBase commands. Option 8, the Hayes online store, is used for ordering items such as parts and manuals. It's actually a TBBS survey file, Cooper notes. Results from it are printed and taken, by hand, to the same people who take orders by phone.

Cooper is proudest, however, of his product information area. This is an online catalog of everything Hayes sells. The information there is often more complete and current than that appearing in a typical brochure. When Hayes announces a new product, for instance, it's usually accompanied by a feature overview that goes into a lot of detail; such overviews don't usually make it into the printed brochures.

Hayes tries to keep its online policies as loose as possible. This means that anyone—even a first time modemer—can look at everything in the system. Cooper hasn't had any problems with that policy. There are no public message bases, as on hobbyist boards, so there's limited interactivity and few ways a user can get into trouble.

Cooper says that many people started BBSs after dialing into the Hayes board, and he still gets two messages each day from individuals asking about what it takes to run a BBS. What it takes, he says, is as much or as little as you're willing to give. And what you get, he adds, is immeasurable.

Cooper's concluding comments could be made by the head of any company smart enough to offer its customers bulletin board access to its employees—that he and the firm learn something through the board every day, with every question, every problem, and every suggestion.

12

Online Etiquette

ABOUT THIS CHAPTER

In this chapter we'll explore how emotional overreaction is a chronic problem in online communications, since this text-only world lacks:

- Facial cues

- Gestures

- Intonations

- Immediate feedback

Therefore, attention to the details of online etiquette is essential if business is to be conducted smoothly.

INTRODUCTION

"Better to remain silent and be thought a fool, than to open your mouth and remove all doubt."

—Mark Twain

"Don't you see how risky it is to say or do what you don't understand? The people you know who do or say things they don't understand—do you think they get praise or blame that way?"

—Socrates (Xenophon's Memorabilia of Socrates)

In the online world, you can't take back what you've said. You certainly can't claim you were misquoted. A thoughtless or ill-conceived statement will remain there for other users to react to. And then you'll have to deal with those reactions, and eventually to their reactions to your reactions to those reactions.

Then there are people who are models of civility in person but who turn into verbal savages when online. Perhaps they feel more secure with the modem holding the other party at arm's length. More likely (we hope), they just don't know how to react within the altered context of the online world.

Consider this conference message thread, based on many we've seen and participated in:

```
------
Conference: ZIP. Message 505. User l.pyre
------
Personally, I think the new postal rates are more than justified,
considering the service you get.
Lance Pyre


------
Conference: ZIP. Message 506. User imp.son
Comment to message 505
------
Then how come my Playboy never gets here on time or intact?


      -----
    /       \
 \/\/         ¦
  ¦   (o)(o)
  C     .---_)
   ¦  ¦.___¦
   ¦   \__/
   /_____\


------
Conference: ZIP. Message 507. User g.flambeau
Comment to message 506
------
Is that all you Eastern Liberal perverts ever think about? Isn't
it enough you've wrecked the court system? Now you have to
subvert the postal system to your own sordid ends? Things like
this never happened when Elvis was around.

    **************************************************
    * Live Every Day As If It Were To Be Your Last. *
    *                 Or Else.                       *
    **************************************************


------
Conference: ZIP. Message 508. User imp.son
Comment to message 507
------
```

Where do you get off? Eastern Liberal? I'm from Kansas! Check the map.
And who said anything about the court system?

```
       -----
      /     \
  \/\/       :
   :  (o)(o)
   C    .---_)
    :  :.___:
    :    \__/
    /_____\
```

```
------
```
Conference: ZIP. Message 509. User g.flambeau
Comment to message 508
```
------
```
So now you're saying I'm stupid? I know where Kansas is. Unless
the courts have moved it. I'm glad the post office can still find
it. It must be lonely out there, huh, just you and that stack of
Playboys?

```
    **************************************************
    * Live Every Day As If It Were To Be Your Last. *
    *                  Or Else.                      *
    **************************************************
```

```
------
```
Conference: ZIP. Message 510. User imp.son
Comment to message 509
```
------
```

FORGET IT. I'M RESIGNING THIS CONFERENCE.

```
       -----
      /     \
  \/\/       :
   :  (o)(o)
   C    .---_)
    :  :.___:
    :    \__/
    /_____\
```

```
------
```
Conference: ZIP. Message 511. User l.pyre
```
------
```
But seriously, can you think of anything else of value any more that
costs as little as a first-class postage stamp....?
Lance Pyre

```
-----------------------------------------------------
```

FLAMING

There are people, like g.flambeau in the preceding exchange, who don't know when they are making a personal attack, or don't care, or simply can't manage to question the opinions of others without sounding like they're attacking. The reasons this is so much more of a problem online than in normal conversation have been debated. The "why" doesn't matter; it happens a lot, and you need to be aware of it. Regular users of online systems call this technique "flaming," as if the user's keyboard were spouting flame aimed at someone else.

Or are we being too hard on g.flambeau? After all, he (she?) could be joking, smirking impishly with each keystroke. If that's true, doesn't that suddenly make imp.son the flamer? Maybe, but the point is that without visual cues you can't tell. Both sides may be at some fault, but without visual cues—or a referee—they may never get on the same wavelength. The advantages of online conversation—immediacy, intimacy, anonymity—become disadvantages very quickly.

Remember, the stark text of a user can provide surprisingly little indication as to what's really on his or her mind. There have been users who waged raging word wars against each other and who, when they finally met face to face, surprised the other users by turning out to be lifelong, bosom friends. Their online repartee just happened to look like bitter feuding.

In addition to the traps laid by the ambiguities of text, you must be aware of certain unwritten rules of behavior—some not so obvious—that stem from the unique character of the online world. Following them can help you become a valued online citizen. (As you'll see, the users in the preceding conference broke most of them.)

RULES OF ORDER FOR THE MESSAGE BASE

1. *Thou shalt not flame.* To disagree without being disagreeable is a concept that eludes, well, everyone at some point. Flaming usually results from someone assuming that he or she knows more than another person. This is a dangerous assumption in the online world, where the aggrieved can sign off for 10 minutes, log into a database service, download reams of material supporting his or her original contention, and come back at you with it. The holder of the first opinion probably won't be mollified—but now is the time for third parties to step in and note that both contestants have had their say, and that the points raised are very interesting but hardly address the original question, etc., etc., etc.

Beyond such simple "Says who?" arguments, there are the more intractable kind based on pure, untestable opinion. And a conflicting opinion can trigger rage, since the self-image of one of the parties may be a little shaky (as in the opening example).

2. *Thou shalt find ways to deal with the flamer, short of flaming back.* However tempting it may be, counterflaming is never the solution, since it starts rounds of abuse and counterabuse—and that may be what the original flamer wanted.

When BIX (McGraw-Hill's commercial Byte Information Exchange™) first opened, it was joined by a raving flamer whose forte was joining conferences and heaping abuse on everyone who did not agree with him. Since his belief system seemed to be based on years of paranoid fantasizing, no one agreed with him. Rational, constructive answers to his perceived concerns triggered further torrents of abuse.

Expelling the flamer was ruled out. So the moderators developed a counterstrategy called "the pledge." Active participants in conferences the flamer had joined were sent private notes suggesting that they not answer any messages posted by the flamer—urging, in short, that they "take the pledge."

The users fell in line, and soon the flamer found himself shouting in an empty room. Conference message threads continued as if his "contributions" didn't exist. Soon, he drifted away.

3. *When in doubt, wait.* "A soft answer turneth away wrath." And no answer at all may duck it altogether. When in doubt, write what you really think. Then wait a day before sending it. The next day, when you read over your first answer, rewording it might seem imperative. You might even decide not to respond.

Parents call this technique "time out," where children are made to sit alone for a few minutes until their rage burns away and they can deal with a problem rationally. But the technique is also useful for adults, online as well as offline.

4. *Guests should be gentle, even genteel.* Typographical errors, or typos, are probably unavoidable when you are typing a message online. But before sending a message, always read it over. If you see a gaffe, just add another line to the message:

"Oops—by 'office' above, I meant 'official.'"

When leaving, use the BBS's Goodbye command to sign off. Simply hanging up may cause problems with the BBS's software. If you're paying by the hour for the BBS service, you may wind up wasting money if you exit via a window and not a door.

5. *When given something for nothing, offer something in return.* BBSs that charge subscriptions will generally grant newcomers a trial membership. During that time you may pay nothing for access and be permitted to download some files. But you are also expected to upload files in a certain

proportion to the number downloaded—perhaps 1 to 4, perhaps 1 to 20; the proportion is set by the BBS. The files you upload should be useful, should not be copyrighted, and should not duplicate ones already in the file list.

6. *Be yourself.* Most BBSs will not let you use an alias; you have to go by your real name. The sysop may make some effort to authenticate your identity—perhaps by sending a postcard for you to fill out and return, mailed to the name and address you gave online, or perhaps by having software call your number while you're online to make sure it's busy, or perhaps just by seeing if you're in the phone book.

But imposters may be using their real names; there are frauds more subtle than pretending to be Marlon Brando online. Corpulent couch potatoes can present themselves as athletes. Wallflowers can pass themselves off as amorous fireballs. Bankrupts can talk like they're financial advisers. Online anonymity lets the world's Walter Mittys take on new personas unhindered by reality.

A little of this may be good for the soul, but what if people start believing you and act on your unexpert advice? It's best not to tell tales, if only because reality is easier to remember.

7. *Respect copyrights.* Posting copyrighted material—without the express approval of the source—is a bad idea. This goes for text as well as software. A quote or two is OK, when the proper reference is given, but throwing up whole pages and chapters of someone else's work (even this work) and claiming it to be your own is called plagiarism. Posting messages that originated on another network may also be forbidden, even if the original messages weren't copyrighted. It's usually best to stick to your own thoughts.

8. *Advertising belongs in its place.* Most public systems will have a conference dedicated to advertising. Offering something for sale elsewhere in the system will be frowned upon.

In this context, "advertising" generally refers to the "classified ad" variety, stating that user A has a particular item that he or she would like to sell to the first interested party. Purely commercial or trade advertising of the "Come on Down to Ralph's Spoilsport Motors" variety will likely be erased by the system operator, who didn't put up the board to give free advertising to your business.

If you really want to advertise on a bulletin board, offer payment. Like newspaper publishers, public sysops know and value cash.

The sociopathic type of advertising characterized by "make money" schemes, which generally involve no product and embody either pyramid recruitment "games" or advice on placing further "make money" advertisements, will also draw the sysop's wrath. (Sysops of the ILink echo network hub say they have removed such notices more times than they can count. Repeat offenders are barred from the network.)

9. *Moderation is power—don't abuse it.* If you are asked to volunteer and moderate a conference, because of either your special knowledge or your interest in a topic, you should know what you're doing. You're chairing a meeting. Here are some hints to help your chairing run smoothly—and if you're not the chair, keep them in mind when you write notes to a conference:

- Keep the conference traffic on the topic.

- Spur new discussions with your own notes.

- Prod long-running discussions toward resolution.

- Suppress excessive chitchat, especially in technical conferences.

- Answer users politely when they ask questions about system policies.

- Step in and referee quarrels before they get out of hand.

- Refer off-topic users to more appropriate conferences.

- Report to your system administrator regularly on the state of the conference.

A moderator generally has the power to remove or move messages and to suspend users who won't "flame off." If you're in a moderated conference, show the moderator the same respect he or she is showing you. If you can't respect the moderator, get out of the conference.

10. *Don't jump into the message pool head-first.* Read the message base of a new conference before you start posting comments. If there are 75 messages and you comment on message number 5, the other joiners will react as if you made a superfluous comment on a subject long ago discussed and dismissed. And you will have.

Don't comment on every message; that's not the way to get a good reputation. Remember Mark Twain's admonition, and Socrates'. Make your contributions knowledgeable and concise. Make them count. Or don't make them.

But do participate. People who come online only to read messages are often called "ghosts" or "lurkers." These people add nothing to the message base—and the message base is what gives the BBS value. Sysops tolerate them, but just barely.

11. *Listen for the echo.* In an echo network, always pay attention to the echo status of your messages (if there is an option to echo them or leave them local). Purely local messages of the "Dinner tonight?" nature should not be echoed; they will only irritate someone overseas who is paying to download your chitchat along with the rest of the conference traffic.

12. *Keep your signature short.* "Macro signatures" (whimsical graphics similar to screen graphics, used in place of a signature at the end of

a message, such as the picture of Homer Simpson used by imp.son in the opening example) add personality to your messages. However, people have been known to get carried away and include cartoon pictures of themselves (like imp.son) or maps of their locations. This is fine on a local area network or similar private system, where online time is not associated with cost, but in BBS conferences such artwork serves to inflate the online charges of other users. Keep macro signatures short.

"Tag lines" (macro signatures that are all text, often including personal information or a motto, such as the sign-off g.flambeau used in the opening example) should also be short and sweet. Be cautious about using a tag line that embodies an advertisement; it will make you unpopular with the sysop.

13. *Don't echo the echo.* When uploading a series of messages automatically, be sure you don't upload the same message more than once.

When you are commenting on a previous message, it is often helpful to quote part of the message you are referring to. But keep such quotes to the minimum length necessary, since they inflate online times for other users. (Continuously quoting long passages, followed by single lines that say "I agree" or some such, will not make you popular.)

14. *Remember your audience.* Irony is often lost on overseas users for whom English is a second language. They may be struggling just to get the literal meaning of what you said. Be witty, sure, but explain yourself.

For-sale ads should be posted only in conferences devoted to them, or else done only with the permission of the moderator. If users begin devoting conference messages to dickering over price, the conference will soon become clogged with off-topic traffic.

ANSI graphics should not be placed in messages, since they will appear as garbage when the message is echoed as ASCII characters.

If posting thank-you notes seems appropriate, perhaps to all the users who sent you best wishes on your graduation, try to combine them all into one message. The recipients won't feel slighted—they'll understand.

15. *Curses will foil you.* Even if the system has no express rules against profanity, you should still avoid it simply on the basis of enlightened self-interest. Remember, this is a text-only world. The other users are incapable of judging you on the basis of the innate goodness you exude or the kindnesses you show your dog. They see only the words you have typed. See to it that they are words that you would want to be remembered by.

CHATTING WITH CLASS AND STYLE

Unlike messages, chats happen in real time. All the users involved in a chat conference will be at their keyboards, reading each other's notes as they appear and replying to them immediately. For this reason, chatting has its own rules.

1. When you are through typing, put in about three carriage returns to signal that you have "stepped aside."

2. Try not to start typing while someone else is typing. Your software may offer a "chat mode," which lets you work on your comment while reading those of others, but not everyone's does.

3. The use of upper case looks like shouting. This sentence is that of a calm man online. THIS SENTENCE WAS WRITTEN BY A RAVING LUNATIC ONLINE. Save the capital letters for SPECIAL occasions.

4. Be aware of line lengths. If you do not break (hit a carriage return) soon enough, the system will likely insert its own, and your thoughts may come out formatted rather grotesquely—long lines alternating with very short lines—reducing the impact of whatever you said and impairing legibility. (Alternatively, the system may let the text trail off the right end of the screen into limbo, hurting legibility even more.)

And Always...

When caught flaming, apologize.

It happens even in the best families: anyone can wake up and suddenly realize he's been flaming.

In that case, never be afraid to apologize—especially in public, in the conference where it happened, in front of all the other users. Remember, if you're gracious and the other person isn't, guess who wins the argument?

13

The Law of the BBS

ABOUT THIS CHAPTER

Welcome to the electronic frontier, pardner. As in the Old West, the law has failed to keep up with the advance of human settlement and technology. It will catch up one day, but that will require new laws, and cases to test them through the appeals process to show what they mean.

Law is made slowly, over many years. In the meantime we are left with old legal doctrines whose application to BBSs is unclear, a host of unresolved legal issues, and a few law enforcement officials who either don't understand modems or regard them as the very spawn of Satan.

But don't lose hope, since there's nothing new about all this. A century ago the law had little to say concerning freeway motorists or private pilots, yet we muddled through on common sense. Your BBS can do the same thing. As the old frontiersman said, "First make sure you're right. Then go ahead." In this chapter we'll explore what's considered right.

We'll also discuss telephone companies' attitudes toward BBSs—or, rather, the absence of any coherent attitudes—and developments in BBS taxation.

INTRODUCTION

"Modems ought to be outlawed."

—U.S. federal agent

The preceding statement was made to Steve Jackson, owner/president of Steve Jackson Games in Austin, Texas, after a raid on his office on

March 1, 1990. The owner of the game company arrived at his office that morning to find the place being raided by agents who had just come from the home of his managing editor, looking for evidence of computer crime. The nation's 911 emergency telephone systems were under attack by a hacker conspiracy, and Steve Jackson's people were involved. Or so the agents believed. After all, the managing editor had a BBS in his home, and a copy of a "hacker newsletter" had been posted there.

Jackson's lawyer stood at his side, nudging him to shut up when the agents said things, he recalled later. (Jackson, a former college journalist, possesses a rapier wit.) He managed to bite his tongue and stay out of further trouble, even as agents carted off 3 of his 13 computers (including the one that ran his firm's BBS), a laser printer, and miscellaneous pieces of hardware and software.

The next day the authorities were boasting of having seized (on one of the confiscated computers) copies of the game "Cyberpunk," taking it, by its title, to be some kind of hacker's handbook. What they didn't know was that "Cyberpunk" was the latest in a series of multiplayer role-playing games the firm produced using a single set of basic rules called General Universal Role Playing (GURP). Previous titles had used scenarios based on the Old West, feudal Japan, Vikings, pirate tales, and space operas—and players were never really taught how to rustle cattle, commit hara-kiri, plunder English villages, sink Spanish galleons, or use a laser gun.

Eventually the authorities figured all this out, since no one from Jackson's firm was ever arrested or even questioned. Jackson wound up with the bulk of his hardware back, and the authorities have remained silent on the incident.

A Missouri college student named Craig Neidorf was finally indicted for wire fraud and interstate transportation of stolen property for posting information about the 911 system on his BBS. The trial slid from high court to low comedy when it was shown that a printed version of the documentation he had posted was for sale by the phone company to the public for $13.

These disturbing events point to a serious problem: There is a freakish amount of computer illiteracy in high places. But take heart—sysops have gotten in trouble for BBS activities, but in numbers no higher than you'd expect in any other randomly assembled community of the same size. And they generally had to do something to get into trouble—knowingly post stolen credit card numbers or pirated software, distribute pornographic graphic files in communities where this is taboo, or (in one case) solicit the kidnapping of a child for the purposes of making a pornographic movie.

In the American BBS community, as in most other communities, you are unlikely to get into trouble if you set out to keep out of trouble— barring freakish events. (The police can always show up at your door if you happen to look like a hunted bank robber.) But as a member of that community, like a member of any other community, you'll want to keep in mind certain rules of behavior, consciously or unconsciously, to stay out of trouble. In the BBS community, some of these rules are pretty obvious, whereas others have obscure origins. But they all seem to relate to questions of privacy, criminal liability, and civil liability.

Our discussion of these topics is based on input from:

The Electronic Frontier Foundation Inc.
155 Second Street
Cambridge, MA 02141
617-864-1550

Lance Rose, Attorney
(revisor of *Syslaw: The Sysop's Legal Manual*)
Greenspoon, Srager, Gaynin, Daichman & Marino
825 Third Avenue
New York, NY 10022
212-888-6880

The Electronic Mail Association
1555 Wilson Blvd., Suite 300
Arlington, VA 22209
703-875-8620

Paul Bernstein, Attorney
The Electronic Bar Association Legal Information Network
333 East Ontario Street #2201-B
Chicago, IL 60611
312-951-8264
BBS: 312-661-1740

PRIVACY

Privacy issues involve the privacy of the messages posted on your board and, by extension, the privacy of your users.

Privacy, it turns out, is about the only BBS legal concern addressed by federal legislation, namely, the Electronic Communications Privacy Act of 1986 (ECPA). The result of this law is that you repeatedly run across opening-screen caveats such as the following on "public" BBSs:

```
N O T I C E
Pursuant to the Electronic Communications Privacy Act of 1986
18 U.S.C. 2701 et. seq., notice is hereby given that there are
no facilities provided by this system for sending or receiving
private or confidential electronic communications! ALL messages
shall be deemed to be readily accessible to the general public.
DO NOT use this system for ANY communication for which the sender
intends only the sender and the intended recipient(s) to read!
At the very least, the operators of this system can and do review
all communications transmitted!
--------------------------------------------
Note that all messages, both public and private, deposited on
this BBS are subject to review and possible deletion at the discretion
of the System Administrator.
----------------------------------------------------------------------
```

The bottom line is that users are told up front not to expect privacy on the BBS. Boards are not compelled by the ECPA to write these notices, but the implications of the ECPA make it wise to do so.

The ECPA is 13 pages long. Its purpose is to extend to digital media the same protection afforded by previous laws to telephone conversations. The gist is that if an electronic service "holds itself out" as providing a private message service to the public, then it has the responsibility for maintaining the privacy of messages. It is expected that, in the course of maintaining the system, some private messages will end up being seen by the staff (as telephone company operators, checking a connection, are likely to overhear conversations), but that's not an issue so long as the staff does not disclose the contents to any third parties. There are exceptions, of course. If the glimpsed material appears to concern criminal activity, staff can freely report it to the police, just as any citizen is expected to report criminal activity he or she comes across.

So far, so good. But how do you, as a sysop whose computer is private property or business equipment subject to momentary reuse, relocation, or disconnection, guarantee that privacy? Do you even want to? If people start to use your message system for criminal activity, you may find the police at your door wanting to cart it off as evidence in someone else's trial (although you may be able to talk them into accepting backups, or at least letting you make your own backup before they take the hard disk). And what if someone starts using your BBS to send out digitized manuscripts of his latest postmodern photo-novella? Are you going to sit helplessly while someone takes over your hard disk with huge graphics files you cannot legally examine? Are you going to be the helpless tool of anyone who calls in?

It would seem, then, that although the privacy guarantee is an appropriate requirement for commercial electronic mail services, it's a huge potential liability for any BBS sysop. Commercial services, after all, charge for the risks they assume, charge according to use, know exactly who their customers are, and have their own legal staffs. (Additionally, by guaranteeing privacy, such services can argue that they have no information about the contents of their message traffic and therefore are not liable for any criminal activity on their systems.)

For a BBS sysop, then, the obvious move is to do as countless others do, and state up front that you do not guarantee anyone's privacy. If you balk at letting narrow legal concerns block you from granting others what should be a common courtesy, a "middle road" has also been suggested: State that you intend to respect the privacy of your users, but note that certain situations (search warrants, subpoenas, and your own suspicions of criminal activity) could force you to violate this promise.

The question of whether you, the owner of a business BBS, have a right to impose censorship, and to what extent, is unsettled, but your power in this regard can be assumed to be broad, even total. After all, the board was presumably set up with private resources to promote private aims, and not as a public forum.

On a corporate BBS, unless management has decided to guarantee privacy, users should be informed that privacy is not guaranteed. The decision of whether personal messages should be forbidden, and whether the traffic should be examined or censored, is best left to management. Whatever policies are established, users should be explicitly informed of them. If management has ever left the implication that users can expect privacy, they may find themselves held to it. (There is a case on record of a corporate electronic mail manager who was fired after assuring users that their messages were private, when in fact her supervisors were reading them.) A printed employee manual for the BBS, one that is posted online as well, seems like a good idea.

Another wrinkle of the ECPA is that after being on your system for 180 days, data change in status from private communications to business records and can be accessed by the authorities with a subpoena instead of a full-scale search warrant (which requires a hearing before a "neutral magistrate"). Usage data and similar user records (as opposed to the mail itself) are always considered business records.

The government, then, can require that you, as a "service provider," provide a backup copy of the data it's seeking on a particular user. You are not allowed to inform the user that this is happening; the government is supposed to do that within three days.

CRIMINAL LIABILITY

What if people use your system for criminal purposes? What is your liability? To have your computer seized because of the actions of other people hardly seems fair. Some liken this situation to a supermarket being shut down because of a criminal message posted among the little "for sale" notices on the cork bulletin board near the entrance. But with BBSs it actually happens.

Worse, what if the store manager is involved in the criminal activity by "solicitation, aiding, and abetting"? What if he's running a drug ring and is announcing the availability of cocaine disguised in tea bags using coded messages on the bulletin board? Closing the store then seems an appropriate part of any police crackdown.

Obviously, the question of criminality on a BBS revolves around the intent of the sysop. Your best defense is a clean conscience, backed by a clear statement that illicit activities are not allowed on the board. Then, of course, you must follow through on that statement.

Pornography

People define pornography in different ways. The U.S. Supreme Court has issued this definition: The material at issue must appeal primarily to prurient interests as defined by local community standards; it must embody no serious artistic, literary, or scientific merit; and it has to be adequately defined as obscene in state law.

The "local community standards" issue has our authorities scratching their heads. Naughty .GIF, .TIF, and other graphic files residing in your board (not to mention steamy text files, role-playing games in very adult settings, and even digitized audio recordings) can be accessed by people across the globe. Does this mean you're in a position to violate pornography laws worldwide?

In fact, such legal hassles that have been reported have been local affairs, and they say more about the local authorities than the law. A sysop was prosecuted in Oklahoma for posting pictures of "things going into things" (as a local constable defined pornography). But other boards in other regions that routinely specialize in such picture files, and the Unix-based Usenet network has conferences devoted to sex. Other general-purpose BBSs post such material but put it in closed conferences, meaning that a user has to apply for admission to the sysop, who can weed out anyone who's underage or an Oklahoma constable.

Certain adult magazines are reportedly planning to offer their graphics online. And national dial-a-porn phone services continue, although FCC regulations pertaining to access by minors to adult material has pressured many into moving from 900-number toll lines to 800-number toll-free lines (billing callers through credit cards and, in the process, weeding out the underaged).

Unless your business BBS is involved in certain "novelty" lines, you need not be concerned about the pornography issue. A private BBS can set narrow bounds for the tone and content of discussions and can simply banish any non-business-related .GIF files that show up.

Freedom of the Press

The First Amendment to the U.S. Constitution reads as follows: "Congress shall make no law respecting the establishment of religion, or prohibiting the free exercise thereof; or of abridging the freedom of speech, or of the press; or the right of the people peaceably to assemble, and to petition the Government for a redress of grievances." Considering the fourth clause in that sentence, can U.S. authorities legally interfere with your BBS in any way?

Yes and maybe. Yes, there is no freedom to yell "Fire!" in a crowded theater, although some say that analogy by Oliver Wendell Holmes is overused in an attempt to ban any speech people don't like. Yes, speech and writing involved in the commission of a criminal act are not protected. Under a number of Supreme Court rulings, obscenity is not protected. And beyond that, your data can still be searched or subpoenaed, provided authorities follow "due process."

As to whether interfering with the operation of your BBS constitutes a violation of "press freedom," again we're in an ambiguous area. Does a BBS constitute a printing press? A publisher—be it of a newsletter, a newspaper, a magazine, or this book—generally has an editorial organization with full control over what gets in and is left out of the product. A BBS's message base, by contrast, is the product of its users, with the sysop seeing nothing in advance of its posting, and exercising control mostly by weeding out anything deemed offensive. This might put a BBS under the heading of a "distributor," who is afforded even broader protection against liability than a publisher, since a distributor has no control over content.

The bottom line: Your first line of defense is the freedom of speech of your users, and then their privacy under the ECPA. In fact, at this writing, Steve Jackson Games Inc. and the Electronic Frontier Foundation are suing the U.S. government for seizing Jackson's BBS on the grounds that it violated users' rights under the ECPA.

CIVIL LIABILITY

Even if you have never broken any criminal laws, you can still end up in court: You can be sued by someone who thinks you have done him or her damage.

Civil liability is harder to anticipate than criminal liability. Under American criminal law, you must be proven guilty beyond a reasonable doubt. In the civil courts, proof turns on a "preponderance of evidence" standard. It's much easier to prove civil liability. For example, in 1991 a Georgian was "convicted" in civil court of murdering his wife and denied her inheritance, even though the district attorney, both before and after the case was filed, refused to prosecute, saying he lacked evidence to obtain a conviction.

In other words, you can't be sent to jail in a civil trial, but you can be punished severely. And defending yourself against a civil suit can be just as expensive, both financially and in terms of publicity, as defending yourself in the criminal courts.

In a civil trial your intentions are not an issue; instead, the court asks whether a "reasonable man" (or "reasonable woman") would have done what you did. Alas, this is the frontier, and it's hard to tell what's reasonable until some pioneers get shot in the back with arrows. Right now, the main areas of concern appear to be copyright infringement, libel, and negligence.

Copyright Infringement

Letting people upload and download copyrighted software puts you in the "stream of commerce" of stolen material, and you could be held liable in an infringement suit from the copyright holder. Intentional infringement, of course, may involve criminal liability.

Posting excerpts from books or magazine articles is also a violation of copyright. Simply citing the copyright of the source (as many people do) is not enough; you are supposed to get the permission of the copyright holder. An exception is made in the case of excerpts amounting to "fair use"—meaning that you have not quoted enough of the original to make buying and reading it superfluous.

But what about material posted on the board by a user, or by you? Who has copyright to it? You have a copyright on anything you write that embodies "authorship" (that is, something more involved than asking another user, "dinner at eight?") from the moment you write it, regardless of whether you registered it with the Copyright Office. (Although registration gives you more rights if you do end up suing.) And you do not abandon that copyright once you post your creation on a BBS. The sysop may be able to claim a copyright to the contents of the BBS as a collection, but the individual authors would still have copyright to their own material (much as many scientific books are collections of individual papers, copyrighted individually and as a collection). Reprints of conference message threads do appear in magazines, but before you emulate this practice, it would be wise to get reprint permissions from the users involved.

Libel

Libel is a defamation of character in print. (Slander is the same thing done verbally, which doesn't concern us.) Of course, if you launch a character assassination attempt against someone, you risk getting sued. But there are two extra facets to libel in the BBS world: identification and press freedom.

The identity issue comes into play because libel is in the eye of the beholder. Reporting that a married man slept with a beauty contest winner half his age can be libelous to an American politician, but it may be "due recognition of the leader's vitality" in certain other countries. Saying that a man's hands shake is merely interesting if he's a rock star, but possibly libelous if he's a brain surgeon.

But on a BBS you ultimately can't be sure who is who. Even if you have made some effort to validate your users, someone may still be using another party's account when posting a cancer cure claim that leads you to denounce the user by name as a charlatan. The advent of automatic number identification, or caller ID service, may let you know exactly where a call came from, but it still won't tell you who was at the keyboard.

On the other hand, there's the doctrine of freedom of the press, as interpreted by the U.S. Supreme Court. There are several levels of consideration. If something is true, you can always get away with saying it, painful as it might be to the subject. If you are a news organization, you can make any potentially defamatory statement about a public figure—unless you do it with "actual malice." A news organization can also say potentially defamatory things about a private person as long as the statements are thought to be true. (If you grossly abuse someone's privacy, that's another issue.)

Of course, what is a news organization, and who is a public figure? Neither question has a real answer. Purely commercial database informational services (such as the Dow Jones News Retrieval Service) have been found by the courts to be nonmedia organizations since they sell to a select group of subscribers instead of the public. The operator of a noncommercial BBS could probably argue that it's more of a news organization, and it is the position of the Electronic Frontier Foundation that it ought to be considered as such for purposes of defamation liability.

People who habitually "interject themselves" into the news are readily identified as public figures. But where does celebrity status stop? With the mayor? The justice of the peace? The policeman? There is no real answer. Lawyers get paid to argue such things.

And what about defamatory statements posted by one user about another? (This can be a real problem if the two people are your employees.)

In this case, the sysop is a distributor instead of a news organization, and a distributor can be held liable only for defamatory material that he or she was aware of—unless, of course, the sysop was actively involved in posting the material or was negligent in removing it. The best course is to avoid personal attacks, and to tell your users not to make any, either.

Negligence

Doing nothing at all can also get you sued, which is why people fence swimming pools and cover old wells to keep children from falling into them. In the BBS world, the obvious danger is viruses. What is the sysop's responsibility if someone downloads a file, runs it, and the virus it contains wipes out the user's system? Should the sysop have fenced this hazard?

There are a number of claims a sysop can make in this case. The user, after all, voluntarily assumed some degree of risk in downloading the software; shareware is widely known to carry the danger of virus infection, much as liquor is widely known to carry the danger of drunkenness. The defense may also argue that the user was involved in "contributory negligence" by running the software without checking for a virus. How a court will decide depends on its mood and the details of the case. But a sysop is well advised to guard against viruses, or at least warn the users if no action has been taken.

More prosaic things than viruses can cause trouble, such as posting stolen credit card and telephone access numbers, or even statements that someone is on vacation and their house is unguarded. The sysop should make prudent efforts to police such things. But what's "prudent"? Reading the files once a week? Once a day? Hourly?

Think of that grocery store again, the experts suggest: If you trip on a banana peel and injure yourself, you might sue the store for leaving that peel on the floor. But the store could argue that it had just fallen there moments before, and there was no time to clean it up, and why didn't you watch where you were going anyway? You could argue that they had plenty of time and were negligent sloths, and that you could not see the danger because of that rickety shopping cart they gave you. Whose story is believed depends on the court, on the judge and the jury. But the jury is not likely to be swayed by a manager who admits that the floors are never cleaned and who claims that anyone who walks in takes his chances.

Sysops have gone on vacation with their boards running, and returned to find copyrighted software posted and a lawsuit in process from the publisher. But they were able to get off the hook by showing that they had been gone, and that normally they did clear such stuff off the board.

TARIFFS AND REGULATIONS

Most American sysops (judging from echo network traffic on the topic) are more concerned about regulatory than legal issues. They wonder when the local phone company will decide that their BBS is a business and charge business rates for the phone lines. This is a major concern for hobbyist sysops because the monthly charge for a business line can be twice that for a residential line. (The pricing presumes that business lines are busier than residential lines, putting more of a load on phone company switches.) The extra money gets you a listing in the Yellow Pages and possibly more attention from the customer service department. (Obviously, this question should not be of concern to a business BBS; it's already paying the higher line rates.)

Residential phone customers can always add a few extra lines, claiming they're for teenagers. But at some point the phone company is likely to ask embarrassing questions about the population explosion. Then, if you as a sysop admit what you are doing, they are likely to regard your multiline BBS as a business, especially if you are charging users a subscription fee.

At that point it's difficult to say what to expect or give advice on how to proceed. Phone companies set their rates for a particular area under the regulation of each state's public utility commission. There are 50 states (plus the District of Columbia, Puerto Rico, and other territories) served by about 1,500 phone companies in the United States. Some are tiny firms serving small rural areas; others are giant regional Bell companies. Thus, regulations differ widely from place to place, even within a state. So do the attitudes of phone companies: some are aggressive in seeking to turn residential lines into business lines, and some aren't.

A solution would be for phone companies to offer a special "sysop" rate for hobbyist BBSs. This could be 20 or 30 percent higher than the residential rate, but still lower than the business rate. The rationale is that although BBSs do impose an extra load on phone switches, this usually occurs at night, when other loads are lower. In exchange for the extra payment, sysops should get separate BBS listings in the "white pages" of the phonebook, and access to an account representative who actually understands BBS phone problems.

TAXES

In September 1991 a controversy erupted that may change the face of hobbyist BBSs forever. As part of its fiscal 1992 budget agreement, New York state lawmakers decided to impose sales taxes on BBS downloads. The legislation (Senate bill 6079, Assembly 8491) went into effect on September 1. A group called New York Bulletin Board Systems (NYBBS) sent 31 representatives to a September 7 meeting with two legislators, Democrat Paul Tonko and Republican James Tedisco, who told them that the tax requirement includes not only commercial software but also shareware and public-domain software. For the latter types, the sysop is required to estimate the "value" of the software and then remit applicable tax. The tax remission requirement is said to be in effect for the sysop whether or not the downloader ever pays for the software.

Tony Mack, a sysop in the Albany area, said that the only exemptions mentioned by the two legislators were for BBSs that did not accept donations of any type and imposed no restrictions on downloading, such as upload/download ratios or membership requirements.

Reaction was swift. Some BBS sysops urged protests and a repeal movement. The New York Amateur Computer Club sysop, Hank Kee, threatened to stop file transfers.

Within a week, however, it was unclear if the state was prepared to back up its contention. Paul Rickard, director of the New York Department of Tax and Finance, assured attorney Lance Rose that hobby boards were not affected and that others could gain exemptions from sales taxes that newspapers and periodicals already enjoy. More important, Rickard's definition of "hobby board" seemed quite loose, covering all nonprofit boards. Texas had previously defined hobby boards as those with fewer than three phone lines, for purposes of applying business or residential rates.

Computer industry leaders were unanimous in damning the proposal, saying it was like demanding that delivery services such as Federal Express pay sales tax on what they deliver, when it is the merchants sending the materials that should be billed.

If New York backs down—and it was unclear as this book went to press whether it would—the movement to tax BBSs could stall. If New York succeeds in collecting more in taxes than it pays in enforcement expenses, however, this movement could rapidly spread across the nation. Sysops need to be aware of applicable tax laws in their state, as well as possible changes in the law, when putting a BBS with file downloads online.

A Final Note

The law cannot be summed up in any book. If you're in trouble, get professional help. If you fear trouble, get professional help. If you use common sense, you'll probably stay out of trouble.

14

Viruses, Hackers, and
Other Dangers

ABOUT THIS CHAPTER

Computer security problems have gotten a lot of press. The BBS world has been able to shrug off most of it. You'll see why, as we discuss:

- Computer viruses
- Antivirus measures
- Hackers
- Security measures

VIRUSES

Viruses are parasitic programs that can alter the way your computer works, perhaps even hanging it up, forcing you to turn it off and lose your recent work, or corrupting disk files. The virus programs add themselves to the end of existing programs, and then overwrite (and damage) sections of existing files. Whenever the infected program is run, the virus emerges—its code runs first—and looks for other programs to infect.

Some viruses lodge themselves in a computer's RAM, waiting for an opportunity to do damage or reproduce. Other viruses add random bytes of code, or phrases like "eddie lives," to files at random. You might not notice it until it's too late, until a program file is hopelessly corrupted.

Other viruses have been known to add words to files, turning "I do love you" into "I do NOT love you." Other viruses make your PC seem to slow down or to have suddenly lost memory. Or insulting messages may appear on the screen. Or the system may die altogether.

John McAfee, chairman of the Computer Virus Industry Association, estimates at this writing that there are about 700 identified viruses in circulation. About half will cause damage when invoked, while the others merely seek to reproduce, such as the famous "Stoned" virus from Australia, which displays a pro-pot message on victims' screens. (This was somehow modified and copied to Chinese PCs in 1991 to display pro-democracy slogans on the anniversary of the Tiananmen Square massacre.) As to who writes viruses and why, there are few clues, but McAfee thinks their places of origin are evenly split among Western Europe, Eastern Europe, and Asia. (And a few, no doubt, originate in the United States.)

McAfee says about 70 percent of reported infections can be traced to computer repair shops. Someone who encounters a virus may think there's a hardware problem and take the machine to a shop. The technician immediately runs diagnostic software, which gets infected and goes on to infect every computer brought into the shop thereafter.

Salesmen who make computer presentations also account for many infections. They go from place to place running demos on clients' computers. Eventually they run into an infected computer, and their demo software gets infected—and it then infects every computer it's run on subsequently.

BBSs, however, probably account for only 1 percent of infections, according to McAfee. When a file is uploaded to a BBS, it does not run on that BBS; it just sits there inertly until someone downloads it, so it has no chance to infect the other software on the board. Files that are uploaded are usually fresh from the vendor or from the user-programmer and haven't had much opportunity to be infected. The chief danger, therefore, is from people intentionally uploading infected files. Fortunately, not much of that goes on, he notes. Moreover, most sysops run uploaded programs through virus checkers before making them available for downloading.

Other high-profile dangers include worms and Trojan horses. Worms are viruses that travel on their own accord from computer to computer through the networks they are attached to. Worms are not a factor in the BBS world, since to travel the worm would have to take control of the modem software package, and there are many incompatible packages out there.

Trojan horses, also called logic bombs, are destructive programs that do not try to reproduce. Some event, usually the arrival of a particular date, sets them off. Computer folklore has it that many of these bombs are left in software by freelance programmers who are worried about getting paid. If they get their money, they disarm the bomb. Otherwise, at some future date, when the programmer is gone and forgotten, the client suddenly has no computer system—all files are erased. In the BBS world, any Trojan horse would likely be the result of intentional vandalism.

Stopping Viruses

Predictably, a "disinfectant" industry has sprung up. Antiviral programs take one of two approaches. The program may monitor the size of all program files, since a sudden change can indicate an infection. Or it may sit in the background and watch the system for virus-like activity, especially suspicious disk activities.

Since new viruses continue to crop up, antivirus vendors offer updates at frequent intervals, often through their own BBSs. Here are the major PC antivirus vendors:

Parsons Technology, 375 Collins Road NE, P.O. Box 3120, Cedar Rapids, IA 52406-3120, 1-800-223-6925

ViruCide scans all the files on a disk, looking for the "signatures" of known viruses and removing the ones it finds. Updates are mailed out.

McAfee and Associates, 4423 Cheeney Street, Santa Clara, CA 95054, 408-988-3832

McAfee sells three programs: Viruscan, which scans the disk for viruses; Cleanup, which removes viruses; and VShield, a memory-resident program that examines program files as they are being loaded, looking for viruses and preventing the program from loading if one is found. Updates are posted on the firm's BBS at intervals of four to six weeks. The prices listed, incidentally, pertain to home use only. Corporate "site licenses" are available, at prices depending on the number of machines in use. Updates are mailed quarterly to corporate sites.

IMSI, 1938 Fourth Street, San Rafael, CA 94901, 415-454-7101, 1-800-833-4674

VirusCure Plus comes with two years of free upgrades, posted every few weeks on the firm's BBS. The main feature is a memory-resident module that examines files as they are loaded for viruses and watches system activity for signs of viruses at work. It can also clean up damaged files in many cases.

*Peter Norton Product Group, Symantec Corp., 100 Wilshire Blvd.,
Santa Monica, CA, 90401, 213-319-2000.*

Norton Anti-Virus comes in two parts. The first is a memory-resident program called Virus Intercept that can watch the system for viral activity, check the boot section for problems, and scan all files being loaded for virus signatures. The second, Virus Clinic, can scan the disk for viruses, remove them, and repair files. The firm posts updates about every other week on its BBS and on CompuServe, and it will disinfect any disk sent in with about a seven-day turnaround.

*Central Point Software Inc., 15220 NW Greenbrier Parkway,
Beaverton, OR 97006, 1-800-888-8199, 503-690-8090,
BBS 503-690-6650*

Central Point Anti-Virus can both scan the disk looking for signatures and leave a TSR to examine file loads for viruses. Updates are posted immediately, and quarterly updates are also sent out.

Several organizational bulletin boards also offer virus information and antivirus utilities. Here are their main menus, listing the features available:

*Computer Virus Industry Association Virus Information Bulletin
Board: 408-988-4004.*

```
==========
The Homebase BBS
==========


<P>=Shareware Validation Data Base
<Q>=How To Download
<M>=VIRUS DETECTORS AND DISINFECTORS   ********

<V>=Virus Information Board
<R>=Upload Infected Program or Suspected Virus
<!>=CVIA General Information
<U>=Utilities Misc. System Options
<E>=EMAIL Electronic Mail
<Z>=Review Agent Uploads (For McAfee Agents Only)
<S>=Sigs (Uploads/Downloads)
<B>=Bulletin-Boards All Topics
<H>=Help Tips For This System
<A>=Combine Read All Boards (Except Group Therapy)
<C>=Pacific Standard Time
<T>=Terminate Connection

Command:
```

The National Computer Security Association Bulletin Board:
203-364-1305.

```
                    Welcome to the NCSA Bulletin Board!
Washington, D.C.:
        Voice & Fax: 717-258-1816   BBS: 202-364-1304, -1305
        NCSA, Suite 309, 4401-A Connecticut Ave NW, Wash. DC 20008
Exeter, England:          BBS: +44 392 433566 (2 lines)
Hayward, California:      BBS: 415-786-0471
Coming soon to...
        Cedar Rapids, Iowa:         BBS: 319-366-3724
        Charlotte, North Carolina:  BBS: 704-545-7076; -1205
        Denver, Colorado:           BBS: 303-962-9536
        Hudson, Ohio:               BBS: 216-656-1046
        Ottawa, Ontario, Canada:    BBS: 613-521-6108

                    Information about this BBS
                1 - Purpose of this Board
                2 - Policies of this Board
                3 - Statistics on this Board
                4 - Rules Governing this Board

        NCSA Information                 COMSEC Information
5 - NCSA's Policy Statement          8 - Benefits of joining the
    Concerning Product Reviews           COMSEC Assocation
6 - Benefits of joining the NCSA     9 - Answers to some common
7 - Answers to some common               questions about COMSEC
    questions about the NCSA        10 - COMSEC Bulletin #1

                Information about Our Books
            11 - About "Computer Viruses" (book)
            12 - About "Computer Security" (book)
            13 - About "Defend Your Data" (NCSA's book on Data Recovery)

                Information about Viruses
14 - Intro to the Virus problem    22 - Are LANS safe?
15 - Anatomy of a Virus            23 - Preventing Trojans/Viruses
16 - Preventing Viruses            24 - Virus Detection
17 - Trojan Horse Recovery         25 - Advice on Virus recovery
18 - Advice on Virus recovery      26 - Anti-Virus Software
19 - Virus protection programs     27 - How to update our information.
20 - Definitions menu              28 - Lists of Trojans, Hacks
21 - Write-protecting a hard disk  29 - Virus Researcher Agreement
35 - Checking for changes in files

    Other Information
30 - Comp. sec. in modern lit.     31 - Security product vendors
32 - NCSA Events Calendar          33 - National Personnel Recruiters
34 - NCSA needs donated equipment!      Job List

Read what bulletin(s), L)ist, S)ince, N)ews ([ENTER] = none)?
```

The National Institute of Standards and Technology's National Computer Systems Laboratory Computer Security BBS: 301-948-5717 or 5140.

```
                    BULLETIN TOPICS MENU

1    Using the BBS - READ THIS!        NOTE: Viewing Bulletins is NOT
                                       straightforward! The BBS makes
2    Computer Security Alerts          you view all bulletins from this
                                       menu only.   For example, after
3    New Publications                  displaying sub-menu 1 you want to
                                       view Bulletin 16, return to this
4    Upcoming Events & Activities      menu and then enter '16' at the
                                       prompt at the bottom of this menu.
5    Of General Interest
                                       TO DOWNLOAD BULLETINS, first note
6    Resources                         the bulletin numbers.  Quit this
                                       menu, go to the Main Menu & type
7    Computer Security Organizations   'F' to go to the File Menu. Then
                                       type 'D' to download. To download
8    Virus-l and Risks Forum           Bulletin 24, ex., use filename
                                       'BULLET24'


Read what bulletin(s), L)ist, S)ince, N)ews ([ENTER] = none)? 1
```

HACKERS

Hobbyist BBSs offer few thrills to hackers, since they are open to the public. Why go to the trouble of hacking your way in when anyone can initially log in free with a "guest account," even on boards that charge subscriptions? Hackers more often go to the other extreme and set up their own boards for themselves and their cronies.

Private business boards, however, represent a real challenge to hackers. The public is not invited, and an intruder might find something of genuine commercial value. There are two ways a business sysop can protect the board: password management and physical isolation.

Passwords

Hackers make enormous headway as a result of human torpor: operators never change the system-default ("factory-installed") passwords. If you dial in and enter USER=SYSTEM PASSWORD=SYSTEM (or GUEST-USER, or FIELD-MAINTENANCE, or some such) you can get into a shocking number of nonpublic systems.

Even if the corporate sysop is paying attention and changes these defaults, users present a major security threat. They may be allowed to pick their own passwords, and the passwords often end up being their first and last names, single letters of the alphabet, or common epithets. A hacker can often get in if given the opportunity to try a list of 200 or so words.

As a sysop, you should use gibberish passwords of the maximum length allowed by the software. Do not use words that appear in the dictionary. You should also see to it that passwords are changed at regular intervals. Also, usage should be examined, to see if any particular account is suddenly getting an abnormal amount of use. You may also consider limiting the number of times a user can try a password—in case a hacker is guessing.

These precautions should prevent a hacker from getting into your board through educated guessing. There are other approaches, however.

Hackers can rummage through your office garbage during the night, looking for discarded computer manuals or slips of paper with passwords written on them. (They may also find discarded credit card purchase slips showing valid card numbers, which is useful in credit card fraud.) You don't have to work for the CIA to need a paper shredder.

Hackers may also converge in the parking lot at night outside steel and glass office buildings and peer through the windows with telescopes, looking for computer screens that have been left on, from which they can glean log-on information.

They may try "people hacking," calling your users at the office during business hours, engaging them in conversation and trying to get them to reveal their log-ons through some pretext. Or they may simply try to get to know them well enough to guess what password they would have chosen; hackers have boasted that they can examine a person's wallet and determine their password. (Safecrackers take a similar approach, guessing at a string of numbers that would be significant to the user.)

Military systems are protected according to specifications called Tempest. All conventional computer terminals emit radio noise that can be picked up and analyzed, and from it the contents of the screen can be reconstructed. Tempest shielding prevents the emissions. You need be concerned about Tempest only if you are doing secret government work.

In sum:

- Use long, gibberish passwords.
- Change them at intervals.
- Monitor use.
- Beware of intrusions through trashcans and windows.
- Beware of glad-handers.

Physical Security

Physical security doesn't mean sealing your BBS in a vault in the basement. It means physically isolating it from your other computers.

Presumably, the BBS is being used for message traffic and for posting notices—not for processing payrolls, keeping customer files, doing market analyses, or anything else "mission-critical." Those activities should remain on your bookkeeping system. To ensure that any penetration of the BBS will not compromise the security of the bookkeeping computer, it's best to have no physical connection between the two. Data that you want to post from the bookkeeping computer to the BBS or vice versa should be put on a floppy disk and then loaded into the other computer. Program files that show up on the BBS should be examined for viruses before anything is done with them.

Thus, having a BBS can actually enhance your business's security. Penetrations will be limited to the BBS and will not affect the conduct of business. Of course, if you are using the BBS to handle credit card sales, transmit invoices, or move electronic mail, security remains a concern. Corporate computer security is a discipline in itself. Still, a BBS can isolate your "non-savvy" computer traffic in a user-friendly environment that can be isolated from sensitive data. This protects not only against hackers, but also against naive users, who will, after all, make mistakes.

Networked BBSs that share a local area network with mission-critical applications can also be kept logically isolated from the rest of the LAN, as is done with a system called BBServer from Mustang Software. The approach is logical; time will tell whether or not it works.

15

The BBS Future

ABOUT THIS CHAPTER

Enhancements in BBS technology hinge on enhancements in:

- Microprocessors
- The public phone system
- Sound synthesis
- Video compression

As we'll see, dramatic advances are brewing in all fields.

"NO LIMITS"

In just 13 years, BBSs have gone from being a hobbyist's dream to a growing industry. A handful of pioneers now make their livings running BBSs, or writing software for them.

Jack Rickard of Boardwatch Magazine (which covers the BBS scene) predicts that, although a few dozen public boards now have cash flow of $3,000 per month, the best BBS sysops could become millionaires in a few years. "The opportunities as a business are enormous. Most operators have no business acumen, yet they're still drawing a crowd. I would be safe in saying that in three years there will be 20 people walking around, clear-cut millionaires running bulletin board systems. Several hundred will be making a good living at it."

And you ain't seen nothing yet.

The world is changing fast, warns Dennis Hayes, founder of Hayes Microcomputer Products, the leader in the PC modem business. Aside from getting away from a dependence on paper, we are finding that the implosion of technology is not finite. We can continually integrate more functions onto semiconductor devices and continue to make interesting application software. The only limitation is the ability of institutions—computer companies, phone companies, businesses, and (most importantly) our own minds—to handle it.

MICROPROCESSORS

Two forces are driving these big changes in BBSs. The first is the microprocessor itself. Today's chips are 10 to 100 times faster than those first programmed by Ward Christensen and Randy Seuss. Tomorrow's chips will be faster still. This means that a Galacticomm™ system that can now handle 64 users will be able to handle 128, or more. With a local area network, a PC Board system will be able to handle hundreds of users at once, easily.

A common refrain heard by the authors while researching this book was: "I'm going to compete with CompuServe." The giant mainframe-based online system in Columbus, Ohio, has 600,000 users and is spreading its network around the world through joint ventures in Europe and Japan. This year, the refrain was laughable. In a few years, it won't be.

Again, the reason is the microprocessor. PCs just cost less to run than mainframes. Shrink-wrapped software costs less to maintain than any mainframe application. Thus, bulletin boards already have a substantial cost advantage over mainframe-based systems. As the power of microprocessors grows, as it gets easier and less expensive to access such systems using X.25 packet networks, and as BBSs gain ever-cheaper magnetic storage—plus CD-ROM systems, which put gigabytes online for a few thousand dollars—BBSs will become full-fledged competitors with mainframe systems, at a fraction of the cost.

Some sysops are already going head-to-head against the mainframe operators, and winning. Jim Appleby of the Business BBS laughs when he hears of trade groups spending millions to put a few thousand users into a private network on CompuServe. "I can give them the same services, free, for what they're now spending on monthly maintenance," he says. "And I can give their users customized menus, using familiar buzzwords, which CompuServe can't match."

Just as many corporations are now junking their mainframes or minicomputers in favor of local area networks, Appleby predicts that many will begin junking their mainframe-based communication systems in favor of bulletin board software. "Make the BBS a node on a LAN, and any other node can dial in and use its services without making a phone call," he says.

ISDN

The second driver of BBS change is less obvious, because it's part of the phone system itself. The Integrated Services Digital Network, or ISDN, is a set of digital standards for phone services, best known for letting telephones, fax machines, and modems share a single line while passing information back to central phone company switches (see Chapter 5). The phone networks, in other words, are becoming data networks.

This has huge implications for anyone using BBSs, according to Dennis Hayes. Hayes is the person who brought out the first PC modem and patented the key escape sequence, which controls interaction between PC modems and communication software. He has now bet a substantial part of his company on ISDN, building adapters that can link PCs to those services.

The computer industry is blind to what's about to happen with ISDN, he complains. The seven regional Bell companies serving the United States expect to have half their lines "ISDN-capable" by the end of 1992. Those deployment plans will be published by the time you read this book. That means your phone company is now telling businesses in your area where and when they can expect the service.

Many people in the computer industry have ignored ISDN because the phone companies have been using the acronym for a decade now. As mentioned earlier, many joke that it stands for "I Still Don't Need (it)." But the joke's now on the skeptics. Telephone time frames and computer time frames are completely different. To the phone companies, all this change has been very sudden, Hayes notes.

But that's not all. The phone companies will create a standard form for ISDN parameters, making it easier to order. Users will order standard packages of service and find out right away what it will cost. Generally, Hayes explains, basic-rate ISDN lines are being priced at between 1.3 and 1.7 times the price of regular business phone lines. That's a bargain, because a single ISDN phone line can handle two channels of 64,000 bps service plus a 16,000 bps signaling channel.

By contrast, modem companies are now reaching the technical limits on the volume of data they can push through analog phone lines. Today's 9,600 bps modems frequently slow down because of line noise.

Yes, Hayes says he can smell ISDN coming. In the next year every large phone company in North America will be funding ISDN within their networks. That's why Hayes has been building packet assembler-disassemblers, or PADs, into his Ultra 9600 modems, so that when ISDN is installed he can offer a natural connection between today's analog service and digital. Hayes says he wants the analog-digital conversion to go through packet switchers in your computer, not through a telephone company's central office. It's on the verge of happening.

With ISDN, boards will be capable of providing 64,000 bps data channels, as well as voice-data applications nobody knows how to use yet. ISDN will turn today's bulletin boards into multimedia boards, with audio, text, and compressed pictures all sent in the time it now takes to send program files, Hayes notes. With current levels of compression, a 64,000 bps data channel can squeeze 256,000 bytes down the line per second—the equivalent of a digitized movie frame every 6 seconds. The bottleneck here will be the serial ports of older PCs, and Hayes' company has addressed this with its Enhanced Serial Port, or ESP, found on its newer modems. The ESP technology has also been offered to Hayes' competition.

Hayes says it it will be up to the BBS community to prove him right. He expects sysops to totally redo the way bulletin board systems work, so that multimedia can use the basic-rate service in ways no one has thought of before.

For instance; there are already boards that are devoted to .GIF files (see Chapter 8). Any picture can be turned into a .GIF file. Using bulletin boards, news wires could sell their photo libraries, doctors could offer inside views of surgical procedures, and stores could offer online catalogs that are just as good as those they now produce for mailing.

Another example: A few boards now offer MIDI (musical instrument digital interface; see the next section) files to run music synthesizers. Currently, the boards are offering only tiny "samples" of sound effects—everything from the barking of dogs to classic Keith Richard guitar riffs. They also offer utilities for various MIDI synthesizers, and interfaces between those synthesizers and PCs. But what if a board could offer whole concerts, which you could not only record and play on your CD player, but alter and sample into your own compositions?

Using ISDN lines and video compression schemes such as those of JPEG (the Joint Photographic Experts Group, to be discussed), movie studios could deliver copies of classic films into your home equal in quality to what they can put on the largest movie screen. Colleges could offer multimedia courseware—pictures, sound, computer instructions, and text—with which students could interact outside the classroom. You could download pictures of Saturn, in their original resolution, as delivered by the Voyager spacecraft, into your home PC for your kids to play with.

With ISDN, in other words, the current speed limits on BBS operations will disappear. The ability to pass around PC files will finally match the PC's ability to create them.

How will BBS operators, and BBS software vendors, react to these changes? No one knows. The BBS future is limitless. In the meantime, since ISDN opens the BBS world to MIDI and JPEG technologies, let's look at them.

MIDI

A discussion of MIDI may not belong in a chapter on the future of BBSs. Such files are already a feature on some BBSs. There is even an echo network, the MidiLink Network, sharing messages about the technology.

MIDI was first put together in 1983 by the International MIDI Association. It was created by a number of synthesizer manufacturers as a standard way to pass musical files. As such, it has technical weaknesses, such as the fact that it's oriented strongly toward keyboards rather than computers; it can be used to "stack" synthesizers so that a musician can get a more complex sound from them. But those weaknesses are offset in large part by its massive acceptance not only by synthesizer makers, but by the PC community.

Our information on MIDI comes from two primary sources. Bob Mc-Queer wrote a primer on MIDI for the Usenet network. Bob Tullis of the AV-Sync BBS in Atlanta, which specializes in MIDI files, recommended the primer and helped us understand it.

You can easily identify a synthesizer that takes MIDI input. It will have two round, five-pin connectors on the back clearly labeled "MIDI IN" and "MIDI OUT." The pins (or holes, depending on whether the connector is male or female) form a semicircle on the upper portion of the socket. Some machines also contain a "MIDI THRU" socket used to pass the input of one device directly to output.

MIDI data pass along this async serial interface at 31,250 bits per second, with 8 data bits, 1 start bit and 1 stop bit—320 microseconds per byte. (It's something like passing data between computers using a serial cable and a null modem.) The basic concept is that one device acts as a "transmitter"—or "master," in computer terms—and the other as a "receiver," or "slave." Messages take the form of status bytes, with the seventh bit always being a 1, followed by data bytes with a seventh bit being a 1. Thus, all the data bytes can have a value between 0 and 127.

MIDI uses a logical-channel concept. There are 16 logical channels, which are put into bits 0 to 3 of the status bytes of a message. This leaves three bits for describing the message type. Complex orders can be given using multiple bytes. A sequence of notes in the same voice can also be sent without resetting the status byte. The pitches of notes are given numbers, with middle C equal to 60.

What's most important to note is that MIDI songs use an eight-bit, non-ASCII code and are used with synthesizers clearly marked to accept them. There are a number of "MIDI-boards" on the market to use MIDI files, and different boards work with different synthesizers. To control a synthesizer from a PC, you need three elements: a synthesizer that can handle MIDI input and output, a MIDI board that can handle the specific inputs and outputs of your synthesizer, and a program file.

Since the MIDI specification is based on combining or "daisy-chaining" synthesizers, McQueer writes, most devices always shovel whatever they play to their MIDI OUT port, whether they got it from the keyboard or from a computer through MIDI IN. So instruments sometimes echo input back if you're in an interactive session with a synthesizer.

There are many different types of files on a board that supports MIDI. There are program files for various types of synthesizers. There are files used on various types of hardware; Apple, IBM, and Atari are the most heavily supported. And there are MIDI sound files, which range in complexity from simple effects to entire songs. On a commercial basis, MIDI songs cost from $10 to $30.

Since real-time MIDI inputs must run at 31,250 bits per second, MIDI music can take up lots of disk space. Fortunately, such files can be compressed; ZIP appears to be the most common compression routine. But a MIDI fanatic can still use many, many megabytes. ISDN, with its ability to dial up or dial down any data rate from 300 to 56,000 bits per second, could for the first time allow MIDI music files to be passed in real time. That's an exciting point for the future.

JPEG

JPEG is a graphics compression standard sponsored by the Joint Photographic Experts Group and submitted to the International Standards Organization (ISO) and CCITT.

The lack of a compression standard has prevented the use of color images on a desktop. A single 24-bit color image, 4 × 5 inches, at 300 dots per inch, may take 5 megabytes of space. Even in a compressed .TIF format, it could take over 2.5 megabytes. Color-prepress systems routinely prepare images that take up to 40 megabytes each.

According to Tony Bove, editor of the *Bove & Rhodes Inside Report on Desktop Publishing and Multimedia* (Bove & Rhodes, P.O. Box 1289, Gualala, CA 95445, 707-884-4413) and author of numerous books on those subjects, JPEG simply removes information from an image. It can be dialed up or dialed down to create the impression of anything from "broadcast quality" to mere " VHS tape quality." In the latter case, compression ratios can reach 80:1. These types of images are often acceptable in multimedia applications. Video editors can send images of the highest quality directly to ½-inch tape for broadcast.

Just as the PostScript standard was created specifically for digital printing, and the MIDI standard was created for digital keyboards, so JPEG has a specific application in mind: digital photography.

Among the first compression utilities to support JPEG were ColorSqueeze™ from Kodak (343 State Street, Rochester, NY 14650, 716-724-1336) and PicturePress™ from Storm Technology (220 California Avenue, Suite 101, Palo Alto, CA 94306, 415-322-0506). They can take advantage of JPEG hardware such as SuperMac's SuperSqueeze (485 Potrero Avenue, Sunnyvale, CA 94086, 408-245-2202).

Although the authors have not yet found any BBSs devoted to JPEG—it has nowhere near the market acceptance of .GIF in the BBS community—JPEG does have many advantages over the older format. Its compression scheme lets you pass around much more complex images. Its acceptance by makers of digital cameras and video equipment will mean that there will be lots of images to pass around. And its acceptance for use in desktop publishing applications, on platforms such as the NeXT workstation and Macintosh II computer, as well as high-end IBM PC compatibles and the PS/2, will mean that there will soon be thousands of savvy users with a need to exchange such images.

In the next few years BBSs devoted to JPEG should spring up like wildfire. Among the first will be corporate boards created by JPEG hardware and software vendors, used to pass software patches and technical data to users. We also expect that many will be located in large cities, to take advantage of ISDN lines—at least on a local basis. Faster data delivery is still needed to pass huge data files economically.

16

Glossary of Jargon and Abbreviations

alphanumeric Refers basically to data that can be represented by one of the keys on the keyboard, transmitted as a character code, usually in ASCII. The variants are graphical data, consisting of arrays of pixels, and numeric values encoded as binary numbers.

analog Communication method where information in one medium is converted to analogous information in another medium. In the phone system, for example, sound is turned into electrical vibrations.

archive A compressed file, created through any of several available compression methods, which usually decompresses into a collection of files.

arithmetic coprocessor A chip that extends the command set of the microprocessor to include calculator functions, such as arithmetic, higher math, and trigonometry, and performs those calculations many times faster than software. The use of such a chip can greatly speed up calculation-intensive software, such as in computer-aided drafting.

ASCII (American Standard Code for Information Interchange) The character code used in the PC and BBS worlds. There are two versions: ANSI and eight-bit.

ASCII, ANSI   The seven-bit American Standard Code for Information Interchange as defined by the American National Standards Institute is the character code used in the PC world to represent alphanumeric data. The 128 characters are as follows:

Code	Character	Name	Note
0	ˆ@	NUL	Null, filler for time delays
1	ˆA	SOH	Start of header, used in bisync
2	ˆB	STX	Start of text, used in bisync
3	ˆC	ETX	End of text, follows STX
4	ˆD	EOT	End of transmission (or file)
5	ˆE	ENQ	Enquiry (who are you?)
6	ˆF	ACK	Acknowledge (the text arrived intact)
7	ˆG	BEL	Bell, rings the bell or triggers a beep.
8	ˆH	BS	Backspace
9	ˆI	HT	Horizontal tab
10	ˆJ	LF	Line feed
11	ˆK	VT	Vertical tab, moves cursor down a line
12	ˆL	FF	Form feed, go to next page/screen
13	ˆM	CR	Carriage return
14	ˆN	SO	Shift out, "supershift" for special printers
15	ˆO	SI	Shift in
16	ˆP	DLE	Data link escape, used in bisync
17	ˆQ	DC1	Device control 1, used for XON
18	ˆR	DC2	Device control 2, for custom use
19	ˆS	DC3	Device control 3, used for XOFF
20	ˆT	DC4	Device control 4, for custom use
21	ˆU	NAK	Negative acknowledge (text garbled)
22	ˆV	SYN	Synchronous idle, used for timing
23	ˆW	ETB	End of transmission block
24	ˆX	CAN	Cancel, error signal
25	ˆY	EM	End of medium
26	ˆZ	SUB	Substitute, filler for garbled character
27	ˆ[	ESC	Escape, switch from text to control codes
28	ˆ\	FS	File separator
29	ˆ]	GS	Group separator
30	ˆˆ	RS	Record separator
31	ˆ_	US	Unit separator
32			Space
33	!		Exclamation point
34	"		Quotation mark
35	#		Pound sign
36	$		Dollar sign
37	%		Percent sign
38	&		Ampersand

(continued)

Code	Character	Name	Note
39	'		Apostrophe, close single quote
40	(		Open parenthesis
41	)		Close parenthesis
42	*		Asterisk
43	+		Plus sign
44	,		Comma
45	-		Hyphen
46	.		Period
47	/		Slash
48	0		Zero
49	1		
50	2		
51	3		
52	4		
53	5		
54	6		
55	7		
56	8		
57	9		
58	:		Colon
59	;		Semicolon
60	<		Less than
61	=		Equal sign
62	>		Greater than
63	?		Question mark
64	@		"At" sign, "apiece"
65	A		
66	B		
67	C		
68	D		
69	E		
70	F		
71	G		
72	H		
73	I		
74	J		
75	K		
76	L		
77	M		
78	N		
79	O		
80	P		
81	Q		
82	R		
83	S		
84	T		

(*continued*)

Code	Character	Name	Note
85	U		
86	V		
87	W		
88	X		
89	Y		
90	Z		
91	[		Open bracket
92	\		Backslash (gray key slash)
93	]		Close bracket
94	^		Circumflex, "caret"
95	_		Underline
96	'		Open single quote
97	a		
98	b		
99	c		
100	d		
101	e		
102	f		
103	g		
104	h		
105	i		
106	j		
107	k		
108	l		
109	m		
110	n		
111	o		
112	p		
113	q		
114	r		
115	s		
116	t		
117	u		
118	v		
119	w		
120	x		
121	y		
122	z		
123	{		Open brace
124	|		Vertical line, "pipe"
125	}		Close brace
126	~		Tilde
127	.		Delete, rubout

ASCII, Eight-Bit   The nonstandard version of ASCII that covers the code values between 128 and 255. The most common version contains the following characters:

128 Ç	144 É	160 á	176 ░	192 └	208 ╨	224 α	240 ≡
129 ü	145 æ	161 í	177 ▒	193 ┴	209 ╤	225 ß	241 ±
130 é	146 Æ	162 ó	178 ▓	194 ┬	210 ╥	226 Γ	242 ≥
131 â	147 ô	163 ú	179 │	195 ├	211 ╙	227 π	243 ≤
132 ä	148 ö	164 ñ	180 ┤	196 ─	212 ╘	228 Σ	244 ⌠
133 à	149 ò	165 Ñ	181 ╡	197 ┼	213 ╒	229 σ	245 ⌡
134 å	150 û	166 ª	182 ╢	198 ╞	214 ╓	230 µ	246 ÷
135 ç	151 ù	167 º	183 ╖	199 ╟	215 ╫	231 τ	247 ≈
136 ê	152 ÿ	168 ¿	184 ╕	200 ╚	216 ╪	232 Φ	248 °
137 ë	153 Ö	169 ⌐	185 ╣	201 ╔	217 ┘	233 Θ	249 ∙
138 è	154 Ü	170 ¬	186 ║	202 ╩	218 ┌	234 Ω	250 ·
139 ï	155 ¢	171 ½	187 ╗	203 ╦	219 █	235 δ	251 √
140 î	156 £	172 ¼	188 ╝	204 ╠	220 ▄	236 ∞	252 ⁿ
141 ì	157 ¥	173 ¡	189 ╜	205 ═	221 ▌	237 φ	253 ²
142 Ä	158 ₧	174 «	190 ╛	206 ╬	222 ▐	238 ε	254 ■
143 Å	159 ƒ	175 »	191 ┐	207 ╧	223 ▀	239 ∩	255

assembler   Highly complicated programming language that directly controls the inner workings of a computer. Used mostly by professionals on projects where high-speed execution is essential.

asymmetrical   Lacking symmetry. In a modem, to transmit faster in one direction than in the other.

async   Asynchronous—the start-stop style of data communication used in the PC and BBS world.

asynchronous   In data communications, signals that are not synchronized to any timing signal but consist of discrete bytes whose spacing may be random.

AT command set   The set of modem control commands pioneered by Hayes Microcomputer Products Inc. These commands are normally sent to the modem by the computer's modem control software in a manner that is invisible to the users. However, the user often has to specify the "modem initialization string" that the software is to send to the modem, and with a Hayes-compatible modem that will be an AT command. With some software setups it is possible or even necessary for the user to send AT commands directly from the keyboard, by typing the command and pressing Enter. The modem should respond as if it got the command from the software.

Once online, you are dealing with the other computer, and any further commands to the modem will require the sending of another AT command.

The syntax for the AT command is to send the prefix **AT** or **at** (but not **At** or **aT**) followed by as many as 40 characters making up the command, plus Enter (carriage return). Following the **AT** prefix, you can have:

D   Dial

T   Tone dialing

P   Pulse dialing

,   (comma) Pause for two seconds

0–9   Phone number numerals

Enter   Ends the command

Thus, a typical dial command might be **ATDT9,5551212** followed by the Enter key. **AT** gets the modem's attention. **D** tells it to dial, and **T** tells it to use tone dialing. It dials **9** to get outside of the corporate switchboard, sends a comma to cause the modem to pause for two seconds to give the outside dial tone time to emerge, and then sends the phone number for the modem to dial.

Other commonly used AT commands include:

W Wait for the second dial tone (when dialing out of a PBX)

@ Wait for an answer

! Send a flash-hook signal (equivalent to pressing the switch hook)

A Wait for and answer a call

Many brands of modems have their own, extended versions of the AT command set, and to learn about one of these you'll have to check the documentation that came with the modem. However, for getting online, **ATDT** or **ATDP** is generally all you need to know.

autotyping Another word for file uploading or downloading to send a text file from disk as if it were being typed very quickly, without error correction.

BASIC Fairly simple programming language often included with a PC operating system, generally used by amateurs for their own projects or for self-education, although it has also been used for commercial projects.

baud The rate at which signals are introduced into a line; it is not the same as the bits-per-second speed of a line. Lately, "baud" has fallen from favor, replaced by "symbols per second."

baudot Five-bit character code used in older, electromechanical telex machines.

BBS Bulletin board system—meaning, of course, a computer bulletin board system.

Bell standards North American data communications standards established by the Bell System of phone companies before its breakup in 1984.

binary A base-2 number system, using only the integers 1 and 0. The first eight numbers look like this:

Decimal	Binary
1	1
2	10
3	11
4	100
5	101
6	110
7	111
8	1000

Binary numbers lend themselves to electronic representation, since the 1s and 0s can be represented by opposing line values, such as plus and minus voltage, or current above and below a certain value.

bit A single binary integer—a single 1 or a single 0.

BITNET (Because It's Time Network) A worldwide network connecting more than 500 universities, colleges, and research organizations, with gateways to Internet, Usenet, and other networks.

bits per second The speed rating of a data communications connection, referring to how many bits—including data and framing bits—can be moved in a second. It is not the same as the baud rate.

BTW "By the way," as in "BTW, the access number is changing next Thursday."

buffer Special computer memory used to hold data in transit from one place to another.

byte A group of eight binary integers, which gives 256 possible code permutations (2 raised to the power of 8). All character codes in the PC world represent alphanumeric characters (that is, a character you can generate by pressing a key on the keyboard) with bytes.

C Programming language commonly used by professionals for commercial projects. Popular variants include C++ (pronounced "cee plus plus").

Call Waiting A special service offered to telephone subscribers whereby someone talking on the phone can answer a second, incoming call, and switch between the two conversations. (A third person calling the line will get a busy signal.)

CCITT Comité Consultatif International Télégraphique et Téléphonique (Consultative Committee on International Telegraphy and Telephony), the United Nation's standard-setting body for the global telecommunications industry.

cellular phone A modern car radio-telephone, a car radio that automatically tunes to the antenna of the "cell" it is in. Crossing between cells, as well as "contention" among radios in a crowded cell, can cause momentary problems that garble data traffic.

COMMAND.COM The basic MS-DOS file that must be present on a disk if it is to be a "system" disk. You don't need to worry about it for application and data disks.

compatibility Refers to the ability of hardware and software to work together, regardless of their origins.

conference A message base devoted to discussion of a specific topic. Conferences may be local or echoed.

CONFIG.SYS The data file that MS-DOS checks when it "boots," to determine details of the system's configuration.

CP/M (control program for microprocessors) A disk operating system for eight-bit computers that preceded DOS.

crash The complete failure of a computer system, usually signaled by locking and ignoring of further input. A software crash (the most common kind) can usually be rectified by rebooting. A disk crash may require the replacement of hardware.

cursor The flashing spot on the screen where any impending screen activity will take place.

DCE (data communications equipment) The serial port arrangement used by modems and certain printers and terminals.

DES (data encryption standard) A method codified by the National Bureau of Standards for encrypting online data using a 56-bit key.

digital Communication method in which data are encoded in binary form.

door A program called by an online user of a BBS program to perform some specialized activity, such as running a game or gathering conference mail for a user. The BBS normally exits to DOS, and the door program is invoked. The door continues to use the serial port to communicate with the user, with the call having already been set up by the BBS program. After its use, the door exits to DOS, and the BBS program is reloaded.

DOS (disk operating system) The basic system software that actually controls the machine. Application software that uses specific machine functions (for example, writing or reading disk files, writing to the screen, or handling keyboard input) generally does so through DOS functions. Application software, therefore, is generally not written to run on a particular machine but rather on a particular operating system. For the PC, the most common systems are MS-DOS from Microsoft, PC-DOS from IBM, and DR DOS from Digital Research. Application software intended for DOS will run on any of these.

DTE (data terminal equipment) The serial port arrangement used by computers.

duplex Refers to the ability of a telecommunications connection to carry data in both directions.

EBCDIC   (Extended Binary-Coded Decimal Interchange Code) A character code used by IBM mainframes.

echo conference   A "message base" that is echoed—regionally, nationally, or even globally—among multiple BBSs, which are normally members of an organized echo network.

echo flag   With certain echo networks, a flag on a conference message that means it will be echoed to other members of the network.

echo network   An organized network of BBSs that exchange (echo) the contents of selected conferences.

emulation   The use of software to make a PC act as if it were a particular kind or brand of terminal.

encryption   The process of turning text or other data into what appears as gibberish to anyone who does not have the decryption key.

escape   (ESC) ASCII code used to signal to a device that the following data should be interpreted as commands rather than as text.

ESP   (Enhanced Serial Port) A PC add-in card from Hayes Microcomputer Products Inc. that replaces a serial port with what is essentially a dedicated communications coprocessor to handle data transmission at speeds higher than the PC would be able to handle unassisted.

.EXE   File extension of an executable program file in MS-DOS. (Certain executable files use the .COM extension.)

fax   Facsimile transmission, where the image of a page is sent to be reproduced by a distant fax machine. Digital methods are used, but fax is not compatible with data communications equipment.

file transfers   The sending of text, data, program, or graphics files in a fashion such that the file arriving at the remote computer is identical to the one on the sending computer.

file uploading   To transmit an existing text file as if the material were being typed very quickly by the user.

flamers   Online users engaged in producing flames. Self-conscious flamers often begin and end their flames with <flame on> and <flame off>, as if they want you to envision them holding a flame thrower.

flames   Online messages that constitute a heated discussion, quarrel, or feud between two or more users. Covers polemical, ad hominem, and insulting communications.

format   The command that tells the computer to write the basic data storage tracks onto a disk. This wipes out any existing data on that disk, making the use or misuse of the Format command a common source of system crashes.

FOSSIL (Fido Opus SEAdog Serial Interface Layer) A layer of device-driver software added to DOS to handle incompatibilities found in some off-brand PCs, used mostly by echo mail and related software in the FidoNet echo network.

framing bits Bits used in async connections to separate bytes from each other.

front-end Refers to a program similar to a door that temporarily replaces a BBS program to perform some specialized purpose, such as sending network echo mail. However, whereas a door is generally invoked by the user, a front-end program is normally invoked by the software itself.

FWIW "For what it's worth," as in "I don't think he ranks as a flamer, FWIW."

Goodbye Command used by most BBS software packages to let a remote user log off the BBS.

graphics Refers to a computer's ability (if present) to plot individual pixels on the screen rather than simply displaying alphanumeric text. The PC was introduced in 1981 without graphics, and the marketplace rushed to fill the void, producing a welter of different graphics standards for the PC. These include:

Monochrome: No graphics at all. It's often called an alphanumeric display, meaning that it can display characters and numbers like a typewriter, on a screen of 24 (sometimes 25) lines by 80 columns. Since the PC character set includes some nonalphabetic characters intended for graphical use (eight-bit ASCII), you can create some interesting graphical effects. But this is still not a true graphics capability; there is no way to control individual dots on the screen.

Hercules®: Produces true black and white graphics (but no shades of gray) on an ordinary monitor designed for an alphanumeric display. (The following video adaptors require special, more expensive monitors.) Like the PC itself, the Hercules board is now widely cloned. Resolution: 720 × 348 pixels per screen.

CGA: (Color Graphics Adapter) This was IBM's first stab at a graphics adapter for the PC, and it shows. It's now rendered obsolete by the EGA card. Resolution: 320 × 200 pixels per screen, using four colors.

EGA: (Enhanced Graphics Adapter) For a long time this has been the standard color graphics card for the PC, although it's quickly being obsoleted by the VGA card. Resolution: 640 × 200 pixels per screen, using 16 colors.

VGA: (Video Graphics Array) This card, with more color and higher resolution than EGA, was introduced with the PS/2 but has since been adopted and cloned for standard PCs. VGA also comes in a monochrome variant that displays shades of gray. Resolution: 640 × 480 pixels per screen, using 16 colors. Super VGA can offer twice the resolution or 256 colors, or sometimes both.

MCGA: The graphics circuitry built into the PS/2 Model 30, compatible with CGA. Resolution: 640 × 480 pixels per screen with 2 colors, 320 × 200 with 256 colors.

Others: High-density graphics designed for large monitors, used in engineering, design, and graphic arts settings. Such displays often come with "screen driver" software to make them compatible with more common DOS applications packages.

GUI Pronounced "gooey," an acronym for "graphical user interface," such as Microsoft Windows or the Apple Macintosh interface.

hack An elegant programming solution, as in "He solved it with a good hack."

hacker (1) A dedicated programmer who uses intuitive, seat-of-the pants methods to feel his or her way to the solution of a problem, hacking at it until it's solved. (2) An online intruder who gains unauthorized entry into a computer system, generally by "hacking" at the password protection, that is, making educated guesses until a password is found that works. The name also applies to intruders in voice mail systems. Some online enthusiasts prefer the word "cracker" or "worm."

hexadecimal A base-16 number system that programmers use to represent binary numbers. For instance, 13B is easier to write than 100111011; both mean 315 decimal. Similarly, 640K is really 655,360 but is A0000 in hex. The hexadecimal numbers run from 1 through F (15), so that hexadecimal 16 is 10.

hiragana The Japanese phonetic syllabary, used for local words.

IC (integrated circuit) A "chip."

Internet A network that serves most academic and research institutions in the United States and many outside the United States, with features resembling a BBS echo network. It is based on the high-speed National Science Foundation Network (NSFnet), which joins various academic supercomputing centers, with links to various regional, state university, and even corporate networks. (At last count, there were more than 2,000 sub-networks in Internet, with the number of nodes easily exceeding 100,000.) Internet (upper-case *I*) refers to any hard-wired node, whereas internet (lower-case *I*) refers to any other computer whose user has log-on access to an Internet node. At this writing, commercial use is not allowed.

interrupt An internal signal generated when a part of a computer system needs to get the attention of the central processor. The keyboard issues an interrupt when a key is pushed, forcing the computer to pay attention to the incoming data. The serial port similarly issues an interrupt when a byte has arrived from the outside.

IMHO "In my humble opinion," as in "IMHO, the sysop made a mistake."

IOW "In other words," as in "IOW, you don't agree?"

ISDN (Integrated Services Digital Network) A plan for converting the phone system to digital technology.

K Refers to 1,000 in discussions of salaries, but in computer science (where everything is based on the binary number system) it actually stands for 2 to the tenth power, or 1,024. Hence, 640K is actually 655,360 bytes.

kanji The Japanese style of writing based on ideograms, of which there are several thousand.

katakana The Japanese phonetic syllabary, or alphabet, used for foreign words.

kilobytes Bytes measured in increments of 1,024.

LAN (local area network) An arrangement whereby computers can share each other's disk files and other peripherals, usually through coaxial cable or some other method of direct connection.

log off To issue the commands necessary to end a connection with a remote BBS in a controlled fashion, generally with the Goodbye command (as opposed to simply hanging up).

log on To complete the steps necessary to connect with and use a remote computer.

M Refers to million, not thousand, in computer science.

macro A simple program that (usually) plays back a series of keystrokes and thus automates a chore or task, such as setting up a word-processing document or drawing a screen particle. Many application programs include some sort of "macro language" for this purpose, varying from simple keystroke playback utilities to elaborate programming facilities.

mail door   A door running on a network node that, when invoked, gathers the user's current conference mail, puts it (usually) in a .ZIP file, and downloads it to the user.

megabyte   1,048,576 bytes.

megahertz   One million cycles per second. In radio it refers to transmission frequency, but in computer science it refers to the speed of the computer's internal clock. The original PC ran at about 5 million cycles per second, and the latest 80486 machines run at about 50 million. (Keep in mind that any meaningful action by the computer requires multiple clock cycles.)

message base   A node's text file that contains all the messages posted in a particular conference.

MIPS   (millions of instructions per second) Since there is no clear agreement on the definition of "instruction," this is more of a marketing term than an engineering term, but it is still used to rate computers. A 16 MHz 80386 PC is generally rated at 3 MIPS, and a 33 MHz 486 PC at 15 to 20 MIPS.

MNP   (Microcom Networking Protocol) A network protocol covering both error correction and data compression.

modem   The interface device between a computer and the phone line.

moderator   A sysop or volunteer who monitors the traffic in a particular conference, at either a local-node or echo-network level, settling quarrels and keeping discussion on track.

MS-DOS   (Microsoft Disk Operating System) The basic PC system software that defines the interactions of the disk drives, serial port, keyboard, and other system components. Compatible variants include PC-DOS from IBM and DR DOS from Digital Research.

node   A computer that is a participating member of an established network.

offline reader   Software that lets you read and write electronic mail offline. Such readers designed for use with echo conferences can present an offline mirror of the conference message base.

online   The act of communicating with a remote computer of any kind.

Opus   A public-domain BBS software package used mostly in the FidoNet echo network.

OTOH   "On the other hand," as in "OTOH, we may both be wrong."

packet switching network Any of several commercial services offering nationwide (or regional) data communications services through shared use of high-speed data lines leased from the phone companies. Each line is shared through "packet switching" in which "packets" of data from users are interspersed on the line at one end and sorted out at the other. In metropolitan areas the services can be reached through local phone calls.

parallel Refers to a data connection where each bit in a byte has its own line. Used for printers and similar peripherals.

parity An error-checking bit optionally added to each async byte.

PBX (private branch exchange) An organization's internal phone system that lets it use fewer outside lines than it has telephones. Phones inside the PBX can dial each other directly, but it takes special codes to dial outside.

PBX, digital A private branch exchange based on digital technology, often comparable to ISDN.

PC A microcomputer based on the Intel chip set that can run software written for the MS-DOS operating system. The "architecture" of the PC was defined by the original IBM PC in 1981, but it is now cloned by hundreds of vendors—which is legal as long as they don't copy the IBM PC ROM BIOS. The chips that have been used in the PC to date are as follows:

8088: Original version

8086: Original with 16-bit bus

80186: Faster version of 8086

80286: Heart of the PC/AT, three times faster than 8088

80386: 32-bit chip, four times faster than 80286

80486: Enhanced 80386 with internal arithmetic coprocessor.

Each chip is available with various clock speeds. Software for earlier chips will run on later ones, but the reverse is not always true.

phone phreak A hacker who takes control of phone company switching equipment to make free long-distance phone calls or to prevent his or her calls from being traced.

PIN (personal identification number) The primary form of password protection used by automatic teller machines, security "tokens," and smartcards.

pixel One dot on the display screen.

PSTN   (public switched telephone network) The system that allows you to pick up a phone and dial another phone that is outside your organization.

QWERTY   The standard American keyboard, so named because of the arrangement of the left-side keys in the second row. The main variant is the Dvorak keyboard, named after its inventor.

RAM   (random-access memory) The memory embodied in the memory chips inside the computer, as opposed to the data stored on the hard disk or the diskettes. The name refers to the fact that you can address one byte without having to scan through all the others first, as you would with magnetic tape, at one time the main alternative to RAM. Data stored in RAM are "volatile," meaning that they are lost when the power is turned off.

reboot   To boot when the machine is already turned on, usually after a software glitch has locked up the system or sent it into an infinite loop. This can be done on a PC by pressing the Ctrl, Alt, and Del keys at the same time. Many PCs also include a red Reboot button, in case the computer is ignoring the keyboard. Rebooting wipes the slate clean: you might as well have turned the system off and back on.

ROM   (read-only memory) Software that has been hard-wired into a chip, so that it survives when the computer is turned off.

ROM BIOS   (read-only memory basic input/output system) The BIOS is the heart and soul of the PC, since it is the only memory that survives when you turn the computer off. It contains the "intelligence" that loads the operating system when the computer is turned back on, and it also contains the software used by the operating system to perform certain basic internal functions, such as writing data on the screen.

Romaji   Japanese word for the Latin alphabet.

ROTFL   "Rolling on the floor, laughing," as in "Comment re: your previous statement: ROTFL."

RS-232C   Designation for the technical description of the serial ports used by PCs.

RTFM   "Read the famous manual," as in "The question was cleared up after he RTFMed."

RYFM   "Read your famous manual" (Variant of RTFM).

salami method   A bank embezzlement scheme whereby the programmer diverts the fractional cent left over from the daily interest calculation of each savings account and deposits it in the programmer's own, secret account.

screen particles In ancient Greek, a "particle" was a one-syllable word that carried a meaning that would have been expressed, in face-to-face conversation, by some nonverbal gesture or sign. (In many of the Platonic Dialogues, Socrates' interrogatees respond mostly in particles and come across in translation as rather tongue-tied.) To make up for the lack of verbal cues in online conversation, BBS users have developed a wealth of screen particles; some users have developed their own repertoires of particles reflecting their personalities. The particles are generally produced as needed by macros within the user's word processor.

If you are going to use particles, you should develop your own. But here are some examples:

->	Tongue firmly in cheek
(o.-)	Wink
(O.O)	Wide-eyed amazement or interest
(@.@)	Total shock
(*.*)	Wake me when it's over
:-)	Smile face (sideways)
:-(	Frown face (sideways)
B-)	Smile face with glasses (sideways)
B-(	Frown face with glasses (sideways)
;-)	Winking and smiling (sideways)
!@#$%&*	Generic expletive (QWERTY keyboard)

script file A record of the commands necessary to (usually) log on to a remote system, used with a modem software package to automate the procedure.

serial Refers to a data connection in which all the bits of every byte are sent sequentially and serially down the same line. Used for modem connections and for certain peripherals.

serial port Input/output connection on a computer designed to be used with a modem or modemlike device (such as certain printers or scanners).

session The time between log-on and log-off that a user spends on a system. Some systems can support multiple simultaneous sessions.

software The digitally encoded instructions a computer follows in performing any task. Without software the computer can do nothing.

switchboard   The control panel of a PBX, where the organization's telephone operator sits.

symbols per second   The CCITT's replacement phrase for "baud rate"—the rate at which the modem is putting signals on the line. It is generally not the same as the bits-per-second rate.

sync   Refers to synchronous communications, where two devices are locked in a continuous communications link, and the meaning of each bit is determined by its place in the data stream.

sysop   Short for "system operator," generally of a BBS.

telex   Electromechanical teleprinter formerly relied on for data communications, generally using the five-bit Baudot code or upper-case ASCII.

thread   Messages within a conference that address the same theme; usually they are comments on the same original posting. Some software allows you to read a particular thread in a conference to the exclusion of other messages.

time bomb   A computer program, usually hidden in a legitimate program, that will crash the system on a given date unless the programmer has intervened in the meantime. Sometimes used by programmers who are afraid they won't be paid.

TINAR   "This is not a review/recommendation" (for lawyerly types who need to qualify their opinions, and also seen on some commercial boards that don't allow people to post any reviews) as in "BTW, TINAR."

token   Pocket-sized intelligent devices used to authorize access to a computer system.

trap door   Usually, a shortcut that lets programmers get around a system's password protection.

TSR   (terminate and stay resident) A program that, once invoked, stays in the PC, even if it is not doing anything visible to the user. Essentially, it becomes part of the operating system. Examples include "pop-up" or "memory-resident" programs invoked with special keystrokes, and antivirus programs that monitor system activity for software sabotage.

Unix   (also UNIX) An operating system originated by AT&T, and designed for multi-user systems, with built-in telecommunications functions. It is most popular in the academic and scientific communities. There are versions that will run on the PC.

Usenet   A semiformal echo network composed of Unix systems at industrial, academic, and industrial institutions.

V standards Official standards accepted by the CCITT for telephone equipment, so called because their names start with the letter *V*.

vendor conference A conference devoted to technical support for a particular product, usually with official participation by personnel of the vendor's technical or customer support department.

virus In the computer world, a self-replicating program that attaches itself to a legitimate program (such as an operating system utility) and seeks to attach copies of itself to other programs. It may also cause damage to the system, intentionally or otherwise.

worm A self-replicating program that attempts to take over the computer it is resident in and that also propagates copies of itself through whatever network it is attached to.

WORM (write once read many) An optical storage disk on which data can be written but not overwritten; thus, it is used as an online data archive.

APPENDIX **A**

BBS Echo Networks

ABOUT THIS APPENDIX

We'll examine the "echo networks" that have arisen in the hobby BBS world, creating a unique, globe-spanning communications medium that businesses can also use.

INTRODUCTION

Computers scattered across the globe, calling each other daily and automatically updating each other's databases—it sounds like a multimillion-dollar management information system set up by a huge corporation, but it's not. It's an ad hoc "echo network" organized and managed by hobbyists. Thanks to such networks, a BBS is not limited to its own resources. By joining a network, a BBS can offer organized conferences on virtually any topic. Netmail can also be sent between boards linked on an echo network, and specialized software is available for sending and reading the mail. Although most of the networks are run by volunteers, they are surprisingly sophisticated, and they form the heart of the BBS community.

Businesses can use the tools of echo networks to improve productivity. Product support conferences can have worldwide participation and offer up-to-the-minute information. Workers in remote locations can be linked at low cost.

HOW DOES IT WORK?

There are a number of automatic netmail packages available, ranging from free packages such as BinkleyTerm to commercial packages such as

QNet. They combine elements of a database program with a communications package.

Each night the netmail program goes through a complex updating routine. First it collects all new messages on your board, noting what topics they cover, and compresses them. Then the software dials another board—a "hub" or "host," which carries all the topics of the network your board belongs to. It then passes the new notes to the hub board in their compressed form, and it collects all the new messages left (by other boards) within chosen topics since the last time it called. These messages are compressed and downloaded to the linked board, after which the software decompresses them and adds them to the local conference.

Mail is passed in the same way, except that it's addressed to users at boards, not conferences on the network. Many sysops will pass a message to another board; they may ask a nominal charge for the cost of the call. Sometimes, however, messages are passed along the same hub-and-link system used by conferences. To get a note from a hobbyist board in Peoria to one in Singapore may take four or five board-to-board calls—from the local board to a regional hub, then to a national hub for the United States, then to a hub for the Far East, and then (if that hub is not in Singapore) a call to the regional hub for Singapore, from which it's passed on to the addressee board.

Usually, this process takes place late at night, at 3:00 or 4:00 in the morning. Phone bills are then at their lowest, and so is usage on both the hub and linked boards. By combining the fastest possible modems with data compression for both the file and the transmission, costs are reduced further.

(Many retail chains do much the same thing with financial data. A headquarters mainframe will dial each store in turn, polling each computerized "point-of-sale terminal" cash register for the day's receipts. Such systems can update the totals for use in an executive spreadsheet the next day, and report them directly to a bank's computer for overnight deposits and the collection of interest.)

Files may attract users to a BBS, but once the file list is picked through, it takes something more to keep users coming back. A well-run message base will keep users calling back forever, because it delivers the same thing that bars, salons, clubs, and watercoolers have offered since the dawn of time: a means of interacting with like-minded people. To talk about topics of mutual interest, to pose a question and have it answered, to help someone else a continent away by answering a question—these things are good for the soul and the ego.

They can also be good for your career. Imagine you're using WordPerfect and are stuck on a complex file conversion. Simply add your question to the message base at a local BBS with a WordPerfect conference, and the answer will likely come back to you within days. The same process applies no matter what your software or hardware question. Conferences also exist on virtually any profession you care to mention, or on any hobby or intellectual interest. If you run a collector's shop, an echo network can help you find that rare item you need for a special customer. If you're a politician, it can help you find allies and ideas for the next campaign.

Local conferences on any topic can dry up. The number of BBS users interested in WordPerfect in Elko, Nevada, or Port Arthur, Texas, may be limited. But with an echo conference your note is read, and responded to, by thousands of other people around the continent and around the world.

ECHO SOFTWARE

Several types of software have sprung up that make it easier to use and run echo networks: echo mailers, mail doors, and offline readers. It is fair to say that the arrival of such software is what made BBSs and echo networks a practical and popular messaging medium, since they dramatically reduce the costs involved. Properly used, such programs let you make full use of a BBS while remaining online only a few minutes at a time; all reading, writing, organizing, musing, and so forth happens offline. Mark "Sparky" Herring, author of the first offline reader, QMail, estimates that you can download 300 to 400 messages at 9,600 bits per second in the time it would take you to read and fully comprehend about 5 messages online.

Some of these programs are commercially produced and supported. Others were written (and new ones are continually added) by network users, who turned their software adrift as shareware or freeware on the networks, making it hard to track down details. But the following examples are thought to be representative of what's available.

Again, we'll show price ranges using the following codes:

!	free
$	to $20
$$	$20 to $50
$$$	$50 to $75
$$$$	$75 to $150
$$$$ +	above $150

Echo Mailers

The sysop of a network node needs to gather the new conference messages placed on the board and upload them to the next hub. He or she must then gather the new conference traffic from the hub and post it in the correct conferences.

Echo mailers automate this procedure. Often they don't handle the actual transmission, but merely unpack a compressed traffic file that's already been downloaded and parcel the messages out to the correct conference message bases. Echo mailers can work either with a specific BBS package or with a broad selection of packages.

PCRelay, $$, Kip Compton, available from the Running Board (301-229-5623 or through Relaynet mail)

PCRelay is the echo mailer of choice for Relaynet (described later). The current version creates outgoing message packets and distributes incoming ones (using compressed .ZIP files), but it does not handle the actual transmission.

PCRelay is able to run with the disparate BBS packages used on Relaynet because it uses a universal text interface (UTI) to link with them. The message traffic is translated to a format PCRelay can handle, and then to the format the BBS package expects. Each BBS software vendor is asked to provide a UTI, and most have done so.

Qnet, $$, Sparkware, P.O. Box 605, Cordova, TN 38018, 901-373-6245, BBS: 901-382-5583

Qnet only works with PCBoard BBS software. It unpacks or decompresses a file of network traffic with the extension .QWK and distributes it to the message base of a remote BBS. It can also pack or compress a file with the extension .REP for uploading new message traffic. Qnet is available through the Sparkware BBS.

Tnet, $$, Technique Computer Systems, 110-1841 Oak Bay Avenue, Victoria, British Columbia, V8R 1C4 Canada, 604-598-2141, BBS: 604-598-1546

Tnet is a shareware program that generates echo mail packets for Wildcat BBS systems. (It is the only such program for Wildcat systems, at this writing.) It does not handle the actual communications. Tnet is available through the BBS of Technique Computer Systems or from Mustang Software.

BinkleyTerm, !, *Bit Bucket Software Co., P.O. Box 460398, Aurora, CO 80046*

BinkleyTerm (named after a character in the "Bloom County" and "Outland" comic strips) is used to send network mail on FidoNet or on networks using FidoNet protocols. Unlike other packages, which concentrate on compressing or decompressing message files, BinkleyTerm handles the actual file transmission, unattended. (You could write a script file to do the same thing using many modem software packages—but you'd have to be pretty good at it.) It can run on a BBS waiting for a mail call, and if a user calls in the meantime, it can unload itself and invoke the BBS system. The package is free for noncommercial users, and commercial users can negotiate a site license at about $25 per machine. The source code is included with the program so that you can modify it to suit your needs.

SEAdog, **$$$$**, *Systems Enhancement Associates, 21 New Street, Wayne, NJ 07470, 201-473-5153*

SEAdog is used for unattended echo mailing. It can send message files in a number of different formats using its Import facility. SEAdog can be left running on a BBS, and it will turn control over to the BBS software if a user calls in. It can also be used in "slotted mail" mode, in which the BBS software turns control over to SEAdog at a specified time, and SEAdog passes control back after the mailing is finished.

SEAmail, **$$$$+**, *Systems Enhancement Associates, 21 New Street, Wayne, NJ 07470, 201-473-5153*

SEAmail is the enhanced version of SEAdog and has a list of added features, including compatibility with more types of software and the ability to send fax messages through a fax modem.

TIMS (the Integrated Mail System), **$$$$+**, *eSoft Inc., 15200 E. Girard Avenue #2550, Aurora, CA 80014, 303-699-6565*

TIMS runs with TBBS and handles incoming mail only, although future versions are expected to handle outgoing mail as well. TIMS waits in RAM and examines incoming calls to see if they are mail packets in the FidoNet protocol. (This process is transparent to the caller.) If it is such a packet, TIMS takes control and handles the reception.

Mail Doors

Mail doors are external programs on a BBS that a user invokes when online. A mail door gathers the user's current conference messages (plus any bulletins or program files the sysop wants the user to have); compresses them into a file, usually with the extension .QWK; downloads them to the user; and then returns control to the BBS system. The user can upload conference postings by invoking the door and choosing its Upload command. Mail doors may work with a specific BBS package, or with a broad selection. (Doorway, a shareware utility touted as being able to turn nearly any character-based program into a door, is available from Marshall Dudley, 406 Monitor Lane, Knoxville, TN 37922, BBS: 615-966-3574.)

Qmail Door, $$, Sparkware, P.O. Box 605, Cordova, TN 38018, 901-373-6245, BBS: 901-382-5583

Qmail Door was the first mail door on the market, and it established the .QWK file format. It works only with PCBoard BBS software. The sysop can configure it to automatically add programs, bulletins, and other files to a user's download. It can be purchased through the Sparkware BBS (it's not shareware), and each copy of Qmail Door includes a copy of Qmail Deluxe2.

Tomcat! Mail Door, $$, Technique Computer Systems, 110-1841 Oak Bay Avenue, Victoria, British Columbia, V8R 1C4 Canada, 604-598-2141, BBS: 604-598-1546

This shareware package generates .QWK files for Wildcat BBS systems. Apparently the only mail door for Wildcat systems, it is available for downloading from the vendor or from many Wildcat BBS systems.

Mjrmail, $$$$+, Farwest BBS, P.O. Box 1296, Station E, Victoria, British Columbia, V8W 2W3, CANADA, 604-381-6462, BBS: 604-381-3934

This program runs with the Major BBS, producing .QWK mail packets. Although the vendors try to disguise the fact, Mjrmail is written by the same people who produce the Tomcat! mail door.

Offline Readers

An offline reader lets a user read and reply to computer conference messages while offline. The software may even compose a duplicate of the conference message base. Some readers work with a specific mail door, and others work with a wide selection; many use the .QWK file format for downloads and the .REP format for uploads.

The .QWK file is assembled by the mail door and downloaded to the user, employing whatever modem software the user is running. Then the user leaves the modem software and invokes the mail reader, which unpacks the .QWK file and creates a local model of the BBS's conference message base. The user composes replies using an editor that's part of the offline reader, or using a separate text editor to create an ASCII file. The offline reader will then pack the replies into a .REP file for uploading to the mail door of the BBS.

> *Qmail Deluxe2,* **$**, *Sparkware, P.O. Box 605, Cordova, TN 38018, 901-373-6245, BBS: 901-382-5583*

This offline reader works with any mail door that produces a .QWK file. An editor is included, but you need your own archiving software to compress or decompress the file. The offline message base it creates includes only messages from the last download. Qmail Deluxe2 is not shareware, but a free demo version is available that works only in the main conference of a BBS. The full version is available through the Sparkware BBS or through other major BBSs that have distribution agreements.

> *SLMR (Silly Little Mail Reader),* **$$**, *Mustang Software Inc., P.O. Box 2264, Bakersfield, CA 93303, 805-395-0223*

Advertised as working with most mail doors that produce .QWK packets, this shareware package includes a "twit filter" that saves you from having to read conference messages from someone you particularly loathe or on subjects you're tired of. ANSI animation and color is supported in offline viewing.

> *Session Manager,* **$$** *shareware, Pat Hart, the Exchange BBS, 804-552-1010 or 1018, voice: 804-420-7506*

Session Manager works with .QWK files and any file-archiving utility, and was reportedly the first offline reader to include a fully functional editor. The message base it creates embodies only the last download. The software can also be ordered through the Session Manager conference on Relaynet.

> *EZ-Reader,* **$$** *shareware, Eric Cockrell, Thumper Technology, P.O. Box 471346, Tulsa, OK 74147-1346, 918-355-4311, BBS: 918-355-4409*

This offline reader works with standard .QWK files and produces standard .REP reply files. The message base it creates embodies only the latest download. It works with any text editor you choose. EZ-Reader is touted as being very fast and easy to use.

ECHO NETWORKS
FidoNet

Main North American BBS sysop: George Peace
717-657-8699
Main BBS (in Australia) sysop: Matt Whelan
+61-2-665-0941

FidoNet is the oldest of the BBS echo networks. It is also the oddest.

Fido was created with high ideals, few rules, and a loose structure. Tom Jennings of San Francisco wrote the original Fido BBS software and offered it to the public domain. FidoNet emerged as a way for users of the software to share tips.

But it grew far beyond that. The system currently carries over 450 individually named conferences and has 10,000 member boards—8,000 in the United States and Canada. Most conferences are computer-related, but many aren't; one of the hottest topics is genealogy.

FidoNet conferences are passed along a hierarchy, although all FidoNet member boards offer local messaging. At the top are the five zone coordinators, who keep all the conferences online. (In the United States there are two boards used for this, called "superstars.") Regional coordinators pass the zones their new note collections and download messages from other regions. Hosts collect new messages from regional coordinators and pass along what's new from their areas. Hubs pass messages on to hosts and collect notes from their localities. Just like all the boards above them in the chain, nodes offer local messaging, pass their new messages to hubs, and collect notes for the lowest level of the hierarchy, called points.

George Peace of Harrisburg, Pennsylvania, is currently the North American coordinator for FidoNet, while founder Tom Jennings now serves as editor of the group's newsletter, *FidoNews*. Their appointments followed a long period during which Fido tried, unsuccessfully, to get itself organized.

The zone coordinators, such as Peace, form a zone council, which passes for the ruling body of FidoNet today. The council tries to act as a democracy, but most sysops are fairly anarchistic, notes Richard Couture, a zone coordinator in San Francisco.

As Peace recalls, the issue that drove FidoNet to distraction was off-topic notes. How was a Fido sysop to determine when a note to a conference was off the topic and should be deleted? More important, who would decide? A group called the International FidoNet Association (IFNA) tried for a number of years to set down some rules, but each proposal was met with opposition. Eventually, they gave up.

As Couture explains, "The real problem is money. It costs money to do this, and none of us are publicly funded. I pay $300/month in phone bills to run my BBS. I run at a deficit. I don't know of anyone in the black."

Since the failure of IFNA to set down hard-and-fast rules, says Peace, the group's 10,000 sysops, 2,000 of whom are outside the United States, live by two simple commandments: "Do not be excessively annoying, and do not be excessively annoyed. The interpretations are vague and hard to pin down," he admits. "It's left to local interpretation how to handle situations. We have a policy document I look at for guidance, which tries to define 'excessively annoying,' but it leaves us a good amount of leeway."

Joining FidoNet is an equally vague process. "What it takes to become a Fido sysop is to inquire with virtually any FidoNet sysop," says Peace. "We all hope that in our unstructured environment they'll filter to a net coordinator, who is prepared to accept and issue a node number. It doesn't cost anything; it simply requires that you send a little information on your board, and exchange mail to prove that you actually are FidoNet-capable."

Anyone can start a topic on FidoNet, says Peace. "You start a topic on a local system, advertise it in conferences like 'echo_req,' then the backbone operates as a transport medium. If people in different parts of the country are looking for a topic and it can be located, it's our job to transport it," says Peace.

The 450 backbone conferences attract a lot of notes. They're all compressed using PKZIP for transport among the nodes, and sent using Xmodem or Zmodem error correction. "We're moving a minimum of 3 megabytes zipped each day. Add everyone else's traffic and there's a lot" of traffic moving over FidoNet.

Any software that can collect, organize, and pass messages to another board will work with FidoNet, Peace says. Two public-domain packages, called BinkleyTerm and QM, are used most often. But Peace estimates that 20 to 50 percent of sysops use shareware programs such as Front Door and commercial packages such as DBridge, QMail, and MarkMail. The Fido BBS software itself includes network facilities, as do some other BBS packages.

Any free-standing BBS can be interfaced with FidoNet, from the freeware RBBS to Clark Development's PCBoard. Peace's own board, the Other BBS, runs TBBS software. But the Fido BBS package is still used, and it has gone through several phases—from free to commercial to shareware. The software is still owned by Tom Jennings.

As zone coordinator, Peace's job is to keep track of the official list of Fido boards, called the nodelist, and to maintain the group's documents. In his own file collection, the basic Fido documents, including the nodelist, have filenames starting with FTS. Technical standards and other miscellaneous documents have filenames starting with FSC. As one of the two North American "superstar" boards, the Other BBS maintains all Fido conferences, takes calls from regional coordinators, and exchanges mail with the other zones in Europe, South America, the Pacific, and Asia/Africa. The person who actually links the zone coordinators together is international coordinator Matt Whelan in Sydney, Australia.

Because of the costs of passing the mail, Peace says, FidoNet sysops are always looking for faster modems and cheaper long-distance rates. Some sysops are using a compression scheme called ARJ because it makes files 6 percent smaller than ZIP does. Nearly all the mail today is moved using 9,600-baud modems, usually in the middle of the night, when phone rates are lowest. And long-distance calling plans such as MCI's "Friends and Family" always attract a crowd. Many of the "friends" listed by Fido sysops on that plan, Peace says, are other Fido sysops.

Peace himself started using FidoNet in 1986, as an ordinary user interested in the old CP/M operating system. Today he works as a data-processing consultant for Unisys.

SmartNet

Host board: The Sound of Music
Sysop: Paul Waldinger
BBS: 516-536-8723

SmartNet was formed in 1987 by Paul Waldinger, operator of the Sound of Music board on Long Island. Waldinger had been running his board for two years before starting his own echo network. It began as a joint venture with Hayes, the modem company. The name SmartNet came from the Hayes SmartModem. "The idea was to offer an online substitute to CompuServe," says Waldinger.

What has emerged is a network with strict rules on content, but loose rules on technology, and 125 conferences. It's devoted mainly to supporting common software and hardware products.

SmartNet has been able to get important companies to devote the time of professionals to tracking SmartNet conferences. Quarterdeck's Gary Faxer keeps track of conferences on DesqView, Hayes' Randy Cooper runs conferences on his company's products, and Juan Jimenez of Borland runs topics on that company's products. Not all the SmartNet experts, however, are employed full-time to support their products. "Doctor Hard Drive" for SmartNet, the man to whom all questions about such drives are addressed, is a hobbyist, Richard Driggers of Monroe, Louisiana, whose day job is with South Central Bell.

"We reserve the right to purge a message," says Waldinger. "That sets us apart. We also reserve the right to remove a message that's off-topic.

When you run a professional network doing professional support, you have to do these things. Factory representatives aren't going to put up with extraneous stuff."

Half of the topics on SmartNet involve computers, none involves sex or religion. But there are conferences on sports, politics, and noncomputer hobbies. The topics to be supported are decided on by the systems that belong to the network, says Waldinger. "I had someone come up with the idea of a cryogenics conference. We put a message into the main SmartNet conference stating that desire. If there are enough sysops to support it, we'll open it."

Like many other conferencing systems, SmartNet does not insist that member boards use all conferences, only the main SmartNet conference, which coordinates the rest.

As the core of the network, the Sound of Music doesn't move the mail; it just tracks it. And it's technologically loose: Waldinger allows member boards to use a number of different mail programs, supporting them on PCBoard doors within the main board. The number 1 door is MarkMail, written by Mark Turner in California. The second is QMail, and then KMail and RoseMail. All are supported by network sysops so they can do their mail exchanges. It's up to them which they use.

Here's how it works. "They scan their messages in QNet, written by Mark Herring, or RNet by Robert Boksreither, or RoseMail. None of them are shareware. They're all commercial packages. We scan for duplicate mail once a day. PCBoard has a package for that built in."

Adds Waldinger, "There's enough room for more than one echo network. All the networks use similar software. But the politics are very different. In most cases a sysop will belong to more than one network." The different networks don't share messages even on the same topic, though. Waldinger says that's because "we don't have recourse on messages entered from other networks."

ILink

Host board: Executive Network Information System
Sysop: Andy Keeves
BBS: 914-667-4684 Voice: 914-667-2151

"Give ILink a few minutes and it will bring you the world!" That's the tag line used in the online promotional literature for ILink, and although it may not actually bring you the world, it comes close.

Hubbed at the Executive Network Information System BBS in Mount Vernon, New York, ILink was organized in September 1988. It boasts of having been born with an experienced set of sysops and a nucleus of 40 boards (or nodes) from the Memphis-based PCB-Echo network, which disbanded in August 1988. The first European ILink nodes were added that October.

At this writing, ILink has about 160 nodes, including several regional or intermediate hubs, located in the United States and Canada as well as Europe, Singapore, Saudi Arabia, and Australia. Mail turnaround is one to two days, although same-day response between major hubs such as New York and Toronto is possible. Sysops call in with mail during the evening or (using automated procedures) after midnight. Many call in twice or even four times a day.

Andy Keeves, a computer consultant and sysop of the 20-line Mount Vernon hub, says the network's success stems from a careful admissions policy. "We recruit sysops very carefully," says Keeves. "We require an application, and we have a review committee that calls the system and looks at it, and checks out how the conferences are managed," among other things. "We weed out more than we admit."

Longevity is the biggest weeding factor: a board must have been up for at least six months before ILink will accept it. Allowing the use of aliases, and tolerating the posting of commercial software, are other reasons for rejection. The committee also steers away from what it calls "kiddie boards," those devoted to games and chatting. "We are looking for a system where professionals gather for serious purposes," Keeves says. "The attitudes of the sysop will reflect that. We also look at how up-to-date the sysop is—is the latest news bulletin two years old? And we look at participation—does the sysop participate in the board himself? When questions are not read by the sysop for six months, that means there is something wrong."

ILink averages 50,000 messages per month, something over 600,000 bytes of information per day. Many of the technical conferences have a healthy amount of traffic, but the most popular conferences, according to traffic statistics, are Chitchat, Opinion, StarTrek, Politics, Religion, and Microsoft Windows.

With all this traffic, storage becomes an issue, even with a hub containing 4.5 gigabytes of online storage. How long messages are kept online depends on the traffic in that conference: they'll last two weeks in a high-volume conference and two months in a low-volume one. But all conferences are backed up on tape; no messages are really deleted, Keeves says. That's less for legal reasons than for the benefit of the occasional user who wants to consult a message in a technical conference that was taken off a year ago.

No censoring of the traffic is attempted. "It's impossible to read all the messages," Keeves admits. "We do have volunteer moderators for most of the conferences, to keep an eye on that conference, to guide it on track and calm down any fights. If need be, they can suspend an offender for 30 days or something."

In fact, legal issues have not been a problem for ILink. "Advertising for firearms was a touchy issue for a while, since we are dealing with national and international mail." A handgun that is legal in the United States may not be in Canada. "So we elected not to allow firearms advertising, as many newspapers and magazines do. The ads may be legitimate, but it is not our place to check them."

No private mail is carried by ILink—which neatly eliminates the electronic mail privacy concern. Individual ILink nodes may, however, pass local, private mail among its users. "Another concern is that we have mail going to countries like Russia. What happens if locals talk about something the government considers sensitive? But our research shows this is not a serious consideration—not a problem at all. It is the sender's responsibility, on a public open network, not ours," to censor himself.

The elimination of private mail also tends to eliminate the problem of stolen credit card numbers. "If they were posted, dozens of people would complain," Keeves notes. "If someone accidentally uploads a commercial file, as happens from time to time, we get dozens of complaints within hours. New files are posted between 3:00 A.M. and 5:00 A.M. New York time, and by 11:00 A.M. a dozen boards would have told us about the commercial file. So we go in and kill it."

Program files are examined only to make sure that they contain no known viruses, don't duplicate existing files on the network, don't hawk pyramid schemes, and don't advertise other BBSs. Files compressed with PKZIP are unZIPed and scanned using automated procedures. Novices often compress a whole directory, including the compression program itself and COMMAND.COM: these files are removed to make space before the file is compressed again.

Being an ILink sysop is a labor of love, Keeves says. Some of his sysops may put in as little as an hour a day running their boards, but some may put in 10 hours, while holding down full-time jobs! A great deal depends on how many conferences the sysop personally follows. Because of its tight admissions policies, there is relatively little turnover among ILink sysops. In the last year 2 boards had dropped out, while 30 joined.

Sysops get no money from ILink. Any subscription fee they charge is between them and their users. The hub's phone bills average $1,300 to $1,600 per month, largely from the number of lines (20) the hub has, Keeves said. An individual-node sysop will usually have phone bills of less than $200 per month; with a high-speed modem, echoing mail costs only a few dollars a day.

All ILink hubs use PCBoard BBS software. Keeves says he likes the interface the software offers, and using the same BBS software across the network makes echoing easier. For hardware, Keeves favors US Robotics™ dual-standard modems, saying that they were the first affordable 9,600 bps modems on the market. But there's no requirement there.

NorthAmeriNet

Host: Canada Remote
Sysop: Jud Newell
BBS: 416-620-1439

NorthAmeriNet was founded in September 1988 by Jud Newell, system operator of the Canada Remote board in Mississauga, Ontario. The basic idea is that this is a Canadian echo network, meant primarily for Canadian bulletin boards. But the topics covered are familiar to other echo nets, and there is a network of large, regional U.S. bulletin boards on the system. As of July 1991 there were 244 systems participating in NorthAmeriNet.

Like other echo networks, including FidoNet, NorthAmeriNet has a treelike structure. Canada Remote is the root, but there are a number of regional "hubs" through which smaller boards can access conferences at a lower cost. Newell likes his hubs to be large systems, distributed in rough equivalence to the spread of BBSs generally. There might be two in New York but only one in British Columbia, for instance. Hubs are up 24 hours a day and carry all conferences.

One unique aspect of NorthAmeriNet is that it doesn't cost anything to belong to it. Regional hubs are given secure access to a toll-free line for handling their mail functions, uploading new messages from their boards and downloading new messages from other boards.

Newell's goal is a professional network of the best bulletin boards. "Size is not as important as approach," he wrote in starting the net. "We'd like to turn this into North America's premier mail system. Larger systems may wish to act as regional hosts, but we envision a totally open net where any qualifying system may participate, either directly with CRS or through a regional host."

NorthAmeriNet, however, does have stiffer rules than some other echo networks. This isn't a bad thing, if you like conferences that stay on their topics and a man at the top who keeps things humming along smoothly. In this case, the man is Newell, who now has more time to devote to the net since passing the business end of Canada Remote on to Neil Fleming.

One cast-iron rule is that NorthAmeriNet specifies a single mailing package for uploads and downloads: Mark Herring's Qmail/Qnet package. Canada Remote distributes registered copies of it free to participating system operators. Qnet is designed for use with PCBoard software, but it can be adapted for use with other software, says Newell.

Membership terms in the net are pretty simple. Sysops agree that they're participating voluntarily, that they're independently choosing which conferences to echo (there is no requirement to echo all conferences), and that they choose which notes to echo as well. Regional hubs have to take all conferences, but individual nodes don't.

The major requirements involve the NetMail Admin conference, which controls net activity. That conference should be read every day, and notes should be sent to it on messages or echoes that are routinely denied access to an individual system. A note in the NetMail Admin conference is deemed private; it can't be passed outside the group without Newell's approval and notification of any other sysop within the system referenced by the note. Distribution of notes from NorthAmeriNet to outside systems is forbidden unless permission is requested first. The terms note that such permission is usually granted.

Also, a sysop retains the right to join other networks, although messages can't be routinely exchanged with other echo systems. You can withdraw from the net with notice to Canada Remote, and sysops are urged to eliminate or make private any messages "that are not suitable for viewing by the general public, including minors."

Although Canada Remote itself echoes a number of outside echo networks—including ILink, PCRelay, Intelec, HyperNet, RIME, EchoNet, and even an all-adult net called ThrobNet—NorthAmeriNet tries to stick to pretty standard topics. Conference titles are shared with ILink, but the general NorthAmeriNet list includes 14 topics on Apple, 3 on CP/M systems, and 13 on the Commodore 64. There are 30 different business conferences, 34 with buy/sell ads, and 28 opinion conferences, along with computing conferences on PKware (the makers of ZIP), NeXT, Quarterdeck's DesqView, and artificial intelligence, among other topics.

Relaynet

Host board: The Running Board
Sysop: Dr. Bonnie Anthony
BBS: 301-229-5623
Voice: 301-229-7028

"It's an addiction," says Dr. Bonnie Anthony about BBS use. She should know—the Bethesda, Maryland, resident is not only a practicing psychiatrist, she's also the sysop of the central Relaynet hub. "I once said I would give it up, turned off the computer, and walked out of the house. I was back in 30 minutes."

And there was a lot to come back to; at this writing, the Relaynet Information and Message Exchange (sometimes known as RIME) has about 850 nodes (including 54 regional hubs and 5 "super-regional" hubs that call in three times a day), making it the biggest PC-based hobbyist echo network. The nodes are scattered throughout North America, Europe, Brazil, Taiwan, Japan, the Middle East, Australia, and New Zealand. (During Operation Desert Shield/Storm, 49 nodes in Saudi Arabia closed down because their sysops were called to military service. Those that remained open relayed messages to American service people, offering much faster service than the U.S. mail.)

There are about 250 conferences, and conference message traffic amounts to about 3 megabytes a day. The echo mail turns around in about 24 hours. Unlike the situation for some other networks, old messages that are dropped from a conference are gone for good; there is no effort to save everything forever. Topics covered by the conferences are notably broad, ranging from the usual technical conferences, to self-help groups such as Survivors of Incest, to conferences devoted to trivia about individual TV shows.

From its inception, Relaynet was purely a hobby affair: Bronx native Dr. Anthony wanted to exchange messages with her brother back in New York. Both were into BBSing, and they decided to set up boards and exchange messages in 1986. The software used to update their message bases was written by Kip Compton, then 15 years old, during his spring break from school. Twelve other people wanted to join the plan, and soon they had 50 boards exchanging traffic.

"But we had this 15-year-old software author and 49 novice BBS operators, and it took a while to gain some respectability," she recalls. "We were a kind of joke. We had no famous BBSs, no programmers who had written lots of shareware, we were just nobodies. Initially, 50 kilobytes of mail was a lot. The system was unreliable, it would not work, people fought over how things should be run. But people joined us, and it got better and better."

And they keep joining. "Whenever we grow a little bigger, I figure we've exhausted the market," Dr. Anthony says. So far she's been wrong.

What attracts boards as members, she says, is RIME's openness: they'll take almost any board. There is no minimum age for sysops: ages run from 14 to 74. They'll take brand new boards. The main requirements are that the boards not allow aliases or illegal activity and that they pay the network $15 a year. Yet the turnover is less than 5 percent a year, she notes. The main case of burnout (besides her own) was the sysop of a regional hub that carried 50 nodes whose wife announced he had to choose between her and the computer. "He turned off the computer that minute; I had no warning," she says.

RIME can accommodate so many disparate boards and sysops because of Compton's software, now named PCRelay. It can interface with all major BBS software packages. Dr. Anthony sells it to the sysops for $30 a copy. Compton has since gone on to attend the Massachusetts Institute of Technology.

RIME also differs from other major echo networks in that it will carry private mail—or, at any rate, a form of private mail called "courtesy mail." Such mail moves from point to point rather than being echoed to all nodes. Any user can ask for a mailbox, and if mail gets sent to a user without a mailbox, it ends up in limbo—which at least means no one else can read it.

Normally, however, four people are entitled to read courtesy mail: the sender, the recipient, the sender's sysop, and the recipient's sysop. Allowing the sysops to read the mail lets them assure themselves that nothing illegal is happening. And by advertising the fact that the mail is not private, the network follows electronic privacy laws (see Chapter 13).

"We expected to get suits from users whose private messages turned up public, but that has never happened," Anthony says. "We have had no problems with mail and don't see why you should. And mail lets you moderate conferences better: you can tell someone to tone it down without everyone else being involved." Lately, mail traffic has amounted to 20 percent of the network traffic.

RIME is also distinctive in that there is no corporate sponsorship at all; everything is a hobby effort. This causes Dr. Anthony to worry about the rise in the traffic volume, since it means greater expenses to the hub sysops. However, she has no plans to turn Relaynet into a money-making enterprise. "It would be something different. It would not be as much fun," she says. But her own phone bills run to $1,000 a month (mostly for talking new sysops through the software, including one in Taiwan, whose Bronx accent matched her own).

Dr. Anthony's hub system has five 386 machines and five phone lines: three for the Relaynet mail traffic and two for her BBS. She has "only" 660 megabytes of storage; she does not offer files on the network, and that cuts down the storage requirement. (Files can be sent point to point as mail, however.) Her subscription fees brought in about $10,000 in the past year, but she spent $18,000 on new hardware; obviously, no profit is being made.

Meanwhile, it's her professional opinion that there's a good reason why BBSs are addicting. "It's a way of communicating that's very safe. On your computer you're not black or white, tall or short, fat or skinny. You are what you put out in front of you in terms of words. We have paraplegic sysops [using voice-activated systems or mouth pens]. They are like anybody else."

APPENDIX **B**

BBSs Around the World

ABOUT THIS APPENDIX

BBSs are in use around the world. We'll look at the situation in:

- Western Europe

- Eastern Europe

- The (Former) USSR

- Japan and the Far East

- The Third World

INTRODUCTION

"Everything's connected to everything else everywhere!"

Dave Hughes

After a slow start, the BBS movement is spreading rapidly around the globe. There are a number of reasons for this. The opening up of Eastern Europe and Russia has stimulated demand for knowledge. Universities are more interested than ever in some form of linking to the West. Not only are they using PCs and networks such as Fido, they're also using Unix-based machines and their networks, such as Bitnet or Internet. Third World upper classes, with incomes and education representative of the American middle class, are quickly learning how to start and operate BBSs.

But most important has been the advent of fast, error-correcting modems using such schemes as MNP 5 and V.42 bis. Combined with echo mail packages, these modems allow a BBS anywhere in the world—no matter how poor the phone lines it's connected with—to transfer mail efficiently, not only within that country's borders but overseas. Overnight, when rates are lowest, a backwoods BBS in Africa can compress its new postings, send them at the equivalent of 38,400 bits per second to another BBS, and receive a similar packet in return.

The technology is irresistible. If the world is becoming a global village, BBSs are the post offices.

WESTERN EUROPE

Although Western Europe is the second most active BBS community in the world, after the United States, government regulations have until recently worked against its growth.

In the United Kingdom, where telecommunications are rapidly being deregulated, the problem is ignorance, says journalist Steve Gold. "Most people here don't understand modems," so even as prices drop, few new BBSs come online. The most popular hangout for the modem-literate in that country is a Unix-based system called CIX, for CompuLink Information Exchange. That's not to say that there aren't BBSs; there are. But Gold says the vast majority have only a few phone lines, and a surprisingly high percentage are run by teenagers. It's a market that's ripe for development.

In France, the government-owned France Telecom has been working for a decade to bring its people online, but not using BBSs. Instead, the Minitel system is the rage. Minitel is a simple terminal, using a standard called Teletel, that was originally given away free so that the government could avoid the expense of printing phonebooks. Although looking up phone numbers remains its most popular use, a number of information services have arisen to serve the millions of Minitel users throughout the nation. Some receive millions of minutes of use per year. Unfortunately, the most popular services are those offering sexually explicit talk. This has dampened the enthusiasm of American politicians to emulate the Minitel model, although it is still sometimes mentioned.

In Germany, the situation until recently was quite the opposite. The state-owned PTT discouraged modem use by licensing all modems put on its lines and charging extra for "data lines." "The situation is changing drastically now," says journalist Detlef Borchers, with about 500 hobbyist boards open and more expected.

There are still unusual requirements for starting or even calling a BBS in Germany, Borchers adds. "We have two license structures. Private users must have a modem with a test number of the German Telecom," but this is more a technical quirk than anything else. Germany's telephone network is still state-owned, but privatization is coming, Borchers says, and this may free things further.

As a result of the license requirements, "The modem prices for official modems are very high. On the other hand, if you have a PBX, you're free to choose whatever modem you like. A private user phoning from home must adhere to the government standards, but companies with in-house systems can choose any modem." Once a PBX system has been tested — and nearly every company has one — components running off that system are their owners' business. This means that it can actually be cheaper for a business to run a BBS for its workers than it would be for a worker to run one.

Regulations on content also go beyond those found in the United States, Borchers adds. "Sysops of BBSs are responsible for content. They are like a press editor: they can be reproached under law if the BBS contents violate rules. A fascist organization which posts a flyer on a BBS can lead to the sysop being reproached." In the United States, hate groups freely run, and use, BBSs. Partly due to the regulations, Borchers says, "I don't see much political discussion here."

Germany is also embracing two technologies that are moving slowly in the United States: X.400 and ISDN. X.400, a scheme for allowing large systems to pass messages, isn't used much in the United States because of difficulty in addressing the "envelope"; addresses used by MCI Mail, CompuServe, and GEnie vary widely in approach. In Germany, the PTT has its own standardized addressing scheme, so many boards are moving toward it. ISDN is also becoming available, Borchers says, and this will cause another revolution among German BBSs.

EASTERN EUROPE

"Eastern Europe is changing even more rapidly," Borchers says. "They have only one telephone system there. The only way to get good communication is to use a bulletin board, and dial it all night until you can get the mail."

Dave Hughes, who runs the Old Colorado City board in Colorado Springs, Colorado, has been online all around the world. "From having no BBSs three years ago, Eastern Europe has exploded with a flood of them," he says.

Some of the boards are mysterious and secretive, like one in Bulgaria "where you can upload or download any existing virus source code in exchange for your copy of another virus," according to a journalist who's heard about it.

Far more typical, however, is George Lamac's system in Prague, Czechoslovakia. The BBS, which runs on an Atari ST computer but does have a 9,600-baud V.32 modem, has become a haven for local musicians interested in MIDI files. It also runs echo conferences with the West and has many local conferences on the usual hobbyist topics: role-playing games, .GIF files, and programming problems. Lamac also stands ready to chat with international callers at any hour of the day or night. Some of those conversations have been loaded onto the Well, a Unix-based online service in San Francisco.

Of all the Eastern European countries, Czechoslovakia and Hungary seem the most modem-literate, Hughes says. And what happens on their boards can be pretty exciting. A Hungarian network called Magyar echoed dozens of eyewitness accounts of fighting in the Yugoslav republic of Slovenia, which in the spring of 1991 began attempts to break away from the federation. The former East Germany, Poland, Rumania, and Bulgaria trail in their use of BBSs, but that could change quickly, says Hughes.

"What you're getting is a simultaneous accelerated development throughout Eastern Europe. It's force-fed by the fact that they couldn't do it for years, but they were reading computer magazines all that time. Their modem development was retarded, but the minute the lid came out, not only did they get sophisticated equipment," but that equipment went right into the hands of sophisticated users. As a result, "You're getting a quicker, faster, and more serious development" than in the West. "Not only are they able to direct-dial to the West, but they can exchange information at a cost that's tolerable, using the techniques of distributed conferencing," fast error-correcting modems, and echo mail. "We're talking about more development in one year than you'd see in U.S. cities in five years."

Still, Hughes says, a BBS is a BBS. "Every BBS has the same culture on it; it's the funniest thing you've ever seen. There are techie discussions, sysop discussions, some unique thing like MIDI, and increasing numbers of them in Eastern Europe are seen by their operators as having some business connection."

THE FORMER USSR

Some of the most exciting BBS activity anywhere has taken place in the former Soviet Union. As the central government broke down and its edicts were ignored in many spheres, thousands of people turned to used computers, cheap modems, and BBSs as a form of political discussion and protest. Estonia, one of the three Soviet Baltic republics that broke from the federation, even put its laws on Eesti BBS #1 in its capital, Tallinn.

Kirill Tchashchin, Moscow bureau chief for the Newsbytes News Network, which covers technology, reported on this during the summer of 1991 and counted 24 systems in Moscow, 5 in St. Petersburg, a half-dozen in Tallinn, Estonia, and small numbers in other cities in the country—about 50 in all. As elsewhere, some drop offline, others come on, and still others keep going.

"There was a long discussion on how those lists should be compiled and what kind of information should be included in them," he said in an electronic mail message to Blankenhorn. "The standard joke is the inclusion of the phone number for a Fido mailer installed in a sysop's girl's grandmother's flat in Tallinn, Estonia. Current boards have names like Angel Station, Blue House, Red Rat's Nest, Call or Die, and Nice Landing."

Eesti #1 was the first BBS to go online, helped by its location near Finland, the relative wealth of its Baltic citizenry, and technical help from the West. "It is still the only one operated using PCBoard software," writes Tchashchin. "Others use mostly Fido packages with Maximus, a public domain package, being the most popular." Another reason to use Maximus, besides its low price, is that American-made packages haven't yet been translated for the 31-character Cyrillic (Russian) character set. This isn't a problem in the Baltics, however, where the native languages are written with a Latin character set and thus can handle ASCII with few modifications.

JAPAN AND THE FAR EAST

According to the New Media Development Association in Tokyo, there were 1,387 computer services in Japan as of July 31, 1991, with 170 operated by government offices. The services were used by 1.1 million people and 13 of them had at least 10,000 members each.

Users can choose from five packet service networks. KDD's Venus-P is the largest, linking to 53 foreign countries, but Trip and TYMPAS are more popular among BBS, or "pasocom tsushin," operators. DataCall Plus, operated by Sprint Japan, is also popular.

TYMPAS offers access to dozens of free BBSs via a simple menu. The nation's ministry of posts and telecommunications has been active in stimulating BBS traffic, and it even held a major conference at Sendai in 1989, followed by a BBS trade show in Tokyo under the theme "Think Globally, Act Locally."

To handle the Japanese language, local BBSs use local software such as Assist BBS. Such systems require two eight-bit words to describe a single kanji character. Dialing into such a system from the West is nearly impossible, unless your PC can handle kanji or the Japanese sysop has an English-language section. Normal eight-bit computer traffic from a Japanese BBS looks like so much garbage.

The complexities of kanji have slowed Japanese use of PCs. As recently as two years ago, specialized word processors were still the rage. That changed with the advent of 6-pound PCs built around standards such as DOS/V or, more likely, the NEC 9801 standard. Such systems are helping many Japanese learn to type, using a system in which they enter a number of hiragana or katakana characters, and then press a translation key for kanji at intervals.

Tympas, notebook PCs, a government push, and the other factors mentioned earlier have made Japan a hub for BBS traffic from throughout the Pacific Rim, says Hughes. "I'm seeing a tremendous amount of Manila and Singapore traffic. Other Far East and Pacific Rim places are chitchatting on BBSs, because they're all Fido-connected. The BT Tymnet packet net is hooked to TYMPAS, and you have a gateway that lets people in Japan access services in other cities" at packet net prices and without having to pay extra for the BBS. "There are an amazing number of individual BBSs, accessible by TYMPAS in a gateway from Tokyo. Someone from Osaka can talk to Tokyo, which in turn echoes to Singapore and Hong Kong. And I see an amazing number of Americans on the Tokyo systems through echoes."

Korea, meanwhile, is saturated with boards using the NAPLPS videotex code. "It's their solution to their language," which features 24 unique characters rather than ideographs, which are used in Japanese and Chinese. "You can stick it on a PC or a Mac. It's universal. It's absolutely critical in the Bitnet, Internet, Usenet world because it's the only way to send binary files," says Hughes. Put memory-resident translation software on any PC, he adds, and link that PC to BBSs or other networks, and a graph put into NAPLPS can accompany an ASCII text file and be translated on the fly. "Suddenly every mail system in the world can be a dual graphics-text system, and nothing has to be on the host machine." And it's being developed and first used overseas, because language makes it necessary.

The situation in Australia is a little like that in the United Kingdom. The state-owned Telecomm monopoly is being broken, which is stimulating traffic, and there is a core group of very active hobbyists. This group includes Matt Whelan, the international coordinator for FidoNet, and the authors of a BBS package called RemoteAccess. As competition drives domestic phone rates down, large numbers of new BBSs are expected to emerge, giving people in that far-flung country a chance to communicate as one at last.

THE THIRD WORLD

Operation Desert Storm actually helped make BBSs more popular throughout the Middle East. Hughes served on the periphery of the conflict, putting his communications expertise to use.

"There are 30 to 40 boards in Dhahran alone," Hughes reports. "Saudi Arabia was saturated" with them." Why? "Anywhere there are U.S. air bases someone puts up a BBS on the base. They use it for more than chitchat. Sometimes it's for technical information." Hughes said that, had he used some of his Japanese contacts, he could have even reached boards in Baghdad, Iraq. One board in Kuwait stayed open until AT&T turned off the international circuits, and it came back immediately after liberation.

Of course, "Israel has boards coming out their ears. The Middle East is loaded because engineering people are there. Users of the Saudi Arabia BBS I went into were mainly Aramco employees—Brits, Americans, and Saudis." But there are plenty of other boards that are used by locals.

In Latin America, Hughes says, Argentina and Mexico were leaders early on, "but there's a tremendous amount of activity on the university level elsewhere. That spawns other things," especially off-campus boards and boards run by alumni.

Hughes is aware of at least a few boards in nearly every country on the globe but says, "I am probably only dimly aware of 1 percent of what's really out there. I think there's an enormous underground of BBSs around the world. Finding them is not easy, but they're beginning to link to each other. The overseas evolution is in the linkable ones." For those interested in learning more, he recommends a book entitled *The Directory of Computer Networks* by Tracy Laquey, published by Digital Press.

PROBLEMS

The toughest limits on BBS usage worldwide today come from China and, ironically, the United States. Hughes says the American attitude toward any technology transfer overseas stiffened during the Gulf War, with fears that such technology might end up in the hands of Iraq.

Beyond that, "China remains supertight." Hughes' own son married a Chinese girl in 1990, and Hughes managed to transfer files directly with him. "I can send e-mail into Beijing, with interconnections" through Germany. That's not BBSing, but in Hughes' view, "It's hard to talk about BBSs in isolation from other systems; they're too interconnected. You can jump among systems transparently."

The 1990s will be very exciting everywhere, for anyone with a modem, Hughes concludes. "Now you have many ways to move data overseas, despite the costs, with a $269 V.32 modem. Suddenly every phone system is connectable, and data is error-checked. The worst phone lines can handle the data cheaply."

Concludes Hughes, "Conferences, files, and e-mail remain the basic building blocks. We take software out of the public domain and make it self-installing" on any computer. "I go somewhere and stick software into a PC I've never seen. Suddenly its user is looking at his PC through a reader, and he's reading notes as though he were logged on to my PC all the time."

It's a miracle. Thirteen years after CBBS went online in Chicago, it's still a miracle.

C

Commercial BBS Services

ABOUT THIS APPENDIX

With the population of BBS users now representing a significant market, various commercial services have arisen whose use can cut the costs of long-distance calls for BBS users. These services are based on the marketing of packet-switching network capacity for small users. Phone company calling plans and related offerings can also serve the BBS user. We'll examine some of the major plans and services, explaining their use and the cost savings attainable.

INTRODUCTION

Instead of dialing a BBS directly, you can save money by reaching it through a packet-switching network. Packet-switching networks are national or regional networks, made up of phone lines whose long-distance signal boosters are "conditioned" not to make hash of data traffic. They have racks of modems located in major metropolitan areas, often reachable with a local phone call. At these centers, data from many modems calls are "packetized" (chopped up and intermixed on one channel) and sent between cities on one high-speed data line. The data are sorted out in another city, using the X.25 and X.75 data protocols.

All this saves money because the average voice call requires the equivalent of 56,000 to 64,000 bits per second in data bandwidth to transmit. Modems send data at 1,200, 2,400 or 9,600 bits per second. By sharing a single voice line, a number of modem users can save money. Large businesses have used packet networks for years, mainly for short bursts of data used in financial transactions—verifying credit cards or dealing in stocks, for instance. Lately, packet networks have become popular ways to connect individual modem users nationwide to commercial services such as Dialog and CompuServe. Commercial services are linked directly to the networks as "nodes," and you can reach them by entering their access code once you're connected to their network. From that point, there's little practical difference between a packet link and a direct call, except that response time may not be quite as fast, and the call may have a different "rhythm." File transfers may also require a little extra attention. But even when the cost of using the network is added in, you can save a lot of money over the cost of calling the service directly.

Most commercial traffic occurs during business hours. At night the paid-for data capacity is unused. This gives a further discount to BBS users.

Few BBSs are themselves "nodes" on packet networks, however. (Meaning they are not hard-wired to the network; they're located in someone's office at the end of an ordinary phone line.) Thus, dialing a BBS through such a network requires an extra step. After dialing into your packet network (hopefully, with a local call), you route the call through that network to a city near the BBS you want to reach. There another modem will "outdial" back into the public phone network and connect you to the BBS.

Charges for using the networks are not "distance-sensitive": you can call coast-to-coast or across the hill for the same per-hour fee. The charges can be dramatically lower than long-distance phone charges, but there are usually both sign-up and minimum monthly fees.

Although primarily aimed at BBS users going online during low-usage evening hours, the packet networks are also offered to link with BBSs during business hours—often at higher prices.

PC PURSUIT

800-736-1130

PC Pursuit is the BBS access service offered by US Sprint on its Sprint-Net (more popularly called Telenet, its former name) packet-switching network.

User-to-BBS connections can be carried by the network at 2,400, 1,200, and (sometimes) 300 bits per second. The rate is about a dollar an hour during "non-prime-time" hours: 6:00 P.M. to 7:00 A.M. local time Monday through Thursday, plus 6:00 P.M. Friday to 7:00 A.M. Monday. Holidays, with non-prime rates all day long, include New Year's Day, July 4th, Thanksgiving Day, Labor Day, and Christmas Day.

Regular membership in PC Pursuit costs about a dollar a day. For that you get 30 hours of non-prime online time. Anything over that is charged at a few dollars an hour. There is also a moderately higher family membership fee that gives you 60 hours of non-prime online time. You can use the service during prime time, but you will be charged about $10 an hour—which may still be less than the cost of a direct, long-distance phone call. (PC Pursuit originally offered unlimited use for a set monthly fee. This was changed after some users were found to be online more than 300 hours a month!)

Disabled users can get a special low rate. To qualify, you must demonstrate a "permanent impairment that substantially limits that individual's ability to take care of himself or herself, perform manual tasks, walk, see, hear, speak, breathe, learn, or work," according to Sprint documents. Sprint accepts a letter from a physician, or a Social Security Administration Supplemental Security Income award letter, as proof of disability. Disabled membership includes up to 90 hours of non-prime online time for one-third the normal price. Non-prime-time usage over 90 hours and prime-time use are billed in the usual ways.

Using PC Pursuit

Using PC Pursuit is not particularly difficult, but you will need to have several pieces of information handy before dialing: the local Telenet access number, your PC Pursuit account ID and password, the code of the "outdial" city nearest the BBS you want to reach, and that BBS's phone number. Once you dial the local number and get the CONNECT message from your modem, the log-on procedure is as follows (user input is in boldface):

```
@D < enter>
TELENET
port ###s
TERMINAL= D1 < enter>
@ C D/CITYCODE/24,ACCOUNTID <enter>
PASSWORD= Password < enter>
D/CITYCODE/24 CONNECTED
AZT< enter>
OK
ATDT 12125551212 < enter>
CONNECT
```

The initial @**D**<**enter**> input is called the Hunt/Confirm command. It tells the Telenet port to wake up and configures it to your modem's speed, duplex, and "framing bits." @**D** represents settings of 2,400 bits per second, full duplex, 8-N-1. (See Chapter 5.) Telenet can also run at both 8-N-1 and 7-E-1 in full and half duplex at all three speeds (300, 1,200 and 2,400 bits per second). There is a Hunt/Confirm code for each combination, but the one shown has the widest applicability in the BBS world.

At the TERMINAL= prompt, a simple carriage return will also work in place of the **D1** shown.

In the city code, the **24** input could be replaced by a **12** or a **3**, if your modem runs at only 1,200 or 300 bits per second.

After getting the CONNECTED signal from the modem in the outdial city, you then input **AZT**< **enter**> to put that modem into command mode. When the remote modem responds with OK, you input **ATDT** and the number of the BBS you want to reach. (ATDT is the Touch-tone dial prefix used by modems with the Hayes AT command set; see the AT entry in the glossary, Chapter 16.)

There can be a tense wait after input of the dial command, since you cannot hear the phone ringing or otherwise gauge the progress of the connection, as you can with a voice call. If you don't get the CONNECT message, it is common to get a BUSY message. BUSY may mean the line is busy, but it could also mean that the line is not in service or that Telenet decided this was a long-distance call from the outdial port and refused to make it.

If nothing happens for about 90 seconds, disconnect and try again. Local access numbers to get into Telenet will be included in your documentation when you subscribe. After getting online with Telenet, you can also get a list of local access numbers by inputting, after the @ prompt:

MAIL<**enter**>
User Name? **PHONES**<**enter**>
Password? **PHONES**<**enter**>

Of course, getting this list of numbers requires that you already know your local access number. The list can be useful if you're going on a business trip. However, a city with a local access number doesn't necessarily have an outdial facility. The latest list of outdial cities, their area codes, and their dialing codes appears in Appendix F.

Phone Geography

Determining the outdial city for the BBS you want to reach is only the first step. As pointed out, PC Pursuit outdial modems will not make long-distance calls (since that would complicate the billing); therefore, you have to make sure that the BBS you want to reach is within the local call distance from a Telenet modem.

The only way to do this is to log on to PC Pursuit's own BBS, the Net Exchange in Reston, Virgina, and download the list of exchanges served by each outdial city you're interested in. (For example, in the phone number 212-555-1212, 555 is the exchange number.) At the @ prompt, type: **C PURSUIT**<**enter**>

The connection to the Net Exchange is free. After various preliminaries, you will get the main menu, shown in Figure C.1. **F** will get you a list of files, one for each outdial city, with a list of exchanges served, sometimes under more than one area code. If the phone exchange you want is not listed, it probably can't be reached through PC Pursuit.

Text files of technical information are also listed on the Net Exchange. The **R** command will get you a list of files, one for each letter of the alphabet. **B** will give you a list of bulletins about the system, spelling out such things as pricing and rules of use.

File Transfers

For file transfers, PC Pursuit recommends using the Zmodem protocol, which can achieve 99 percent of the speed you'd get with a direct connection over the network. Xmodem, by contrast, only averages 40 percent of the speed of a direct connection. Ymodem gets about 75 percent and Kermit gets about 65 percent.

The reason for these differences are the time lags resulting from the network's "packetizing" of the data. For instance, an Xmodem data block contains 131 bytes (128 data bytes and 3 "overhead" bytes). The network sends the first 128 bytes as a full data packet. It then takes the next 3 bytes and waits for any further data the PC might be sending. After a tenth of a second the network decides there aren't any more, and it sends those 3 bytes. At the other end, Xmodem requires that the receiving computer send a 1-byte acknowledgment. This byte must also wait a tenth of a second before being forwarded, so for this purpose the network has an effective throughput of 100 bits per second. The network may also impose a quarter-second turnaround delay between the end of one side's

```
M(essage section)    F(ile section)       T(oggle page) B(ulletins)
N(ew user msg)       W(elcome message)    R(ead files)  C(omment to Sysop)
Q(uestionnaire)      G(oodbye)            ?( help )

Commands: M,F,T,B,N,W,R,C,Q,G,? ===> r
```

Figure C.1 The Net Exchange Main Menu

transmission and the start of the other's. So protocols such as Zmodem that use larger data blocks and do not require repeated acknowledgments work much better.

PC BusinessCall

PC BusinessCall℠ is the daytime version of PC Pursuit. It works in the same way, on the same network, but the pricing structure and hours of service differ. There are actually two PC BusinessCall services: the Initiator program, for low-volume business users, and the Professional program, for those with consistent monthly usage. The Initiator plan has a sign-up fee and a low monthly account fee. Usage rates vary among peak-time (10:00 A.M. to 3:00 P.M.), prime-time (7:00 A.M. to 10:00 A.M. and 3:00 P.M. to 6:00 P.M.), and non-prime-time use. For the Professional plan there is no monthly account fee. Instead, a monthly minimum prepayment buys a block of time at about half-price. There is also a sign-up fee. Online rates also vary between peak, prime, and non-prime times.

CONNECT USA

1-800-ATDT-USA

Connect USA was founded by Tom Scott, who also runs the Galaxy bulletin board in Albuquerque. The network consists mainly of 56,000-baud trunk lines linking cities around the country and is centered in Scott's home base in Albuquerque. Connect USA is offered as an alternative to other packet network services specifically for the BBS community.

Connect USA was opened in July, 1991. Its network offers 9,600-baud service under the V.32 modulation standard in about 50 cities. In some locations, such as New York, you can also get 14,400-baud service under the V.32bis standard, and the company expects to upgrade its entire network to this speed in time.

What It Costs

Connect USA is not as extensive as the older SprintNet and CompuServe networks, but it offers faster modems and a single price, day-or-night. You pay $10 to start an account and a $10 monthly minimum.

In over 50 cities around the country a "leisure-time account" is available, using equipment installed by Connect USA. Since the company is expanding rapidly, it's best to call them to find out if your city is covered. This account costs $30 for 30 hours of service, day or night, or you can pay $60 for 60 hours of service.

Using the Connect USA Network

The first step in using Connect USA is to dial your local Connect USA access number. A list of these numbers is available from the company. Set you communications software at 8-N-1 for best results; these are the parameters used by most BBSs.

At the first prompt you see, "Please login:", type your assigned Connect USA user name and a carriage return. At the next prompt, "password:", type your Connect USA password.

Next, you'll be asked for a destination. This can either be a BBS name, such as EXECPC (19 BBSs were served directly in this way as of December 1991), or a 10-digit telephone number, with the area code first. If you are using a 9,600-baud, V.32-compatible modem, enter a V in front of the phone number to get the faster service. Otherwise, service is at 2,400 baud.

At 19 locations around the country, specifically those with boards reachable through mnemotics such as EXECPC, you can use an outdial port to reach other boards in the immediate area. Simply enter the seven-digit local phone number of the board you want to reach at the prompt on the transferring board. You don't need to be a member of one of these BBSs to use its outdial facility, as long as you have a Connect USA account.

If the line you're calling is busy, or if there is some other problem in making the connection, you'll get a detailed error message informing you of the fact. Simply redial the number in the same way, or dial another number.

Conclusions

Connect USA had been a dream of Scott's for years before he opened the service. Starting in 1988, he offered a similar service, called Starlink, reselling the packet network services to Tymnet. That service closed in September 1991, when Tymnet, now owned by British Telecom, decided to leave that part of the market.

Originally, Scott's plan was to get 9,600-baud service through the CompuServe network, using it as the centerpiece of his Connect USA operation. Scott claimed in a 1991 lawsuit, however that CompuServe was late in offering 9,600-baud operation throughout its system, so he decided to go it alone.

That decision represents both the strength and the weakness of Connect USA. Tom Scott understands BBSs and is committed to offering their users fast data service at low prices. But Connect USA is a start-up, and depending on it for communications entails the same risks you'd find in dealing with any small long-distance carrier.

ACCU-LINK

1-800-945-7272

Accu-Link opened for business in March 1991. It is owned by Paragon Communications of Charlotte, North Carolina, a company that creates data communications networks for banks and other large businesses. Paragon's president is James E. Oswell.

Accu-Link acts as a reseller of time on various packet networks through 1,000 access ports throughout the United States. These ports can be easily reached for the cost of local call from most cities. Once linked to such a port, you can dialout through an Accu-Link modem to most cities in the United States. "We say we serve 92 percent of the United States population with a local phone call," says director Terry Rossi.

Accu-Link offers 9,600-baud service under the V.32 modulation standard through all ports of its member networks that support this speed. Other ports get 2,400-baud service.

Accu-Link only recently began advertising its services through *Boardwatch Magazine* and through cooperative ads with major BBSs around the country.

What It Costs

Accu-Link designed its rate structure to be as simple as possible. There's a $20 sign-up fee and a $10 monthly account maintenance fee. There is also a $20 charge if your credit card isn't honored and a $5 reprint charge for bills.

The hourly costs of using Accu-Link vary depending on whose network you're actually using. If you are linked through CompuServe in the United States or Sprintnet, the cost is $4 per hour, day or night. If you are linked through one of the regional Bell companies' networks, it's $5 per hour. From Canada, where service is available only through CompuServe, the cost is $8.50 per hour.

You can sign up for Accu-Link by dialing a local CompuServe or Sprintnet node and entering **Accuinfo** at the "host name:" prompt. You can also sign up for the service and learn the number of a nearby node by calling 800-945-7272 and talking to Accu-Link support personnel.

Using Accu-Link

First set your communications software for the fastest baud rate your modem can support. Then select the 8-N-1 parameters. After dialing a local access point, hit the + key and then Return after a connection is made in order to reach the "host name:" prompt.

At the "host name:" prompt, simply type **accumenu** to reach the main Accu-Link menu. If you want to dial a board immediately, enter **Acculink** and you'll be in an "expert mode," prompted merely to enter a 10-digit phone number, area code first. This direct-dial capability is also available from the Accu-Link menus, however. You may also enter **accuinfo** from this prompt to reach a 24-hour online help systems, along with a free database of common questions and answers. Questions left here will usually be answered 8–15 hours after posting.

After responding to the "host name:" prompt, you'll need to enter your Accu-Link user ID at the "UIC:" prompt and your password at the "password:" prompt.

The Accu-Link main menu offers five major choices. The "Full Service" option lets you reach menus containing the names of over 1000 boards, any of which can be accessed by entering its menu number at the resulting prompt. You can reach smaller menus of choices by selecting "Adult BBSs," "Product Support BBSs," or "Special Interest Systems" from this prompt. Manual dialing is also available from all menus.

If you choose the "Manual Dial" option from any menu, simply enter a 10-digit phone number, area code first. If the destination is accessible from an Accu-Link outdial port, your call will be routed to it automatically.

While a remote system is being dialed, you may see the following on your screen:

Dialing . . . .

Each dot represents a ring heard by the answering modem. If the modem is not answered within 60 seconds, the system will give up and report that there was no answer. Other possible informational and error messages that might be reported are as follows:

Unable to wake up the modem. The initial "wakeup" codes sent to the modem did not receive a successful response. Please try the selection again.

Unable to init the modem. The initialization codes sent to the modem did not receive a successful response. Please try the selection again.

Remote end disconnected. This message indicates that the remote BBS hung up.

Busy. The remote modem is busy. Try the call later.

No carrier. This usually indicates that the remote end answered the call, but a successful connection could not be established. This could be caused by a modem failure or by a voice answering the call.

No answer. The remote modem never answered the call, or you dialed incorrectly.

Time out. A time-out is caused by the outdial modem not seeing the result code of the call. The call was unsuccessful.

Call refused. The X.25 call was refused because no modems are available in the outdial city. This sometimes happens when demand for packet network services is at a peak.

No dial tone. This is an error message caused by the modem not having a dial tone. Retry the call, and if the problem persists call Accu-Link customer service.

Connect. This is the normal connect message. The next thing you should see is the welcome for the system you've called. If you need to switch to other parameters, such as 7-E-1, do so at this point.

Conclusions

Until the fall of 1991, Accu-Link was set up to resell time on the Tymnet packet network. British Telecom's decision to leave that end of the business forced Accu-Link to make some rapid adjustments.

Accu-Link represents a good alternative to Connect USA. Costs are higher, but access is through existing packet networks. Accu-Link's system of menus also makes it easier for users who merely want to sample a lot high-profile BBSs at a minimal cost.

NATIONAL VIDEOTEX NETWORK

201-242-3119
Fax: 201-242-1662

National Videotex Network (NVN) marks AT&T's entrance into the consumer packet-switch market. Until now, the company's Accunet network was accessed only by large businesses, either for internal traffic or for short "bursts" of financial data. NVN has over 600 local nodes points around the United States.

Roger Charland wants to make Accunet a consumer service. National Videotex Network plans to do this by offering not only packet service, but what amounts to protocol conversion as well. If your online service uses the Minitel teletel standard or the NAPLPS standard—the same graphic standard used by Prodigy—your users could access it from ordinary PCs via NVN. All you need do is maintain NVN's emulation software at your end of the link.

What It Costs

Information providers pay moderate setup fees for each "service code" they establish. They also need to buy a digital service unit, or DSU, to link with the X.25 network. An X.25 link to Accunet costs about $500 per month.

Unlike the other services, NVN provides a way to bill users directly for your service. If you're charging for access to your BBS, in other words, you can take on casual users with NVN and have them billed through the network. Information providers will pay about 10 cents per minute, but NVN will automatically collect 20 cents per minute access to their services. There is also a small user surcharge when the average usage is greater than 1,500 128-byte packets per month, but this won't apply unless users are spending all their time online moving large files.

Beyond these usage charges, there is a $4.95 monthly charge for the basic user connection to NVN. Software to use it is free. There are a number of "free" services offered to spur usage, including USA Today's Decisionline newspaper, a classified ad function, and some electronic mail. Charland sees his service as a "national clearinghouse for data providers" that clears up the protocol problems now plaguing modem users.

Conclusions

NVN has been slow to get off the ground. A major marketing push, using AT&T's logo, was pushed back from the fall of 1991 to March 1992.

For most BBSs, there is no extra value in NVN's protocol emulation service. The idea of a packet network billing users directly for BBS services holds promise, but the BBS operator must still buy some expensive equipment to take advantage of it. This could prove crucial to BBSs offering product support, either to customer or resellers. Although, NVN's basic costs are low, users will in the end face higher bills than they're used to with other networks, since they'll be billed 20 cents per minute for accessing remote services.

NVN bears watching, but its time may not yet have arrived.

OTHER WAYS TO SAVE

If you have a fast, 9,600-baud modem that you use for uploading and downloading large files, 1,200 or 2,400 bps services won't help you much. You'll waste time online, and you won't get the most your modem can deliver.

But there are many ways in which you can still save money. The easiest, and most common, way is to schedule modem calls for after 5:00 P.M. on weekdays. Better yet, call after 11:00 P.M. on weekdays and during the weekends. Generally, "evening calls" cost 25 percent less than daytime calls, and "nighttime" calls cost 40 percent less.

Beyond that, each of the major long-distance companies—AT&T, MCI, and Sprint—has crafted low-cost dialing plans aimed at increasing the savings and thereby winning all of your business. Generally, the residential plans require payment of an up-front fee and a monthly fee; with the business plans, savings increase the more you use the company.

The rules underlying calling plans are subject to change based on the marketing aim of the long-distance carriers, so consider this section only a rough guide. Contact carriers directly for details.

AT&T

There are a number of AT&T calling plans, but they all involve the same principle: You pay a monthly fee to secure a set rate for a set amount of time.

- *AnyHour Saver*. This is AT&T's "premium" calling plan, for consumers making heavy use of the phone at any hour of the day. A small monthly fee buys one hour of direct-dialed, out-of-state calling any time of the day or night. After that, charges are about 20 cents per minute by day and about 12 cents per minute at other times. There's a 5 percent discount on in-state and international direct-dial calls, and the plan automatically fits the most expensive calls into that hour of free service.

- *Reach Out America*. This is the most popular plan with hobbyists for echo-mailing and late-night modeming. A small amount per month buys one hour of direct-dialed, out-of-state calling after 11:00 P.M. weekdays or on weekends. For a little more, you can get a 15 percent discount on evening calls, making those prices comparable with the normal night rates. A small additional charge provides a 10 percent discount on daytime calls plus a 5 percent discount on international and in-state calls. You can also get an AT&T Calling Card for any plan.

- *Reach-Out Half Hour.* A small monthly charge buys you 30 minutes of direct-dialed out-of-state calls on nights and weekends, plus a 10 percent discount on evening calls.

- *SelectSaver.* If you're making heavy use of one bulletin board, either to download files or for other work, this plan works best. A couple of dollars per month buys a daytime rate of about 20 cents per minute and a night/weekend rate of about 12 cents per minute, for calls to any area code of your choice.

In addition, AT&T has Reach Out plans for 15 different states, but, again, all work on the same principle: Pay a set monthly fee and get one hour of calls within the state in which you live. It's worth inquiring about if the BBS you need to reach is inside your state's borders.

As with all special deals, AT&T calling plan rates are subject to change with little notice. But the principle of a set fee for a set amount of calling, and more discounts for higher fees, seems well established.

MCI

MCI calls its residential plans MCI Premier, and the company offers two business calling plans.

- *MCI PrimeTime.* This plan offers one hour of direct-dialed interstate calls per month, starting at 5:00 P.M., for a small monthly fee, with additional calls billed at about 11 cents per minute. The same plan offers a 10 percent discount on daytime calling.

- *International Plans.* These are designed for callers who make a habit of calling one particular country. There are special low rates for Canada, most of Europe and the Pacific Rim, and Mexico.

- *Personal 800.* This is an inbound toll-free line you can provide to a select group of callers. For a low monthly subscription fee, you get low day or night rates from anywhere in the United States using a toll-free line, plus a four-digit security code that differs for each user.

- *Friends & Family.* Many BBSs that do a lot of echo-mailing have expressed interest in this plan, MCI's newest consumer calling plan. Customers specify a list of up to 12 numbers, which form a calling circle. There are no sign-up or monthly fees for joining a circle, and members may be added to a circle at any time. Each call within a circle gets a 20% discount on MCI's regular rates, and the plan works in conjunction with other MCI calling plans; it's not a replacement. The savings apply even when calls are made with MCI's Calling Card. Of course, every BBS involved in a circle must have MCI as its default long-distance company in order to get the savings.

- *MCI Preferred.* This is MCI's main calling plan for small-business customers. If you're paying business rates to your local phone company, you're ineligible for the residential calling plans, but you can get MCI Preferred. The plan combines all business calling—even calls placed by owners in their own homes—into one statement with one discount, which increases with calling volume. There's a single low rate on daytime calls, with discounts of 30 percent in the evening, and 45 percent on weekends and at night, and calls are billed in six-second increments with a 30-second minimum. There's a 10 percent discount on all calls to the most frequently called area code, and a 10 percent discount for combined usage of $200 per month. Inbound 800 services and calling card calls can be added to the plan as well. You can also add accounting codes for client billing and detailed usage reports so that you know which employees are doing what.

- *MCI Vision.* MCI's latest calling plan for the business marketplace is aimed at firms making at least $500 worth of calls per month. As with the Preferred plan, Vision offers a single bill that details calls from each location and adds codes for employees, departments, and calling cards. Volume discounts of up to 20 percent are offered when calling is consolidated through MCI. There are also clever services such as remote exchange, which gives callers in another city a local number that is answered in your remote location, and the ability to add dedicated lines to the bill. You can even have your monthly statement sent on magnetic tape instead of paper.

U.S. Sprint

Sprint's calling plans are more like those of MCI than those of AT&T. One difference is that Sprint is trying to use an MCI strategy designed for the business market in the residential arena. Sprint also advertises that it can analyze your bill to choose the best calling plan.

- *Sprint Select.* Like MCI Premier, this plan offers one hour per month of night and weekend calling for a low monthly fee. Calls beyond that hour are billed at set low rate per minute, with one-minute increments. There are additional 5 percent discounts on calling card, intrastate, and international calls.

- *Select with Day Option.* If your modem calls are placed during the day, this option gives you a 10 percent discount on those calls, but the monthly minimum is higher. The 5 percent discounts on calling card, intrastate, and international rates also apply.

- *Sprint Plus.* This is Sprint's main calling plan for the small-business market. It offers per-minute rates computed using 12 mileage bands, and rates are discounted with increased usage. Callers who spend $20 per month under the plan get a 20 percent discount on evening, night, or weekend calls and a 10 percent discount on daytime calls over $20 per month. As usage increases further, discounts can rise to up to 30 percent. In addition, there's a 15 percent on calling card calls, and 5 percent discounts on international calls and evening or weekend calls. Plus, there's a 1 percent discount on intrastate tariffs. This plan was recently reconfigured to raise rates 2.7 percent, but the company says callers spending $20 per month or more will see their bills go down.

- *Sprint World.* Like the MCI international plans, this offers special rates to a number of different countries. The rates are the same as MCI's, with the same countries covered. In addition, there's a 5 percent discount when a business combines this plan with Sprint Plus.

- *Priority Customer Program.* Sprint's latest marketing move is to remove all this complication within the residential marketplace. All residential calling plan customers are given a toll-free number for customer service, annual reviews of their calling patterns to make sure they're on the best possible discount plan, and automatic enrollment in an awards program with such benefit as free long-distance, merchandise, and travel discounts.

Service Alternatives

Large businesses should talk to their long-distance carriers, and their local phone companies, about the following alternatives to regular service.

Packet Connections. Becoming a node on SprintNet (Telenet), Tymnet, AT&T® Accunet, Infonet, or CompuServe may cost a few thousand dollars up front, for set up fees and for X.25 PADs. (For more information on these topics, see Chapter 5.) But you can save money if you have a large number of regular callers. Users dial the packet net's local number, then enter a special "node number," or code, for your system. Generally, larger systems have their own mnemonics, and smaller systems have numbers that start with their respective area codes.

Leased Lines.   Using leased lines is the "traditional" method for large companies to save on data communications costs. Renting "conditioned" lines gives you a regular connection at a set speed between two points. These were a good deal before 9,600-baud modems became effective on regular voice lines. You could combine, or multiplex, a number of modem lines onto the data stream and save money over making the calls individually.

T1 or Fractional T1.   T1 is the new way for large companies to save on data communications. Today's digital phone networks let you dial up a 1.544 million bps line, or part of such a line in units as small as 56,000 bits per second. You can combine fax, data, and voice traffic on such a line, and even hold videoconferences. Both regional phone companies and long-distance firms are pushing this technology heavily. (For more on T1, see Chapter 5.)

Frame Relay.   In just the last few months most major long-distance companies, including AT&T, MCI, Sprint, and CompuServe, as well as BT Tymnet and Williams Telecommunications, have announced what they call Frame Relay Service. Like T1 and fractional T1, these are digital links, purchased in units of 56,000 bits per second, going up tp T1 speeds of 1.544 million nits per second. These lines lack most the of the error correction features of X.25 lines, but much of the transmission equipment you may buy for these speeds includes such error correction as a standard feature. Frame Relay is being pushed as a way to link local area networks, but you can also multiplex a large amount of data or fax traffic onto them. It's something worth learning about, and an offering you'll hear much more about in the next few years.

Toll-Free Lines.   If you want many remote salesmen or steady customers to call your board, offer them toll-free access. This isn't a money saver; you pay for all calls to the line, even wrong numbers. But toll-free lines do encourage marginal callers to make an effort to link with you. If you are offering toll-free voice numbers to your customers, offering toll-free modem numbers could save money by shortening the time of the call and increasing the volume of information that can be delivered in one call.

ISDN. As ISDN becomes available in more and more cities, you may be able to take advantage of it. Like fractional T1, this alternative offers you flexibility; data, voice, fax, and videoconference traffic can share the line, dynamically. It's not a leased line, so you don't pay for it at night when you're not using it. And basic ISDN service will offer two 64,000 bps channels, plus a 16,000 bps channel, for little more than the cost of a single business line. Plus, ISDN offers the services of that signaling channel. Right now, that means you can track where your calls are coming from, and additional services will eventually emerge. The one disadvantage to ISDN is it's not available everywhere, and it won't be for some time. If you've got a lot of calls going between Podunk and Juneau, it may be years before ISDN service becomes available. (See Chapter 5 for more information on ISDN.)

Negotiate. As your need for telephone service of all kinds increases, negotiation is the best option of all. If you can keep 24 lines busy all day within a city, you probably don't need your local phone company; you might look into accessing a "bypass" ring instead. If you're shelling out millions per year for long-distance calls, you can easily play off long-distance companies against each other to get the best deal. And whenever you make such a deal, consider the cost of data transmission both to and from your BBS as part of the mix. Don't rely on plain old telephone service (POTS) to get the job done.

Selected BBSs

Here is a list of significant BBSs, as selected by *Boardwatch Magazine* in August 1991 (used with permission).

ADA 9X Project Bulletin Board, 800-232-9925
ADA programming language revisions and news
Chris Anderson/Susan Carlson, Eglin AFB, FL

ADA Information Clearinghouse, 703-614-0215
Information on ADA programming language/military specs
Department of Defense, Washington, DC

American Cybernetics BBS, 602-968-1082
Multi-edit product support BBS
American Cybernetics, Tempe, AZ

ANARC BBS, 913-345-1978
World radio/TV handbook; Shortwave Frequency lists/schedules
Association of North American Radio Clubs, Mission, KS

Applied Modeling Research RBBS, 919-541-1325
Environmental Protection Agency atmospheric models
William Peterson/EPA, Hurdle Mills, NC

Aquila BBS, 708-820-8344
2 GB, 14 nodes, FidoNet/Interlink/Metronet MCe IL/CHI Graphi
Kevin Behrens/Steve Williams/Chris Babb, Aurora, IL

Ashton-Tate Technical Support, 213-324-2188
dBase and Multimate support, CIS HOST NAME:ATBBS
Ashton-Tate Corporation, Torrance, CA

AST Technical Services BBS, 714-727-4723
Superb support system for AST computer products
AST Research Inc., Irvine, CA

AT&T Support BBS, 201-769-6397
Support for PC 6300 and other AT&T PC models
American Telephone/Telegraph PC Division, Plainfield, NJ

ATI Support BBS, 416-756-4591
Support for ATI modems and video cards
ATI Technologies, Scarborough, Ontario, Canada

Audiophile Network, 818-988-0452
High-end audio components, music, video reviews
Guy Hickey/Quatre Speakers, Van Nuys, CA

Automobile Consumer Services, 513-624-0552
New car pricing reports, used car value reports
Automobile Consumer Services Inc., Cincinnati, OH

Back Room, 718-849-1614
America's largest exclusively gay BBS—home of Gaycomm
Artie Kohn, Richmond Hill, NY

BBS Press Service, 913-478-9239
Home of INFOMAT Online Weekly PC News Magazine
Alan Bechtold/BBS Press Service, Topeka, KS

BellSouth's TUG Gateway, 404-594-3964
Transtext Universal Gateway, *Atlanta Journal-Constitution*
BellSouth, Atlanta, GA

Best Friends BBS, 714-832-5902
DLX multiline chat/match social/sexual
Ann and Joe Wiseman, Fountain Valley, CA

Big Peach BBS, 404-446-6650
Home of Automenu and Treeview software
Marshall Magee/Magee Enterprises, Norcross, GA

Big Sky Telegraph, 406-683-7680
Education/Economic development info to Montana rural community
Montana Rural Education Network, Dillon, MT

Bird Info Network, 303-423-9775
Breeding, raising, taming exotic birds
Terry Rune/Dave McClauggage, Arvada, CO

BMUG BBS, 415-849-2684
Support for Macintosh owners—files, conferences
Berkeley Macintosh Users Group, Berkeley, CA

Boardwatch Magazine Online Info, 303-973-4222
Distribution Service for USA Today/Boardwatch/Closing NYSE
Boardwatch Magazine, Littleton, CO

Book BBS, 215-657-6130
Information on 2,000 computer books; 800 order number
Business & Computer Book Store, Willow Grove, PA

Borland Download BBS, 408-439-9096
Utilities, macros, programming examples for Borland Products
Borland International/Mike Fitz-Enz, Scotts Valley, CA

Bruce's Bar & Grill, 203-236-3761
24-line social system, chat, games, downloads
Bruce Lomasky, West Hartford, CT

Bucks Telematics 273/201, 215-493-5242
Local, national, international message conferences
Richard Press, Yardley, PA

The Business BBS, 213-477-0408
Microsoft Windows support
Jim Appleby, Los Angeles, CA

C.A.R.L Library Service, 303-863-1350
Citations to 2 million texts in Colorado library system
Colorado Alliance of Research Libraries, Denver, CO

Canada Remote Systems, 416-798-4713
19 GB/400,000+ files, 2,500 conferences, USENET, IBM/Amiga/Mac
    and more
Jud Newell, Mississauga, Ontario, Canada

Cape Cod Bungalow 101/870, 508-759-1168
Multiline service, shopping mall, games, tourist info
Crawford Communications/Daniel Crawford, Cape Cod, MA

Capital PC User's Group BBS, 301-738-9060
One of the oldest PC user's groups, 5,500 members
Capital PC Users Group/Roger Fajman, Rockville, MD

Castle Tabby 107/412, 201-988-0706
Home of TABBY FidoNet interface program for Apple Macintosh
Michael E. Connick, Bradley Beach, NJ

Census Bureau Office Automation, 301-763-4576
Microcomputers and office automation
U.S. Dept. of Commerce/Nevins Frankel, Suitland, MD

Census Bureau Personnel Division, 301-763-4574
Employment opportunities within the Census Bureau
U.S. Dept. of Commerce/Nevins Frankel, Suitland, MD

Channel 1, 617-354-8873
45-line PCBoard system, 3.7 GB of files, 250 message conferences
Brian Miller/Tess Heder, Cambridge, MA

Chicago SysLink, 312-622-4442
Special interest areas for ferret/pet owners, TRS80/aviation
George Matyaszek, Chicago, IL

chinet, 312-283-0559
Unix system offering Internet mail
Randy Suess, Chicago, IL

Classi Computer Fieds, 317-359-5199
Online system for classified advertisements
Steve Edsall/*Trader* Newspaper, Indianapolis, IN

Clean Air BBS, 408-298-4277
Environmental health/cigarette smoking topics
American Lung Association/Sheila Blash, San Jose, CA

Cleveland Freenet, 216-368-3888
Cleveland city information/Ohio governor's office online
Case Western University/AT&T/Ohio Bell, Cleveland, OH

CocoNet, 619-456-0815
CocoNet support/demo, hires graphics BBS for Unix systems
Brian and Patricia Dear, La Jolla, CA

The Comm-Post 104/666, 303-534-4646
Astronomy, 725+ MB of files
Brian Bartee, Denver, CO

Compact Audio Disk Exchange, 415-824-7603
Buy/sell/trade compact audio disks online
Wayne Gregori, San Francisco, CA

CompuCom Customer Support BBS, 408-738-4990
Support for CompuCom SpeedModem (9,600 bps, $279)
CompuCom, Sunnyvale, CA

Computer Business Services, 714-396-0014
Computer columnist John C. Dvorak's office BBS
John C. Dvorak and Nick Anis, Jr., Diamond Bar, CA

Computer Garden, 301-546-1508
Treasure hunting, metal detectors, online catalog
Milford P. Webster, Salisbury, MD

Computerized Bulletin Board Sys, 708-849-1132
First electronic bulletin board, creator of Xmodem protocol
Ward Christensen, Chicago, IL

Computing Canada Online, 416-497-5263
Adjunct to excellent Canadian PC newspaper
Computing Canada Newspaper, Willowdale, Ontario

Corporate Data Exchange CDX-, 609-683-4422
PR news wire/business wire, log-on: hello user.cdx
LaFountain Research Corp/Tad LaFountain, Princeton, NJ

Crosstalk Communications BBS, 404-740-8428
Product support for Crosstalk for Windows/MK4/XVI
Digital Communications Associates, Roswell, GA

CTC IEEE Employment Database, 508-263-3857
Online database of 20,000 resumes for engineering
Career Technologies Corporation, Andover, MA

Cul-de-Sac Bar & Grill, 508-429-1784
Multiline service, ham radio, humor, TDBS applications
Pete White, Holliston, MA

CyLink, 719-520-5000
Online chat/multiplayer interactive games, 12 lines
Klaus Dimmler, Colorado Springs, CO

Dante Project BBS, 603-643-6310
Commentary/research on Dante's *Divine Comedy*
Dartmouth College, Hanover, NH

Dark Side of the Moon, 408-245-7726
Home of WAFFLE, Unix uucp BBS software for DOS and Unix
Thomes E. Dell/Darkside International, Mountain View, CA

Data Core BBS, 213-842-6880
25-line Major BBS
Matthew Schoen/Delta Enterprises, Los Angeles, CA

Data Point, 501-442-8777
Online publications, excellent TBBS system
Gary Funk, Fayetteville, AR

DataLink RBBS System, 214-394-7438
Weather satellite imaging, NOAA satellite tracking—AMSAT
Dallas Remote Imaging Group/Jeff Wallach, Carrollton, TX

DayDreamer BBS, 886-2-3122452
10-line remote-access BBS, largest BBS in Taiwan
Allen Wu, Taipei, Taiwan

Denver Deaf-Net, 303-989-9245
Hearing-impaired/computing
David Sheneman, Lakewood, CO

DigiBoard Support BBS, 612-922-5604
Multiport serial cards
DigiBoard Inc., St. Louis Park, MN

DragonNet 386/451, 409-765-5459
Multiline Major BBS with 4 GB, 64 lines of interactive games
Robert Michal/Dragon Profit Systems, Galveston Island, TX

East Bay X-Change 372/888, 803-556-7485
Home of XRS offline mail reader
Mike Ratledge, McClellanville, SC

Echo, 212-989-8411
New York emulation of The Well, Unix caucus conferencing
Stacy Horn/Echo Communications Group, New York, NY

Economic Bulletin Board, 202-377-3870
Economic statistics/GNP/CPI/employment, trade opportunities
U.S. Department of Commerce, Springfield, VA

Electic Dialectic BBS, 708-705-6774
40 online game doors, graphic files
Bruce Johnson, Palatine, IL

Energy Info Admin E-Publications, 202-586-8658
Variety of petroleum/coal/electricity energy statistics
U.S. Department of Energy, Washington, DC

eSoft Product Support BBS, 303-699-8222
Home of the Bread Board System TBBS, BBS software
Phil Becker/eSoft Inc., Aurora, CO

Event Horizons, 503-697-5100
32-line digitized graphics image library, Adult .GIF file
Jim Maxey, Lake Oswego, OR

Exactus Information Service, 707-524-2548
12,500 Amiga files, USA Today, closing NYSE stocks
David Salas/Robert Cohen, Santa Rosa, CA

The Exchange BBS, 713-521-2191
Largest gay/bi/lesbian multiline BBS in Houston
James Craig/John Fields, Houston, TX

EXEC-PC, 414-789-4210
Largest U.S. BBS: 230 lines, 70,000 files, 7 GB
Bob Mahoney, Shorewood, WI

Executive Network, 914-667-4567
Interlink netmail national host, multiline PCBoard system
Andy Keeves, Mt. Vernon, NY

Eye Contact BBS, 415-255-5972
22-line Oracomm—gay issues, popular chat system
Bill Montgomery, Mill Valley, CA

Falken Support BBS, 703-803-8000
Support for FALKEN software—16 lines, doors, chat
Herb Rose, Woodbridge, VA

Farwest BBS, 604-381-3934
Large western Canada Galacticomm info system
Ren L'Ecuyer, Victoria, British Columbia

FCC Public Access Link, 301-725-1072
Equipment authorization status advisory service
Federal Communications Commission, Columbia, MD

Federal Job Information Center, 313-226-4423
Federal job opportunity lists available online
U.S. Office of Personnel Management, Detroit, MI

FEDLINK ALIX II, 202-707-9656
Info on federal libraries, excerpts Library of Congress news
Federal Library Information Network, Washington, DC

Fido Software BBS 1:125/111, 415-863-2739
The first Fido BBS and home of Fido BBS 12s
Tom Jennings, San Francisco, CA

Fido Tech Stand, 31-30-735900
FidoNet technical information for Holland
J.J. van der Maas, Utrecht, Holland

FOG City BBS 125/10, 415-863-9697
Gay community BBS, AIDS info, desktop publishing, Macs
Bill Essex, San Francisco, CA

Fred the Computer, 508-872-8461
Newspaper BBS, Weirdnet news wire, list of Massachusetts libraries
Middlesex News, Framingham, MA

GDP Technologies, 303-673-9470
Outstanding IBM shareware on a small system
Tom Getty's, Lafayette, CO

Gilmore Systems BBS, 818-706-9805
Support for Magnum BBS, OS/2 BBS software, up to 8 lines
Chuck Gilmore, Thousand Oaks, CA

GLIB, 703-578-4542
Gay and lesbian information bureau, 11 lines, 9,600 bps
Community Educational Services Foundation, Arlington, VA

Greenpeace Environet, 415-512-9108
Ecological and peace issues, disarmament/toxics/wildlife
Dick Dillman/Greenpeace, San Francisco, CA

GT PowerComm BBS, 713-772-2090
Home of GT Power Communications software
Paul Meiners/P&M Software, Houston, TX

Hay Locator, 317-494-6643
Database of hay/straw suppliers and buyers
Purdue University Agricultural Computer Net, West Lafayette, IN

Hayes Advanced Systems Support, 800-874-2937
Customer support line for Hayes customers, V-series/Ultra
Hayes Microcomputer Products, Norcross, GA

Heartland Free-net, 309-674-1100
Community online service, free Internet e-mail boxes
Peoria County Board/Bradley University, Peoria, IL

Herpnet/Satronics TBBS, 215-698-1905
Reptile and amphibian studies—poison snakes/toads/fish
Mark Miller, Philadelphia, PA

HH Info-Net BBS, 203-246-3747
Specializes in MS Windows and OS/2 files
Lee Winsor, New Hartford, CT

HOLLIS, 617-495-9500
Harvard On-Line Library Information System, 7E1 VT100
Harvard University, Cambridge, MA

IBM National Support Center BBS, 404-835-5300
IBM PC User Groups Database, newsletter exchange
IBM National Support Center, Atlanta, GA

Imaging GraphicsLine BBS, 415-968-1834
Paradise/Verticom graphics products, .GIFs
Western Digital, Mountain View, CA

Inbound/Outbound/Teleconnect, 212-989-4675
Telephone sales trade magazine online service
Harry Newton Publications, New York, NY

Index Systems, 404-924-8414
Excellent list of Atlanta BBS systems online
Rodney Aloia, Marietta, GA

Infinity World, 606-271-6556
Eight-line Galacticomm system, many good text publications
Daniel Diachun, Lexington, KY

InfoHost Demo BBS, 201-288-7792
Demo BBS for InfoHost BBS software, multiline, database
A-Comm Electronics Inc., Hasbrouch Heights, NJ

Infolink for Upper East Tennessee, 615-434-2551
Space database, online store, chat
John Williams, Johnson City, TN

Intel PCEO Support BBS, 503-645-6275
Support for Intel PC products, Inboard 386/AboveBoard 286
Intel Corporation PCEO Division, Hillsborough, OR

Invention Factory, 212-431-1194
32 lines, 100 directories, good shareware catalog, 3.2 GB
Mike Sussell, New York, NY

Investor's Online Data, 206-285-5359
Online investment/stock market information/tech analysis
Don Shepherdson, Bellevue, WA

JAG-NET, 703-325-0748
Navy judge advocate general's information network
U.S. Department of the Navy/Chris Buechler, Arlington, VA

JDR Microdevices BBS, 408-559-0253
Online hardware order catalog, 1.1 GB of files, quizzes
JDR Microdevices, San Jose, CA

JEPP/LINK, 800-767-7000
7E1 pilots weather service, NWS data and maps
Jeppeson Data Plan Inc., Los Gatos, CA

JOBBS, 404-992-8937
Online job listings—2,186 technical positions, 10,000 corporations
Alpha Systems Inc./Bill Griffin, Roswell, GA

Joe's Place BBS 1:367/15.6, 809-254-3566
Colorful Spitfire BBS in Puerto Rico
Jose Frias, Lajas, PR

Kimberley BBS, 612-340-2489
Prime rate/fed funds/T-bill/discount rate/economic data
Federal Reserve Bank of Minneapolis, Minneapolis, MN

King's Market BBS 104/115, 303-665-6091
400 MB, books, writers' area, TRS 80 support
Jim and Karen Burt, Boulder, CO

LANtastic BBS, 602-293-8065
Support for LANtastic local area network
Artisoft Inc., Tucson, AZ

Late Night BBS, 315-592-7300
Home of Genesis BBS software, multinode LANable
Carter Downer, Hannibal, NY

Late Night Software 125/555, 415-695-0759
Home of UFGATE, software to connect PCs to uucp/Usenet
Tim Pozar, San Francisco, CA

Leading Edge Auto Info Line, 508-836-3967
Support for Leading Edge computer owners
Leading Edge Computer, Westborough, MA

The Ledge PC Board, 818-352-3620
Home of Textview door for PC Board systems
Joseph Sheppard, Tujunga, CA

LegalEase, 509-326-3238
Legal issues/forms, law BBS list
Bill Sorcinelli, Spokane, WA

LUMINA, 612-626-2206
Libraries of University of Minnesota Integrated Net Access 7E1VT1
University of Minnesota, Minneapolis, MN

Macalot Bulletin Board, 412-846-5312
Support for Second Sight BBS software for Macintosh
Jeff Dripps/FreeSoft Company, Beaver Falls, PA

MacInternational, 803-798-3755
Largest Mac BBS on East Coast
Ralph Yount, Columbia, SC

Magpie BBS, 212-420-0527
Support/demo system for Magpie BBS/conferencing software
Steve Manes, New York, NY

Maxi-Micro TickerScreen, 212-809-1160
2,000 closing stock quotes/market research/order entry
Max Ule & Company, New York, NY

MaxiHost Support BBS, 209-836-2402
MaxiHost BBS—small, very easy to run
Don Mankin, San Ramon, CA

Maxtor Technical Support BBS, 303-678-2020
Installation/troubleshooting/support for Maxtor hard disks
Maxtor Corp./Chris Bowers, Longmont, CO

McAfee Associates BBS, 408-988-4004
Computer virus information, VIRUSCAN and CLEANUP programs
John McAfee/CVIA, Santa Clara, CA

METRO Online Entertainment, 212-831-9280
32-line DLX with city guide/ski database, matchmaker
Bruce Kamm/Metro Online Services, New York City, NY

The Micro Foundry, 415-598-0398
2.2 GB downloads, Your Online Software Source, Boardwatch
Thomas Nelson/Clockwork Software, San Jose, CA

Micro Message Service, 919-779-6674
USA Today/Boxoffice Magazine, large download area
Mike Stroud, Raleigh, NC

Micro Tech BBS, 314-334-6359
Support for OSIRIS multiline BBS software, IRIS mail
Micro Tech, Cape Girardeau, MO

Microlink B, 303-972-9600
Over 2.5 GB of IBM software, multiline, USA Today news
Girard Westerberg, Littleton, CO

Microrim Technical Support BBS, 206-649-9836
Support for popular RBase relational data base system
Microrim Corporation, Redmond, WA

Microsoft Product Support BBS, 206-646-9145
Word/Works/multiplan/flight simulator application notes
Microsoft Corp./Scott J. Honaker, Bellevue, WA

Microsystems Software Inc., 508-875-8009
HandiWare software for handicapped, CodeRunner C utilities
MSI/Reed Lewis, Framingham, MA

Minnesota Spacenet, 612-920-5566
Minnesota Space Frontier Society, NASA news
Ben Husset, Minneapolis, MN

N8EMR Ham BBS, 614-895-2553
login:hbbs HAM radio/AMSAT Unix system, satellite/packet
Gary Sanders, Westerville, OH

NARDAC BBS, 804-445-1627
Zenith computer support, list of federal micro user groups
Navy Regional Data Automation Center, NAS Norfolk, VA

NASA Headquarters Info Tech, 202-453-9008
Shareware and technical info for NASA PC users
National Aeronautics and Space Administration, Washington, DC

NASA Spacelink, 205-895-0028
NASA Educational Affairs Div., flight data/space history
Marshall Space Flight Center, Huntsville, AL

Nashville Exchange, 615-383-0727
Eight-line TBBS, games/TDBS software development
Ben Cunningham, Nashville, TN

National Agricultural Library, 301-344-8510
Agricultural info/research resources
U.S. Department of Agriculture, Beltsville, MD

National Genealogical BBS, 703-528-2612
Family history/genealogical research/gravestone hunting
National Genealogical Society, Arlington, VA

Nautilus BBS, 316-365-7631
32-line TBBS with 5 GB of files on 80486, CD/WORMS
Nautilus Communications, Iola, KS

NAVWESA, 202-433-6639
Naval Weapons Engineering Support
Department of the Navy/Bill Walsh, Washington, DC

Network World Bulletin Board, 508-620-1178
LAN and WAN issues and technology
Network World Magazine/CW Communications, Framingham, MA

Neuropsychology Bound 157/3, 216-356-1431
Support groups for disabled/physically impaired
Butch Walker, Rocky River, OH

NIST ACTS, 303-494-4775
Automated computer telephone service, sync PC to NBS time
National Institute for Standards/Technology, Boulder, CO

NIST Computer Security, 301-948-5717
Computer security and virus protection issues
National Institute for Standards/Technology, Gaithersburg, MD

Nixpix, 303-920-1263
Large library of adult .GIF graphics images
Nick De Wolf, Aspen, CO

NOAA Space Environment Lab, 303-497-5042
Solar flare/geomagnetic data online
National Oceanic and Atmospheric Administration, Boulder, CO

NoGate Consulting, 616-530-3392
Home of PAK archive utility
Mike Neuhaus/Gus Smedstad, Grand Rapids, MI

Numisnet, 301-498-8205
Collecting of coins, medals, and exonumia
The Mitchell Group, Laurel, MD

OASis BBS, 404-627-2662
Home of Atlanta Bulletin Board List (ABBL)
Robert Orr/Online Atlanta Society, Decatur, GA

Occupational Health/Safety BBS, 212-385-2034
Job safety issues for artists, musicians, entertainers
Mike McCann/Center for Safety in Arts, New York, NY

Odyssey, 818-358-6968
Adult multiline chat system, games, magazines, download
Michael Allen, Monrovia, CA

OERI BBS, 800-222-4922
Educational statistics and data, performance stats
U.S. Department of Education, Washington, DC

Old Colorado City Communications, 719-632-4111
Political discussions, Unix uucp public access, multiline
Dave Hughes, Colorado Springs, CO

Online Now, 807-345-5522
5 CD-ROMs plus 3 MB of new software per week
Gary Walsh/Tom Haavisto, Thunder Bay, Ontario

Online with Hayes, 404-446-6336
Hayes public bulletin board—conferences/SIGs/support
Hayes Microcomputer Products, Norcross, GA

Oracle PC, 6108 260-6222
South Australian TBBS multiline system
Don Crago, Pooraka, South Australia

Oracomm Support BBS, 619-346-1608
Sales and support for Oracomm multiline BBS software
Surf Computer Services, Rancho Mirage, CA

Osprey's Nest, 301-989-9036
Birdwatching, bird feeding, naturalist/ecology issues
Fran and Norm Saunders, Colesville, MD

The Other BBS 1:1/0, 717-657-2223
FidoNet zone coordinator for North America 1:1/0
George Peace, Harrisburg, PA

PacComm BBS, 813-874-3078
Packet radio equipment supplier, TNC/PSK modems
Gwyn Reedy/PacCom Inc., Tampa, FL

PC Ohio, 216-381-3320
Shareware library with 100 percent USR HST access, five years up
Norm Henke, Cleveland, OH

P.D.S.L.O. BBS, 516-938-6722
Home of The List national BBS list
James Toro, Hicksville, NY

PHYSICS Forum BBS, 413-545-1959
Physics and astronomical sciences
University of Massachusetts Department of Physics/Astronomy,
Amherst, MA

Pinecliffe BBS 104/28, 303-642-7463
Large shareware library, echo mail conferences since 1985
Craig Baker, Pinecliffe, CO

PKWare BBS, 414-354-8670
Home of PKZIP 1.10 compression utility
Phil Katz/PKWare Inc., Glendale, WI

Pleasure Dome, 804-490-5878
Sexually explicit fantasy chat system—adults only
Tom Terrific, Tidewater, VA

Popular Mechanics Online BBS, 212-582-8369
Automotive, home/shop, electronics/photography, science
Popular Mechanics Magazine, New York, NY

PowerNet, 407-834-3326
Commercial distributor for Remote Access BBS software
Richard T. Brannon, Altamonte Springs, FL

Practical Peripherals BBS, 818-706-2467
Support BBS for Practical Peripherals modems
Practical Peripherals, West Lake Village, CA

ProComm Support BBS, 314-474-8477
Home of ProComm 2.4.3 and ProComm Plus communications
    programs
Thomas Smith/DataStorm Technologies Inc., Columbia, MO

The Professional System, 303-740-2223
Writers, lawyers, EDP auditors
Bob Voorhees, Littleton, CO

The Promised Land, 715-387-1339
16-line/2.5 GB/11,000+ files/ windows, chat and more
Tim Brown/Computer Solutions, Marshfield, WI

Public Brand Software BBS, 317-856-2087
Commercial shareware vendor
Public Brand Software, Indianapolis, IN

QMail Deluxe Support BBS, 901-382-5583
Support for QMail, offline conference mail reader
Mark "Sparky" Herring, Germantown, TN

Qualitas Inc. BBS, 301-907-8030
386MAX and BlueMAX memory management software support
Qualitas Inc., Bethesda, MD

QuickBBS Support BBS 363/34, 407-896-0494
Product support for QuickBBS software
Richard Creighton/Steve Gabrilowitz, Orlando, FL

Random Access Information Service, 503-761-8100
10,500 IBM/Mac/Amiga files, 3,000 MaxiPic graphics
Janice Stevens, Portland, OR

Remote Access HQ 3:690/625, 61 9 389 8048
Home of Remote Access BBS software
Andrew Milner/Continental Software, Perth, Western Australia

RGB Computing, 519-824-3997
Multiline information service/PC sales/large file selection
Ronald Spencer/RGB Computing, Guelph, Ontario

Rose Media, 416-733-2780
Excellent Canadian PCBoard system—publications/conference
Vic Kass, Willowdale, Ontario

Rusty & Edie's, 216-726-0737
Large ML PC Board run by husband and wife—NFL/tradeware
Rusty and Edwina Hardenburgh, Boardman, OH

Salt Air BBS, 801-261-8976
Home of PC Board BBS software, national list of PC Board systems
Clark Development Company/David Terry, Murray, UT

San Diego NeXT User's Group BBS, 619-456-2522
Support for NeXT computers
Brian Dear/San Diego NeXT User's Group, San Diego, CA

Science Resource Studies BBS, 202-634-1764
Federal R&D budget, technical labor market statistics
National Science Foundation, Washington, DC

Scooters Scientific Exchange, 215-657-5586
Biotechnology/chemistry/physics/astronomy/space sciences
Brian Moldover, Willow Grove, PA

SEAboard!, 201-473-1991
Support system for ARC, SEADOG, and AXE software
System Enhancement Associates, Wayne, NJ

Seagate Technical Support BBS, 408-438-8771
Installation and specifications for hard-drive models
Seagate/Shelley Toich, Scotts Valley, CA

Searchlight BBS, 516-689-2566
Support system for Searchlight BBS software
Searchlight Software, Stonybrook, NY

SemWare Support BBS, 404-641-8968
Home of QEdit, a superb shareware text editor
Sammy Mitchell/SemWare Software Products, Marietta, GA

Sistema Profesional Informacion, 525 590-5988
Largest BBS in Mexico—Spanish-language TBBS
Tecnologia Uno Cero S.A. de C.V., Mexico City

SNAFU BBS, 202-547-6238
Advice for government whistle blowers—fouled DOD program
Greg Williams/Project on Military Procurement, Washington, DC

Society for Technical Communication BBS, 703-522-3299
STC job service, freelance registry—technical writers
Society for Technical Communication, Washington, DC

Sonshine Express BBS, 415-651-2440
Family-oriented Christian BBS
Anton Johnson, Fremont, CA

Sound Advice BBS, 816-436-4516
20-line PCBoard with 2 GB storage—HST modems
Roy Timberman, Gladstone, MO

Southern Arizona Birding BBS, 602-881-4280
Rare bird alerts online, birdwatching in Southwest
Chuck and Sharon Williamson, Tucson, AZ

StarLink Network BBS, 718-972-6099
Nine nodes, 2.1 GB, Ilink, 75,000 programs
Michael Keylin, Brooklyn, NY

State and Local Emergency Management, 202-646-2887
Hazardous materials/National dam watch/Emergency info
Federal Emergency Management Agency, Washington, DC

Stillwaters BBS, 708-403-2826
Home of Stillwaters Chicagoland BBS List—over 500 systems
Colby Jordan (BBS)/Peter Anvin (list), Orland Park, IL

Talk Channel, 818-506-0620
DLX-based multiline chat/talk service—sexual orientation
Gary Clarkson, North Hollywood, CA

TAXACOM, 716-896-7581
Botany, herbaria, Flora Online newsletter, Latin translation
Clinton Herbarium, Buffalo Museum, Buffalo, NY

TEAMate Unix Bulletin Board, 213-318-5302
Demo/support for TEAMate BBS software for Unix
Bob Baskerville/MMB Development Corp., Manhattan Beach, CA

Telegodzilla, 503-621-3746
Home of ZModem file transfer protocol/YModem/YAM
Chuck Forsberg/Omen Technology Inc., Portland, OR

Telepath, 415-364-8315
DBMS/Dr. Dobbs Journal online service
M&T Publishing, Redwood City, CA

Telix Support BBS, 416-439-8293
Support service for Telix Communications software
Colin Sampaleanu/Exis Inc., West Hill, Ontario

That Old Frog's Swamp, 715-362-3895
Zen Buddhist monk/PC consultant
Ryugen Fisher/The Old Frog, Rhinelander, WI

Trinity 1 BBS, 44 392 410210
United Kingdom distributor of Boardwatch Magazine
John Burden, Exeter Devon, UK

TurboTax Support BBS, 619-453-5232
Income tax information, Turbotax 1040 program support
Chipsoft Inc., San Diego, CA

Twilight Zone, 415-352-0433
Rare bird alerts, birdwatching
Ken Jones, San Leandro, CA

U.S. Naval Observatory BBS, 202-653-1079
Time, date, sunrise, sunset; enter @TCO for commands
U.S. Department of Commerce, U.S. Naval Observatory,
Washington, DC

US Robotics—Sit UBU Sit, 708-982-5092
Support for US Robotics HST 9600 bps modems
US Robotics Corporation, Skokie, IL

USGS Quick Epicenter Determin., 800-358-2663
Earthquake epicenter data—Geomagnetism 7E2
U.S. Geological Survey, Earthquake Information Center, Denver, CO

USNO Time of Day for Clocks, 202-653-0351
Transmits ASCII time string; sync your PC to USNO atomic clock
U.S. Naval Observatory, Washington, DC

UT Library Online Catalog, 512-471-9420
Online library card catalog listing 3.5 million entries
University of Texas, Austin, TX

VA Property Listing BBS, 602-640-2371
List of VA-held property foreclosures
Veterans Administration—Phoenix Regional Office, Phoenix, AZ

Ventura Professional Forum, 408-227-4818
Ventura Publisher user's group BBS
Gene Rodriguez/Ventura Professional, San Jose, CA

Ward and Randy's CBBS, 312-545-8086
World's first and oldest micro-based BBS, since 2/16/78
Ward Christensen/Randy Suess, Chicago, IL

WeatherBank, 800-827-2727
Online weather forecasts for any city; download radar data
Steve Root/WeatherBrief Data Services, Salt Lake City, UT

The Well, 415-332-7190
Unix conferencing system—$10 monthly plus $2.50 hourly
Whole Earth Lectronic Link, Sausalito, CA

Western Digital Tech Support, 714-753-1068
Hard drive/controller installation and configuration data
Western Digital Corporation, Irvine, CA

Wildcat HQ BBS 210/12, 805-395-0650
Multiline support system for Wildcat BBS software
Mustang Software, Bakersfield, CA

Windsor Manor, 203-688-4973
Over 27 online adventure games
Jim Taylor, Windsor, CT

WordPerfect Customer Support, 801-225-4444
WordPerfect 4.2/5.0/5.1 support/printer drivers
WordPerfect Corporation, Orem, UT

WWIV Support BBS, 213-208-6689
Support for WWIV BBS software
Wayne Bell, Rolling Hills Estates, CA

XTree BBS, 805-546-9150
Support for XTree Pro Gold DOS shell program
XTree Company, San Luis Obispo, CA

XyQuest Support BBS, 508-667-5669
Support for XyWrite word processor, custom keyboard files
XyQuest Inc./Christine Madsen, Bellerica, MA

Yellow Dream Machine BBS, 512-473-2702
Disability rights issues, Variety of Disability newsletter
Bill Scarborough/Cyanosis Rex, Austin, TX

Zenith Technical Support BBS, 800-888-3058
Technical support for Zenith desktop and laptop units
Zenith Data Systems Customer Service, Chicago, IL

Bulletin Boards Contacted for This Book

ADT BBS
Sysop: Aaron Thompson
602-881-8570

Ashton Tate
Sysop: Roger Wegehost
213-538-7489

AST Research
Sysop: Jim Bergaman
714-727-8237

Auntie Support
Sysop: Wes Meier
415-937-0156

AV-Sync
Sysop: Bill Tullis
404-320-6202

Bare Bones BBS
Sysop: Mike Hancock
404-987-3972

BBS Concepts
Sysop: James E. Toro
516-983-6722

Big Peach (Automenu Support)
Sysop: Marshall Magee
404-446-6650

Bitwiz Opus
Sysop: Michael Katz
312-935-6809

The Black Hole Literary Review
Sysop: Bill Allendorg
513-821-6670

Boardwatch Magazine
Sysop: Jack Rickard
303-973-4222

The Business Board
Sysop: Jim Appleby
213-477-0408

Canada Remote
Sysop: Jud Newell
416-629-7000

Capital City Computer Users' Club
Sysop: Roger Fajman
301-738-9060

CBBS
Sysop: Ward Christensen
312-545-8086

Celebration Station
Sysop: Paul Stookey
207-374-2303

Channel 1
Sysop: Tess Miller
617-864-0741

Chicago Computer Society
Sysop: Colby Jordan
312-942-0706

Chicago Syslink
Sysop: George Matyasak
312-622-4442

Colorado TravelBank
Sysop: Jay Melnick
303-671-7669

The Compact Disc Exchange
Sysop: Wayne Gregori
415-824-7603

CONNECT 19.2 (PC Relay)
Sysop: Kip Compton
703-690-7361

Darwin BBS
Sysop: Bob Blacher
202-547-3037

DCA Support
Sysop: Mark C. Miller
404-740-8428

Deafcom
Sysop: Murray Mattenson
312-262-6173

Down n Dirty PC Board
Sysop: Scott Foster
Albuquerque, NM
505-299-5402

The Economic Bulletin Board
Sysop: Paul Christy
202-377-0433

Exec-PC
Sysop: Bob Mahoney
414-420-4210

Faster than Light
Sysop: Rob Vostreys
404-292-8761

Fido #1
Sysop: George Peace
717-657-8699

FidoNews
Sysop: Tom Jennings
415-764-1629

Front Porch
Sysop: Jeff Freeman
404-695-1889

Galaxy
Sysop: Tom Scott
505-881-6964

HomeBase (anti-viral software)
Sysop: John McAfee
408-988-4004

IBBS
Sysop: Gene Plantz
708-882-4227

IBM's Product Support
Sysop: Wyn Easton
404-835-6600

ILink
Sysop: Andy Keeves
914-667-4567

KLMS Radio
Sysop: Michelle Chase
402-489-2515

LawMUG
Sysop: Paul Bernstein
312-661-1740

The Lively Arts
Sysop: Andy Prestigiacomo
312-348-7269

National Computer Security Association
203-364-1305

The Net Exchange (PC Pursuit)
C PURSUIT on Telenet (SprintNet)

NIST Computer Security Bulletin Board
301-948-5717

Nitelines by Multicomm
Sysop: Mike Stone
815-282-2428

Online Atlanta Society OASis
Sysop: Chris Camacho
404-627-2662

Online with Hayes
Sysop: Randy Cooper
404-446-6336

PCBoard Support
Sysop: Fred Clark
601-261-8979

PDSLO
Sysop: Jim Toro
516-938-6722

PKWARE Support
Sysop: Phil Katz
414-352-7176

Plywood PC
(Technique Computer Systems)
604-598-1546

ProStar
Sysop: Bob Michnick
206-946-0579

Public Brand Software
Sysop: Tony Moletta
317-856-2085

Random Access Support
Sysop: Paul Painchaud
603-357-8941

RBBS Support
Sysop: Doug Azzarito
407-627-6969

RBBSnet
Sysop: Rob Bowman
714-381-6013

Rock n Roll
Sysops: Mark Leff & Bob Helbush
404-982-0960

The Running Board
Sysop: Dr. Bonnie Anthony
301-229-5623

Rusty & Edie's
Sysop: Rusty Hardenburgh
216-726-0737

San Francisco PC Users' Group
Sysop: Richard Couture
415-621-2609

SEAdog & Arc Support
Sysop: Thom Henderson
201-473-1991

Searchlight Support
Sysop: Frank LaRosa
516-689-2566

The Sound of Music
Sysop: Paul Waldinger
516-536-8723

Sparkware
Sysop: Mark Herring
901-382-5583

SQLBBS
Sysop: John F. Prior
312-589-0508

TBBS Product Support
Sysop: Phil Becker
303-699-8222

Thumper Technologies
Sysop: Eric Cockrell
918-355-4409

Wildcat Support
Sysop: Jim Harrer
805-395-0650

Winthrop College
803-328-0762

Ye Olde Bailey
Sysop: Reg Hirsch
713-520-1569

Zmodem and Pro-Yam Support
Sysop: Chuck Forsberg
503-621-3746

ZSoft Support
Sysop: Shannon Donovan
404-427-1045

F

PC Pursuit OutDial Modems

City	Area Code(s)	Access Code
Ann Arbor, MI	313	D/MIAAR/
Atlanta, GA	404	D/GAATL/
Austin, TX	512	D/TXAUS/
Boston, MA	617	D/MABOS/
Chicago, IL	312, 708, 815	D/ILCHI/
Cleveland, OH	216	D/OHCLE/
Colton, CA	714	D/CACOL/
Columbus, OH	614	D/OHCOL/
Dallas, TX	214, 817	D/TXDAL/
Denver, CO	303	D/CODEN/
Detroit, MI	313	D/MIDET/
Glendale, CA	213, 818	D/CAGLE/
Hartford, CT	203	D/CTHAR/
Hempstead, NY	516	D/NYHEM/
Houston, TX	713	D/TXHOU/
Indianapolis, IN	317	D/ININD/
Kansas City, MO	816, 913	D/MOKCI/
Los Angeles, CA	213, 818	D/CALAN/
Memphis, TN	601, 901	D/TNMEM/
Miami, FL	305	D/FLMIA/
Milwaukee, WI	414	D/WIMIL/
Minneapolis, MN	612	D/MNMIN/
New Brunswick, NJ	908	D/NJNBR/
New York, NY	212, 516, 718, 914	D/NYNYO/
Newark, NJ	201, 908	D/NJNEW/
Oakland, CA	415	D/CAOAK/
Orlando, FL	407	D/FLORL/
Palo Alto, CA	415	D/CAPAL/
Philadelphia, PA	215	D/PAPHI/

(continued)

City	Area Code(s)	Access Code
Phoenix, AZ	602	D/AZPHO/
Pittsburgh, PA	412	D/PAPIT/
Portland, OR	503	D/ORPOR/
Research Triangle Park, NC	919	D/NCRTP/
Sacramento, CA	916	D/CASAC/
Salt Lake City, UT	801	D/UTSLC/
San Diego, CA	619	D/CASDI/
San Francisco, CA	415	D/CASFA/
San Jose, CA	408, 415	D/CASJO/
Santa Ana, CA	714, 213	D/CASAN
Seattle, WA	206	D/WASEA/
St. Louis, MO	618, 314	D/MOSLO/
Tampa, FL	813	D/FLTAM/
Washington, DC	202, 301, 703	D/DCWAS/

Resources

Abstract Data Technologies
2805 North Highland Avenue
Tucson, AZ 85719
BBS: 602-881-8570

AccuLink
P.O. Box 688
Pineville, NC 28134
800-945-7272

Associated Information Services
P.O. Box 13711
Albuquerque, NM 87192
BBS: 505-299-5974

Bernstein, Paul, Attorney
The Electronic Bar Association Legal Information Network
333 East Ontario Street #2201-B
Chicago, IL 60611
312-951-8264
BBS: 312-661-1740

Bit Bucket Software Co.
427-3 Amherst Street, Suite 232
Nashua, NH 03063

Borchers, Detlef
011-49-541-45-258

Bove & Rhodes Inside Report
P.O. Box 1289
Gualala, CA 95445
707-884-4413

Buffalo Creek Software
913 39th Street
West Des Moines, Iowa 50265
515-225-9552

Capital City PC User Group
51 Monroe Street, Plaza East Two
Rockville, MD 20850
301-670-1737

Central Point Software Inc.
15220 NW Greenbrier Parkway
Beaverton, OR 97006
800-888-8199
503-690-8090

Clark Development Co. Inc.
P.O. Box 571365
Salt Lake City, UT 84157-1365
801-261-1686
Fax: 801-261-8987
BBS: 801-261-8976 or 8981

Compton, Kip
P.O. Box 206
MIT Branch
Cambridge, MA 01239

CompuCom
1186-J Miraloma Way
Sunnyvale, CA 94086
408-732-4500
Fax: 408-732-4570

CompuServe Inc.
5000 Arlington Center Boulevard
Columbus, OH 43220
614-457-8600

Connect USA
1330 San Pedro NE #201
Albuquerque, NM 87110
800-ATDT-USA
505-255-2553

Continental Software
625 Greencove Terrace #128

Altamonte Springs, FL 32714
407-788-3736

Curtis, Paul
Intercom
1302 North Catalpa Avenue
Anaheim, CA 92801
714-774-1827

Datastorm Technologies Inc.
P.O. Box 1471
Columbia, MO 65205
314-443-3282

Dhesi, Rahul
GEnie: r.dhesi

Digital Communications Associates Inc.
1000 Alderman Drive
Alpharetta, Georgia 30202
404-442-4000

Directory of Computer Networks
Tracy L. LaQuey
ISBN 1-55558-047-5
Digital Press
12 Crosby Drive
Bedford, MA 01730

Dudley, Marshall
406 Monitor Lane
Knoxville, TN 37922
BBS: 615-966-3574

Eesti BBS #1
Sysop: Lembit Pirn
+0142-422-583

Electronic Frontier Foundation Inc.
155 Second Street
Cambridge, MA 02141
617-864-1550

Electronic Mail Association
1555 Wilson Boulevard, Suite 300
Arlington, VA 22209
703-875-8620

eSoft Inc.
15200 E. Girard Avenue #2550
Aurora, CA 80014
303-699-6565

Exis Inc.
P.O. Box 130
West Hill, Ontario, Canada
416-289-4641

Farwest BBS
P.O. Box 1296, Station E
Victoria, British Columbia, V8W 2W3, Canada
604-381-6462
BBS: 604-381-3934

Feathernet Software
810-F Vernon Circle
Mountain View, CA 94043
BBS: 415-967-3484

Forbin Project Inc.
P.O. Box 702
Cedar Falls, IA 50613
319-266-0543

Frey, Russell E.
35 Fox Court
Hicksville, NY 11801
BBS: 516-873-8032

FrontDoor
OCI—Online Communications Inc.
22 State Street
Bangor, ME 04401

Galacticomm Inc.
4101 SW 47th Avenue, Suite 101
Fort Lauderdale, FL 33314
305-583-5990
BBS: 305-583-7808

Mark D. Goodwin
P.O. Box 187
Orland, ME 04472
BBS: 207-469-6556

Gordon, Fabian
P.O. Box 851
East Brunswick, NJ
908-668-6468

GW Associates
P.O. Box 6606
One Regency Drive
Holliston, MA 01746
508-429-6227
BBS: 508-429-1784

Hart, Pat
The Exchange BBS
BBS: 804-552-1010 or 1018
Voice: 804-420-7506

Hayes Microcomputer Products Inc.
P.O. Box 105203
Atlanta, GA 30348
404-840-9200

Hilgraeve Inc.
111 Conant Avenue, Suite A
Monroe, MI 48161
313-243-0576

Hughes, Dave
719-636-2040

Ibis Software
625 Second Street Suite 308
San Francisco, CA 94107
415-546-1917

IMSI
1938 Fourth Street
San Rafael, CA 94901
415-454-7101
800-833-4674

Infinetwork
P.O. Box 1241
Laurel, MD 20725
301-498-6352
BBS: 301-498-6183

Inset Systems
71 Commerce Drive
Brookfield, CT 06804
800-828-8088
203-775-5866
Fax: 203-775-5634

Jung, Robert K.
2606 Village Road West
Norwood, MA 02062
617-255-0061
Fidonet: 1:16/390.7
Internet: robjung@world.std.com
CompuServe: 72077,445

Kingdom Enterprises
Round Rock, TX
BBS: 512-255-8297

Kodak
343 State Street
Rochester, NY 14650
716-724-1336

Kowaliski, Curtiss
2312 Vincinda Circle
Knoxville, TN 37924
BBS: 615-522-2498

Laforet, Christopher
BBS: 919-226-6984
CompuServe: 76120,110
GEnie: XTX74591
BIX: laforet

Lamac, George
Prague sysop
BBS: +422 842 424

Lockhart, Jim
317 San Miguel Street
Winter Springs, FL 32708

Logicom Inc.
1371 NW 80th Terrace
Plantation, FL 33322
305-474-4850
BBS: 305-473-8203

McAfee and Associates
4423 Cheeney Street
Santa Clara, CA 95054
408-988-3832

McGuire, Jay
Telesaurus
21832 Green Hill Road
Farmington Hills, MI 48335-4310
Order line: 800-488-9831
313-477-0067

MicroCom Communications Services
P.O. Box 17854
Irvine, CA 92713-7854
714-552-5971
BBS: 714-639-7725

Mikronetics
2114 Weatherton Drive
Wilmington, DE 19810
Fidonet: 1:150/199

M.B. Murdock and Associates
P.O. Box 2194
Pinellas Park, FL 34665
813-545-8050

Mustang Software Inc.
915 17th Street
P.O. Box 2264
Bakersfield, CA 93303
800-999-9619
805-395-0223
Fax: 805-395-0713
BBS: 805-395-0650

National Videotex Network
111 Mulberry Street, Suite 1A
Newark, NJ 07102
201-242-3119
Fax: 201-242-1662

NoGate Consulting
P.O. Box 88115
Grand Rapids, MI 49518-0115
616-455-6270

BBS: 616-455-5179
Fax: 616-455-8491

Nordevald Software
P.O. Box 280138
Tampa, FL 33682
BBS: 813-961-0788

Omen Technology
503-621-3406
BBS: 503-621-3746

Online Computer Resources
4330-J Clayton Road
Concord, CA 94521
415-687-0236
BBS: 415-687-0236

Onlinestore
Stadtle 2 Fl-9490
Vaduz, Liechtenstein
+41-75-20366
BBS: +41-75-82084
Fax: +41-75-20367

Parallax Development Co.
#21 Lower Concourse
2016 Sherwood Drive
Sherwood Park, Alberta T8A 3X3, Canada
403-452-3626
BBS: 403-449-9199

Parsons Technology
375 Collins Road NE
P.O. Box 3120
Cedar Rapids, IA 52406-3120
800-223-6925

PC Pursuit (US Sprint)
12490 Sunrise Valley Drive
Reston, VA 22096
800-835-3638
703-689-5177
Fax: 703-689-5177

Peter Norton Product Group
Symantec Corp.

100 Wilshire Boulevard
Santa Monica, CA 90401
213-319-2000

Pinnacle Software
P.O. Box 714
Airport Road
Swanton, VT 05488
514-345-9578
BBS: 514-345-8654

PKWare Inc.
9025 North Deerwood Drive
Brown Deer, WI 53223
414-354-8699

Pocket, Richard
BBS Caller's Digest
P.O. Box 416
Mount Laurel, NJ 08054
609-953-9110

Prostar Software
1821 South Central, Suite N
Kent, WA 98032
206-949-0579
BBS: 206-941-0317

QuickBBS Group Inc.
P.O. Box 621735
Orlando, FL 32862
407-228-9096
BBS: 407-856-0356

RBBS (D. Thomas Mack, Ken Goosens, and Doug Azzarito)
5480 Eagle Lake Drive
Palm Beach Gardens, FL 33418
407-627-9767
BBS: 407-627-6969

Rickard, Jack
Boardwatch Magazine
5970 South Vivian Street
Littleton, CO 80127
303-973-6038
BBS: 303-973-4222

Rose, Lance, Attorney
Greenspoon, Srager, Gaynin, Daichman & Marino
825 Third Avenue
New York, NY 10022
212-888-6880

Softklone
327 Office Plaza Drive, Suite 100
Tallahassee, FL 32301
904-878-8564

Software Connection
5237 SW 31st Terrace
Topeka, KS 66614

Solot, Ned
Faxts Now
1633 Westwood Boulevard, Suite 204
West Los Angeles, CA 90024
213-477-2707

Sparkware
P.O. Box 605
Cordova, TN 38018
901-373-6245
BBS: 901-382-5583

Storm Technology
220 California Avenue, Suite 101
Palo Alto, CA 94306
415-322-0506

Streamline Design
1 Herron Place
Bramalea, Ontario L6S 1P3, Canada

SuperMac
485 Potrero Avenue
Sunnyvale, CA 94086
408-245-2202

Surf Computer Services
71-540 Gardess Road
Rancho Mirage, CA 92270
Voice: 619-346-9430
BBS: 619-346-1608

System Enhancement Associates Inc.
925 Clifton Avenue
Clifton, NJ 07013
Voice: 201-473-5153
Voice: 201-614-9605

Technique Computer Systems
110-1841 Oak Bay Avenue
Victoria, British Columbia V8R 1C4, Canada

Thumper Technology
P.O. Box 471346
Tulsa, OK 74147
918-355-4311
BBS: 918-355-4409

Virkkala, Risto, and Aki Antman
Porslahdentie 23 G 40
SF-00980 Helsinki, Finland
BBS: +358-(9)0-341-1398

W & W Associates
1988 Via Appia
Walnut Creek, CA 94598
BBS: 415-937-0156

White, Pete
GW Associates
P.O. Box 6606
One Regency Drive
Holliston, MA 01746
508-429-6227
BBS: 508-429-1784

Yoshizaki, Haruyasu
Nifty Serve PFF00253
ASCII PCS: pcs02846
GEnie: K. Obuko
PC-VAN: FEM12376
Compuserve: 74100,2565
Internet: c00236@sinet.ad.jp.

Using the Diskette

The enclosed diskette contains a number of different files that will be of value to users or operators of bulletin board systems.

Before using the files here, please copy them into separate subdirectories on your computer's hard disk. You might use the structure of this disk: one subdirectory for Smartcom EZ, one for Mustang's SLMR and Wildcat.FRM, another for the bulk of the shareware offered here, and one for this file and PKZIP110.EXE, which is necessary to decompress and use the other shareware programs.

For the files to be usable by you, most will need to be decompressed. The decompressed files will take far more space than what is allotted to them here.

PKZIP110.EXE

PKZIP Version 1.1, from PKWare in Glendale, Wisconsin, is the key to unlocking most of the other files on this diskette.

The file itself comes in the form of a self-extracting archive. Again we recommend that you copy the file from this diskette into a separate subdirectory on your hard disk. You might also want to make that subdirectory part of the Path command in the AUTOEXEC.BAT file, which is part of your root directory. That way, the program can be invoked from any other subdirectory.

Once you've copied the file and reached the DOS prompt, type the name of the program:

PKZIP110 (return)

where (return) denotes the Return or Enter key on your PC keyboard. At this point, all the files that make up PKZIP Version 1.1 will decompress and become available for use. Included are both a manual and order form for a licensed copy of the program, as well as updates.

If you find PKZIP of use to you, please register it with PKWARE. Single-user copies cost $47 plus $2.50 shipping and handling ($5 from overseas), and prices are lower when you buy more copies. A complete price list is in the MANUAL.DOC file.

(*Note*: By the time you read this, it's very likely that PKWARE will have released PKZIP 2.0. This version of the program has many new features and is even easier to use. If the update has been released when you register your copy, you will be given PKZIP 2.0, along with an additional free upgrade.)

Once the file is decompressed, you'll find complete documentation in the .DOC and .TXT files created by PKZIP110.EXE. The two files you will use most often are PKZIP.EXE and PKUNZIP.EXE. PKUNZIP, in fact, is the key for "opening up" most of the other files on this disk.

Now, to decompress any of the other files on this disk that have the extension .ZIP, you'll only need to reach the DOS prompt and then enter the following:

    PKUNZIP (filename) (path)

Example. To decompress the file CNGBEEP.ZIP and put it in a subdirectory called BOOK, type the following:

    PKUNZIP a:\execpc\cngbeep c:\book

When you type this command, the file CNGBEEP.ZIP will be taken from the floppy drive a: and decompressed, with the result put into the subdirectory c:\book. If you've put this floppy disk in drive b:, use that letter. If you want the result put onto a different drive, or into a different subdirectory, use that name.

README.DOC

This is the file you are now reading. It contains information on the programs found in this diskette and on how to use them. It is not compressed, and it is also printed in the book.

HAYES SUBDIRECTORY

Not all the files on this diskette are compressed. A file in the Hayes subdirectory, for instance, can be used as is.

Smartcom EZ

Smartcom EZ is a communications program from Hayes Microcomputer Products Inc. Included with it is a special upgrade offer to Smartcom

Exec, a fuller-featured program designed for business users. Smartcom Exec was given the PC Magazine Editors' Choice Award in April 1991.

This program is not shareware. It's a $49 value and is a personal gift to you from Hayes. Since it's a single-user commercial program and not shareware, two important rules apply:

- *Do not place this on your BBS.*

- *Hayes has a copyright on Smartcom EZ.*

To load the software, place the disk in drive A, type **cd \hayes**, and then type **a: install (return)**. To read the manual, type **a: (return) guide (return).** Again, (return) means the Return or Enter key.

If you have trouble, call Hayes customer service at (404) 449-8911 or (404) 441-1617.

MUSTANG SUBDIRECTORY
Shareware versus Freeware

Smartcom EZ is free when you buy this book. Most of the other programs here are shareware.

As the word implies, shareware is software that is meant to be shared. It's distributed free, on bulletin boards and by mail. But if you use it, you're expected to pay for it within 30 days. Each of the shareware programs here contains an order form you can use to pay for the program. By registering, you can get access to program updates and support as well.

Over the years, shareware has become the best way for new software companies to reach the market. As sales grow, shelf space follows. The authors of these programs, then, represent tomorrow's software industry. If you like their work, they deserve your financial support.

SLMR20.ZIP

The Silly Little Mail Reader (SLMR) is one of the most popular shareware utilities of its type, and it is the only one that lets you access, download, and then read offline mail messages from most of the major programs described in this book. SLMR runs with PCBoard, Wildcat, Major BBS, and most of the other BBS packages found here. In late 1991, the program was purchased by Mustang Software Inc., publishers of Wildcat, who are creating a version of the program for the commercial market.

This program lets you read and respond to messages offline, using your favorite word processor. You save money and time by downloading a mail packet with the extension .QWK, in a fraction of the time it would take to respond online. You can also schedule mail uploads and downloads late at night, saving all your users money in responding to messages from remote systems.

WCORDER.FRM

This form, when printed, filled out, and mailed to the address provided, can bring you a "test-drive" copy of Wildcat 3.0, a popular BBS program that has been redesigned for easy use with local area networks and corporations.

EXEC-PC SUBDIRECTORY

Exec-PC

Most of the shareware programs on this disk came to us from Exec-PC, the largest BBS in the world, with 250 phone lines. The board is often the place where other sysops get their stuff, and many shareware authors who want to distribute new updates make it a point to call Bob Mahoney's board first.

The authors of the book want to thank Bob for his help in producing this disk. The main line for the board is 414-789-4210.

CNGBEEP.ZIP

This is a nifty little utility that will change the pitch of that nasty little "beep" you hear on your computer. It will even let you replace that beep with a song if you like. It's free, so enjoy it.

DLYMG2-4.ZIP

This is one of those utilities that can help distinguish your board from the competitors. It lets you create a customized "quote of the day" file, a simple message that changes every day and is displayed to all callers after they log on. This could be an alert of a sale, a general message to employees, or the words of a great man or woman. It's copyrighted by Daniel Kempton, and if you use it send him $20 plus $2 shipping to 375 West Main Street #5, Monmouth, OR 97361.

DRU_225.ZIP

This utility lets you appoint "assistant sysops" who can perform their duties remotely, from another office, from their home, or on the road. It's called within your BBS. If you like it and use it, Jeremy Slade and Delta Software Productions hold the copyright. The fee is $15. Send it to 1308 Alford Street, Fort Collins, CO 80524..

GOTTA_GO.ZIP

This program will let you "hang up" on obnoxious or long-winded callers with style. Select from any number of sound effects, such as a police siren, which will be played on the caller's PC. It's free and is meant as a working advertisement for a number of interesting shareware utilities from Charles Eglington of Electronic Technologies, 2985 S. Rochester Road, Suite H, Rochester, MI 48063.

KBD.ZIP

This program is usually used in batch files to control the actions of the keyboard, changing the functions of various keys. It's part of a broader product line and costs $10 plus $3 for shipping. It is available from Marc Perkel, Computer Tyme, 411 North Sherman, Suite 300, Springfield, MO 65802.

LIST76B.ZIP

List is a filing and browsing utility that is a favorite of many system operators. Since it was first written in 1983, it's been enhanced into a complete file management utility, a fine example of what shareware support can do for a program. Vernon Buerg is the author, and the program is often called "Buerg's list" for that reason. The single-copy price is $30, and bulk discounts are available. Send the cash to Vernon Buerg at 129 White Oak Circle, Petaluma, CA 94952.

SMRTZP11.ZIP

The Smart Zip program is used to optimize the compression of files made with PKZIP. Both Version 1.1, included in this collection, and Version 0.9 are supported by the program. Author Joseph Vincent is already working on a version for PKZIP 2.0, which could be available as you read this. The single-user license fee is $12. Send it to Joseph A. Vincent Consulting, 805 Pine Way, Anchorage, KY 40223.

TSRBOOT.ZIP

This is really two packages. TSRBOOT itself is a memory-resident program that lets you reboot a computer at a specified time, regardless of other activities occurring on the system. This is especially useful for beginning automated cleanup tasks late at night. BATTIME will create a report on "error levels" in your system, telling you, for instance, when TSRBOOT ran and began maintenance of your system. They cost $25, and quantity discounts are available from Horizons Consulting, 1432 E. Commercial Street, Springfield, MO 65803.

UPCHKDT.ZIP

This is a great utility for testing uploads. It tests for viruses and checks the integrity of files, and you can configure it for use with nearly any BBS. It's a "test-drive" version—not every feature is implemented—so if it looks useful, be sure and register it. You can buy it for use with different BBSs, and it is priced at $16 to $26. The "user" version, as opposed to the sysop version, cost just $16. Send those checks to Al Maynard, 1409 Cedar Creek, Racine, WI 53402.

DUPCHECK.ZIP

When uncompressed, this program will help you identify duplicate files across all subdirectories and disk drives in your system. As your BBS grows, a shortcut such as this can become very important. You invoke it by typing its name, DUPCHECK, from the subdirectory where you locate the program. The result is a file called DUPLIST showing the names of duplicated files and where they're located. If you like it, send $20 to Ravendale Systems, 31818 Tanglewood, St. Clair Shores, MI 48082.

MELT.COM

This file is quite simple. Since it's only 128 bytes long, it's too small to be compressed. Invoke it from the subdirectory where it's located, and it will clear your screen in a new and interesting way. If you like it, put it in the Path of your AUTOEXEC.BAT file, which will let you invoke it with the word Melt from any subdirectory. This is a good example of the kinds of utilities you can find on a well-run BBS.

PW.ZIP

This program lets you create passwords that won't be obvious to hackers but that users can remember easily. That's very useful for any corporate system interested in security. It was written by Lars Hedbor, a member of the U.S. Air Force most recently stationed in Alaska. If you find it useful, he'd like a small donation of $5 sent to Barnesbay Software, 509B Price Street North, Anchorage, AL 99508.

SS#INFO2.ZIP

Not all files found on a BBS are software programs. Some are useful text files, such as this one. Not only will you learn here your legal rights and responsibilities in using Social Security numbers to track your users, but it will also decrypt the meaning of those nine simple digits and make them understandable.

XCON3.ZIP

When compressed, this program can be useful in helping you convert between different bulletin board packages. You invoke it by typing its name from the subdirectory where it's located. If you like it, send $15 plus $2 for shipping to Karshedan Software, P.O. Box 70, Oak Creek, WI 53154.

EXEC700.COM

In order to show you the files and utilities most common to a well-run BBS, this program will, when invoked, display a list of the 700 most popular downloads in Exec-PC, the largest and most popular BBS in the United States. Most of the other files on this diskette are found on this list. Looking at this list will also give you a feel for the file downloading atmosphere on a typical BBS.

To run the program, copy the file to a subdirectory and type EXEC700. The program simply delivers a listing of the files and an explanation.

If you have any questions about how to use this diskette, please feel free to call the author, Dana Blankenhorn, at (404) 373-7634.

Index